Socialism and International Law

THE HISTORY AND THEORY OF INTERNATIONAL LAW

General Editors

NEHAL BHUTA
Chair in International Law, University of Edinburgh

FRANCESCA IURLARO
Max Planck Institute for Comparative and International Private Law Hamburg

ANTHONY PAGDEN
Distinguished Professor, University of California Los Angeles

BENJAMIN STRAUMANN
ERC Professor of History, University of Zurich

In recent decades, the understanding of the relationship between nations has undergone a radical transformation. The role of the traditional nation-state is diminishing, along with many of the traditional vocabularies that were once used to describe what has been called, ever since Jeremy Bentham coined the phrase in 1780, 'international law'. The older boundaries between states are growing ever more fluid, new conceptions and new languages have emerged, which are slowly coming to replace the image of a world of sovereign independent nation-states that has dominated the study of international relations since the early nineteenth century. This redefinition of the international arena demands a new understanding of classical and contemporary questions in international and legal theory. It is the editors' conviction that the best way to achieve this is by bridging the traditional divide between international legal theory, intellectual history, and legal and political history. The aim of the series therefore is to provide a forum for historical studies, from classical antiquity to the twenty-first century, that are theoretically informed and for philosophical work that is historically conscious, in the hope that a new vision of the rapidly evolving international world, its past and its possible future, may emerge.

PREVIOUSLY PUBLISHED IN THIS SERIES

A Century of Anarchy?
War, Normativity, and the Birth of Modern International Order
Hendrik Simon

The Individual in International Law
Anne Peters, Tom Sparks

Pufendorf's International Political and Legal Thought
Peter Schröder

Victims
Perceptions of Harm in Modern European War and Violence
Svenja Goltermann

Sovereignty, International Law, and the Princely States of Colonial South Asia
Priyasha Saksena

Sepúlveda on the Spanish Invasion of the Americas
Defending Empire, Debating Las Casas
Luke Glanville, David Lupher, Maya Feile Tomes

The World Bank's Lawyers
The Life of International Law as Institutional Practice
Dimitri Van Den Meerssche

The Invention of Custom
Natural Law and the Law of Nations, ca. 1550–1750
Francesca Iurlaro

Socialism and International Law

The Cold War and Its Legacies

Edited by
RALUCA GROSESCU
AND
NED RICHARDSON-LITTLE

Great Clarendon Street, Oxford, OX2 6DP,
United Kingdom

Oxford University Press is a department of the University of Oxford.
It furthers the University's objective of excellence in research, scholarship,
and education by publishing worldwide. Oxford is a registered trade mark of
Oxford University Press in the UK and in certain other countries.

© the several contributors 2025

The moral rights of the authors have been asserted.

All rights reserved. No part of this publication may be reproduced, stored in a retrieval system, transmitted, used for text and data mining, or used for training artificial intelligence, in any form or by any means, without the prior permission in writing of Oxford University Press, or as expressly permitted by law, by licence or under terms agreed with the appropriate reprographics rights organization. Enquiries concerning reproduction outside the scope of the above should be sent to the Rights Department, Oxford University Press, at the address above.

You must not circulate this work in any other form
and you must impose this same condition on any acquirer.

Public sector information reproduced under Open Government Licence v3.0
(https://www.nationalarchives.gov.uk/doc/open-government-licence)

Published in the United States of America by Oxford University Press
198 Madison Avenue, New York, NY 10016, United States of America.

British Library Cataloguing in Publication Data
Data available

Library of Congress Control Number: 2024943773

ISBN 9780198920175

DOI: 10.1093/9780198920205.001.0001

Printed and bound by
CPI Group (UK) Ltd, Croydon, CR0 4YY

The manufacturer's authorised representative in the EU for product safety is
Oxford University Press España S.A. of el Parque Empresarial San Fernando de
Henares, Avenida de Castilla, 2 – 28830 Madrid (www.oup.es/en).

In memory of Philippa Hetherington

Preface

It has been thirty-five years since the end of the Cold War, and the dissolution of the Soviet Bloc and its constituent socialist states. If we date the beginning of the Cold War to around Churchill's famous 1946 Iron Curtain speech, this means that the duration of the Cold War (1946–1989) will soon be eclipsed by the length of time that has passed since its conclusion. Self-declared socialist governments are still with us, and indeed one of them (China) has achieved such significant economic, political, and military power since 1989 that we are considered to be approaching a new period of Great Power confrontation. But we without a doubt live in a post-Soviet world, and have done so for at least two generations.

Since 1989, the sweeping and triumphalist economic and political liberalization of former Soviet states and societies across the globe resulted in at least a decade during which a historical reckoning with the Cold War comprised mostly postmortems for Soviet-style government. However, the global history of the Cold War has attracted scholarly attention over the last twenty years. In the last ten years, an interest in the history of Cold War international law has begun to emerge. Long viewed as a period of stagnation in international law because of an over-reliance on western-centric foreign-office narratives of legal developments, recent historical work has shown the Cold War to be a period of significant transformation in the geological structure of the international legal order—a result of the combined tectonic pressures of decolonization and Soviet-Western rivalry.

The present edited volume brings a new depth of insight and research to our understanding of international law and the Cold War by focusing on the role of socialist states (admittedly, primarily Eastern European ones). Combining intellectual histories of Soviet legal thinkers across diverse national spaces with studies of state socialist legal contributions to particular debates and fundamental legal concepts (such as the crime of aggression, and self-determination), the book makes an exceptionally nuanced and complex contribution. It shows how the theoretical armaments furnished by Marxist and socialist theories of Imperialism and colonialism not only interpreted the world but were deployed very effectively to help change it by Soviet jurists and diplomats. The structural alignment between anti-imperialism, decolonization, and the strategic necessity of avoiding encirclement and containment by the Western capitalist powers resulted in numerous important legal developments that today we perceive as indispensable building blocks for a universal international legal order: self-determination, sovereign equality, and the criminalization of aggression, to name but three.

At the same time, all-too-human stories of intellectual contradiction, political repression, and self-preservation under politically unfree regimes leave us with a clear sense that the inspiring promise of a universal socialist international law was without question mired in its own constitutive contradictions—made starkly evident in the efforts to explain the USSR's invasions of Hungary (1956) and Czechoslovakia (1968) as justifiable exceptions to principles long championed by the Soviet bloc, such as sovereign equality and self-determination. The death of Marxist legal theorist Evgeny Pashukanis, condemned and extrajudicially executed as a Trotskyite saboteur, opened the window of opportunity for the rise of Aron Trainin as a disciple of Stalin's chief inquisitor (and notable Soviet law theorist in his own right), Andrei Vyshinsky. Trainin's prolific and insightful writing would decisively influence the concepts of aggression and crimes against peace used at Nuremburg, and beyond. Trainin himself would be politically purged for his 'cosmopolitan bourgeois' tendencies after 1948. The productive alliance between the decolonized world and the Soviet bloc was also subject to contradictions of interest, as a detailed chapter on the regulation of aircraft hijacking shows.

The cunning of unreason would shape the history of actually existing socialism, as much as it governed the development of bourgeois capitalism. The legacy, as the volume editors observe, is a quintessentially historical one: innovation, combined with contradiction, and also failure, in different measures. As we enter once more a period of dissolution after the brief unchallenged hegemony of one system, we might discern in these recollected pasts some intimations of our future too.

Nehal Bhuta
Edinburgh, September 2024

Acknowledgements

This volume is the result of a long-standing collaboration between Nelly Bekus, Bogdan Iacob, and the editors. In 2020, we successfully submitted a collective research project to the Romanian Research Council to reflect on the overlooked contributions of state socialist experts and governments to international law. We are grateful to both Nelly and Bogdan for their conversations and friendship.

At different stages in the development of this book, Steven Jensen, Sandrine Kott, Michal Kopeček, Wim Muller, Alanna O'Malley, Umut Özsu, Thuc Linh Nguyen Vu, and Tor Krever provided valuable feedback on the project and helped us enlarge the scope of our research. Their criticism has motivated, challenged, and inspired us.

We would like to express our heartfelt thanks to Alessandro Iandolo for his support in allowing us to reprint Sonja Dolinsek and Philippa Hetherington's article 'Socialist Internationalism and Decolonizing Moralities in the UN Anti-Trafficking Regime, 1947–1954'. We also thank the VolkswagenStiftung for their financial support, through the Freigeist Project 'The Other Global Germany' at the University of Erfurt, in securing this article for the book.

We are also grateful to Robert Cavooris, Nehal Bhuta, Anthony Pagden, Benjamin Straumann, and Lisa Butts at Oxford University Press for their support of this project.

Finally, we thank Julia Sittmann, our copyeditor, who has been integral to the process of bringing together our diverse contributions into a cohesive whole. Mircea Vâlceanu, Roxana Robu, and Cornelia Mareș were also key in developing this project: their support in organizing workshops and conferences, as well as in dealing with time-consuming bureaucracy, was invaluable.

We acknowledge the support of the Romanian Research Council (UEFISDCI), through the Exploratory Research Grant, 'The Contributions of State Socialist Countries of Eastern Europe to the Development of International Criminal and Humanitarian Law after 1945' PN-III-P4-ID-PCE-2020-1337, implemented at the National University of Political Science and Public Administration (Bucharest) between 2021 and 2024. In addition, our collaboration with colleagues at the Imre Kertész Kolleg, Friedrich-Schiller Universität Jena, has contributed to the improvement of many chapters in this volume at various conferences and seminars.

Contents

List of Abbreviations — xv
Editor Biographies — xvii
Contributor Biographies — xix

1. Socialism and International Law: Legacies of Innovation, Contradiction, and Failure — 1
   Raluca Grosescu and Ned Richardson-Little
   Introduction — 1
   Global Socialism and Progressive Ideas of International Law — 6
   Law on the Books versus Law in Action — 8
   Socialist Legal Projects and Their Pluralism — 10

2. A Socialist Legal Universalism? Cold War Struggles Over International Law — 17
   Sebastian Gehrig
   Introduction — 17
   From the October Revolution to the Second World War — 20
   Soviet International Law after De-Stalinization — 25
   The Impact of Decolonization, the Sino–Soviet Split, and Détente on State Socialist Theories of International Law — 31
   Accepting Universalism while Abandoning a Socialist Legal Universalism — 36
   Conclusion — 42

3. Socialism and Self-Determination: Lenin, International Law, and National Liberation — 45
   Brad Simpson
   Introduction — 45
   Self-Determination and Socialism Before the Cold War — 46
   Self-Determination, Decolonization, and Socialism in the Postwar World — 52
   Terrorism, Armed Struggle, and National Liberation Movements — 57
   The Soviet Union and Global Secession Movements — 59
   Conclusion: The Contradictions of Socialist Self-Determination — 62

xii CONTENTS

4. Soviet Lawyers and Concepts of Aggression in International Law   69
   Michelle Penn
   Introduction   69
   Aron Trainin and Soviet Engagement with Concepts of Aggression   71
   The Development of Modern ICL: Hitlerite Responsibility at the IMT   77
   Echoes of Crimes against Peace in the 1948 Genocide
       Convention and the 1954 Draft Code of Crimes against
       the Peace and Security of Mankind   82
   Pyotr Romashkin's Crimes against Peace and Humanity   86
   Conclusion   89

5. Decentring Marxism: The Poznań School and Socialist
   International Law in Eastern Europe after 1945   91
   Jakub Szumski
   Introduction   91
   The Vulnerabilities of Socialist Internationalism   93
   The Poznań School and the Field of International Law in Poland   97
   What was Socialist International Law?   107
   Conclusion   113

6. How China Came to Embrace International Institutions   115
   Ryan Martínez Mitchell
   Introduction   115
   International Law and the Discourse of State Sovereignty in China   117
   The Turn to Third World Engagement   121
   From Insurgent Legal Ordering to Institutional Integration   125
   Neo-Statism, Formalism, and Twenty-First Century
       Global Governance   130
   Conclusion   135

7. Health as a Human Right and Eastern European Anticolonialism   137
   Bogdan C. Iacob
   Introduction   137
   Health Anticolonialism in the Early Postwar Period   140
   Health as a Human Right in International Conventions   145
   Health as Anticolonialism and Anti-Racism at the WHO   152
   The 1970s: A Revolution in Health   156
   Conclusion   161

8. Protecting Culture Through International Law in the
   Postwar World   163
   Nelly Bekus
   Introduction   163
   Culture in the Context of War Crimes Prosecution after the Second
       World War   166
   Cultural Genocide: A Rejected International Law Project   172

The 1954 Hague Convention for the Protection of Cultural Property in the Event of Armed Conflict	176
Conclusion	183

9. **Socialist Internationalism and Decolonizing Moralities in the UN Anti-Trafficking Regime, 1947–54** — 185
   Sonja Dolinsek and Philippa Hetherington
Introduction	185
A Genealogy of Law Against Human Trafficking for Prostitution	187
Socialist States Confront the Convention for the International Suppression of Prostitution	191
Consensus Breaks Down: The Debate over the Colonial Clause	197
Conclusion	202

10. **State Socialist Contributions to the Criminalization of Apartheid** — 205
    Raluca Grosescu
Introduction	205
State Socialist Engagements with Apartheid and Self-Determination	207
Apartheid as a Major International Crime	212
Legal Professional Associations against Apartheid	224
Conclusion	227

11. **Terrorists, Revolutionaries, and Migrants: Cold War Conflicts and Convergences over International Air Hijacking Law** — 231
    Ned Richardson-Little
Introduction	231
The Emergence of Hijacking and the Decolonization of Air Law	234
Hijacking Goes Global	239
Failure in Rome and the Turn to Terrorism	249
Conclusion	255

12. **Socialisms and International Law: Epilogue** — 257
    Paul Betts

Index — 265

Abbreviations

AFRO	African Regional Committee (WHO)
CCP	Chinese Communist Party
CENTO	Central Treaty Organization
CERD	UN Convention on the Elimination of all Forms of Racial Discrimination
CESCR	UN Committee for Economic, Social and Cultural Rights
CIJ	International Commission of Jurists
CMEA	Council for Mutual Economic Assistance (also known as COMECON)
CSSR	Czechoslovak Socialist Republic
ECOSOC	Economic and Social Council
GDR	German Democratic Republic
IADL	International Association of Democratic Lawyers
IATA	International Air Transport Association
ICAO	International Civil Aviation Organization
ICC	International Criminal Court
ICL	international criminal law
ICJ	International Court of Justice
IMT	International Military Tribunal
ICESCR	International Covenant on Economic, Social and Cultural Rights (UN)
ICTY	International Criminal Tribunal for Yugoslavia
ICTR	International Criminal Tribunal for Rwanda
IFALPA	International Federation of Air Line Pilots' Associations
ITLOS	International Tribunal on the Law of the Sea
LNHO	League of Nations Health Organization
NIEO	New International Economic Order
NKVD	People's Commissariat for Internal Affairs
OSCE	Organization for Security and Cooperation in Europe
PDPA	People's Democratic Party of Afghanistan
PFLP	People's Front for the Liberation of Palestine
PLO	Palestinian Liberation Organization
PRC	People's Republic of China
ROC	Republic of China (Taiwan)
SEATO	Southeast Asia Treaty Organization
SNT	Supreme National Tribunal (Poland)
UDHR	Universal Declaration of Human Rights
UN	United Nations
UNCLOS	UN Convention on the Law of the Sea
UNCTAD	UN Conference on Trade and Development
UNESCO	UN Educational, Scientific and Cultural Organization

UNWCC	UN War Crimes Commission
USSR	Union of Soviet Socialist Republics
WHA	World Health Assembly
WHO	World Health Organization
WTO	World Trade Organization

Editor Biographies

Raluca Grosescu is Lecturer in politics at the National University of Political Science and Public Administration, Bucharest. Her work focuses on the history of international criminal law and on justice and memory politics in post-dictatorial and post-conflict societies. Her latest monograph, *Justice and Memory after Dictatorship: Latin America, Central Eastern Europe and the Fragmentation of International Criminal Law*, was published in 2024 by Oxford University Press.

Ned Richardson-Little is Research Associate (Wissenschaftlicher Mitarbeiter) in Department V: Globalizations in a Divided World at the Leibniz Centre for Contemporary History, Potsdam (ZZF). He was previously a Freigeist Fellow at the Department of History at the University of Erfurt leading the Volkswagen Stiftung funded research group 'The Other Global Germany: Deviant Globalization and Transnational Criminality in the 20th Century'. His first monograph, *The Human Rights Dictatorship: Socialism, Global Solidarity and Revolution in East Germany*, was published with Cambridge University Press in 2020. He is co-editor of the *Routledge Handbook of the History of International Law: Eastern Europe* (forthcoming 2025) and co-editor, with Michal Kopeček, of a special issue of the *Journal of Modern European History* on '(Re-)Constituting the State and Law during the "Long Transformation of 1989" in East Central Europe' (2020).

Contributor Biographies

Nelly Bekus is Lecturer at the University of Exeter. She defended her PhD in Sociology at the Polish Academy of Science, held research posts at Harvard University, the Institute of Human Sciences in Vienna, New York University, and worked as Assistant Professor at the University of Warsaw (2008–12). She has published several monographs, including *Struggle Over Identity: The Official and the Alternative Belarusianness* (2010), co-authored *Orthodoxy Versus Post-Communism? Belarus, Serbia, Ukraine, and the Russkiy Mir* (2016), and co-edited a special issue of *International Journal of Heritage Studies* on 'Heritage, Socialism and Internationalism' in 2020. Her publications also include over twenty articles and book chapters on heritage, memory, the history of nationalism, and religious and linguistic identity.

Paul Betts is Professor of Modern European History at St Anthony's College, University of Oxford. His publications include *Within Walls: Private Life in the German Democratic Republic* (Oxford University Press, 2010; paperback, 2012) and *The Authority of Everyday Objects: A Cultural History of West German Industrial Design* (University of California Press, 2004; paperback, 2007). He is also the co-editor of various collective volumes, including *Socialism Goes Global: The Soviet Union and Eastern Europe in the Age of Decolonisation* (Oxford University Press, 2022).

Sonja Dolinsek is Research Associate (Wissenschaftliche Mitarbeiterin) in Contemporary History at the Otto-von-Guericke University in Magdeburg. Previously, she worked as a research associate in the Department of Media Studies at Paderborn University and held teaching assignments in Global and European History at Humboldt University and Free University Berlin, and Gender History at Marburg University and Leuphana University. Her dissertation focuses on the transnational politics of prostitution and anti-trafficking after 1945. Her research interests include transnational and global history, with a focus on gender and sexualities, human rights, crime and labour, theory and methods, as well as data histories. With Siobhán Hearne she co-edited a special issue on 'Prostitution in Twentieth-Century Europe' (*European Review of History*, 2022), which includes her article on the negotiations surrounding the 1949 Convention Against Trafficking. With Magdalena Saryusz-Wolska, she co-edited the collection *Histories of Prostitution in Central, East Central and South Eastern Europe* (Brill, 2023).

Sebastian Gehrig is Senior Lecturer in Modern European History at the University of Sheffield. His recent book *Legal Entanglements: Law, Rights, and the Battle for Legitimacy in Divided Germany, 1945–1989* explores how opposing ideological notions of what the law and rights constituted became simultaneously the object and means by which the two German governments contested each other's political legitimacy at home and abroad. His publications include articles on the politics of human rights, the clash of sovereignty doctrines within the United Nations, citizenship rights and freedom of movement, Sino-German cultural diplomacy, Maoism and militant subcultures during the 1960s and 1970s, and 1970s gender politics.

Philippa Hetherington († 2022) was Lecturer in History at the School of Slavonic and East European Studies, University College London. Her research focused on the global history of the Russian Empire and the early Soviet Union, with a particular interest in legal history and feminist theory as well as migration and imperial government. She was the co-editor of two special issues on 'Migration, Sex, and Intimate Labor, 1850–2000' (*Journal of Women's History*) and 'Liberal and Illiberal Internationalisms' (*Journal of World History*), as well as publishing numerous articles in journals such as *Gender and History*, *Journal of the History of International Law*, and *Russian History*. Her book, *Circulating Subjects: Sex and Migration in Russia, 1885–1935*, will appear with Cornell University Press in 2025.

Bogdan Iacob is Researcher at the 'Nicolae Iorga' Institute of History (Romanian Academy). His work focuses on the role of Eastern European experts (historians and physicians) at international organizations and in postcolonial spaces. He contributed to the collective volume *Socialism Goes Global: The Soviet Union and Eastern Europe in the Age of Decolonisation* (2022), and authored 'Malariology and Decolonization: Eastern European Experts from the League of Nations to the World Health Organization' (*Journal of Global History*, 2022) and 'Babel in Bucharest: "Third World" Students in Romania, 1960s–1980s' (*Cahiers du Monde russe*, 2022).

Ryan Mitchell is Law Professor at the Chinese University of Hong Kong. His writing on international law and relations, intellectual history, and modern China has appeared in leading academic journals, and his commentary on related topics has been published in *Foreign Affairs*, *The Diplomat*, and *The National Interest*, among others. His analysis has also been cited in *The New York Times*, *FT*, *NPR*, *Al Jazeera*, *Bloomberg*, *The Wall Street Journal*, and many other major news outlets. His book *Recentering the World: China and the Transformation of International Law* was published by Cambridge University Press in October 2022.

Michelle Penn is Assistant Professor and Law Librarian at the University of Colorado. She received her PhD in History from the University of Colorado, and her MLIS degree from the University of Arizona. Her dissertation focused on the work of Soviet Jewish lawyer Aron Trainin and the development of modern international criminal law. She has been a research fellow at the US Holocaust Memorial Museum.

Brad Simpson is Associate Professor of History and Asian Studies at the University of Connecticut. He is the author of *Economists with Guns: Authoritarian Development and US–Indonesian Relations, 1960–1968* (Stanford University Press, 2008), and *The First Right: Self-Determination and the Transformation of International Order*, forthcoming from Oxford University Press.

Jakub Szumski is Associate Researcher at the Imre Kertész Kolleg, Friedrich Schiller University of Jena, as part of the Volkswagen Foundation project 'Towards Illiberal Constitutionalism in East Central Europe: Historical Analysis in Comparative and Transnational Perspectives'. He earned his PhD at the University of Jena in 2022 with a dissertation on corruption scandals in state socialist Poland and East Germany. He previously studied history and philosophy in Warsaw, Konstanz, and Berlin. His research revolves around the intersection of politics, intellectual history, and law in East Central Europe. His latest publication is 'Consentful Contention in Revolutionary Times: Debating Elite Corruption at Communist Party Congresses in Poland and East Germany' (*Journal of East Central European Studies*, 2023).

1
Socialism and International Law: Legacies of Innovation, Contradiction, and Failure

Raluca Grosescu and Ned Richardson-Little

Introduction

This book provides a new account of international law making during the twentieth and twenty-first centuries by examining the role of socialist states and legal experts from around the world in the development of international conventions and legal practice. The volume challenges two major meta-narratives of international law history: a Eurocentric canon of steady liberal progress, and an anticolonial account focusing on Third Word contestations of the Western international order. Both of these historical schools have ignored or downplayed the role of global socialism, from the Soviet model to African socialism, Chinese communism, and democratic socialism in Latin America. We offer a new interpretation of post-Second World War international law history across three interconnected themes: socialism as a driver of progressive projects; the contradictions between socialist law as theory and as legal practices; and the polycentrism and pluralism of socialist international law.

The history of international law making has long been viewed through a Eurocentric lens, taking the development of law as a self-evidently Western and liberal project, and obscuring the contributions and contestations of actors from other world regions and political systems.[1] This scholarship continued a nineteenth-century teleological narrative in which an idealized (Western) Europe constructed a universal, liberal, progressive path to human dignity and humanitarianism. Within this account, stories of Western domination and oppression were downplayed, if not made invisible, while liberalism emerged as the main driver of democracy and human rights, despite its problematic connections to colonialism, racism, and economic inequality. This literature had little place for the socialist world beyond stock villains impeding Western progress and dismissed socialist

---

[1] On Eurocentrism in international law, see Martti Koskenniemi, 'Histories of International law: Dealing with Eurocentrism', *Rechtsgeschichte* 19 (2011): 152–76; Walter D. Mignolo, 'The Making and Closing of Eurocentric International Law: The Opening of a Multipolar World Order', *Comparative Studies of South Asia, Africa and the Middle East* 36, no. 1 (2016): 182–95.

initiatives as dystopian projects, deemed to generate hypocritical and authoritarian practices.[2]

From the 1960s onwards, various scholars began to challenge this overt Eurocentrism and examine international lawmaking as a system of imperial domination that has been resisted and reimagined by colonial and sub-altern subjects. In the last twenty years, efforts to write a polycentric history of international law have produced an exciting new literature on the protagonism of the Global South and its contestations of Western doctrines and practice. Some have emphasized the theoretical and empirical contributions made by actors from beyond the West including the Afro-Asian bloc, the Non-Aligned Movement, and Indigenous movements.[3] Such narratives engaged with state socialism but usually positioned it in a supporting role within the larger history of anticolonial struggles. It thus often subsumed socialism into the history of Third World international legal battles. Even accounts written through the lens of the global Cold War offer few insights into the role of socialist states and movements in shaping international law. For instance, a ground-breaking volume on Cold War international law, published in 2019, focused on socialism as a theory of law with examples from the Soviet Union and the People's Republic of China (PRC), but in isolation from others socialist states and with very little analysis on how ideology and theory translated into political practice on the global stage.[4] Similarly, a breakthrough volume published in 2021 on the legacies of the Mexican (1910–1920) and Russian (1917) revolutions looked primarily at the early Bolshevik period, with little reference to postwar socialist developments.[5]

In contrast, only a few works have provided in-depth empirical analysis of socialist engagements with international law during the Cold War, and almost all of

---

[2] Geoffrey Robertson, *Crimes Against Humanity: The Struggle for Global Justice* (London: Penguin, 2006); Anton Weiss-Wendt, *The Soviet Union and the Gutting of the UN Genocide Convention* (Madison, WI: University of Wisconsin Press, 2017); Ana Isaeva, 'The Cold War and Its Impact on Soviet Legal Doctrine', in Matthew Craven, Sundhya Pahuja, and Gerry Simpson (eds.), *International Law and the Cold War* (Cambridge: Cambridge University Press, 2019), 256–70. When work does engage with Eastern European state socialism as a relevant actor for global histories of international law, it is almost invariably reduced to the former USSR playing a minor or oppositional role. Bardo Fassbender, Anne Peters, and Simone Peter (eds.), *The Oxford Handbook of the History of International Law* (Oxford: Oxford University Press, 2012).

[3] Steven Jensen, *The Making of International Human Rights: The 1960s, Decolonization and the Reconstruction of Global Values* (New York: Cambridge University Press, 2016); Sundhya Pahuja, *Decolonising International Law: Development, Economic Growth and Politics of Universality* (Cambridge: Cambridge University Press, 2011); Arnulf Becker Lorca, *Mestizo International Law: A Global Intellectual History 1842–1933* (Cambridge: Cambridge University Press, 2015); Luis Eslava, Michael Fakhri, and Vasuki Nesiah, *Bandung, Global History, and International Law: Critical Pasts and Pending Futures* (Cambridge: Cambridge University Press, 2017); Jochen von Bernstorff and Philipp Dann (eds.), *The Battle for International Law: South–North Perspectives on the Decolonization Era* (Oxford: Oxford University Press, 2019).

[4] Matthew Craven, Sundhya Pahuja, and Gerry Simpson (eds.), *International Law and the Cold War* (Cambridge: Cambridge University Press, 2019).

[5] Kathryn Greenman, Anne Orford, Anna Sounders, and Ntina Tzouvala (eds.), *Revolutions in International Law: The Legacies of 1917* (Cambridge: Cambridge University Press, 2021).

those have concentrated on Eastern Europe.[6] Even fewer have sought to explore the consequences of these initiatives for the international order, both during the Cold War and in our contemporary world. Moreover, most of this literature has focused on a specific convention, a particular field, or a single-country case study. In the fields of international criminal and humanitarian law, several scholars have highlighted the crucial role of the Soviet Union at the International Military Tribunal at Nuremberg, in the prosecution of Japanese war criminals, and in the efforts to establish 'economic aggression' and other legal norms through these the trials.[7] Other scholars have addressed the contributions of national tribunals in the PRC and in Eastern Europe to prosecuting war crimes or Soviet and Polish efforts to enforce the non-applicability of statutory limitations to international crimes.[8] In the field of human rights law—where the socialist world has been widely defined by its role in opposition to Western liberal initiatives—recent studies have underlined how Eastern Europe (particularly the Soviet Union, Yugoslavia, and the German Democratic Republic) defined progressive ideas of law on the international stage.[9] Such states objected to the exclusion of the right to self-determination in the Universal Declaration of Human Rights in 1948 and, with the advent of decolonization, engaged in an aggressive international politics that attacked Western racism and imperialism from the 1950s onwards.[10] By the

---

[6] Raluca Grosescu and Ned Richardson-Little (eds.), 'Revisiting State Socialist Approaches to International Criminal and Humanitarian Law', Special issue: *Journal of the History of International Law* 21, no. 2 (2019).

[7] Valentyna Polunina, 'The Soviets at Tokyo: International Justice at the Dawn of the Cold War', in Kerstin von Lingen (ed.), *Transcultural Justice at the Tokyo Tribunal* (Leiden: Brill, 2018), 124–47; Franziska Exeler, 'Nazi Atrocities, International Criminal Law, and Soviet War Crimes Trials: The Soviet Union and the Global Moment of Post-Second World War Justice', in Immi Tallgren and Thomas Skouteris (eds.), *The New Histories of International Criminal Law: Retrials* (Oxford: Oxford University Press, 2019); Kirsten Sellars, 'Economic Aggression: A Soviet Concept', in Nina H. B. Jørgensen (ed.), *The International Criminal Responsibility of War's Funders and Profiteers* (Cambridge: Cambridge University Press, 2020), 17–36. Francine Hirsch, *Soviet Judgement at Nuremberg. A New History of the International Military Tribunal after World War II* (New York: Oxford University Press, 2020).

[8] See the chapters on war crimes prosecutions in Eastern Europe in Morten Bergsmo, Cheah Wui Ling, and Ii Ping (eds.), *Historical Origins of International Criminal Law*, vol. 2 (Brussels: Torkel Opsahl, 2014); Ōsawa Takeshi, 'The People's Republic of China's "Lenient Treatment" Policy towards Japanese War Criminals', in Kirsten Sellars (ed.), *Trials for International Crimes in Asia* (Cambridge: Cambridge University Press, 2015), 145–66; Raluca Grosescu, 'State Socialist Endeavours for the Non-Applicability of Statutory Limitations to International Crimes: Historical Roots and Current Implications', *Journal of the History of International Law* 21, no. 2 (2019): 239–69.

[9] Stefan Troebst, '"Sozialistisches Völkerrecht" und die sowjetische Menschenrechtsdoktrin', in *Toward a New Moral World Order?: Menschenrechtspolitik und Völkerrecht seit 1945*, edited by Norbert Frei and Annette Weinke (Göttingen: Wallstein, 2013). Ned Richardson-Little, Hella Dietz, and James Mark (eds.), 'New Perspectives on Socialism and Human Rights in East Central Europe since 1945', Special issue of *East Central Europe* 46, no. 2–3 (2019); Eric D. Weitz, 'The Soviet Union and the Creation of the International Human Rights System', *Zeitgeschichte-online* (December 2018); Paul Betts, 'Rights', in *Socialism Goes Global: The Soviet Union and Eastern Europe in the Age of Decolonisation*, edited by James Mark and Paul Betts (Oxford: Oxford University Press, 2022), 180–220.

[10] Jennifer Amos, 'Embracing and Contesting: The Soviet Union and the Universal Declaration of Human Rights, 1948–1958', in *Human Rights in the Twentieth Century*, edited by Stefan-Ludwig Hoffmann (Cambridge: Cambridge University Press, 2010) 147–65. Western accusations of Soviet antisemitism and Soviet counter-accusations of American racism are treated as obligatory aspects of international legal debates in the 1960s, but a sideshow to the real process of international lawmaking

late 1960s, state socialist elites in Eastern Europe were convinced, even if their Western and postcolonial critics were not, that they were the global leaders in the realization of human rights through international law.[11]

Although there was little early promise of socialist involvement in the remaking of international humanitarian law after the Second World War, the field became an important site of contestation between East and West. The Soviet Union and Yugoslavia initially boycotted the efforts of International Committee of the Red Cross to revise the Geneva Conventions; no invitation was even sent to the Chinese Communist Party. Yet, by the end of the 1940s, the whole of the Eastern Bloc mobilized to take part in, or at least send observers to, the developing negotiations.[12] As a result, the Soviets and their allies were able to aggressively push for the inclusion of wars of decolonization under the umbrella of international law in an attempt to 'incorporate principles of national self-determination and decolonization into the [Geneva] Conventions' genetic code.'[13] Through the revisions of the 1977 Protocols to the Geneva Conventions, national liberation movements were finally recognized under international law, realizing the common goal of the Soviet Bloc, the PRC, and many African socialist states.[14] As both a socialist state in conflict with the Soviet Union and a leader of the Non-Aligned Movement, Yugoslavia straddled the line between Eastern Bloc and Global South in these negotiations throughout the peak years of the decolonization of international law.[15]

Twentieth-century initiatives to rethink international economics and global equality have been another topic where scholars have underlined state socialist contributions, while narrowly focusing either on Yugoslavia as a leading actor of the New International Economic Order (NIEO), or on the 'international law of solidarity' born of Salvador Allende's democratic socialist experiment in Chile.[16] Both countries played an important role at the United Nations Conference on Trade and Development (UNCTAD) and are evidence that NIEO was primarily

in Rabiat Akande, 'An Imperial History of Race-Religion in International Law', *American Journal of International Law* 118, no. 1 (2023), 25.

[11] Ned Richardson-Little, 'From Tehran to Helsinki: The International Year of Human Rights 1968 and State Socialist Eastern Europe', *Diplomatica* 1, no. 2 (2019): 180–201.
[12] Boyd van Dijk, *Preparing for War: The Making of the Geneva Conventions* (Oxford: Oxford University Press, 2022), 44
[13] Ibid., 127; Gilad Ben-Nun, *The Fourth Geneva Convention for Civilians: The History of International Humanitarian Law* (London: Bloomsbury, 2020).
[14] Giovanni Mantilla, 'The Protagonism of the USSR and Socialist States in the Revision of International Humanitarian Law', *Journal of the History of International Law* 21, no. 2 (2019): 181–211.
[15] Arno Trültzsch, *Sozialismus und Blockfreiheit: Der Beitrag Jugoslawiens zum Völkerrecht 1948–1980/91* (Göttingen: Wallstein, 2021).
[16] Johanna Bockman, 'Socialist Globalization against Capitalist Neocolonialism: The Economic Ideas behind the New International Economic Order', *Humanity* 6, no. 1 (2015): 109–28; Claerwen O'Hara and Valeria Vázquez Guevara, 'Salvador Allende, Populism and an International Law of Solidarity', *Centre for International Law* (blog), accessed 7 May 2024, https://cil.nus.edu.sg/blogs/salvador-allende-populism-and-an-international-law-of-solidarity/.

the brainchild of socialist thinkers—from both the Global South and Eastern Europe.

From this important but still sparse literature, the current volume expands to consider socialist engagements with international law globally and across a broad range of fields, from human rights, international criminal and humanitarian law, transnational criminality, non-interventionism, heritage law, and the law of the sea. It examines both theoretical and practical applications of socialist international law and situates them within a global historical analysis that moves beyond national and treaty-based cases studies. In seeking to rediscover these overlooked contributions, this collection employs a range of methodologies, combining intellectual, political, legal, and biographical approaches to the history of international law in order to offer a comprehensive view of state socialist international law making and practice. Rather than focusing entirely on intellectual history or the formal negotiations underpinning international conventions, the volume integrates a wide configuration of actors (diplomats, epistemic communities, and judicial officials, among others) who contributed to debates on the creation and application of international law. The book examines state interventions at various international organizations—United Nations (UN), UN Educational, Scientific and Cultural Organization (UNESCO), World Health Organization (WHO), and International Civil Aviation Organization (ICAO)— and transnational mobilizations of lawyers and epistemic communities, as well as the enterprises of individual intellectuals, diplomats, and judicial officials (with their own political views, forms of socialization, and legal interpretations).[17] The authors have thus conducted research into a wide range of sources: archival documents from various international institutions, national archives, and research institutes; autobiographies; the scholarly literature; and the press. This integrative methodological approach and the multiplicity of sources helps to disrupt linear stories of socialist entanglements with international law and demonstrates the diversity of approaches and conflicts within the socialist world.

By using global history perspectives, this book makes visible those outside Western-centred narratives of international integration, codification, and convergence: from smaller Eastern European actors to African, Latin American, and Asian socialisms that carried their own traditions and genealogies, to postcolonial experts whose biographies and initiatives are not contained by the classic East–West or North–South axes of analytical specialization. Our deployment of these methods opens the door to understanding and emphasizing diverse geographies

---

[17] See the profiles of the Soviet theorist Aron Trainin and the Polish lawyers Emil Stanisław Rappaport and Stefan Glaser in Frédéric Mégret and Immi Tallgren (eds.), *The Dawn of a Discipline: International Criminal Justice and Its Early Exponents* (Cambridge: Cambridge University Press, 2020). The impact of Bulgarian jurist Nissim Mevorah is examined in Ben-Nun, *The Fourth Geneva Convention*.

inherent to crafting international law, alignments that connected spaces to specific themes, thus challenging simple geopolitical explanations.[18]

Global Socialism and Progressive Ideas of International Law

The socialist world played a crucial role in the development of the theory and practice of international law. While socialist states were indeed often impediments to specific Western liberal initiatives, they did not simply reject international law and made unique contributions to its genesis and evolution in the postwar period and beyond. State socialist governments and experts from across the globe generated new legal theories and led the adoption of key legal principles and norms often in conflict with liberal internationalists in the West. Some of these initiatives were unsuccessful, but many others are recognized today as *jus cogens* or serve as the basis for current transnational mobilizations for social justice and global equality. These original conceptualizations and actions were the result of both socialist ideologies (with their global variations) that challenged the liberal, colonial status quo of the postwar period and realpolitik as part of the global competition of the Cold War and its aftermath.

Complementing Francine Hirsch's work on the role of the Soviet Union at the International Military Tribunal at Nuremberg, Michelle Penn's chapter in this volume underlines the contribution of Soviet theorists in defining 'crimes against peace', the 'crime of aggression' and the associated mode of liability ('complicity'), not only during the early Cold War—via the Nuremberg and Tokyo charters— but also later on, in the 1960s and 1970s. She highlights the evolution of these categories within Soviet legal thinking, as well as the Soviet impact on the creation of a UN-endorsed definition of 'aggression' in the mid-1970s (which became part of the 2010 Kampala proposals to include this crime in the Statute of the International Criminal Court, ICC). Similarly, Nelly Bekus underlines that, while the USSR was instrumental in limiting the scope of the Genocide Convention to avoid liability for political crimes and repression, both the Soviet Union and Poland engaged in a forceful campaign (albeit without success) to include the category of cultural genocide to criminalize the destruction of their cultural heritage during the Second World War but also to condemn attacks against the culture of colonized or Indigenous people. Both Bekus and Raluca Grosescu emphasize how socialist lawyers and governments pushed for sanctioning not only the commission of core international crimes but also of adjacent crimes such as the application of propaganda or public incitement to such crimes. In the 1960s, socialist countries from Eastern Europe and Africa advocated for the non-applicability of statutory

---

[18] For the global approaches to the history of international law, see Ignacio de la Rasilla, *International Law and History: Modern Interfaces* (Cambridge: Cambridge University Press, 2021), ch 5.

limitations to major international crimes and disconnected the category of crimes against humanity from the existence of a war of aggression. Eastern European socialist governments also (unsuccessfully) lobbied for greater accountability in terms of the protection of cultural heritage during armed conflict, including criminal responsibility for heritage destruction, and the elimination of the military necessity clause from the 1954 UNESCO Hague Convention for the Protection of Cultural Property in the Event of Armed Conflict.

The push for anticolonialist law was another key element of socialist international engagements and was evident in many fields. Socialist states contested the Western colonial order and its supposed 'civilizational mission' and aimed to enforce the inclusive application of international law, including in territories and for peoples subject to Western imperialism. The contributions by Sonja Dolinsek and Philippa Hetherington and Ned Richardson-Little reveal how socialist states successfully removed the 'colonial clause' from the UN 1949 Convention on the Traffic in Persons and the 1963 Tokyo Anti-Hijacking Convention, while Bogdan Iacob highlights how socialist states were instrumental in promoting the extension of health as a human right to the entire world, including newly independent countries and non-self-governing and trust territories. The impact of socialist anti-colonialism is also visible in the negotiations over the 1946 Constitution of the WHO and the 1966 International Covenant on Economic, Social and Cultural Rights. State socialist Eastern European struggles to remove this discrimination in international law and erode Western European dominance included the goal of assuring newly decolonized states of their full independence. Removing the colonial clause was a key element in destabilizing and finally ending the ostensible civilizational superiority of Europe that had justified colonialism under the so-called 'discovery doctrine'.

As shown in Grosescu's chapter, African and Eastern European socialist governments were also the most vocal proponents for the criminalization of apartheid under international law in the 1960s and the 1970s. Their actions culminated in the UN Anti-Apartheid Convention of 1973. The condemnation of apartheid was interconnected to radical stances against colonialism that challenged more conformist narratives such as those emerging from the 1970 Friendly Relations Declaration, which promoted strong protection of non-intervention in internal affairs—described by Umut Özsu as 'the high-water mark of efforts by socialist and nonaligned states to win support for an expansive interpretation of national self-determination'.[19] Moreover, the resolve to criminalize the collaboration of multinational corporations with the apartheid regime was connected to broader initiatives for economic change—such as the NIEO and demands to recognize national sovereignty over natural resources. For his part, Bradley Simpson underlines

---

[19] Umut Özsu, *Completing Humanity: The International Law of Decolonization, 1960–82* (Cambridge: Cambridge University Press, 2023), 29.

how the Soviet Union and its Eastern European allies worked together with Third World countries to extend the principle of non-intervention in order to incorporate all forms of political, cultural, and economic coercion. This enterprise aimed in particular to condemn the subordination of economic aid to conditions like the acceptance of military bases on the territory of the receiving state, the adoption of domestic legislation favouring foreign private investments, or the renunciation of the right to nationalize and expropriate foreign property.

When it came to the regulation of transnational criminality, the Eastern Bloc also played a constructive role. In the postwar pursuit to revive and expand interwar global drug regulation, the Soviet Union was integral to the creation of the 1961 Single Convention on Narcotics, the first of three international agreements that have defined the field until today. When the United States sought to expand upon the interwar regulatory system by creating a bloc of six authorized opium-producing states—Bulgaria, Greece, India, Iran, Turkey, the USSR, and Yugoslavia—the Soviet Bloc boycotted the negotiations, which they saw as a Western attempt to limit medical production in the rest of the world. An alternative plan based around universal regulation rather than a cartel system gained momentum at the UN in large part due to strong support from Eastern Europe, which rallied newly decolonized countries around this initiative. Despite Cold War tensions at a near boiling point with the Congo Crisis and the ongoing conflict over divided Berlin, negotiations were held over a matter of weeks early in 1961 resulting in the Single Convention.[20] Similarly, while the Soviets and their allies have often been viewed as opponents of the international criminalization of terrorism, the Eastern Bloc was one of the driving forces behind the mandatory prosecution or extradition of airplane hijackers, as Ned Richardson-Little explores in his chapter in this volume.

Law on the Books versus Law in Action

This collection explores the many contradictions and duplicities of socialist international law when it collided with the complex realities of local and global politics. In contrast to a new wave of neo-Marxist scholarship that has begun to recover an idealized version of socialist law, in particular through the writings of the Soviet theorist Evgeny Pashukanis, as a means of reimagining the international order in the present day,[21] this volume highlights the contrast between socialist *law on the*

---

[20] John Collins, *Legalising the Drug Wars: A Regulatory History of UN Drug Control* (Cambridge: Cambridge University Press, 2021), ch 7. On the further involvement of the Eastern Bloc in the creation of international narcotics law, see Ned Richardson-Little, 'The Drug War in a Land Without Drugs: East Germany and the Socialist Embrace of International Narcotics Law', *Journal of the History of International Law/Revue d'Histoire du Droit International* 21, no. 2 (2019): 270–98.

[21] Some recent works that have sought to draw upon Marxist and Soviet theory to develop new perspectives on contemporary international law include: China Miéville, *Between Equal Rights: A Marxist Theory of International Law* (Leiden: Brill, 2005); John Quigley, *Soviet Legal Innovation and the Law of*

books and *law in action* and addresses the many mismatches between doctrine and practice.

In many cases, socialist states agitated for progressive principles and international conventions but also strongly opposed significant enforcement mechanisms in the name of state sovereignty. This ambivalent position allowed them to evade international accountability for violations of human rights at home and illegal interventions abroad. State socialist legal theorists crafted a historical theory of human rights that generated one standard for those who had evolved to the socialist stage of development and an entirely different standard for states still in the bourgeois phase of history, which created a philosophical basis for political hypocrisy.[22] In other cases, contradictions were simply ignored. For instance, the chapters by Grosescu and Iacob reveal that, despite their anti-racism and anti-apartheid activism at the UN and the WHO, socialist states avoided any self-reflection on the racial and ethnic discrimination ongoing in their own countries—from antisemitism and prejudice against the Roma to the persecution of various minorities in postcolonial states in Africa and Asia.

Although the Cold War competition for the moral high ground did result in the creation of important international legal conventions, the real impact of these instruments was sometimes decades in the future, and only possible after the collapse of state socialism in most of the world. Grosescu emphasizes that although socialist countries promoted broad definitions of core international crimes, they also opposed the creation of an international criminal court and provincialized the principle of universal jurisdiction by endorsing it only for contexts non-applicable to state socialist realities. Similarly, Bekus underlines that Eastern European state socialists agitated for the criminalization of cultural genocide, even as they opposed not only the criminalization of political and social genocide, but also all efforts to create an international tribunal to judge such crimes.

Yet, the socialist tendency to match maximalist theory with weak enforcement mechanisms also explains why the Cold War was such a generative period for international lawmaking without, however, creating the conditions for real implementation. While demonstrating the importance of the Leninist vision of self-determination for the global anticolonial struggle, Bradley Simpson highlights that, after 1945, socialist states advanced a moderate anticolonial conception of

---

the Western World (Cambridge: Cambridge University Press, 2007); Susan Marks (ed.), *International Law on the Left: Re-Examining Marxist Legacies* (Cambridge: Cambridge University Press, 2008); B. S. Chimni, *International Law and World Order* (Cambridge University Press, 2017); Ntina Tzouvala, *Capitalism as Civilisation: A History of International Law* (Cambridge: Cambridge University Press, 2020); Gian-Giacomo Fusco, Przemyslaw Tacik, and Cosmin Cercel (eds.), *Legal Form: Pashukanis and the Marxist Critique of Law* (London: Routledge, 2025).

[22] Michal Kopeček, 'The Socialist Conception of Human Rights and its Dissident Critique: Hungary and Czechoslovakia, 1960s–1980s', *East Central Europe* 46, no. 2–3 (2019): 261–89; Ned Richardson-Little, *The Human Rights Dictatorship: Socialism, Global Solidarity and Revolution in East Germany* (Cambridge: Cambridge University Press, 2020), 82.

self-determination in UN resolutions and the 1966 human rights covenants. This approach aimed to support national independence for former colonies and the right to economic self-determination, while preventing sub-national, secessionist, and Indigenous movements. Simpson also underlines the flexibility and double standards of Soviet conceptualizations of the principle of non-intervention. While militating for a maximalist definition of this principle at an international level, at the regional Eastern European level, the Soviet Union subordinated non-intervention to socialist internationalism and international proletarian solidarity, in order to justify interventions that suppressed counterrevolutionary movements in other socialist countries. Similarly, Ryan Mitchell's contribution argues that the PRC has always had, and continues to maintain, an extremely UN Charter-centric and essentially conservative, statist interpretation of norm enforcement in international criminal and humanitarian law.

Socialist Legal Projects and Their Pluralism

We argue that the plurality and complexity of the socialist world generated multiple and ambiguous projects of international law, resulting in cooperations and competitions that crossed ideological and geographical divides. In the twentieth century, the socialist world existed as an ambiguous and fragile construct with one foot in Eurocentric traditions pursuing peaceful coexistence with the West via the Soviet-led Eastern Bloc and the other foot in the camp of the radical Third World, led primarily by postcolonial Afro-Asian states intent on challenging the status quo. Far from a monolith, the socialist world was a diverse and dynamic space, which often shared common understandings of global affairs and the meaning of the law but also became sharply divided on matters of material and political importance. International law was crafted through the intersections of multiple historical processes including the Cold War, decolonization, and globalization and was not defined only by East–West or North–South divides. Moreover, norms evolved and operated through the interweaving of local, national, regional, and global political, legal, and cultural processes within and beyond the Cold War blocs. Anticolonialism, national liberation movements, and the anti-racist struggle provided common ground for Eastern Europe and the Global South. But Eastern European socialists also shared common values and causes with various Western countries at various stages of the Cold War. At times, the shared military interests and moral imagination of the superpowers generated moments of cooperation between the Soviet Union and the United States, which worked to assure the very status quo questioned by smaller countries from Europe and the Third World.[23]

---

[23] See Roland Burke, 'From Individual Rights to National Development: The First UN International Conference on Human Rights, Tehran, 1968', *Journal of World History* 19, no. 3 (2008): 275–96; Mantilla, 'The Protagonism'.

At other times, shared economic interests between the Eastern Bloc and the West created overlapping legal agendas between erstwhile Cold War rivals.[24]

Socialist international law challenged the (legalized) capitalist and imperialist order with a system that aimed to achieve class equality, as well as the equality of states without colonialist hierarchies. In Eastern Europe, the Soviet model of international law was initially conceived as a radical counter-alternative to the liberal order, despite the fact that it built upon and—in many respects—embraced markers of Western legal thinking such as legal positivism and legal dogmatism. Sebastian Gehrig's contribution explores the efforts, primarily by Soviet and Chinese scholars, to establish a socialist counter-universalism in the field of international law by challenging the theoretical foundations of capitalist law. Prewar Soviet scholars attacked international law as a capitalist and imperialist construct expected to eventually wither away after the global socialist revolution. After de-Stalinization, the work of various legal scholars and organizations—including the International Association of Democratic Lawyers (IADL) and the Chinese Society of International Law—reveal a project of socialist law that was meant to depart from 'bourgeois' legal traditions but used some of its features to secure the socialist world's integration into the international system. Yet, there was no accord amongst these scholars about the nature of an alternative socialist law. Moreover, Détente with the West led Soviet scholars to abandon the idea of a separate socialist international law entirely. Well before the collapse of the USSR, its claims to an alternative world of law had long fallen apart.

Throughout the Cold War, the proliferation of socialist states in Europe produced numerous hybrid models of international socialist law, with certain experts regarding international law as a technical discipline without a core ideological bias, which could nonetheless be employed by socialist states to socialist ends. As Jakub Szumski's chapter shows, certain international law initiatives had definite ideological roots in the socialist project, while others were defined by geopolitical necessity, with socialism providing a weak guide to action and a poor basis for international collaboration. Polish legal academics—especially those coming from the Poznań School of International Law—decentred or ignored the Marxist–Leninist script during the Cold War and continued to be influenced by Western legal positivism. The continuing relevance of pre-socialist legal norms meant that scholars retained their Western legal methodology, which would later facilitate the transition by many state socialist international lawyers to the liberal, post-Cold War order. Iacob also demonstrates that socialist engagements with the question

---

[24] Pierre Thévenin, 'A Liberal Maritime Power as Any Other? The Soviet Union during the Negotiations of the Law of the Sea Convention', *Ocean Development & International Law* 52, no. 2 (2021): 193–223.

of health built upon prewar visions of social medicine and its linkage to state-led health governance that crossed ideological lines. At the same time, a radical break with their prewar activism was visible after 1945 in the systematic state socialist challenge to the capitalist and imperial status quo, through conceptions that merged state-funded medicine, self-determination, and anti-discrimination.

This fragmentation of visions of international law within the Eastern Bloc not only drew from pre-socialist traditions but also from competing contemporary political interests. Individual countries had their own priorities and historical trajectories, and specific political issues shaped idiosyncratic national approaches to international law. East German international law priorities were always refracted through the country's diplomatic isolation and competition with its much more internationally accepted Western counterpart, the Federal Republic of Germany. Bucharest's insecurities and insistence on Romanian national sovereignty as it affirmed its autonomy within the socialist camp led to a cautious approach regarding transnational prosecutions of international crimes, which they saw as an infringement on diplomatic immunity and state sovereignty. Jurists in the Hungarian People's Republic developed the concept of 'crimes against the people', as an alternative to 'crimes against humanity', as a means of prosecuting the elites who had served under the previous regime, which had collaborated with Nazi Germany.[25]

Beyond Europe, alternative socialist visions of international law and politics proliferated according to differing regional and national agendas and types of socialism (Soviet-style, African, Chinese). As shown by Grosescu, while Eastern European and African socialisms were informed by common ideological struggles against Western capitalism, imperialism and racism, various African leaders rejected the doctrine of economic class struggle and the Marxist idea of global proletarian revolution; instead, they insisted on the importance of a cross-class unifying project of nation building and solidarity. In fact, African socialists often looked with suspicion on the Soviet counter-liberal project. They perceived the latter as a new form of imperialism and Eurocentric universalism, characterized at worst by interventionist agendas in the Third World or, at best, a paternalistic, socialist civilizing mission to help 'backward' Third World societies. Simpson explores the criticism against the Soviet doctrine of limited sovereignty within the Eastern Bloc and the subsequent military interventions in Czechoslovakia and Afghanistan. The crushing of the Prague Spring in 1968 was condemned not only by the Western bloc and most non-aligned states but also by certain socialist countries, including Yugoslavia, Romania, Albania, and the PRC and by several sovereigntist leaders of socialist African states, including Julius Nyerere in Tanzania and Ahmed Sékou Touré in Guinea. Yet, here too, the African socialist camp was not a monolith

---

[25] Tamás Hoffmann, 'Crimes against the People—a Sui Generis Socialist International Crime?', *Journal of the History of International Law (Revue d'Histoire du Droit International)* 21, no. 2 (2019): 299–329.

either: as Simpson also explains, in 1978, Somalia initially sought the support of the Soviets to invade Ethiopia under the communist Derg regime, which they justified as a plan to realize Leninist self-determination for separatist Eritreans and the minority populations of the Ogaden region. As Mitchell reveals, the disinclination of the PRC towards global enforcement mechanisms of international criminal and humanitarian law resulted from its opposition of both Western and Soviet conceptions of international law, which it considered to be two sides of the same imperialist First World coin. Communist Chinese visions were not only grounded in socialism but also in long-standing intellectual traditions that drew from Daoist philosophy and its later theoretical application to global politics.

Even at the height of Cold War tensions, there were areas where the East and West had shared visions of international law. Dolinsek and Hetherington demonstrate the ideological overlap between the socialist camp and Western delegations on the desirability of the abolition of prostitution, which resulted in a radical condemnation of all forms of commercial sex. Iacob underlines the overlaps between conceptualizations of health as a human right in Eastern Europe and those advanced by France or the Scandinavian countries.[26] These convergences reflected common histories that predated the Cold War as well as the emergence of the welfare state across Europe and elsewhere, including Latin America. Yet, state socialists stood out because of both their emphasis on the state as the sole provider of the right to health and their unwavering push to extend a comprehensive vision of public health to (former) colonies. Such a stance stood in contrast to French and British unwillingness to carry national health services to colonial peoples. South–East relationships thus fluctuated between solidarity and dissonance on matters of self-determination, non-intervention, and collective well-being. Détente amplified these dynamics, as East–West international alliances grew in importance by the 1970s and postcolonial delegates increasingly slotted socialist countries into a North that perpetuated global inequalities. Richardson-Little shows how the Eastern Bloc's preoccupation with preventing illicit emigration at all costs lined up with Western goals to prosecute hijackers without exception but also created a rift with the Global South. Socialist states in Africa, which represented a diverse ideological spectrum including Algeria, Tanzania, Mali, and the People's Republic of Congo all rejected defending the migration controls of Eastern Europe over the legal protection of national liberation movements.

Furthermore, academics, diplomats, and party leaders drew upon national historical memory and legal traditions to conceptualize the issues raised by international legal debates and to rationalize political choices made in terms of drafting and implementation. Szumski demonstrates that—while still not rebelling against the socialist mainstream—Polish legal scholars from the Poznań

---

[26] Similar Eastern Bloc–French alliances were also to be found in the field of international humanitarian law based on their shared experiences of Nazi occupation. See Mantilla 'The Protagonism'.

School approached international law from a radically different standpoint than those trained in more Stalinist methods in Warsaw, let alone Hungary, Romania, or East Germany. The professional background and legal tradition inherited from the interwar period rendered Polish legal scholarship much closer to Western interpretations of international law. Grosescu exemplifies this argument through the story of the Polish judge Bohdan Winiarski, who in the South West Africa Cases at the International Court of Justice stood with Western judges—and against the general anticolonial politics of his government. By dismissing Ethiopia and Liberia's right to question South Africa's mandate in Namibia, he contributed to a judicial decision that continued the colonial tradition of international law and the reluctance to advance human rights, the anti-apartheid movement, and the end of anti-racial discrimination. Conversely, due to their experience as citizens of a formerly Nazi occupied country and (often) as members of the anti-Nazi resistance, Polish lawyers were keen to expand definitions of core international crimes as well as transnational jurisdictions for prosecuting such crimes. They shared the goal of advancing international criminal law beyond strict sovereigntist approaches with Western legal scholars, who had analogous historical and personal experiences during the Second World War, as underlined by Bekus's chapter, among others.

Similar national and personal histories, as well as shared ideological values, generated complex relations of cooperation and competition that departed from the generally acknowledged East–West and North–South divides. Grosescu underlines the collaboration of Eastern and Western lawyers against apartheid within the IADL. She demonstrates that socialist lawyers cooperated across the Iron Curtain to outlaw apartheid, while also connecting this cause to a radical denunciation of colonialism as a whole and the recognition of wars of national liberation as international armed conflicts. Iacob highlights the intersection between Eastern European advocacy of health as a human right and Chilean experts' activism rooted in the country's struggles for the achievement of state-funded, universally accessible national healthcare.

This collection thus serves as an antidote to both the view that socialist states were actors of stagnation and opposition to liberal progress and the literature that presents socialist endeavours as a absolute alternative to Western international law. Rather, socialist projects have often been ambiguous, inconsistent, and evolving. In addition, clear political self-interest is blended with larger principles to create outcomes that do not sit neatly within abstract categories. This collection should be read as a call for further empirical research on the history of socialist international law. The conceptualization of socialist law as a multifaceted and often flexible project allows us to interrogate the place of Eurocentrism and the legacies of imperialism in international law making from a new angle. The socialist world's combination of states from the European North and the postcolonial South generated new forms of international law, but it also revealed the limits of the socialist project in overcoming its European roots and creating a basis for a global coalition against the West. Socialist international law was constructed as an alternative to the Western order, yet failed to fully realize a total ideological system that could supplant the liberal international project. Ultimately, socialism failed as a project of world making through international law as divisions among Eastern Bloc, Chinese, and African socialist projects made a unified ideological vision for the new world order impossible.[27]

Yet, the legacies of socialist international law are still with us today through the many legal developments that were made possible through state socialist efforts, including the elimination of colonial clauses, the codification of international crimes such as aggressive war, apartheid, airplane hijacking, drug trafficking, and the expansion of humanitarian legal principles, including the protection of national liberation movements. The non-applicability of statutes of limitations for war crimes and the protection of cultural heritage are also the result of socialist initiatives. Although the PRC was often at odds with the Soviet Union and the Eastern Bloc during the Cold War, it has carried on the earlier role of the USSR in promoting statist conceptions of human rights protections and the defence of state sovereignty as the highest priority in international legal negotiations.

We hope that this volume will spur on further work on the role of socialism in the genesis of postwar international law in fields not addressed by our collection, including the environment, economic law, and migration, among others. While this volume has touched on the actions of various socialist countries, the role of smaller Eastern European states such as Albania, or Latin American socialist countries including Castro's Cuba, Nicaragua under the Sandinistas, and Chile under Salvador Allende or the impact of Eurocommunism on international law, the emergence of Marxist–Leninist states in Africa like the People's Republic of Congo, and the initiatives of Vietnam, Mozambique, and other post-revolutionary socialist states are all topics that call out for further study.

Acknowledgements

This research was supported by the Romanian National Authority for Scientific Research and Innovation, CNCS-UEFISCDI, project number PN-III-P4-ID-PCE-2020-1337.

---

[27] On anticolonial 'worldmaking' via the law, see Adom Getachew, *Worldmaking After Empire: The Rise and Fall of Self-Determination* (Princeton: Princeton University Press, 2019); Samuel Moyn, 'The High Tide of Anticolonial Legalism', *Journal of the History of International Law* 23, no. 1 (2020): 5–31.

2
A Socialist Legal Universalism? Cold War Struggles Over International Law

Sebastian Gehrig

Introduction

In 1948, the American Council of Learned Societies finally commissioned a translation of Andrei Y. Vyshinsky's *The Law of the Soviet State*, ten years after its initial publication in Russian. In the first decades after the October Revolution in 1917, leading Soviet legal minds such as Evgeny B. Pashukanis had argued for a merely strategic use of international law to safeguard the revolution at home. This dismissive attitude to international law and the law in general would disappear after the proclamation of the Stalin Constitution in 1936. John N. Hazard's introduction to Vyshinsky's book pointed out that this was as much a book of political theory as it was about law: 'Vyshinsky's aim is to acquaint the Soviet reader with what others [i.e. pre-Bolshevik legal scholars] have said and why he believes it to have lost validity'.[1] The translation was one sign that Western audiences were, often grudgingly, acknowledging that they had to reckon with state socialist approaches to law.

Reviews of Vyshinsky's book, however, quickly moved beyond the issue of propaganda and politics that Hazard highlighted. Franz L. Neumann, for example, whose pioneering work *Behemoth* on the nature of Nazi rule had made him a leading voice explaining dictatorship, went to the heart of the challenge to Western law that Vyshinsky had already posed in 1938 and that had become all too clear in the field of international law at the Nuremberg International Military Tribunal (IMT) in 1946.[2] He highlighted Vyshinsky's proposal that law and the state had a permanent role to play in the building of socialism. By 1948, Western readers such as Neumann realized that Vyshinsky's rehabilitation of law as a tool of revolution in the wake of the Stalin Constitution formed part of a fundamental challenge to non-Marxist–Leninist legal traditions. Neumann stressed that 'Vyshinsky's insistence on the originality of Soviet law and jurisprudence thus serves a double

---

[1] John N. Hazard, 'Introduction', in Andrei Y. Vyshinsky, *The Law of the Soviet State* (New York: The Macmillan Company, 1948), vi–x, ix.
[2] For the Soviet influence on the IMT, see Francine Hirsch, *The Soviets at Nuremberg: A New History of the International Military Tribunal after World War II* (Oxford: Oxford University Press, 2020); Franz L. Neumann, *Behemoth. The Structure and Practice of National Socialism* (London: Victor Gollancz Ltd, 1942).

purpose: to justify state and law and to present them as something radically new, having nothing in common with bourgeois forms and theories.'[3]

This claim of a total separation of socialist law from all other legal traditions meant that Soviet international lawyers had to consider whether this state of a 'new type' not only produced novel domestic law but would also transform international law.[4] This chapter explores the attempt to create theories of socialist international law as part of the fundamental question that Soviet and other state socialist legal professionals grappled to come to terms with: What role should the law play in building socialism and, later, in maintaining 'developed socialism' domestically and internationally? Western scholarship on state socialist approaches to international law often measures socialist legal theory implicitly or explicitly against the liberal tradition of law. While it remains important to point out the gulf between socialist legal texts and the everyday realities of life under socialism, such criticism is today often based on the assumption that the only real law that exists is grounded in Western liberalism. In contrast, early studies of Soviet law acknowledged the openly political function of Soviet law and studied socialist law as a tool for social change and governance as well as for its educational function in the logics of the party-state.[5] During the Cold War, certain Anglo-American scholars also recognized that the gulf between socialist legal scholarship and their own liberal common law tradition was especially wide. While there was a considerable familiarity between European legal thought upon which much—especially pre-revolutionary—Russian writing was based, segments of Western contemporary scholarship even accepted after 1945 that state socialist international law theories were part of 'a larger philosophical and ideological framework with its own distinctive world outlook and language'.[6] While this position did not inherently imply support for Marxist–Leninist legal arguments, it did constitute an acknowledgement that there existed alternative ideological visions of legal universalism opposed to the liberal tradition.

Since the revolutions of 1989 and the dissolution of the Soviet Union in 1991, however, state socialist contributions to legal theory and international law have

---

[3] Franz L. Neumann, 'The Law of the Soviet State by Andrei Y. Vyshinsky, Translated by Hugh W. Babb, Introduction by John N. Hazard', Political Science Quarterly 64, no. 1 (1949): 127–31, 129.

[4] For theoretical discussions of the Soviet Union as a new type of state, see Scott Newton, 'Microcosm: Soviet Constitutional Internationality', in Revolutions in International Law: The Legacies of 1917, edited by Kathryn Greenman, Anne Orford, Anna Saunders, and Ntina Tzouvala (Cambridge: Cambridge University Press, 2021), 134–55.

[5] For such early studies of Soviet law, see John N. Hazard, Law and Social Change in the USSR (Westport, CT: Hyperion Press, 1953); Harold J. Berman, Justice in the USSR: An Interpretation of Soviet Law (Cambridge, MA: Harvard University Press, 1963). Paul Betts has recently pointed to the same issue for the scholarship concerned with socialist notions of rights. See Paul Betts, 'Rights', in Socialism Goes Global: The Soviet Union and Eastern Europe in the Age of Decolonization, coordinated by James Mark and Paul Betts (Oxford: Oxford University Press, 2022), 180–220, 181.

[6] See William E. Butler's introduction in: Grigory I. Tunkin, Theory of International Law (London: George Allen & Unwin Ltd, 1970), xiii–xxi, xiv.

seldom been studied beyond select facets such as Pashukanis' dictum about the withering away of the law. Recently, scholarship on both state socialist visions of human rights in domestic settings and as a new language to build alliances with anticolonial movements and newly independent states have illuminated state socialist agency in shaping legal norms after 1945.[7] Yet, especially for the post-Stalinist period, few studies consider state socialist approaches to international law as part of the wider issue of where law fit into the building of socialism and how socialist legal scholars and politicians tried to connect their visions of international law with their general visions of what the law was in a Marxist–Leninist worldview.[8] In other words, how state socialist legal experts and politicians connected the legal norms they advocated to demands for institutional frameworks that fit their understandings of socialist legality and governance has not yet attracted much scholarly attention.

If we study the state socialist project of defining a new kind of law on its own terms, the attempt to create a legal counter-universe within the Eastern Bloc becomes visible. Soviet international law theories of the mid-century assumed that different kinds of law existed depending on the form of a state's system of governance, just as did Western traditions of the late nineteenth century.[9] Whereas European imperial states justified unequal international legal standards using a hierarchy of civilizational progress, especially as far as their colonies were concerned, state socialist legal thinkers argued for a qualitative difference between bourgeois law and socialist law based on the revolutionary class character and economic base of their countries.[10] This was their starting point when they began to engage with the sphere of international law. Like Western states, the Soviet Union and its Eastern European allies safeguarded domestic legal sovereignty to keep the influences of ideologically opposed legal traditions at bay. And, again similar to manifold Western traditions of thinking about international law from the point

---

[7] For two broader introductions to state socialist rights campaigns geared towards the Third World and global human rights history, see Betts, 'Rights' and Roland Burke, Marco Duranti, and A. Dirk Moses, 'Introduction: Human Rights, Empire, and After', in *Decolonisation, Self-Determination, and the Rise of Global Human Rights Politics*, edited by Roland Burke, Marco Duranti, and A. Dirk Moses (Cambridge: Cambridge University Press, 2020), 1–31.

[8] For a broad overview of the Soviet contribution to law, see John Quigley, *Soviet Legal Innovation and the Law of the Western World* (Cambridge: Cambridge University Press, 2007) and Scott Newton, *Law and the Making of the Soviet World: The Red Demiurge* (London: Routledge, 2014). For studies on domestic legal systems, see Dina Moyal, 'Did Law Matter? Law, State and Individual in the USSR 1953–1982', PhD dissertation, Stanford University (2010). For East Asia, see Fu Hualing, John Gillespie, Pip Nicholson, William Partlett (eds.), *Socialist Law in Socialist East Asia* (Cambridge: Cambridge University Press, 2018).

[9] For the imperialist roots of international law, see e.g. Anthony Anghie, *Imperialism, Sovereignty, and the Making of International Law* (Cambridge: Cambridge University Press, 2005).

[10] For a discussion of Bolshevik perspectives on international law grounded in theories of imperialism and capitalism, see Robert Knox and Ntina Tzouvala, 'Looking Eastwards: The Bolshevik Theory of Imperialism and International Law', in *Revolutions in International Law: The Legacies of 1917*, edited by Kathryn Greenman, Anne Orford, Anna Saunders, and Ntina Tzouvala (Cambridge: Cambridge University Press, 2021), 27–55.

of view of specific national or regional traditions and schools of legal theory, state socialist countries and their legal experts also produced a range of different approaches to international law across Eastern Europe,[11] East Asia,[12] and Africa that adopted, adapted, rejected, or ignored original Soviet theories of international law.

From the October Revolution to the Second World War

Until 1945, Soviet controversies over international law closely mapped upon debates about the function of law within Marxism–Leninism, although theoretical engagement with the subject had remained sporadic. In 1924, Evgeny Korovin published a first doctrinal book on international law. In keeping with the transitional logics of building socialism following the October Revolution and the civil war, Korovin aptly titled his work *International Law of the Transition Period*. Korovin had been appointed to a full professorship at Moscow State University in 1923 and later moved to a dedicated chair for international law. In this role, he taught international law and international relations at a number of leading Soviet academic institutes in Moscow.[13] The book was released in a 5,000-copy print run, which suggests wide circulation and usage in teaching. A second edition was released one year later. From the 1930s, Soviet legal thought was increasingly distributed abroad. In this context, John N. Hazard became an important interlocutor between the Anglo-American and Soviet expert communities. Hazard was the first American to study law in the Soviet Union from 1934 to 1937, and he earned a certificate from the Moscow Juridical Institute. He met Korovin frequently during his studies in Moscow as Korovin pioneered the field of comparative law and shaped Hazard's understanding of Soviet scholarly debate, which he then took back to the United States.[14] A leading scholar of Sovietology after 1945, he supported Justice Robert Jackson in preparing the prosecution of Nazi war criminals at Nuremberg before taking up a chair in public law at Columbia University in New York where he was instrumental in founding the Russian Institute (now the Harriman Institute).

Korovin's pragmatic approach followed Vladimir Lenin's doctrinal writings and stipulated that as long as states existed, there would be international law to regulate relations between them. His work was driven by strategic concerns over how the Soviet state could engage with Western countries diplomatically without compromising the dismissal of bourgeois law, and the rejection of being bound by any agreements made by the Tsarist Russian state and the Provisional Government led by Alexander F. Kerensky. In what he called 'legal instrumentalism', as Boris

---

[11] See Jakub Szumski, Chapter 5 in this volume.
[12] See Ryan Martínez Mitchell, Chapter 6 in this volume.
[13] Boris N. Mamlyuk and Ugo Mattei, 'Comparative International Law', *Brooklyn Journal of International Law* 36, no. 2 (2011): 385–451, 396.
[14] Ibid., 397f.

N. Mamlyuk and Ugo Mattei have argued, Korovin 'openly argued for elastic legal standards as a way to both undermine the bourgeois concept of law and to afford the young Soviet state room to operate in a hostile foreign environment'.[15] The Soviet government had just emerged victoriously from the civil war and Korovin mistrusted existing international law altogether.[16]

Korovin argued, however, that 'old' international law norms and rules could still be useful to insulate the only socialist country in the world from foreign influence. If implemented by the Soviet Union following its Marxist–Leninist interpretation of the law as a means of politics and social transformation in the transition period, he argued, 'old' international law would change its ideological character. In other words, it was not so much the legal norms that mattered but the institutional and ideological logics with which they were applied. In the 1920s, international law was thus just a tool to engage with hostile bourgeois states until the world revolution was achieved. Korovin warned his comrades in 1924: 'As long as the USSR is surrounded by capitalist states it must remain in legal "isolation"—it cannot become either an object or subject of the bourgeois trapeze.'[17] This sceptical position towards opening up the socialist sphere to existing international law was again reinforced in 1946, when Korovin warned of too much enthusiasm for universal international law at the end of the Nuremberg Trial.

The long-term introspective debate on international law within the Soviet Union before 1945 was caused by the ideological battles raging over the fundamental question of the relationship of law and socialism. After Korovin's initial assessment in the 1920s, Evgeny Pashukanis dismissed the existence of any socialist international law altogether in 1935. Already in 1925, Pashukanis had voiced intense criticism of international law, dismissing it as part of the imperialist project of capitalist states: 'The historical examples adduced in any textbook of international law loudly proclaim that *modern international law is the legal form of the struggle of the capitalist states among themselves for domination over the rest of the world*.'[18] In *The General Theory of Law and Marxism* published two years later in 1927, Pashukanis famously contended that law and the state would eventually 'wither away'. For him, law in both domestic and international frameworks was a purely bourgeois tool of domination that had no permanent role to play in the building of socialism. This radical position first propelled him to the directorship of the Institute of Soviet Construction and Law (later the Institute of State and Law at

---

[15] Ibid., 399.
[16] For Soviet engagement with international law in the interwar period and Western reception, see Owen Taylor, 'Law and Socialist Revolution. Early Soviet Legal Theory and Practice', in *Revolutions in International Law: The Legacies of 1917*, edited by Kathryn Greenman, Anne Orford, Anna Saunders, and Ntina Tzouvala (Cambridge: Cambridge University Press, 2021), 156–80.
[17] Cited in Mamlyuk and Mattei, 'Comparative International Law', 401.
[18] Evgeny Pashukanis, 'International Law' (1925), www.marxists.org/archive/pashukanis/1925/xx/intlaw.htm (last accessed: 19.09.2024).

the Soviet Academy of Science) and made him one of the most prominent revolutionary voices on the role of international law for the socialist project.

By the 1930s, however, Stalin's supporters began to attack Pashukanis' radical arguments that proposed that no proletarian law or socialist rights could exist. This internal opposition did not deter Pashukanis. In keeping with his argument about the withering away of state and law as part of his commodity theory of law, he openly dismissed any future of socialist international law in 1935. He argued in *Essays on International Law* that there existed only one bourgeois international law. In Pashukanis' eyes, law was part of the ideological superstructure to the economic base—like commodities. Consequently, it would disappear once the transition to socialism and eventually communism had overthrown existing legal relationships based on property.[19] In the end, world revolution would make international law obsolete. Yet, Pashukanis still conceded, agreeing with Korovin, that international law could be used strategically by the Soviet state to further its political goals until this transformation was complete.

Until the Second World War, the Soviet debate on law remained introspective. When Vyshinsky published his theory of the Soviet state in 1938, a long and protracted process of defining the state in law came to an end. This struggle over the meaning of law under socialism had counted numerous victims by the end of Stalin's purges.[20] The Soviet state now had a legal form. Or as Vyshinsky put it: 'The class structure of Soviet society, its political and economic bases—that is to say, that which in its entirety also constitutes social organization—are defined in extraordinary sharp, and classically exact, juridical form.'[21] Vyshinsky hailed Soviet law and the Stalin Constitution of 1936 as the 'triumph of the socialist system' and the 'realization of socialism'. At this point, he even saw the constitution as internationalist in the sense that it should attract 'honest people in capitalist countries' to put Soviet law into practice in their countries after overthrowing capitalism: 'What has been put into practice in the USSR can perfectly well be put into practice in other countries too.'[22] At the same time, the Moscow government's All People's Discussion of the constitution was meant to signal popular involvement in the codification of Soviet law to its citizens and to the outside world.[23]

The propagandistic value of Soviet law on the eve of the Second World War centred on the goal of exporting the revolution and framed the fight for communism in explicit antifascist terms. After Pashukanis' execution in 1937 at the height of Stalin's purges, the Soviet position moved to a new middle ground during

---

[19] See Newton, *Law and the Making of the Soviet World*, 100–12.
[20] For the history of Stalinist show trials and Vyshinsky's leading role as prosecutor, see David M. Crow, 'Late Imperial and Soviet Show Trials, 1878–1938', in *Stalin's Soviet Justice: 'Show' Trials, War Crimes Trials, and Nuremberg*, edited by David M. Crow (London: Bloomsbury, 2019), 31–79.
[21] Vyshinsky, *The Law of the Soviet State*, 129.
[22] Ibid., 124f.
[23] Benjamin Nathans, 'Soviet Rights Talk in the Post-Stalin Era', in *Human Rights in the Twentieth Century*, edited by Stefan-Ludwig Hoffmann (Cambridge: Cambridge University Press, 2011), 172.

the war, wherein international law was now seen as an amalgam of bourgeois and socialist norms.[24] Yet, the Soviets maintained their position that a separate socialist version of international law existed, and that it had emerged after the October Revolution. In 1938, Vyshinsky repositioned Soviet law and the constitution as central tools in defending and exporting the revolution beyond the boundaries of the USSR.[25] He pointed out that 'the Stalin Constitution mobilizes the masses of toilers of all countries in the struggle against fascism'.[26]

Yet, Soviet antifascist prestige had taken a severe hit before the war. The signing of the Molotov–Ribbentrop Pact in 1939 left many communists around the world deeply disillusioned. The non-aggression treaty between Nazi Germany and the Soviet Union contained a secret protocol that divided Central and Eastern Europe between the two countries. When Hitler invaded Poland in September 1939, Soviet troops did likewise and occupied its Eastern half. Stalin's attack on Finland in November 1939 and the occupation of the Baltic states in 1940 made the Soviet Union appear as an imperialist country in the eyes of many international observers. The enormous human cost that the Soviet Union suffered at the hands of the Nazis after the German invasion in June 1941 would change Soviet perspectives on the need for new international norms, especially the criminalization of aggressive warfare as a crime against peace. By this time the definition of the Soviet state in law was firmly in place and ideological opponents of Vyshinsky's view deposed. Now, the question of how the USSR interacted with other countries and positioned itself in international law had to be discussed anew.

Vyshinky's foundational book on the law served an ideological purpose to the outside world in this repositioning of the Soviet debate on law. Hazard pointed to this aspect in his introduction to the English translation, when he argued that the real target of the book had been Soviet legal professionals in the making, and that the text sought to insulate them from Western Cold War propaganda by exposing them to the great legal thinkers of the past. When they hear Western attacks on Soviet law, the 'Soviet citizen has met these arguments before and is prepared with an immediate response'.[27] With the ideological confrontation between the United States and the Soviet Union escalating after 1945, Western scholars took the potential international impact of Soviet law seriously. They also acknowledged that it would not be necessarily easy to convince Soviet citizens of the superiority of Western notions of law and justice.

The end of the Second World War and the mid-century disjuncture—as Mark Mazower has called the end of European normative dominance in international affairs—provided the Soviet Union with an opportunity to reshape the meaning

---

[24] John N. Hazard, 'The Soviet Union and International Law', *Soviet Studies* 1, no. 3 (1950): 189–99, 191.
[25] Newton, *Law and the Making of the Soviet World*, 112–27.
[26] Vyshinsky, *The Law of the Soviet State*, 125.
[27] Hazard, 'Introduction', ix.

of universal international law.[28] Or at least this was what some Soviet legal experts thought. Soviet international law scholars first and foremost concentrated on the fallout of Adolf Hitler's war of extermination. The wartime alliance and plans for a war crimes tribunal at the end of the war spurred on Soviet legal minds to advance new ideas for such a transitional justice tribunal framed around novel concepts of crimes against peace and crimes against humanity. In 1944, Soviet scholar Aron N. Trainin developed his ideas on aggressive warfare as the basis for the prosecution of Nazi war criminals in his famous book *The Criminal Responsibility of the Hitlerites*.[29] He had worked as a criminologist and justice of the peace before the revolution. After 1917, he became a protégée of Vyshinsky and helped draft the Soviet criminal code. In the years of Stalin's purges, Trainin published *The Defence of Peace and Criminal Law*, in which he decried the League of Nations' acceptance of the legitimacy of war and demanded that waging war be outlawed internationally.[30] The IMT presented him with the opportunity to implement his vision of making wars of aggression an international crime a reality and cement crimes against peace as a central Soviet concern.

As Francine Hirsch has shown, there was much enthusiasm among Soviet legal scholars for the idea of universal new international legal norms and institutions before the beginning of the IMT in Nuremberg.[31] Soon, however, these hopes were dashed by the acquittal of some Nazi defendants and the growing Western dominance in shaping the emerging United Nations (UN) institutionally. The immediate postwar legal cooperation between the wartime Allies had laid bare once more how different Soviet and Western approaches were, not only in terms of international law norms but also their use in courts and other legal institutions. As fundamental new norms of international law and governance were discussed in the early days of the UN, the Soviets found themselves outmanoeuvred by the Western Allies at the IMT, and Soviet delegate Valentin Treplikov was sidelined at the UN Human Rights Commission in 1947. In 1948, the Soviet Union and Eastern European countries refused to endorse the Universal Declaration of Human Rights (UDHR) because a right of self-determination had not been included and it focused too much on individual rights. This abstention, however, did not preclude the Soviet government from styling itself a champion of human rights in the decade that followed, as Jennifer Amos has argued.[32] Since Lenin had endorsed national

---

[28] For the mid-century disjuncture, see Mark Mazower, 'The End of Civilization and the Rise of Human Rights: The Mid-Twentieth-Century Disjuncture', in *Human Rights in the Twentieth Century*, edited by Stefan-Ludwig Hoffmann (Cambridge: Cambridge University Press, 2011), 29–44.
[29] For a detailed description of Trainin's work, see Gleb Bogush, 'Aron Trainin: The Legal Mind Behind a Soviet International Criminal Law Project', in *The Dawn of a Discipline: International Criminal Law and Its Early Exponents*, edited by Frédéric Mégret and Immi Tallgren (Cambridge: Cambridge University Press, 2020), 260–79. See also Michelle Penn, Chapter 4 in this volume.
[30] Hirsch, *The Soviets at Nuremberg*, 20f.
[31] Ibid., 17–43.
[32] Jennifer Amos, 'Embracing and Contesting. The Soviet Union and the Universal Declaration of Human Rights, 1948–1958', in *Human Rights in the Twentieth Century*, edited by Stefan-Ludwig

self-determination in 1914, the principle had turned into a central rallying cry for the Soviet government to secure the revolution at home and support anticolonial movements in their struggle for independence.[33] In the face of continued Western dominance over shaping new international institutions like the UN, voices such as Korovin's consequently grew louder again—starting in 1946, when he argued that instead of shaping a universal international law, as Trainin advocated at the time, a confrontation of Western notions of international law and Soviet interpretations was on the horizon.[34] With this turn away from an agenda to define universal legal norms, Soviet legal scholars such as Fyodor I. Kozhevnikov and S. B. Krylov, in the late 1940s, remained sceptical about granting the UN equal rights as a legal persona of international law on par with the status of the states that had created it.[35] In the late 1940s, Soviet legal theory thus returned to Korovin's position of a separation of legal spheres and renewed attempts to define socialist international law.

Soviet International Law after De-Stalinization

In the immediate years after the Second World War, colonial conflicts returned with a vengeance. Already in 1946, the Viet Minh began a bitter war for independence against French colonial rule. At the same time, the Cold War divided Europe and turned hot in Asia. In 1947, US President Harry S. Truman proclaimed his determination to support democratic countries economically, politically, and militarily against Soviet expansion. Allied cooperation in occupied Germany finally broke down in 1948 when Soviet troops cut off the Western-occupied sectors of Berlin in an effort to drive out the American, British, and French presence from the heart of their occupation zone. Until summer 1949, the Berlin airlift showed Western determination to push back against the Soviets.[36] Meanwhile, the ideological conflict

---

Hoffmann (Cambridge: Cambridge University Press, 2011), 147–65. See also for the GDR, Ned Richardson-Little, *The Human Rights Dictatorship. Socialism, Global Solidarity and Revolution in East Germany* (Cambridge: Cambridge University Press, 2020). For a discussion of the underpinning ideological Soviet position that favoured revolution over rights to achieve 'good society', see Jessica Whyte, 'Human Rights, Revolution and the "Good Society"', in *Revolutions in International Law: The Legacies of 1917*, edited by Kathryn Greenman, Anne Orford, Anna Saunders, and Ntina Tzouvala (Cambridge: Cambridge University Press, 2021), 401–27.

[33] Vladimir Ilyich Lenin, 'The Right of Nations to Self-Determination', in *Collected Works, Volume 20: December 1913–August 1914* (Moscow: Progress Publishers, 1972), 393–454. For various positions on the nature of self-determination as a right, see e.g. Jörg Fisch, *The Right of Self-Determination of Peoples: The Domestication of an Illusion* (Cambridge: Cambridge University Press, 2015), 129–37; Erez Manela, *The Wilsonian Moment: Self-Determination and the International Origins of Anticolonial Nationalism* (Oxford: Oxford University Press, 2007); Adom Getachew, *Worldmaking after Empire: The Rise and Fall of Self-Determination* (Princeton, NJ: Princeton University Press, 2019).
[34] Hirsch, *The Soviets at Nuremberg*, 397.
[35] Chris Osakwe, 'Contemporary Soviet Doctrine on the Juridical Nature of Universal International Organisation', *The American Journal of International Law* 65, no. 3 (1971): 502–21, 503.
[36] See Christian F. Ostermann, *Between Containment and Rollback. The United States and the Cold War in Germany* (Stanford: Stanford University Press, 2021).

turned into an open war in Korea with the North invading the South in 1950. As a result, the United States mobilized a UN coalition in defence of South Korea. At the same time, France and Britain pushed for the retention of the so-called colonial clause within the UN framework to retain legal authority over 'dependent territories' and exclude them from the application of the principles of the UDHR on the grounds that colonial territories first had to achieve a higher level of development. In response to all of this, the Soviet leadership and other countries from the Global South denounced the new international order as a clear continuation of the 'old' unequal international system, which still perpetuated an ideal of the superiority of European civilization.[37]

The shaky legal coalition between the victorious Allies in organizing the Nuremberg and Tokyo war crimes trials had already broken apart at this point. While the Soviets organized their own trials against Japanese war criminals, the United States separately prosecuted German industrialists, military and SS leaders, Nazi bureaucrats, judges, and doctors in a series of twelve separate trials.[38] Soon after, national war crimes trials across the Socialist Bloc such as the Waldheim trials in the German Democratic Republic in 1950 and internal party purges such as the antisemitic Slansky trial in Czechoslovakia in 1952 deepened the gulf between the Eastern and Western Blocs.[39] 'Revolutionary justice' in the tradition of the Stalinist show trials of the interwar period dominated Western portrayals of state socialist governments that cared little for the law, at home or internationally.[40]

At the same time, the Soviet Union was itself accused of imperialist policies from within socialist Eastern Europe. In 1948, the Yugoslavian leader Josip B. Tito challenged Stalin as legitimate leader of the state socialist camp. At the heart of the conflict lay Stalin's unwillingness to support Tito's ambitions for territorial expansion after his partisans had advanced towards Trieste and captured parts of Carinthia in Austria at the end of the war. In March and May 1948, Stalin sent public letters to Tito in which he denounced Yugoslavian attempts to dominate the Balkan region, drew parallels between Tito and exiled Russian Communist Leon Trotsky (who was assassinated by a Soviet agent in 1940), and called for his removal. The conflict triggered an ideological split between the Soviet Union and Yugoslavia and pushed

---

[37] Roger Normand and Sarah Zaidi, *Human Rights at the UN* (Bloomington, IN: Indiana University Press, 2008), 230–32. See also Jessica Lynne Pearson, 'Defending Empire at the United Nations: The Politics of International Colonial Oversight in the Era of Decolonisation', *The Journal of Imperial and Commonwealth History* 45, no. 3 (2017): 525–49.

[38] Valentyna Polunina, 'The Khabarovsk Trial: The Soviet Riposte to the Tokyo Tribunal', in *Trials for International Crimes in Asia*, edited by Kirsten Sellars (Cambridge: Cambridge University Press, 2015), 121–44; Kim Christian Priemel, *The Betrayal. The Nuremberg Trials and German Divergence* (Oxford: Oxford University Press, 2016).

[39] See Katharina Rauschenberger, Joachim von Puttkamer, and Sybille Steinbacher (eds.), *Investigating, Punishing, Agitating: Nazi Perpetrator Trials in the Eastern Bloc* (Göttingen: Wallstein, 2023).

[40] See Crow, 'Late Imperial and Soviet Show Trials, 1878–1938'.

Tito to both cooperate with the West and become a leading supporter of the Non-Aligned Movement (NAM) to gain independence from both superpowers.[41]

Crises in 1956 prompted both the Soviet–Bloc coalition and the Western European powers to face further accusations of imperialist aggression. Soviet troops had first suppressed an uprising of East Germans against their new socialist government in 1953, and then invaded Hungary in 1956 to end reform efforts undermining Soviet principles of governance. At the same time, France and Britain's failed joint military intervention to recapture the Suez Canal from Egypt in the same year suggested that European colonial powers would not easily relinquish their overseas territories. British colonial troops also brutally suppressed anticolonial movements across Africa, most infamously the Mau-Mau Uprising (1952–60). These conflicts, including the Algerian War (1954–62), triggered influential anticolonial critiques of existing international law, for example, by the scholar and politician Mohamed Bedjaoui, who would later become famous for his advocacy of a New International Economic Order (NIEO).[42]

In 1949, despite the Tito–Stalin split and accusations of Soviet imperialism, the project of defining socialist law emerged into a new world as the coalition of socialist states now reached from Eastern Europe to Asia. The explosive growth in the number of state socialist governments reinvigorated visions of socialist international law. While law remained a key tool of party leaderships in the process of 'building socialism', Korovin renewed his claim of an emerging socialist international law.[43] The disappointment of the IMT's outcome and the sidelining of the Soviet Union in the foundation of the UN prompted Soviet legal scholars to revise their notions of international law. While Korovin had been concerned with securing the revolution within the Soviet Union in the 1920s, his postwar work adapted to the new political interests of the Soviet leadership in a changed international environment. Socialism was now no longer confined to one country, Korovin argued, and the emergence of a 'world system' of state socialism had laid the foundations for a new type of socialist international law.[44] By the mid-1950s, Western observers had already noted this realignment of Soviet theory to fit the new Cold War conditions.[45]

---

[41] See Harald Fischer-Tiné, Nada Boskovska, and Natasa Miskovic (eds.), *The Non-Aligned Movement and the Cold War. Delhi – Bandung – Belgrade* (London: Routledge, 2014).

[42] Mohamed Bedjaoui, *Toward a New International Economic Order* (New York: Holmes & Meier 1979); James Thou Gathii, 'Africa', in *The Oxford Handbook of the History of International Law*, edited by Bardo Fassbender and Anne Peters (Oxford: Oxford University Press, 2012), 407–28, 416, 425.

[43] For the role of law within state socialist countries, see e.g. Moyal, 'Did Law Matter?'; Sebastian Gehrig, *Legal Entanglements: Law, Rights, and the Struggle for Legitimacy in Divided Germany, 1945–1989* (New York: Berghahn Books, 2021), 68–102, 183–258.

[44] See Academy of Science of the USSR (ed.), *International Law: A Textbook for Use in Law Schools* (Moscow: Foreign Languages Publishing House, 1960), 20.

[45] W. W. Kulski, 'The Soviet Interpretation of International Law', *The American Journal of International Law* 49, no. 4 (1955): 518–34.

Yet, with the emergence of new socialist states across Eastern Europe, the authoritative voices on the relationship of party-states and international law multiplied as well. Jakub Szmuski shows in this volume that the Soviet school of international law—which had already been divided internally over the correct ideological interpretation of the nature of international law—was now adapted to new national contexts across the Eastern Bloc shaped by various legal traditions. While some party leaderships such as the East German government adhered closely to the Soviet line, other bloc states such as Poland—where liberal traditions remained particularly influential—saw much disagreement and dissent from the Soviet line in the field of law over the coming decades.[46]

After 1945, it was now generally understood among Soviet officials that international law was needed to manage international relations. Gone was the theoretical revolutionary fervour of Pashukanis and the assumption that a quick global victory of world revolution would make bourgeois international law obsolete. Instead, Korovin's theory of a tripartite international legal system regained purchase in Soviet debates. Korovin distinguished between an inter-state regime regulating relations between capitalist states, an inter-state system governing the relations between socialist and capitalist states, and a third—specifically socialist—international law organizing relations between socialist states.[47] He saw socialist international law emerging from the increasing economic relations between state socialist states. Korovin pointed to the 1948 Hungarian–Polish Convention on economic aid and the foundation of the Council for Mutual Economic Assistance (CMEA, more commonly known as COMECON) in 1949 as signs of 'a new, socialist type of international relations founded in equality, sovereignty, non-intervention and other democratic principles of International Law applied in the spirit of proletarian internationalism'.[48] Citing the Soviet–Chinese Treaty on Friendship, Alliance and Mutual Assistance of 1950 and the 1955 Warsaw Treaty on Friendship, Cooperation and Mutual Aid, Korovin argued that 'all these treaties, drawn up in full accordance with the principles of the United Nations Charter, are strictly defensive'.[49] In short, Korovin concentrated on technocratic and economic cooperation as examples for an emerging socialist international legal system. His argument shares striking similarities with the theories of functionalist scholars such as the Hungarian-born British academic David Mitrany or the American

---

[46] Szumski, Chapter 5 in this volume. For the East German context, see Gehrig, *Legal Entanglements*. See also the special issues: Ned Richardson-Little, Hella Dietz, and James Mark (eds.), 'New Perspectives on Socialism and Human Rights in East Central Europe', *East Central Europe* 46, no. 23 (2019) and Raluca Grosescu and Ned Richardson-Little, 'Revisiting State Socialist Approaches to International Criminal and Humanitarian Law', *Journal of the History of International Law* 21, no. 2 (2019). For Hungary and CSSR, see Michal Kopeček, 'The Socialist Conception of Human Rights and Its Dissident Critique: Hungary and Czechoslovakia, 1960s–1980s', *East Central Europe* 46, no. 2–3 (2019): 261–89.
[47] Mamlyuk and Mattei, 'Comparative International Law', 402.
[48] Academy of Science of the USSR (ed.), *International Law*, 72.
[49] Ibid., 73.

scholar Ernst B. Haas on regional integration. Their work has often been applied to explain the technocratic nature of Western European politics of integration on the grounds that political integration followed technocratic cooperation and would lead towards new supranational governmental structures.[50]

This revised understanding clearly was designed to fit the new Soviet Cold War rhetoric of peace and mutual assistance of socialist states. Korovin reminded Soviet law students in a textbook that was translated into English in 1960 that socialist international law was rooted not just in new principles but also method. The 'Science of International Law', he emphasized, was based 'on genuinely scientific foundations'.[51] As such, he linked the legal sciences to Karl Marx and Friedrich Engel's elevation of their study of bourgeois society and the social conditions that would enable a revolution stemming from 'scientific socialism'.[52] Over several pages of this new authoritative textbook, Korovin listed the revised canon of accepted international law writings since the October Revolution, including specialist literature on various fields of international law from the law of the air by Ivan S. Peretersky (1923) and the law of seas by A. D. Keilin and B. M. Vingradov (1939), to A. Sabanin's work on ambassadorial and consular law (1930), Glyadstern's writings on international recognition (1924), Eugen Kelman's conceptualizing of Soviet law abroad (1927) and in foreign courts (1928), S. F. Kechekyan's books on national minority rights (1929), V. V. Yegoryev's book on slavery (1928), Trainin's pioneering texts on aggression, as well as critical engagements with the League of Nations by C. Yavorsky (1928), A. Kolsky (1934), S. Borisov (1936), Khorvatsky (1937), and Notovich (1929). Ushakov's *The Struggle of the Soviet Union to Secure Observance of the UN Charter* (1955) pointed to Soviet international law propaganda and rights diplomacy. Grigory I. Tunkin's *Fundamentals of Present-Day International Law* (1956) and Korovin's own *Fundamental Problems of Present-Day International Relations* (1959) were new guides in international politics. Tunkin would soon be the new rising star of the international law field in the 1960s. The authoritative texts explaining the history of international law were Korovin's own *History of International Law* (1946) and three studies by Fyodor I. Kozhevnikov (1947), who had represented the Soviet Union in the UN International Law Commission from 1952 to 1953, before he took a seat on the bench of the International Court of Justice (ICJ), which he occupied until 1961. Above all, Vyshinsky's five volumes of collected speeches and articles on *Problems of International Law and International Politics* (1949–53) and his *Bibliography of Soviet Literature on International Law* (1955) remained important ideological guides on the relationship of law and socialism.[53]

---

[50] David Mitrany, *The Functional Theory of Politics* (New York: St. Martin's Press, 1975); Ernst B. Haas, *The Uniting of Europe* (Stanford: Stanford University Press, 1958).
[51] Academy of Science of the USSR (ed.), *International Law*, 75.
[52] The term 'scientific socialism' was first used by Pierre-Joseph Proudhon in 1840.
[53] For the full list of titles and legal fields listed, see ibid., 75–81.

The major theme of Soviet international law around 1960 was the safeguarding of sovereignty, non-intervention, and securing international trade. This coincided with the rapid pace of decolonization and the creation of many new sovereign states—seventeen in sub-Saharan Africa gained independence from the United Kingdom and France in 1960 alone. To facilitate this, Korovin emphasized the importance of equal treaties and outlawing unequal treaties. Here, Soviet and anticolonial demands for a reform of international law norms met. In 1949, the UN International Law Commission began to debate universal norms and rules on who could enter into international treaties and how they should be negotiated. In the midst of decolonization, the international community was still far from reaching an agreement on this fundamental issue of international order.[54] Five years after the 1955 Bandung Conference, Soviet international law scholars claimed to have made particularly important contributions to the development of concepts of state sovereignty and self-determination.[55] Yet, such claims must have sounded particularly hollow to Hungarians after the Soviet invasion of 1956 and Germans who faced renewed tensions over the status of occupied Berlin that would culminate in the building of the Berlin Wall in 1961.

The spread of socialism beyond the USSR had created notable new centres of international law. The 1960 Soviet textbook singled out the Institute of International Relations and International Law in Beijing and the Polish Institute of International Problems and its *Yearbook of International Law*. In acknowledging the writings of scholars from 'socialist fraternal states' such as Olimpiu Olteanu's textbook from Romania, the work of Hungarian scholars edited by Gyula Hajdu, M. Genovski's book on international law from Bulgaria, and Polish jurists such as Manfred Lachs, Ludwik Gelberg, Wacław Makowski, Ludwik Ehrlich, and Leon Babinski, the Soviet international law elite gestured to the new multitude of voices within the Socialist Bloc on the issue of international law, but they insisted on a coherent project of building socialist international law.[56] In the same year in which an unprecedented number of colonies reached independence and anticolonial leaders envisioned the transformation of international organizations to a new kind of world government and the emergence of a truly equal international law, V. V. Yevgeneyev nonetheless reinforced a conservative, restricted definition of what the subject of international law was supposed to remain in the future: the sovereign state. Neither international organizations nor individuals were included in Soviet doctrine.[57] This narrow view of international law would

---

[54] Conflicts over 'divided nations' brought this issue into sharp relief in the 1960s, see Sebastian Gehrig, 'Dividing the Indivisible: Cold War Sovereignty, National Division, and the German Question at the United Nations', *Central European History* 55, no. 1 (2022): 70–89.
[55] Academy of Science of the USSR (ed.), *International Law*, 83.
[56] For the discussion of this Eastern Bloc scholarship, see ibid., 86.
[57] Ibid., 89.

increasingly bring Soviet positions into open conflict with socialist voices from Africa and Asia.[58]

The Impact of Decolonization, the Sino–Soviet Split, and Détente on State Socialist Theories of International Law

The anticolonial challenge to European powers birthed widespread debates on alternative concepts of sovereignty to define, but also fundamentally question, the nation-state as the main subject of international law. Adom Getachew has shown how African leaders pushed for the transformation of self-determination from a principle to a foundational right governing international relations.[59] In 1960, the Year of Africa, seventeen independent African countries emerged from colonial rule. At the same time, the outbreak of the secessionist conflict in Congo and the assassination of Prime Minister Patrice Lumumba appeared as a cautionary tale for socialist leaders such as the Ghanaian Kwame Nkrumah who also sought to challenge European hegemony. For Nkrumah, the failed UN peacekeeping mission and Cold War interests of both the United States and the Soviet Union in Congo called for securing independence politically and economically. African socialist leaders who were part of the so-called Casablanca Group led by Nkrumah, Guinea's Ahmed Sékou Touré, and Egypt's Gamal Abdel Nasser shared the belief in the creation of a united African state or federation.[60] Their chief concern, as Nkrumah outlined before the UN General Assembly in September 1960, was preventing their countries from becoming client-states of their former colonizers.[61] Although Nkrumah turned to Eastern European governments and the Soviet Union at this time for material support, he remained wary of the threat of neo-colonialism and replacing European domination with Soviet hegemony.[62]

Ultimately, pan-African socialist efforts were defeated by the Monrovia Group that included Liberia, Nigeria, and much of Francophone Africa, which also argued for African unity, but not at the expense of nationalism and national sovereignty. In 1963, the Organisation of African Unity (OAU) organized postcolonial state cooperation based on the right of self-determination of peoples rather than

---

[58] In the Soviet textbook chapter on the UN, there was some slippage in this argument by acknowledging the UN 'to a certain extent' as a subject of international law by citing the International Court of Justice's decision on the assassination of UN mediator Count Bernadotte in Palestine in 1949. See ibid., 347. The UN's claim to legal persona in international law would finally be endorsed by Tunkin in 1970.

[59] Getachew, *Worldmaking after Empire*, 87–92.

[60] For alternative visions of a postcolonial Africa beyond the nation state, see Christopher Gevers, 'To Seek with Beauty to Set the World Right: Cold War International Law and the Radical "Imaginative Geography" of Pan-Africanism', in *International Law and the Cold War*, edited by Matthew Craven, Sundhya Pahuja, and Gerry Simpson (Cambridge: Cambridge University Press, 2019), 492–509.

[61] Getachew, *Worldmaking after Empire*, 100.

[62] Nana Osei-Opare, 'Uneasy Comrades: Postcolonial Statecraft, Race, and Citizenship, Ghana-Soviet Relations, 1957–1966', *Journal of West African History* 5, no. 2 (2019): 85–111.

pan-Africanism.[63] Recent historical scholarship has pointed to shared initiatives within international rights diplomacy between Eastern Bloc and African socialist states in this period.[64] Meanwhile, the debate among legal scholars has remained focused on the controversies between 'contributionists', who emphasize Africans' role in the development of international law, and critical theorists, who explore the subordination of Africa in international relations and law.[65] More scholarship on African socialist engagements with international law are needed to expand our knowledge beyond rights diplomacy and policy initiatives within the UN. This might also add to debates centring on the question of to what extent we can speak of a uniform African socialism in the legal field.[66] Interestingly, postcolonial legal experts argued in a similar vein to interwar Soviet scholars that decolonized states were entitled to pick and choose which international law to apply at this time, in particular during the heated controversies surrounding demands for an NIEO that was meant to secure the political sovereignty of African states by means of economic independence from global capitalist economic structures.[67]

Before self-determination was enshrined in both UN human rights covenants in 1966, non-European state socialist officials and legal scholars developed their own frameworks of international law. At the core of these debates remained the questions of whether state socialism had created a novel type of polity that generated a new kind of law and what role nationalism ought to play in anticolonial struggles for self-determination. Revisiting the nature of sovereignty as part of the Third World liberation struggle would have direct implications for the conceptualization of international relations and international law.[68]

Although the People's Republic of China (PRC) and the Soviet Union would split ideologically in the 1960s, in the immediate postwar period, there was initially agreement on key issues of international law. In the quest for independence and international recognition, Chinese officials such as Liu Shaoqi rehabilitated patriotism by endorsing Soviet notions of a class-based definition of nation and

---

[63] Taslim Olawale Elias and Richard Akinjide, 'The Charter of the Organisation of African Unity', in *Africa and the Development of International Law*, edited by Taslim Olawale Elias and Richard Akinjide (Leiden: Brill, 1988), 121–48.
[64] For a broader perspective on such alliances, see Betts, 'Rights', 180–220.
[65] Gathii, 'Africa', 407–28.
[66] On politics, see Emma Hunter, 'African Socialism', in *The Cambridge History of Africa*, vol. 2, edited by Marcel van der Linden (Cambridge: Cambridge University Press, 2022), 455–73.
[67] Anna Brunner, 'Acquired Rights and State Succession: The Rise and Fall of the Third World in the International Law Commission', in *The Battle for International Law: South-North Perspectives on the Decolonization Era*, edited by Jochen von Bernstorff and Philipp Dann (Oxford: Oxford University Press, 2019), 124–40; Anna Krueger, *Die Bindung der Dritten Welt an das postkoloniale Völkerrecht: Die Völkerrechtskommission, das Recht der Verträge und das Recht der Staatennachfolge in der Dekolonialisierung* (Berlin: Springer, 2018), 87–121. See also Getachew, *Worldmaking after Empire*, 142–76.
[68] For the East German re-definition of sovereignty drawing on Third World concepts, see Sebastian Gehrig, 'Reaching Out to the Third World: East Germany's Anti-Apartheid and Socialist Human Rights Campaign', *German History* 36, no. 4 (2018): 574–97. See also Brad Simpson, Chapter 3 in this volume.

state as part of the anticolonial struggle. In the early 1950s, Liu was a senior party leader who would go on to serve as Chairman of the PRC, which made him head of state and put him in charge of the military until he was purged during the Cultural Revolution. The national interests of the proletariat, Liu argued in 1952, were one and the same as the basic interests of 'the masses in every nation'.[69] Liu's intervention formed part of the Soviet anti-Tito campaign, intended to counter Yugoslavian accusations that Soviet and Western foreign policies were equally imperialist. After Tito broke with Stalin in 1948, Yugoslavia had begun to establish an independent state socialist position in international relations and law.[70] Against this dissenting voice from within the socialist camp, Liu posited that 'only the Communists and the international proletariat, only the Soviet Union and the New Democracies led by the Communist Parties are the most reliable friends of all oppressed nations fighting for their liberation from imperialist oppression, for national independence'.[71]

Liu endorsed *national* liberation and independence and argued that such nationalist perspectives did not contradict socialist internationalism. Similar to Soviet positions, the Chinese Communist Party (CCP) thus endorsed the idea of a class-based qualitative difference between 'bourgeois' states and socialist countries. Even before the Bandung Final Communique was signed in 1955, Beijing endorsed the so-called Five Principles of Peaceful Coexistence that also guided Soviet theories of international law at the time: mutual respect for territorial integrity and sovereignty, mutual non-aggression, mutual non-interference in internal affairs, mutual cooperation, and peaceful coexistence.[72] These principles, also supported by Indian leader Jawaharlal Nehru, who at the time was a leading figure in the NAM, found their way into the ten-point final declaration of the Bandung Conference.[73] From a state socialist perspective, the core principles of socialist international law doctrine thus spread beyond the 'socialist world system' and shaped debates of newly independent states at this time.[74]

By the late 1950s, Chinese legal experts were plagued by similar ideological problems as their Soviet colleagues in their attempt to position themselves

---

[69] Liu Shaoqi, *Internationalism and Nationalism* (Beijing: Foreign Language Press, 1952), www.marxists.org/reference/archive/liu-shaoqi/1952/internationalism_nationalism/index.htm (last accessed: 19.09.2024).

[70] See Arno Trültzsch, *Sozialismus und Blockfreiheit: Der Beitrag Jugoslawiens zum Völkerrecht 1948–1980/91* (Göttingen: Wallstein, 2021).

[71] Liu, *Internationalism and Nationalism*.

[72] See Mitchell, Chapter 6 in this volume. See also Sophie Richardson, *China, Cambodia, and the Five Principles of Peaceful Coexistence* (New York: Columbia University Press, 2010).

[73] Andrea Benvenuti, 'Constructing Peaceful Coexistence: Nehru's Approach to Regional Security and India's Rapprochement with Communist China in the Mid-1950s', *Diplomacy & Statecraft* 31, no. 1 (2020): 91–117.

[74] For a discussion of Bandung as the starting point for an Asian regionalism from a Chinese perspective, see Chen Yifeng, 'Bandung, China, and the Making of World Order in East Asia', in *Bandung, Global History, and International Law: Critical Pasts and Pending Futures*, edited by Luis Eslava, Michael Fakhri, and Vasuki Nesiah (Cambridge: Cambridge University Press, 2017), 177–95.

towards international law. In the end, as Ryan Mitchell explains in this volume, a high-profile meeting in 1958 tentatively concluded that international law represented a mixed or hybrid system with some rules emerging in the interaction of state socialist countries, while a different set of norms applied universally in the interaction of all states. While Chinese legal scholars still followed Soviet doctrine in 1958 as first cracks in the Sino–Soviet alliance were appearing, the CCP experts insisted that national liberation movements should be recognized as subjects of international law.[75] This went against the more rigid Soviet position of international law as a state-centred endeavour, socialist or otherwise. Here, the ideas Liu Shaoqi had already gestured to in 1952 began to crystallize. The CCP had a vested interest in expanding international law beyond recognized states. The PRC remained excluded from UN politics between 1949 and 1971 as the Republic of China (ROC on Taiwan had assumed representation of China in the UN Security Council and General Assembly. The legal recognition of states and political movements that the Western alliance blocked from access to international politics and international law debates at the UN thus was a chief concern of the CCP at the time and connected Beijing to other Third World liberation movements fighting for self-determination and the international recognition of their sovereignty.[76]

Many of these theoretical debates took on great relevance to real-world conflicts as Cold War tensions boiled over in the early 1960s. When Belgium retreated from Congo, the newly independent country turned into a battleground of Cold War superpower interests. The UN once more became an active part of the conflict, as it had previously in the case of the Korean War. This time, however, the UN mission to Congo was meant to ensure peace rather than rollback an invasion. Yet, UN troops were soon dragged into hostilities and not seen as an impartial peacekeeping force by the belligerents on the ground.[77] In Europe, the building of the Berlin Wall in 1961 cemented the Cold War divide. One year later, the world came close to nuclear war when the Soviet Union, under Premier Nikita Khrushchev, decided to station nuclear missiles in Cuba. During the thirteen days of the Cuban Missile Crisis, the leaders of both superpowers realized that their global rivalry needed urgent de-escalation.

While Third World revolutionary movements radicalized their politics to achieve independence from colonialism, the Soviet answer to these increased Cold War tensions was the promotion of 'peaceful coexistence' in international politics and law. Already in 1958, Grigory I. Tunkin had called for opening a new page in the development of international law. By 1963, the Committee on Peaceful Coexistence of the Soviet Association of International Law had endorsed the

---

[75] Ibid.
[76] This issue crystalized in conflicts over the international legal status of divided countries such as Germany, Korea, Vietnam, and China. See Gehrig, 'Dividing the Indivisible'.
[77] See Alana O'Malley, *The Diplomacy of Decolonisation: America, Britain and the United Nations During the Congo Crisis 1960–1964* (Manchester: Manchester University Press, 2018).

principle, and Tunkin even argued 'there is every ground to call present-day international law the law of peaceful coexistence', a definition that the Soviet delegation also submitted for endorsement to the UN. US scholars such as Leon Lipson argued that although 'peaceful coexistence' was still undefined in its legal meaning as of 1963, Western observers should not dismiss it outright as a concept of international law. He recognized the Soviets' effort to overcome the international law of the past as 'a law of war and peace' with a new focus on peaceful coexistence.[78] As part of this new rhetoric of peaceful coexistence, the Soviet Union supported a UN convention on universal rules on international treaties to underline its new position on the nature of international law as a law of peace; in 1969, the Vienna Convention on the Laws of Treaties stipulated new rules for inter-state treaties. Hailed as a major success by many state socialist governments, it would take until 1980 for the convention to take effect.

Yet, the CCP took issue with Nikita Khrushchev's new course of 'peaceful coexistence' with the capitalist West. Since the emerging Sino–Soviet split, which saw the recalling of Soviet experts from the PRC, the CCP had moved to take up the mantle as leader of the Third World revolution, participating in the Tricontinental Conference in Havana in 1966 and extending its international support to liberation movements in Africa.[79] In 1971, the ROC was expelled from the UN and the PRC assumed China's seat on the Security Council and at the General Assembly. The entry of the PRC into the UN came at a time when the international community was hotly debating nation-state sovereignty as a foundational principle of international law anew. Decolonized states now also called for new global criminal prosecution mechanisms of individual perpetrators—a debate that peaked in the controversies surrounding the 1973 UN Apartheid Convention.[80] In parallel, PRC leader Mao Zedong revised his theory of international politics into the Three-World-Theory that Deng Xiaoping would officially proclaim at the UN General Assembly in 1973. Deng told the world that Mao saw the world dominated by the First World, the capitalist West, and the Second World, the 'social imperialist' Soviet Union and its allies. Against these two oppressive forces in international politics, the Third World would harbour the revolutionary forces of the era.[81]

---

[78] Leon Lipson, 'Peaceful Coexistence', *Law and Contemporary Problems* 29, no. 4 (1964): 871–81, 871.
[79] Priya Lal, 'Maoism in Tanzania: Material Connections and Shared Imaginaries', in *Mao's Little Red Book: A Global History*, edited by Alexander C. Cook (Cambridge: Cambridge University Press, 2014), 96–116; Ian Taylor, 'The Ambiguous Commitment: The People's Republic of China and the Anti-Apartheid Struggle in South Africa', *Journal of Contemporary African Studies* 18, no. 1 (2000): 91–106.
[80] Sebastian Gehrig, James Mark, Paul Betts, Kim Christiaens, and Idesbald Goddeeris, 'The Eastern Bloc, Human Rights, and the Global Fight against Apartheid', *East Central Europe* 46, no. 2–3 (2019): 290–317. See also Raluca Grosescu, Chapter 10 in this volume.
[81] See Jennifer Altehenger, 'Social Imperialism and Mao's Three Worlds: Deng Xiaoping's Speech to the U.N. General Assembly, 1974', in *Revolutionary Moments: Reading Revolutionary Texts*, edited by Rachel Hammersley (London: Bloomsbury, 2015), 175–82; Chen Jian, 'China, the Third World, and the Cold War', in *The Cold War in the Third World*, edited by Robert J. McMahon (Oxford: Oxford University Press, 2013), 85–100.

Similar to the Soviet Union's aim of safeguarding the revolution at home in the 1920s and 1930s when it came to conceptualizing and engaging with international law, it would take the PRC until the 1990s to engage fully with international law making and turn away from revolutionary Maoist frameworks.[82] As with the codification drive in the Soviet Union at the end of Stalin's purges in the 1930s, the PRC had already begun to engage in prolonged debates on a return to law in the midst of the Cultural Revolution's upheaval. Party officials encouraged Chinese citizens to debate new constitution drafts first in 1970 and then again in 1975; after Mao's death in 1976, a new constitution was proclaimed in 1978. Yet, party reformers quickly pushed further once Deng Xiaoping, now leader of the PRC, announced his Reform and Opening policies in the same year to have these reflected in constitutional law. In 1982, a revised constitution was meant to return PRC society to law-based governance.[83] After this period of internal consolidation, the CCP's bloody suppression of the Tiananmen protests in June 1989 and the demise of the Eastern Bloc and the Soviet Union, the PRC government eventually turned to an agenda of actively setting international law rules.[84] This renewed engagement with international law coincided with Deng's 'Southern Tour' in 1992, during which he endorsed special economic zones to implement the economic opening to the West at home.[85]

Accepting Universalism while Abandoning a Socialist Legal Universalism

Soviet legal theories moved away from notions of a separate socialist international law during the 1960s when the CCP radicalized its perspective on the nature of international politics. De-Stalinization also led to changed attitudes towards international law. Since the early 1960s, Grigory I. Tunkin had spearheaded a theoretical reorientation that denounced both Vyshinsky's 'incorrect, dogmatic conceptions particularly on the essence of international law' and Korovin's thesis of the existence of a separate socialist international law.[86] Against the views of 'the Chinese dogmatists', Tunkin moved the Soviet position to an acceptance of the universality of one international law. By the 1960s, he had risen to prominence

---

[82] See Mitchell, Chapter 6 in this volume.

[83] Jennifer Altehenger, *Legal Lessons: Popularising Laws in the People's Republic of China 1949–1989* (Cambridge, MA: Harvard University Asia Center, 2018), 173, 197–204.

[84] For the domestic return to an emphasis on socialist legality, see Glenn Tiffert, 'Socialist Rule of Law with Chinese Characteristics: A New Genealogy', in *Socialist Law in Socialist East Asia*, edited by Fu Hualing, John Gillespie, Pip Nicholson, and William Partlett (Cambridge: Cambridge University Press, 2018), 72–96.

[85] For the 'Southern Tour', see Ezra Vogel, *Deng Xiaoping and the Transformation of China* (Cambridge, MA: Belknap Press, 2013), 664–92.

[86] Tunkin, *Theory of International Law*, xv.

within and outside the Soviet Union as a leading authority on socialist international law. Tunkin served on diplomatic postings from Iran to Canada and Korea in the 1940s; from 1952 to 1965, he led the legal and treaty section of the Foreign Ministry and held various appointments at leading academic institutions in Moscow. Tunkin became known internationally through his appointment to the UN International Law Commission, which he served on from 1957 to 1966 and chaired as president in 1961. With Tunkin's star rising in the era of Détente, he scaled back Korovin's arguments to the basic assumption that international law was essentially regulating agreements between states based on legal norms. As such, international law was universal as evidenced by the diplomatic practice of the Soviet state. If international law was not universal, how could international agreements be binding between ideologically opposed states?[87]

This assumption, however, did not preclude Socialist Bloc countries from fighting for hegemony in defining these international norms. In a volume entitled *Contemporary International Law*, published in English in 1969, Tunkin argued that 'since international law is now universal, its development is influenced by the struggle and cooperation of states on the world-wide scale'.[88] He thus endorsed that there was only one international system that had become possible by the move of both superpowers towards 'peaceful coexistence'. Still, the Soviet Union and its allies—and not the capitalist West—propelled the development of international law in his eyes: 'The forces championing peace and peaceful coexistence are the forces that stand for the progressive development and consolidation of international law.'[89] He argued that the threat of nuclear war had made peaceful coexistence and common rules a necessity. The fallout of the Cuban Missile Crisis showed here in Tunkin's explanation for a reorientation of international law doctrine. While 'states of the two systems' were still marked by class struggle, Tunkin argued, peaceful coexistence as a socialist principle had to be understood in its historical context: 'In our day, peaceful coexistence—especially between states of the two diametrically opposed social systems—differs very much from peaceful coexistence before the Second World War.'[90] While the socialist world system was a 'new system of international *relations* of the highest type' and not only based on peaceful coexistence but also on proletarian internationalism, Tunkin claimed that the development of contemporary international *law* applied to the relation

---

[87] Ibid., xix.
[88] Grigory I. Tunkin, 'Peaceful Coexistence and International Law', in *Contemporary International Law*, edited by Grigory I. Tunkin (Moscow: Progress Publishers, 1969), 5–35, 17. Tunkin's chapter seems to date from before 1968 judging from the sources cited. The English-language book continues his work in the field based on earlier works from 1962 and 1967 that were published in Russian and translated into German. See Grigory I. Tunkin, *Das Völkerrecht der Gegenwart: Theorie und Praxis* (Ost-Berlin: Staatsverlag der Deutschen Demokratischen Republik, 1963); Grigory I. Tunkin, *Voprosy teorii mezhdunarodnogo prava* (Moscow 1962); Grigory I. Tunkin, *Ideologicheskaĭa bor'ba i mezhdunarodnoe pravo* (Moscow 1967).
[89] Tunkin, 'Peaceful Coexistence', 19.
[90] Ibid., 17.

between all states.[91] However, Tunkin's arguments would soon ring hollow in light of the Brezhnev Doctrine's claim of limited sovereignty, which was used to legitimize the invasion of Czechoslovakia that ended the Prague Spring in 1968.[92]

Tunkin's acknowledgement of the universality of international law in the mid-1960s occurred at a time when the Soviet Union acknowledged the growing influence of Afro-Asian socialist countries on international law debates. Tunkin's revised version of international law was full of enthusiasm for the opportunity of state socialist and Third World states to redefine existing norms together and develop new 'progressive' international law in the future.[93] As Michelle Penn's chapter in this volume and recent studies on Second–Third World links have shown, the Soviet Union and Eastern Bloc states used the advocacy for human rights and international law norms throughout the 1960s and 1970s to forge new alliances against Western countries within the UN.[94] Particularly in the 1960s, Tunkin's work mirrored Soviet confidence that control over the development of international law would soon be pried away from Western states. With decolonization, a coalition of state socialist countries and newly independent states was seen as capable of revising the 'old' imperialist international law into 'contemporary' international law, which would mirror socialist priorities.[95] V. M. Shurshlov further spelled out this idea of new international legal norms that should emerge from the new type of international relations between socialist states. No longer arguing for a distinct socialist international law, the project had now become even more ambitious—redefining universal international law in a socialist image.[96] In that sense, Tunkin still called for a 'fighting international law' to expand the reach of Soviet influence to accelerate this process of transformation.[97]

By declaring international law universal, Tunkin also tacitly suggested that such law had an impact on domestic legal spheres: 'We have a complicated interaction of different phenomena in which international law, subjected to the influence of the economic system and other parts of the superstructure, itself exerts an influence on other parts of the superstructure and the economic system of society.'[98] Even more, the basic principles of contemporary international law, as Tunkin's colleague R. L. Bobrov pointed out, were of 'a normative nature'.[99] In particular, Bobrov cited peaceful coexistence, outlawing of wars of aggression, and friendly relations between states as the Soviet foundations of international law organizing inter-state

---

[91] Ibid., 18. My emphasis.
[92] See Simpson, Chapter 3 in this volume.
[93] Tunkin, 'Peaceful Coexistence', 22f.
[94] For an overview, see Betts, 'Rights'.
[95] Tunkin, 'Peaceful Coexistence', 34f.
[96] V. M. Shurshalov, 'International Law in the Relations Among Socialist States', in *Contemporary International Law*, edited by Tunkin, 59–76.
[97] Cited in: Oskawe, 'Contemporary Soviet Doctrine', 502.
[98] Tunkin, 'Peaceful Coexistence', 31.
[99] R. L. Bobrov, 'Basic Principles of Present-Day International Law', in *Contemporary International Law*, edited by Tunkin, 36–58.

relations. In this context, Tunkin also emphasized that the UN as an international organization embodied sovereign rights of a legal persona under international law. Soviet scholarship in its majority thus accepted that nation-states no longer held a monopoly on international personality.[100]

Tunkin meanwhile expanded the definition of international law beyond an expression of a society's economic system to a more complex view. In his discussion of law as superstructure, he pointed out that 'the development of international law is influenced not only by society's economic system but by different parts of the superstructure: politics, national law, philosophy, ethics, etc'.[101] He therefore implicitly recognized that national traditions of legal theory and practice played a role in how legal professionals from different national, regional, and ideological backgrounds approached international law. In doing so, he suggested that there was a greater variety of approaches to international law than just the capitalist and socialist doctrines, but that these ideologically opposed camps were also internally divided, which implied an acceptable level of national pluralism within the socialist world.

The Soviet invasion of Czechoslovakia in 1968 to shut down the reforms of the Prague Spring dealt another serious blow to the legitimacy of claims to inter-state relations of a new type based on proletarian internationalism between state socialist countries. In 1970, Tunkin published what was hailed as the first comprehensive Soviet theory of international law. By 1974, the book had been translated into English for an international audience by William E. Butler, who had spent a year as senior scholar at the Department of Law at Moscow State University while working on the translation. In his chapter on 'Relations Between Countries of the World System of Socialism', Tunkin sidestepped the Brezhnev Doctrine's retrospective explanation of a justified intervention and merely referred to the Soviet military suppression of the Prague Spring as 'protecting socialist gains and [...] sovereignty and independence from sudden swoops of imperialism'.[102] The Western outcry denouncing the invasion of Czechoslovakia, Tunkin dismissingly argued, was mere 'ballyhoo' of the 'bourgeois press' about a supposedly existing 'doctrine of limited sovereignty'.[103]

In opposition to earlier doctrines of state socialist inter-state relations based on a separate emerging socialist international law, Tunkin moved the goalposts of developing a new type of law once more:

> With the development of relations among socialist states, the principles of proletarian internationalism as moral and political principles of qualitatively new state

---

[100] This still meant that nation-states as the founding entities of the UN underpinned the institution's claim to be a legitimate actor under international law. See Oskawe, 'Contemporary Soviet Doctrine', 503.
[101] Tunkin, 'Peaceful Coexistence', 31.
[102] Tunkin, *Theory of International Law*, 427–48, 436.
[103] Ibid., 440.

relations gradually also are becoming international legal principles in relations between states of the world system of socialism. That is to say, a legal dimension has been added to the moral and political aspect of these principles; legal obligations, to the moral and political obligations. The principles of proletarian internationalism have become legal principles of relations between countries of the socialist system by way of custom and, partially, treaty.[104]

Expanding on his claim of a new type of international relations between socialist states, he thus doubled down on the notion that socialist internationalist principles now structured state socialist inter-state relations. Treaties between state socialist states showed what Tunkin stipulated as the new mission of Soviet legal experts mentioned above: to inject new content into the norms and institutions of international law globally.[105]

In his foreword to the volume, Butler pointed to Tunkin's attempt to differentiate much more carefully in his analysis of foreign law. As with his hints at various national strands of socialist legal science, which Korovin had also already acknowledged (as mentioned above), Butler reported that Tunkin criticized the broad-brush discussion of 'bourgeois' law by many Soviet legal experts. At the annual meeting of the Soviet Association of International Law in January 1972, Tunkin called on his peers to pay more attention to diverse trends of thought in Western legal debates and not be content with the mere ideological rejection of bourgeois law. Butler noted that Western, and particularly Anglo-American, lawyers had created a similar echo chamber and 'internal' literature that paid equally little attention to the actual arguments of state socialist legal scholars beyond pointing to logical flaws in their argumentation based on a prima facie ideological rejection of socialist legal science.[106]

Beyond Butler's English translation, Tunkin continued to directly engage with foreign audiences himself. In 1975, his lectures at The Hague Academy of International Law were published. Tunkin's reading of the nature of international law was now firmly grounded in an extended historical narrative of international law's development. Tunkin's main claim was that the fundamental principles of international law had shifted since the October Revolution. The Soviet focus on state sovereignty, peaceful coexistence, national self-determination, and socialist internationalism had transformed the unequal imperialist international law of the nineteenth century into a system based on the equality of sovereign states. In a telling adoption of Western rhetoric, Tunkin accused Western powers and their 'cold war' of preventing the development of international law until the

---

[104] Ibid., 432.
[105] Ibid., 442.
[106] Ibid., xiii (footnote 1). For the early reception of Soviet international law debates in the West, see also Taylor, 'Law and Socialist Revolution', 160–64.

era of 'international détente'. This stalemate had occurred as 'the use of the term "peaceful coexistence" was considered in some Western countries as subversive propaganda'.[107] In other words, the capitalist West and not state socialist countries had blocked the development of international law. Now, Tunkin went on, it was finally time for the world to acknowledge the pivotal role of state socialist and new independent states in smashing the colonial system and ending 'old' international law as 'the law of the strong'. Tunkin claimed that this transformation had its roots in the Soviet insistence on banning wars of aggression and war in general as an accepted tool of international politics after the Second World War, which he now saw successfully implemented in international law.

Even more, he claimed that 'contemporary international law is in essence anti-colonial. It is a law of equality, self-determination and freedom of peoples'.[108] The next frontier, Tunkin urged, was to turn to the individual human being and ensure respect for human rights. In the spirit of Détente, Tunkin argued that further development of international law was possible as it was neither capitalist nor socialist but 'democratic' in nature.[109] In the changed world of the mid-1970s and with the Helsinki Accord negotiations underway, Tunkin tried to reassure critical reviewers—such as John Hazard—of his 1970 *Theory of International Law* that it was not his aim to remould 'international law in a socialist image'. Instead, Tunkin now argued—ignoring his earlier assertions about a turn to universal international law that should be infused with socialist meaning—that a 'new international law' had evolved with the end of colonialism.

He ended his lecture at The Hague on 'The Emergence of Contemporary International Law' with a call to action: 'The concept of a new international law does not imply that the existing international law is perfect. It is evident that in our age of rapid change international law must constantly develop to keep pace with the development of international relations.'[110] There it was again: the Soviet flexibility in reinterpreting the nature of international law in the logics of Marxist historical materialism. While Western reviewers had tried to pin down socialist thinkers of international law since the 1920s on their logical mistakes and frequent changes in course of argument, for Tunkin, it was the most natural assumption that international law, as domestic law at home, could and perhaps had to continuously change to defend 'developed socialism' domestically and internationally.

---

[107] William E. Butler and Vladimir G. Tunkin, *The Tunkin Diary and Lectures: The Diary and Collected Lectures of G. I. Tunkin at The Hague Academy of International Law* (The Hague: Eleven Publishing, 2011), 256.
[108] Ibid., 259.
[109] Ibid., 260.
[110] Ibid., 261.

Conclusion

By the late 1970s, the Soviet Union and its Eastern European allies accepted international law as a universal system. It had been a winding and contentious process in the Soviet Union alone, not to speak of state socialist controversies over the nature of international law elsewhere in the Eastern Bloc. With the decline of Afro-Asian cooperation and the failure to implement the NIEO in the 1970s, the Soviet Union and its bloc allies remained focused on the now established rhetoric of peaceful coexistence of states grounded in inter-state treaties as the basis of international law. The 1979 Soviet invasion of Afghanistan would of course deal yet another blow to this argument. By the 1980s, the strong focus on the protection of legal state sovereignty extended to state socialist initiatives to define an international law of space exploration. This endeavour was in no small part driven by the escalation of US–Soviet relations after the Soviet invasion of Afghanistan and the attempt to counter Ronald Reagan's Strategic Defense Initiative (SDI), better known under its nickname 'Star Wars'. Yet, there were also renewed negotiations on separating fields of international law to protect the socialist project. The failed plan of a regional socialist human rights convention, discussed by Soviet and Eastern European legal experts in the early 1980s, is one example of several attempts to reform state socialist perspectives on international law after Soviet leader Mikhail Gorbachev took office in 1985. As happened so often in the history of state socialism, this project collapsed due to internal struggles within Eastern Bloc party leaderships, split between orthodox party cadres and reformers supporting Gorbachev's reform agenda of Glasnost and Perestroika.[111]

The project of defining and establishing a separate socialist universe of international law had its heyday between the foundation of new socialist states in 1949 and the beginning of the era of Détente. In this period, hopes of a Soviet-Eastern Bloc and Afro-Asian alliance to overthrow and redefine existing international law in the image of socialism proved utopian. Nonetheless, as the chapters in this volume show, the Soviet Union and legal experts from Eastern Bloc countries nonetheless took part in shaping new international law norms and impacted the UN's agenda of what international legal fields and norms ought to be codified by the institution. Future studies are needed to shed more light on how state socialist legal scholars and politicians perceived the relationship between domestic and international legal institutions and what kind of new international institutions and implementation mechanisms they envisaged (both in the period of advocating a

---

[111] Ned Richardson-Little, 'The Failure of the Socialist Declaration of Human Rights: Ideology, Legitimacy, and Elite Defection at the End of State Socialism', *East Central Europe* 46, no. 2–3 (2019): 318–41.

separate socialist international law and after). This also applies to the history of scholarly legal networks across the state socialist world, transnational influences on socialist legal doctrines from within and outside the bloc (as well as their impact abroad), and dissenting socialist legal ideas of law and international law that opposed state socialist party doctrine and one-party rule. Further research based on recent studies particularly on Third World approaches to international law and human rights and Second–Third World connections are thus needed to look beyond Cold War frameworks of thinking in blocs—East, West, and Global South—and also study emerging state socialist ideas of international law grounded in professional networks and national and regional legal traditions, the logics of emerging international institutions, and the importance of their staffing at different moments in time.[112] Such studies will further illuminate state socialist initiatives in creating, moulding, and obstructing international legal norms in the twentieth and early twenty-first century.

---

[112] Recent studies have stressed the importance of tracing personal networks, the staff of key legal international institutions and courts, and the exchange of ideas and knowledge. See e.g. Marcus M. Payk and Kim Christian Priemel (eds.), *Crafting the International Order: Practitioners and Practices of International Law since c.1800* (Oxford: Oxford University Press, 2021); Jochen von Bernsdorff and Philipp Dann (eds.), *The Battle for International Law: South–North Perspectives on the Decolonisation Era* (Oxford: Oxford University Press, 2019).

3
Socialism and Self-Determination: Lenin, International Law, and National Liberation

Brad Simpson

Introduction

Shortly after the start of the invasion of Ukraine in February 2022, Russian President Vladimir Putin addressed his nation to justify Moscow's actions. Putin lamented the decline and collapse of the Soviet Union and alleged Western support for separatist movements in Chechnya before arguing that Moscow's military intervention was an act of self-defence and a just response to the desire of the Russian-speaking peoples of Ukraine for self-determination. In 2014, he had offered a similar justification for Russia's annexation of Crimea. In doing so, however, he suggested the former Soviet Union's embrace of a Leninist vision of self-determination had been a 'bomb' placed at the heart of the socialist project, one that facilitated its disintegration after 1991.[1] While one claim on self-determination required armed Russian support, other similar claims led only to destruction and chaos.

Putin's seemingly contradictory views are not new. Rather, they reflect long running debates over the scope and meaning of self-determination stretching back more than a century; debates in which socialist and Soviet thinkers were crucial and, at times, decisive interlocutors. The idea of self-determination is one of the most significant and contentious in modern international politics. For more than a century diplomats, lawyers, scholars, activists, and ordinary people around the world have wrestled with the meaning and implications of self-determination for decolonization, human rights, sovereignty, and the international order. Socialist theorists, organizations, and states, this chapter will argue, advanced a distinctive and evolving position on self-determination as a collective right initially rooted in their understanding of the so-called 'national question' in the early twentieth

---

[1] Letter dated 24 February 2022 from the Permanent Representative of the Russian Federation to the United Nations addressed to the Secretary-General, https://digitallibrary.un.org/record/3959647?ln=fr, accessed 1 May 2024; Brad Simpson, 'Self-Determination in the Age of Putin', *Foreign Policy*, 21 March 2014; Bill Bowring, 'The Soviets and the Right to Self-Determination of the Colonized: Contradictions of Soviet Diplomacy and Foreign Policy in the Era of Decolonization', in *The Battle for International Law: South–North Perspectives on the Decolonization Era*, edited by Jochen von Bernstorff and Philipp Dann (Oxford: Oxford University Press, 2019), 425.

century. This position was most famously advanced by Bolshevik revolutionary Vladimir Lenin, and later expanded upon by Soviet leader Josef Stalin as a critique of the more radical position of Marxists such as Rosa Luxemburg and the liberal vision of self-determination described by US President Woodrow Wilson. Like their liberal counterparts, however, many socialist theorists harboured concerns about the potentially disruptive force of proliferating self-determination claims among smaller territories, nations, and peoples, especially in Eastern and Southern Europe, concerns which persisted throughout the twentieth century.

During the interwar period, the socialist position on self-determination as advocated by the League Against Imperialism and the Second International began to cohere around a more consistent anticolonial position, while also embracing 'Black self-determination' in the southern United States. Through the 1940s, however, these positions had little standing in international law. This would change after the formation of the United Nations (UN) in 1945, when the Soviet Union and other socialist states argued for enshrining a right to self-determination in the UN Charter. After 1945, socialist states advanced what I argue was a moderate anticolonial vision of self-determination in UN resolutions and the 1966 human rights covenants—supporting national independence for former colonies and the right to economic self-determination but generally opposing sub-national, secessionist, and Indigenous movements in ways that at times mirrored their non-socialist brethren. Socialist self-determination, however, like its liberal, Western counterpart was riddled with contradictions that would become apparent when socialist states like Czechoslovakia exercised it in ways that Soviet officials considered a threat to the Socialist Bloc or their broader geopolitical interests.

Self-Determination and Socialism Before the Cold War

Historians have traced ideas about self-determination to the French Declaration of the Rights of Man, the US Declaration of Independence, continental philosophers such as Johann Gottlieb Fichte, and Italian political agitator and intellectual Giuseppe Mazzini. Writing in the 1850s, Mazzini argued that self-determination 'would best be realized in the context of independent and democratically governed nation-states', and that these would be territorially defined, bound by common language, religion, culture, and identity. The sovereignty of these new nation-states would also be conditioned by the emerging reality 'that Europe and indeed our entire planet is a vast common market'.[2] Late nineteenth- and early twentieth-century

---

[2] Jörg Fisch, *The Right of Self-Determination of Peoples: The Domestication of an Illusion*, trans. Anita Mage (New York: Cambridge University Press, 2015), 59–112; Eric D. Weitz, 'Self-Determination: How a German Enlightenment Idea Became the Slogan of National Liberation and a Human Right', *American Historical Review* 120, no. 2 (2015): 462–496; 'Introduction: Giuseppe Mazzini's International Political Thought', in *A Cosmopolitanism of Nations: Giuseppe Mazzini's*

Marxists and social democrats expanded upon these ideas and extended them to the colonized world, while engaging in fierce debates about the relationship between nation-state formation, global capitalism, and the liberation of colonized peoples. Vladimir Lenin argued as early as 1903 that the territorial nation-state was the effective building block of international society and the precondition for the emergence of capitalist social relations. For Lenin 'the multi-national state represents backwardness', and 'self-determination of nations' meant 'political self-determination, state independence, and the formation of a national state'. He argued that this right extended to colonized peoples as well as Russia's own subject nationalities, and included in theory the right to secession via plebiscite or revolution, a position Stalin endorsed in his 1913 treatise on Marxism and the National Question.[3] Like most of his contemporaries, Lenin believed that nations-states must be large in order to survive, and he insisted that 'the masses know perfectly well [...] the advantages of a big market and a big state'.[4] Rosa Luxemburg, on the other hand, criticized both Leninist and liberal theories of self-determination as a 'false promise' which delivered the political form of sovereignty while ignoring its economic embeddedness. 'So long as capitalist states exist', Luxemburg wrote in 1914, 'so long as imperialistic world policies determine and regulate the inner and the outer life of the nation, there can be no 'national self-determination' either in war or in peace'.[5]

Until the outbreak of the First World War debates about the scope and meaning of self-determination remained an abstraction on the European Left, much of which had little direct contact with anticolonial movements overseas. The Bolshevik embrace of self-determination as a universal right for all peoples during the war fundamentally changed this dynamic, transforming the global politics of the war and the looming peace. Warring armies and social collapse had uprooted millions across Europe. Both the Central and Allied powers had conscripted the

---

Writings on Democracy, Nation Building, and International Relations, edited by Stefano Recchia and Nadia Urbinati (Princeton: Princeton University Press, 2009), 1–30; Giuseppi Mazzini, 'On Public Opinion and England's International Leadership (1847)', in ibid., 199–207.

[3] Matt Qvortrup, 'A Brief History of Self-Determination Referendums Before 1920', *Ethnopolitics* 14, no. 5 (2015): 547–54; Sarah Wambaugh, *Plebiscites Since the World War: With a Collection of Official Documents* (Washington, DC: Carnegie Endowment for International Peace, 1933); Johannes Socher, *Russia and the Right to Self-Determination in the Post-Soviet Space* (Oxford: Oxford University Press, 2021), 18–19; Joseph Stalin, *Marxism and the National Question, Selected Writings and Speeches* (New York: International Publishers, 1942).

[4] Vladimir Lenin, Programme of the Russian Social Democratic Labour Party, 1903, www.marxists.org/history/international/social-democracy/rsdlp/1903/program.htm, accessed 1 June 2024; Vladimir Lenin, 'The Right of Nations to Self-Determination (1914)', in *Lenin's Collected Works*, vol. 20 (Moscow: Progress Publishers, 1972), 393–454; Bowring, 'The Soviets and the Right to Self-Determination of the Colonized', 409–12.

[5] Deborah Whitehall, 'A Rival History of Self-Determination', *European Journal of International Law* 27, no. 3 (2016), 719–43; Kimberly Hutchings, 'Revolutionary Thinking: Luxemburg's Socialist International Theory', in *Women's International Thought: A New History*, edited by Katharina Rietzler and Patricia Owens (Cambridge: Cambridge University Press, 2021), 52–71.

labour and bodies of millions more colonial subjects, and anticolonial movements everywhere were mobilizing amidst the war's dislocation to demand radical reform of colonial rule or outright independence.

Upon seizing power in November 1917, the Bolsheviks issued a Declaration of the Rights of the Peoples of Russia, which 'asserted the right of the non-Russian peoples to self-determination, including the right to secede from the Russian polity'. The following month they insisted that peace talks be based on the principle of self-determination for colonial areas. In both cases, the Bolsheviks viewed self-determination as a stepping stone on the road to achieving the higher goal of socialism, not as the goal itself. But anticolonial activists embraced the anticolonial formulation. When Woodrow Wilson finally described self-determination among the Allied war aims in February 1918, he did so defensively, hoping to slow a runaway train. He framed self-determination in narrow, liberal terms as political self-government by independent nation-states integrated into a liberal world economy, rather than as emancipation for colonial territories. Since self-determination, like the categories of 'race', 'nation', or 'ethnicity' had no fixed meaning in international law or diplomacy, Allied officials assimilated these ideas into their pre-existing conceptions of national or imperial interest and world order. All sought to narrow and contain self-determination's meaning, ignoring the pleas and petitions of anticolonial representatives who gathered in Paris for the Versailles Conference or who protested in colonial capitals from North Africa to Southeast Asia.[6]

Expansive visions of self-determination, however, were not confined to the colonies. The postwar settlement and the dismantling of the Habsburg and Ottoman Empires led to the creation of new nation-states in southern Europe whose fate would shape future debates about the meaning of sovereignty as well as the promise and perils of national self-determination and ethnic identity as the basis of state formation. The new USSR embraced these new nations and the principle of self-determination, though unevenly. It acknowledged the right to secession of some of its constituent states in the treaties binding them to the Soviet Union, and in 1920 even recognized the secession of Latvia, Lithuania, and Estonia (though not Poland or Finland) from the Russian Empire on the basis of their right to self-determination. At least in theory, Stalin also acknowledged the right of various nationalities within the Soviet Union to cultural self-determination through linguistic, educational, and religious autonomy. But Soviet officials also recognized

---

[6] Erez Manela, *The Wilsonian Moment: Self-Determination and the International Origins of Anticolonial Nationalism* (New York: Oxford University Press, 2009); Derek Heater, *National Self-Determination: Woodrow Wilson and His Legacy* (Basic: New York, 1994); Arno J. Mayer, *Political Origins of the New Diplomacy, 1917–1918* (New Haven: Yale University Press, 1959); Betty Miller Unterberger, 'The United States and National Self-Determination: A Wilsonian Perspective', *Presidential Studies Quarterly* 26, no. 4 (1996): 926–41; Trygve Throntveit, 'The Fable of the Fourteen Points: Woodrow Wilson and National Self-Determination', *Diplomatic History* 35, no. 3 (2011): 445–81; Lauri Mälksoo, 'The Soviet Approach to the Right of Peoples to Self-Determination: Russia's Farewell to Jus Publicum Europaeum', *Journal of the History of International Law* 19, no. 2 (2017): 212–13.

the tensions between acknowledging the right of 'nations' to self-determination and 'their strong desire to hold on to all of the lands of the former Russian Empire' and integrate its land, peoples, and resources into the socialist economy they hoped to build.[7] Early Soviet jurists such as Evgeny Korovin did not consider self-determination a 'purely legal' right, but rather one 'necessary to the real interests of a socialist Russia'.[8] Soviet legal theorist Grigory Tunkin argued that the nations that chose to join the Soviet Union had permanently exercised their right to self-determination, rendering exit a betrayal of the higher good of socialist brotherhood.[9]

Though few legal scholars acknowledged a right to self-determination in international law, much less agreed on how to define it, an ever-widening range of self-described nations, movements, and organizations made sovereignty and rights claims in its name. These include pan-Islamic organizations, pan-racial movements such as Marcus Garvey's United Negro Improvement Association, and petitioners before the League of Nations Mandate Commission.[10] The Third International, Socialist International, and League Against Imperialism all embraced the orthodox Leninist position equating self-determination with an end to colonialism and the emergence of territorial nation-states.[11] These transnational movements helped to vernacularize the idea of self-determination as liberation from colonial rule through bottom-up activism, aided by 'the transnational circulation of activists, texts, ideas, and imaginings via steamships, telegraph, and print'.[12] We might

---

[7] Volker Prott, *The Politics of Self-Determination: Remaking Territories and National Identities in Europe, 1917–1923* (Cambridge: Cambridge University Press, 2016), 51; Natasha Wheatley, *The Life and Death of States: Central Europe and the Transformation of Modern Sovereignty* (Princeton: Princeton University Press, 2023) 21–53; Jeremy Smith, *The Bolsheviks and the National Question, 1917–23* (New York: St Martin's Press, 1999); Lauri Mälksoo, 'The Soviet Approach to the Right of Peoples to Self-Determination', 205–07; quote from Francine Hirsch, *Empire of Nations: Ethnographic Knowledge & the Making of the Soviet Union* (Ithaca, NY: Cornell University Press, 2005), 6.

[8] Boris Mamlyuk, 'Decolonization as a Cold War Imperative: Bandung and the Soviets', in *Bandung, Global History, and International Law*, edited by Luis Eslava, Michael Fakhri, and Vasuki Nesiah (Cambridge: Cambridge University Press, 2017), 204.

[9] Grigory I. Tunkin, *Theory of International Law*, edited and translated by William E. Butler (Cambridge, MA: Harvard University Press, 1974), 10–11.

[10] Megan Donaldson, 'The League of Nations, Ethiopia, and the Making of States', *Humanity: An International Journal of Human Rights, Humanitarianism, and Development* 11, no. 1 (2020): 6–31; Susan Pedersen, *The Guardians: The League of Nations and the Crisis of Empire* (New York: Oxford University Press, 2015), esp. 260–85; Andrew Arsan, '"This Age Is the Age of Associations": Committees, Petitions, and the Roots of Interwar Middle Eastern Internationalism', *Journal of Global History* 7, no. 2 (2012): 166–88.

[11] Fredrik Petersson, 'Hub of the Anti-Imperialist Movement', *Interventions* 16, no. 1 (2014): 49–71; Michele Louro, *Comrades against Imperialism: Nehru, India, and Interwar Internationalism* (Cambridge: Cambridge University Press, 2018); Michele Louro, Carolien Stolte, Heather Streets-Salter, and Sana Tannoury-Karam (eds.), *The League Against Imperialism: Lives and Afterlives* (Leiden: Leiden University Press, 2020); S. A. Smith, 'The Russian Revolution, National Self-Determination, and Anti-Imperialism, 1917–1927', in *Left Transnationalism: The Communist International and the National, Colonial, and Racial Questions*, edited by Oleksa Drachewych and Ian McKay (Toronto: McGill-Queens University Press, 2019), 73–98.

[12] S. A. Smith, 'The Russian Revolution, National Self-Determination, and Anti-Imperialism, 1917–1927', 75.

consider this a 'socialist vernacular' vision of self-determination which placed a wide range of anticolonial struggles within a common conceptual frame.

Like Wilson and Lenin, however, the socialists, communists, anarchists, and anticolonial activists who comprised these movements were unclear on what postcolonial political and economic sovereignty might look like. And they struggled to envision non-territorial constellations of sovereignty, focused as they were on territorial nation-states. This became apparent in the late 1920s when Black communists like Harry Haywood pressed the Communist International to declare that African Americans and Black South Africans counted as oppressed nations.[13] In response, in 1928 the Sixth Communist International passed a resolution on 'The Negro Question in the United States', which demanded 'the right of Negroes to national self-determination in the southern states', including the creation of a Black Belt state where they might relocate.[14] For the next decade, the Communist Party of the United States (CPUSA) made Black Belt self-determination central to its national strategy. Alabama gubernatorial candidate Walter Kelly called for a Black Belt state in 1930, as did the CPUSA's 1932 vice-presidential candidate Alabaman James W. Ford.[15] The CPUSA's demand for a Black Belt state provoked strong opposition from anti-Stalinist Marxists such as Trinidadian journalist C. L. R. James, who denounced the idea as a form of 'inverted segregation' foisted on southern Blacks by white-dominated revolutionary movements.[16]

The outbreak of war in Europe and Asia in the late 1930s and the seeming collapse of European empires once again galvanized anticolonial activists around the world to demand self-rule. In order to articulate a set of Allied war aims that would rally British and American citizens, and perhaps defang these anticolonial demands, British Prime Minister Winston Churchill and US President Franklin D. Roosevelt in August 1941 jointly proclaimed the Atlantic Charter. The charter

---

[13] Oleksa Drachewych, 'Race, the Comintern, and Communist Parties in British Dominions, 1920–1943', in *Left Transnationalism* edited by Drachewych and McKay, 255–57.

[14] 'The 1928 and 1930 Comintern Resolutions on the Black National Question in the United States' (Washington, DC: Revolutionary Review Press, 1975), 13; Harvey Klehr and William Tompson, 'Self-Determination in the Black Belt: Origins of a Communist Policy', *Labor History* 30, no. 3 (1989): 354–66; Oscar Berland, 'The Emergence of the Communist Perspective on the "Negro Question" in America: 1919–1931: Part One', *Science & Society* 63, no. 4 (1999): 411–32; Oscar Berland, 'The Emergence of the Communist Perspective on the "Negro Question" in America: 1919–1931: Part Two', *Science & Society* 64, no. 2 (2000): 194–217.

[15] Robin D. G. Kelley, *Hammer and Hoe: Alabama Communists during the Great Depression* (Chapel Hill, NC: University of North Carolina Press, 2015), 17, 43–47; 'Suggest Black Belt Should Govern Itself; Reds for Complete Race Equality', *Baltimore Afro-American* (11 June 1932), 17; James S. Allen, *Negro Liberation: The American Negroes as an Oppressed Nation, the Struggle for Equal Rights and the Right of Self-Determination*, International Pamphlets, no. 29 (New York: International Pamphlets, 1933), 29–32.

[16] C. L. R. James, 'Preliminary Notes on the Negro Question', in *C.L.R. James on the 'Negro Question'*, edited by Scott McLemee (Jackson, MI: University Press of Mississippi, 1996), 4–10; Glenn Richards, 'C.L.R. James on Black Self-Determination in the United States and the Caribbean', in *C.L.R. James: His Intellectual Legacy*, edited by Selwyn Reginald Cudjoe and William E. Cain)Amherst, MA: University of Massachusetts Press, 1995(,320–26; 'A Report and Assessment: The Communist Party Convention', *The Militant* 30, no. 27 (11 July 1966), 6.

pledged that the Allies would 'respect the right of all peoples to choose the form of government under which they will live' and 'see sovereign rights and self-government restored to those who have been forcibly deprived of them'. Anti-colonial activists around the world seized upon the Atlantic Charter's implied support for self-determination and Roosevelt's apparent endorsement to lend legitimacy to their own ongoing struggles. As the Bolsheviks had done during the First World War, Soviet officials like Ambassador to the United Kingdom Ivan Maisky also embraced this more expansive vision of self-determination, arguing that the Atlantic Charter applied to all peoples, including colonized ones.[17] Crucially, however, Soviet officials denied that the principle applied to the Baltic states, which the USSR had reoccupied as a result of the 1939 Nazi-Soviet pact, formally incorporating them into the Soviet Union in August 1940.[18]

Through the remaining years of the war, US and Western officials attempted to walk back from expansive interpretations of the Atlantic Charter for the colonized world. Soviet officials walked a similar tightrope, calling for self-determination for the colonies while insisting that the Baltic states had already exercised it by joining the Soviet Union and ascending to the socialist stage of development. By the time US, British, Soviet, and Chinese officials met at the Dumbarton Oaks estate in Washington, DC in August 1944 to develop proposals for the UN Organization, however, self-determination had emerged as a vernacular discourse for describing Allied war aims and the postwar hopes of liberated and colonized peoples in many parts of the world. Supporters of self-determination continued to press their case in May at the San Francisco Conference establishing the UN, where more than 1,500 representatives from dozens of nongovernmental organizations gathered at US invitation. Weeks of debate in San Francisco highlighted a simple fact: After decades of discussion diplomats, scholars, lawyers, and activists could not even agree on the meaning of self-determination, much less its place in the UN Charter. Stalin eased the logjam when he directed the Soviet delegation, with support from smaller, non-colonial powers, to introduce a proposed amendment to Article I of the UN Charter describing the purpose of the UN as 'respect for the principle of equal rights and self-determination of peoples'.[19] Soviet delegates also tried

---

[17] Mark Reeves, '"Free and Equal Partners in Your Commonwealth": The Atlantic Charter and Anticolonial Delegations to London, 1941–3', *Twentieth Century British History* 29, no. 2 (2018): 259–83; Gabriel Gorodetsky (ed.), *The Maisky Diaries: Red Ambassador to the Court of St James's, 1932–1943* (New Haven, CT: Yale University Press, 2015), 417.

[18] Lauri Mälksoo, *Illegal Annexation and State Continuity: The Case of the Incorporation of the Baltic States by the USSR* (Leiden: Brill Nijhoff, 2022).

[19] Foreign Relations of the United States (*FRUS*) 1945. General: The United Nations: The United Nations Conference on International Organization, San Francisco, California, April 25–June 26, 1945, 551; 'Self-Determination of Nations: Reaction to Molotov's Plan', *The Times of India* (10 May 1945), 5; Susan Waltz, 'Universalizing Human Rights: The Role of Small States in the Construction of the Universal Declaration of Human Rights', *Human Rights Quarterly* 23, no. 1 (2001): 44–72; UNARMS, Item S-1018-0009-11-00001, UNCIO Press Release no. 107, 17 May 1945, UNCIO (1945) New proposals to Commission II and Technical committees.

unsuccessfully to insert language into Chapter XII of the Charter, outlining the purposes of the newly created Trusteeship system as expediting self-determination for inhabitants of Trust territories with the goal of achieving 'full national independence'.[20] The Soviet shift from supporting 'national self-determination' to 'self-determination of peoples' was significant, even if its full implications were dimly understood, since it acknowledged that many decolonizing territories would emerge as heterogenous states. Still, delegates could not agree on the definition of peoples, or nations, or self-determination itself.[21] Principle or right, self-determination had no agreed-upon legal content, which made its relegation to a vague goal in Article I and the preamble to Chapter IX outlining the purposes of the Economic and Social Committee probably the best that could be hoped for.[22]

Self-Determination, Decolonization, and Socialism in the Postwar World

By 1945 Soviet officials and legal theorists considered self-determination a binding international legal principle, a position roundly rejected by the colonial powers and especially the United States and Britain.[23] In UN General Assembly and committee debates Soviet delegates defended self-determination as a legal basis for supporting the demands of anticolonial movements for independence and sought to include guarantees to this end in the mandate of the Committee on Trusteeship.[24] In the Committee charged with drafting what became the Universal Declaration of Human Rights (UDHR), Soviet representatives criticized the absence of any language on self-determination. On 8 December 1948, shortly before final adoption of the UDHR in the General Assembly, the Soviet delegation proposed to include a clause stating that 'Every people and every nation have the right to self- determination', noting that 'establishment of that right was one of the major achievements

---

[20] *Documents of the United Nations Conference on International Organization, San Francisco, 1945,* vol. 10 (New York: United Nations Information Organization, 1945), 618.

[21] Jesse Kauffman, 'National Self-Determination and Political Legitimacy after Versailles: Leon Wasilewski and the German-Polish Borderlands, 1919–39', in *Beyond Versailles: Sovereignty, Legitimacy, and the Formation of New Polities after the Great War,* edited by Marcus Payk and Roberta Pergher (Bloomington, IN: Indiana University Press, 2019), 60.

[22] Summary Report of 22nd Meeting of Coordinating Committee, 15 June 1945, *Documents of the United Nations Conference on International Organization, San Francisco, 1945,* vol 17-E(1) (UN Information Organization: New York, 1945), 141–44; 'China Takes Firm Stand on Colonial Self-Rule: U. S. Holds Decision Balance China and Russia Lined Up Against Britain, France', *New Journal and Guide* (19 May 1945), 1–2; Rupert Emerson, *Empire to Nation: The Rise to Self-Assertion of Asian and African Peoples* (Boston: Beacon Press, 1960), 295–328.

[23] Socher, *Russia and the Right to Self-Determination,* 26.

[24] Soviet officials were especially critical of US plans to build bases on its Strategic Trust Territories. See AG-033-002—Division of Trusteeship: Office of the Director Ralph Bunche, Subject Files, 1946–1956, Box 22, Memo from Ralph Bunche to A. Cordier, Executive Assistant to the Secretary General, 27 November 1946, 'Tenth Meeting of Sub-Committee 1 of the Fourth Committee'.

of the internal policy of the USSR'. The General Assembly roundly rejected the proposal, much to the relief of Western delegations. The UDHR's silence on self-determination was an important reason that anticolonial movements seized on the Charter and not the UDHR as the ideological framework for national liberation struggles. But decolonizing movements everywhere were already loudly conflating the two.[25]

Having lost the fight over the UDHR itself, advocates turned to the task of drafting binding enforcement covenants, consideration of which would last for the next sixteen years. The Soviet Union, frustrated in its attempts to include the right to self-determination in the UN Charter and the UDHR, proposed to include language in Article 20 declaring that 'Every people and every nation shall have the right to national self-determination' and requiring all administering powers to promote the right in territories under their control.[26] The Soviet proposal was both a riposte to the United States and Great Britain, then attempting to limit the application of human rights in colonial areas and federal states, and a gesture of support for Saudi Ambassador Jamil Baroody, who was emerging as one of the most effective human rights advocates in the world body.

The Soviet proposal raised a host of questions that the UN had not yet answered: What exactly is self-determination? Who or what is a people or a nation? What were the implications of extending a right of national self-determination to all self-governing peoples? Soviet officials and Marxist writers framed Wilsonian self-determination as a reactionary, imperial construction whose aim was the creation of liberal, bourgeois, capitalist states still under the control of the colonial powers.[27] They pointed to the Federal Republic of Germany's Basic Law of 1949, which rejected the legitimacy of the German Democratic Republic (GDR) and demanded 'the unity and freedom of Germany in free self-determination', and its campaign to prevent recognition of the GDR. The socialist critique of liberal self-determination, shorn of its dogmatic language, resonated powerfully with many anticolonial thinkers and movements, who viewed colonial concern with minority rights, internal self-government, and support for federalism as schemes for weakening postcolonial states.[28]

---

[25] Samuel Moyn, *The Last Utopia: Human Rights in History* (Cambridge, MA: Harvard University Press, 2010), 84–119; Fisch, *The Right of Self-Determination of Peoples*, 191; Bowring, 'The Soviets and the Right to Self-Determination of the Colonized', 414–15.

[26] UNCHR, fifth session, Draft International Covenant on Human Rights: Text of Article 20/Union of Soviet Socialists Republics, Document E/CN.4/237, 20 May 1949.

[27] Leon Shields, 'For Self-Determination in Palestine: Against the Slogan of Majority Rule', *New International* XII, no. 6 (1946): 180–81; Albert Gates, 'The Meaning Of Self-Determination, A Reply to Leon Shields', *New International* XII, no.6 (1946): 181–82; Boris Mamlyuk, 'Decolonization as a Cold War Imperative: Bandung and the Soviets', in *Bandung, Global History, and International Law*, edited by Luis Eslava, Michael Fakhri, and Vasuki Nesiah (Cambridge: Cambridge University Press, 2017), 196–214.

[28] William Gray, *Germany's Cold War: The Global Campaign to Isolate East Germany, 1949–1969* (Chapel Hill: University of North Carolina Press, 2003). This is Talbot Imlay's point in 'International

When the Third Committee convened in October 1950 to begin debating the follow-on covenants, pent-up frustration with US efforts to stymie discussion of self-determination erupted. In this setting, however, Washington could not control the agenda. The Soviet delegate criticized the colonial powers for failing to acknowledge the right to self-determination and minority linguistic and cultural rights.[29] Two weeks later, Jamil Baroody and Afghanistan's UN representative Abdul Rahman Pazhwak submitted a resolution directing the Commission on Human Rights to 'study ways and means which would ensure the right of peoples and nations to self-determination' and to prepare recommendations for the General Assembly moving forward. On 4 December, the General Assembly voted to accept the resolution.[30] Over the course of 1951 the United States, Britain, France, and other colonial powers engaged in a fierce rear-guard effort to block discussion of self-determination in the Commission on Human Rights. In frustration, Afghanistan and Saudi Arabia, with Soviet support, proposed adding an article to the draft covenant simply stating that 'all peoples shall have the right to self-determination'. The General Assembly adopted the resolution on 5 February 1952, over bitter objections from the colonial powers.[31] At the end of April 1952, the Human Rights Commission passed resolutions affirming the right or peoples and nations to self-determination; recommending that administering states voluntarily submit information on progress to self-determination under Article 75; and calling on member states to promote self-determination of non-self-governing and Trust territories and to grant the right to self-government through UN-sponsored plebiscites, again with Soviet support.[32] Soviet delegates argued that only 'states with responsibilities for the administration of non-self-governing territories' faced obligations to report on progress towards self-determination.[33] Washington insisted that states should extend the right of self-determination to 'the peoples of all territories or nations under their control' and 'to the peoples of states which were

Socialism and Decolonization during the 1950s: Competing Rights and the Postcolonial Order', *The American Historical Review* 118, no. 4 (2013): 1105–32.

[29] A/C.3/SR.289, Draft first international covenant on human rights and measures of implementation, 19 October 1950, 114.
[30] Draft International Covenants on Human Rights and Measures of Implementation: Future Work for the Commission on Human Rights. A/RES/421(V)[D]. Resolutions adopted by the General Assembly during its 5th session, vol I, 19 September–15 December 1950; for a summary of the arguments made, see E/CN.4/516, 'The right of peoples and nations to self-determination: Note by the Secretary General', 2 March 1951.
[31] A/C.3/L.186 Draft International Covenant on Human Rights and Measures of Implementation: Joint Draft Resolution: Inclusion of the Right to Self-determination in the Covenant on Human Rights, 7 December 1951; 375th Plenary Meeting, item 545, Inclusion in the International Covenant or Covenants on Human Rights of an article relating to the right of peoples to self-determination, 5 February 1952.
[32] UN General Assembly, Seventh Session, Resolution A/RES/637(VII)[C] 'The right of peoples and nations to self-determination', 16 December 1952.
[33] ANA, A 856-13-16 Part 1—Rights of Peoples to Self Determination 1951-1953, 'Statement on US proposal on self-determination', 17 April 1952.

once independent and which have lost that independence', formulations aimed squarely at the Soviet Union and its control of the Baltic states and domination of Eastern Europe.[34]

Over the course of the 1950s, French, British, and US officials slowly began to acknowledge the right to self-determination in principle while emphasizing its necessary limits and the need for its gradual realization. They did so partly in response to the quickening pace of decolonization and the growing momentum of demands for self-determination in the UN, and partly in response to the Soviet Union's consistent support for anticolonial visions of self-determination following Stalin's death in 1953. Soviet Premier Nikita Khrushchev endorsed this vision at the UN and in international forums such as the 1955 Asia–Africa meeting in Bandung, Indonesia, the 1957 Afro-Asian Peoples Solidarity Conference in Cairo, and the 1958 Pan-African Summit in Accra, Ghana.[35] Beginning in 1952, Soviet officials likewise supported UN General Assembly resolutions declaring economic self-determination a human right, supported the nationalization of foreign-owned firms and resources in Iran and Egypt, and endorsed the concept of permanent sovereignty over natural resources as a means of 'liquidating the economic consequences of colonialism and of safeguarding the interests of the developing countries in relation to foreign monopolies'.[36] Speaking in the Third Committee in November 1958, Soviet delegates emphasized that 'there could be no political independence without economic independence' and that permanent sovereignty was 'a basic constituent of the right of peoples to self-determination'.[37]

These efforts culminated in December 1960 with the passage of UN Resolution 1514, the Declaration on the Granting of Independence to Colonial Countries and Peoples, Article 2 of which states that 'All peoples have the right to self-determination; by virtue of that right they freely determine their political status and freely pursue their economic, social and cultural development'. The Soviet Union had first proposed a draft resolution on 23 September calling for the

---

[34] Document A/C.3/L.294, US Recommendations concerning international respect for the self-determination of peoples. New York: UN, 18 November 1952; Eleanor Roosevelt Statement to General Assembly, US Mission to UN Press Release 1851, 18 November 1952.

[35] Elliot R. Goodman, 'The Cry of National Liberation: Recent Soviet Attitudes Toward National Self-Determination', *International Organization* 14, no. 1 (1960): 92–106; James Meriwether, *Tears, Fire, and Blood. The United States and the Decolonization of Africa* (Chapel Hill: University of North Carolina Press, 2021), 33–71; Boris Mamlyuk, 'Decolonization as a Cold War Imperative: Bandung and the Soviets', 196–214.

[36] W. E. Butler, 'Self-Determination in Soviet International Law: The Roles of Law and Policy', *SAIS Review* 12, no. 1: 32–39; quote from Artemy Kalinovsky, 'The Soviet Union and Mosaddeq: A Research Note', *Iranian Studies* 47, no. 3 (2014): 401–18.

[37] Quote from Recommendations concerning international respect for the right of peoples and nations to self-determination, 21 November 1958, General Assembly, 13th Session, 3rd Committee, 889th Meeting, A/C.3/SR.889 (A/3829, A/3775); see also The National Archives of the UK (TNA): POWE 61-40 Oil and the UN Commission on Permanent Sovereignty Over Natural Resources, UN Economic and Social Council 32nd Session—Geneva—July/August 1961, Notes on Report of Committee on Permanent Sovereignty.

immediate and total independence of remaining colonies by the end of 1961, universal suffrage in non-self-governing territories, and the dismantling of foreign military bases, a formulation which alarmed the colonial powers.[38] Over the next several months, members of the Afro-Asian Bloc worked to advance a more moderate resolution shorn of calls to dismantle foreign military bases and implement universal suffrage, and assiduously lobbied the United States and other Western delegations to refrain from opposing. The Afro-Asian draft passed on an eighty-nine to zero vote, with nine abstentions.[39] By the time the UN General Assembly passed Resolution 1514, Western observers widely acknowledged the political importance of the Soviet Union's support for enshrining self-determination as a human right at the UN and in international law.[40]

Throughout the 1960s the Soviet Union remained a consistent supporter of enshrining anticolonial self-determination as a human right. Soviet diplomats introduced the 1966 human rights covenants, both of which declared self-determination the first right from which all other rights derived. They also helped in 1962 to initiate one of the most ambitious UN attempts to codify international law regarding decolonization, an effort that culminated in 1970 with the passage of the Declaration on Principles of International Law Concerning Friendly Relations and Cooperation Among States. British, US, French, and other metropolitan officials, tired of responding to innumerable UN resolutions against colonialism, most backed by the Soviet Union, turned to establishing general principles of international law that might contain self-determination of the world's remaining colonies with acceptable boundaries. In December 1962, the General Assembly passed a resolution calling for such a study, setting off a nearly decade-long debate about the basic principles of international law.[41] Yugoslavia's UN delegation offered the socialist Principles of Peaceful Coexistence as a model, a proposal endorsed by attendees at the second Non-Aligned Movement conference in Cairo in 1964.[42] Over the next eight years, the UN International Law Committee and

---

[38] UN Digital Library, https://digitallibrary.un.org/record/1304736, accessed 1 June 2024; A/4501, Request for the inclusion of an additional item in the agenda of the 15th regular session, 23 September 1960; William Butler, 'Self-Determination In Soviet International Law: The Roles of Law and Policy', *SAIS Review* 12, no. 1 (1967): 32–39.

[39] Mary Ann Heiss, 'Exposing "Red Colonialism": U.S. Propaganda at the United Nations, 1953–1965', *Journal of Cold War Studies* 17, no. 3 (2015): 82–115; Kattan, 'Self-Determination in the Third World', 135–38; Bowring, 'The Soviets and the Right to Self-Determination of the Colonized', 420–22; Cindy Ewing, '"With a Minimum of Bitterness": Decolonization, the Right to Self-Determination, and the Arab-Asian Group', *Journal of Global History* 17, no. 2 (2022): 1–18.

[40] Elliot R. Goodman, 'The Cry of National Liberation: Recent Soviet Attitudes Toward National Self-Determination', *International Organization* 14, no. 1 (1960): 92–106; Quincy Wright, 'Recognition and Self-Determination', *Proceedings of the American Society of International Law at Its Annual Meeting (1921–1969)* 48 (1954), 28; Gleb Starushenko, *The Principle of National Self-Determination in Soviet Foreign Policy* (Moscow: Foreign Languages Publishing House, 1964).

[41] Consideration of Principles of International Law Concerning Friendly Relations and Cooperation Among States in Accordance with the Charter of the United Nations [1962] UN General Assembly 88; A/RES/1815 (XVII), 18 December 1962.

[42] 'The United Nations, Self-Determination and The Namibia Opinions', *The Yale Law Journal* 82, no. 3 (1973): 533, 541; Airgram A-229 from Belgrade to State, 20 September 1963, RG 59 Central

the General Assembly held dozens of meetings to consider how decolonization, the UN Human Rights covenants, the Declaration on Permanent Sovereignty over Natural Resources, and two decades of UN resolutions had reshaped international law.

The United States and other Western powers, having spent years trying to narrow the scope and reach of self-determination, sought a broadly conceived declaration of international law that acknowledged such a right but limited it within strict bounds. The Soviet Union sought an expansive declaration which would acknowledge the legitimacy of armed struggle in pursuit of self-determination and other positions backed by the Afro-Asian Bloc. The compromise declaration expanded the definition of self-determination from an act of colonial emancipation to a process linked to representative government, one that could be equally applied to South Africa under Apartheid and the states of Eastern Europe under Soviet domination. Dissident groups within Baltic states like the Estonian Democratic Movement and the Estonian National Front, formed in 1972, invoked the Friendly Relations Declaration in an appeal to UN member states to urge the withdrawal of Soviet troops from the Baltics and the holding of free elections there.[43] The Declaration also stated that self-determination could take forms other than independence, including 'the free association or integration with an independent State or the emergence into any other political status freely determined by a people'. This created ample wiggle room for the semi-sovereign futures the colonial powers imagined for their remaining dependencies but also for Eastern Bloc states like the GDR, which sought to legitimize socialist one-party rule as a freely chosen political status analogous to the decolonization of non-self-governing territories.[44]

Terrorism, Armed Struggle, and National Liberation Movements

The Soviet attempt to codify armed struggle as part of the right to self-determination in the Friendly Relations Declaration was consistent with its broader support

---

Foreign Policy File 1963, Box 4234, NARA; Borislav Blagojevic, 'Codification of the Laws of Active and Peaceful Coexistence', *Yugoslav Review of International Affairs*, 5 September 1963, 9–13; A/RES/2181(XXI) Consideration of Principles of International Law Concerning Friendly Relations and Co-Operation among States in Accordance with the Charter of the United Nations, 12 December 1966.

[43] TNA, FCO 61-1402, Letter from Ints Runners, President of Baltic Appeal to Sir Keith Unwin, British Representative to the UN Commission on Human Rights, 14 February 1975; and Memorandum to the General Assembly of the United Nations from the Estonian Democratic Movement and the Estonian National Front, 24 October 1972.

[44] Samuel Moyn and Umut Özsu, 'The Historical Origins and Setting of the Friendly Relations Declaration', in *The UN Friendly Relations Declaration at 50: An Assessment of the Fundamental Principles of International Law*, edited by Jorge E. Viñuales (Cambridge: Cambridge University Press, 2020), 23–48; Martti Koskenniemi and Ville Kari, 'Sovereign Equality', in ibid.,166–88.

for armed anticolonial movements.[45] UN efforts in the 1960s to enshrine self-determination as the foundation of global decolonization emerged out of countless local and transnational movements, many committed to armed struggle. The colonial powers and their supporters rejected the legitimacy of armed struggle as a matter of course unless they were doing the arming. Liberation movements, postcolonial nations, and socialist states likewise defended armed struggle with sacramental, unless restive internal minorities, occupied peoples, or unruly satellites claimed the right for themselves. A succession of disputes within the UN Economic and Social Council (ECOSOC), the Decolonization Committee, the Terrorism Committee, and the Legal Committee on Armed Conflicts reveals a terrain of debate over the meaning of human rights and terrorism almost wholly alien to liberal sensibilities.

Few national liberation movements or postcolonial states claiming the right to self-determination practiced internal democracy or acknowledged the civil and political rights that were the focus of human rights activism in the West during the 1970s. The focus of debates at the UN, acknowledged directly or not, was the tactics of the alphabet soup of guerrilla movements fighting against occupation, colonial, or racist rule in South Africa (ANC), Mozambique (FRELIMO), Angola (MPLA and UNITA), Rhodesia (ZANLA and ZIPRA), and Palestine (PLO, PFLP) and the Cold War concerns (in Washington and other capitols) that Soviet, Cuban, and/or Chinese support for them engendered. The practical question was whether the UN could or would acknowledge that, if self-determination was indeed a fundamental human right, peoples living under colonial domination had the right to use any means at their disposal—including armed struggle—to achieve it.[46]

The UN Decolonization Committee (Committee of 24), increasingly dominated by newly independent Asian and African states and the Soviet Union, suggested that the answer was yes. Beginning in 1967, it began passing a series of resolutions urging member states to offer all possible support for liberation movements in South Africa, Southern Rhodesia, Namibia, and the Portuguese territories and called for an arms embargo against Portugal and Southern Rhodesia.[47] Over the next several years, the Fourth Committee, pressed by members of the Organization of African Unity, granted observer status to FRELIMO, PAIGC, the PLO, and other armed movements it recognized as legitimate representatives of

---

[45] Johannes Socher, 'Lenin, (Just) Wars of National Liberation, and the Soviet Doctrine on the Use of Force', *Journal of the History of International Law* 19, no. 2 (2017): 219–45.

[46] For a discussion, see Christopher Quaye, *Liberation Struggles in International Law* (Philadelphia, PA: Temple University Press, 1991); Heather A. Wilson, *International Law and the Use of Force by National Liberation Movements* (Oxford: Oxford University Press, 1988).

[47] NARA, RG 59, Central Files, 1967–1969, POL 19 UN, Box 2575, Telegram 78188 from State to Diplomatic Posts, 2 December 1967; A/Res/2270 Resolution 2270 (XXII), 21 November 1967, adopted by the UN General Assembly; the Soviet Bloc served as a crucial ally in the UN on these votes. See Natalia Telepneva, *Cold War Liberation: The Soviet Union and the Collapse of the Portuguese Empire in Africa, 1961–1975* (Chapel Hill, NC: The University of North Carolina Press, 2022).

the national aspirations of their territories. Soviet Bloc members of the UN Special Committee on Principles of International Law Concerning Friendly Relations and Cooperation Among States pressed for acknowledgement of 'the legitimacy of armed struggle by colonial peoples towards the right of self-determination' as a foundational principle of international law.[48] Soviet diplomats told the Ad Hoc Committee on Terrorism in 1973, as it debated one of the first definitive UN statements on terrorism that 'it is unacceptable to give a broad interpretation to the term 'international terrorism' and to extend it to cover national liberation movements'.[49]

The Soviet Union and Global Secession Movements

Though broadly embracing the anticolonial vision of economic and political self-determination as a human right, including the legitimacy of the use of force, Soviet jurists and officials during the era of decolonization often took a position indistinguishable from their Western and postcolonial counterparts on the question of secession. While early Soviet writings on self-determination embraced the legitimacy of secession, after 1945 Soviet officials embraced the principle of *uti possidetis*, under which nations emerging from colonial rule should preserve their boundaries. Mindful of the fears of many decolonizing and newly independent states of secessionist movements, and eager to appeal to the Afro-Asian Bloc, they took the position that while colonies had the right to 'secede' from imperial rule, internal regional, ethnic, or religious minorities did not. Thus Soviet diplomats supported Indonesian demands for self-determination from Dutch colonial rule between 1945 and 1949 but rejected the legitimacy of secessionist movements such as the Republic of South Molucca or Darul Islam, which themselves were seeking to secede from postcolonial Indonesia.

Rapid African decolonization after 1960 pressed many of the most urgent questions concerning the nature and limits of self-determination to the surface, especially after the Congo plunged into civil war following the attempted secession of Katanga. The newly independent states which formed the Organization of African Unity in 1963 took a strong and unequivocal stance in favour of the preservation of colonial-era borders. The UN, with African members in the lead, repeatedly condemned attempts by secessionist movements to redraw the borders of often fragile

---

[48] Quote from 'Liberation Movements and the Use of Force', *Objective: Justice. A periodical Review of UN Activity against Apartheid, racial discrimination and colonialism* 1, no. 1 (New York: UN Office of Public Information, 1969), 45; Yassin El-Ayouty, 'Legitimization of National Liberation: The United Nations and Southern Africa', *Issue: A Journal of Opinion* 2, no. 4 (1972): 36–45; see also Georges Abi-Saab, 'Wars of National Liberation and the Laws of War', Annales d'études internationales 3 (1972): 93–117; Socher, *Russia and the Right to Self-Determination*, 34.

[49] Leon Romaniecki, 'The Soviet Union and International Terrorism' Soviet Studies 26, no. 3 (1974): 417–40. On the Eastern Bloc's cooperation with the West on defining hijacking as a form of terrorism rather than a form of national liberation, see Ned Richardson-Little, Chapter 11 in this volume.

multi-ethnic states, and explicitly or tacitly authorized countries threatened by such movements to take whatever actions necessary to preserve their territorial integrity. Nikita Khrushchev, eager to gain allies among African states, opposed both the attempted secession of Katanga province from the Congo and Biafra's attempt to secede from Nigeria.[50]

Biafrans had posed this question in May 1967, when the Eastern region of Nigeria voted to secede, followed shortly after by Chukwuemeka Odumegwu Ojukwu's announcement of the independence of the Republic of Biafra. For the next two and a half years Nigeria's Federal Military Government, backed by both the United Kingdom and the Soviet Union, waged a fierce war against the breakaway republic. This included a devastating blockade of the land-locked territory, resulting in the deaths of an estimated one million civilians from fighting and starvation before the Republic finally surrendered on 12 January 1970.[51] Although Biafra's self-styled leaders spoke of self-determination, much of the world recognized their actions as secession. And despite widespread empathy for civilian suffering, support for Biafran self-determination was always a minority proposition. The Soviet Bloc was nearly united in opposition.[52] The lone exception was the People's Republic of China, still reeling from the Cultural Revolution, which denounced the 'imperialist' and 'revisionist' (i.e. Soviet-allied) powers for supporting Nigeria.[53]

Three years later, however, Soviet officials backed India in supporting the secession of East Pakistan to form Bangladesh. This, however, would prove to be an exception, the sole Cold War example of a successful secessionist movement leading to a new, independent country. There are many reasons why Bangladesh's situation was comparatively unique: its geographic isolation; the democratic mandate of the Awami League, the East Pakistan political party, which won an overwhelming

---

[50] Alanna O'Malley, *The Diplomacy of Decolonisation: America, Britain and the United Nations during the Congo Crisis 1960–1964* (Manchester: Manchester University Press, 2018); Alessandro Iandolo, 'Imbalance of Power: The Soviet Union and the Congo Crisis, 1960–1961', *Journal of Cold War Studies* 16, no. 2 (2014): 32–55.

[51] Daniel Sargent, *A Superpower Transformed: The Remaking of American Foreign Relations in the 1970s* (New York: Oxford University Press, 2015); Lasse Heerten, *The Biafran War and Postcolonial Humanitarianism: Spectacles of Suffering* (Cambridge: Cambridge University Press, 2017); Lasse Heerten and Dirk Moses (eds.), *Postcolonial Conflict and the Question of Genocide: The Nigeria-Biafra War, 1967–1970* (London: Routledge, 2017); Robert DeChaine, 'Framing Humanitarian Action: Médecins Sans Frontières', in *Global Humanitarianism: NGOs and the Crafting of Community*, edited by Robert DeChaine (Oxford: Lexington Books, 2005), 67–104; Joseph Thompson, *American Policy and African Famine: the Nigeria-Biafra War, 1966–1970* (New York: Greenwood Press, 1990); John Stremlau, *The International Politics of the Nigerian Civil War, 1967–1970* (Princeton: Princeton University Press, 1977).

[52] Frederic L. Kirgis, 'The Degrees of Self-Determination in the United Nations Era', *American Journal of International Law* 88, no. 2 (1994): 304–08; Redie Bereketeab, *Self-Determination and Secession in Africa: The Post-Colonial State* (London: Routledge, 2015); Freddy D. Mnyongani, 'Between a Rock and a Hard Place: The Right to Self-Determination versus Uti Possidetis in Africa', *The Comparative and International Law Journal of Southern Africa* 41, no. 3 (2009): 463–79.

[53] American Jewish Congress, 'The Tragedy of Biafra: A report by the American Jewish Congress', New York (27 December 1968), 4.

victory in 1970 parliamentary elections; and India's decisive, Soviet-backed military intervention. Moreover, the sheer scale of the suffering in Bangladesh raised the profound question of whether human rights abuses on a sufficiently massive scale could justify the dissolution of a sovereign state.[54] For most of the international community the answer remained no; the principle of territorial integrity and 'the non-interference principle trumped the interference principle of the human rights/genocide rhetoric'. Only the Soviet Union and its allies backed India in opposing UN resolutions that called for a ceasefire in Bangladesh and a withdrawal to international borders.[55]

Though the Soviet Union sided with India over Pakistan on the issue of self-determination for Bangladesh, Soviet leaders matched their Western counterparts in basing their support for self-determination as a human right on geopolitical rather than principled grounds—hailing the notion when it suited their interests and denouncing it when it did not. Moscow's response to the conflict between Somalia and Ethiopia in the late 1970s was more typical. As Arne Westad has described, Moscow switched its support from Somalia to Ethiopia after a military junta known as the Derg took over in Addis Ababa in 1974, viewing the revolutionary regime there as more reliable allies than the revanchist Siad Barre regime in Mogadishu.[56] Upon coming to power in Somalia Barre began laying claim to the Ogaden territory, home to a substantial Somali minority, as well as offering support to Eritrean separatists, telling Soviet officials in Mogadishu that Derg Chairman Mengistu Haile Mariam 'does not abide by Leninist principles in the nationality issue', that is, support for self-determination of peoples. In 1977, Somalia launched a disastrous war to try and retake the Ogaden, only to be stymied by a massive Soviet and Cuban military campaign in support of Mengistu. Soviet analysts denounced Barre and other Somali officials for 'using as a cover demagogic declarations about the right of nations to self-determination' to mask Somalia's irredentist ambitions. They were no more supportive of Eritrean efforts: 'It is especially necessary', R. A. Ulyanovsky of the Soviet Central Committee told his East German counterpart, to convince the Eritrean Liberation Movement 'that self-determination for the Eritrean people will be achieved within the framework of an Ethiopian state'.[57]

---

[54] Briefing book prepared for Josif Tito on the upcoming Visit of the President of UAR Anwar El Sadat to Yugoslavia, 3 March 1972, Cold War International History Project Virtual Archive, Cold War in the Middle East Collection; M. Rafiqul Islam, 'Secessionist Self-Determination: Some Lessons from Katanga, Biafra and Bangladesh', *Journal of Peace Research* 22, no. 3 (1985): 211–21; Nanda, 'Self-Determination in International Law', 335; Charles R. Nixon, 'Self-Determination: The Nigeria/Biafra Case', *World Politics* 24, no. 4 (1972): 476.

[55] A. Dirk Moses, 'The United Nations, Humanitarianism and Human Rights: War Crimes/Genocide Trials for Pakistani Soldiers in Bangladesh, 1971–1974', in *Human Rights in the Twentieth Century*, edited by Stefan-Ludwig Hoffmann (Cambridge: Cambridge University Press, 2010), 258–83.

[56] Odd Arne Westad, *The Global Cold War: Third World Interventions and the Makings of Our Times* (Cambridge: Cambridge, 2007), 250–88.

[57] Cold War International History Project Digital Archive, Horn of Africa Collection, 'Memorandum of Conversation between Soviet Ambassador to Somalia G. V. Samsonov and Somali President

Conclusion: The Contradictions of Socialist Self-Determination

At the UN the Soviet Union generally sided with the Afro-Asian Bloc and postcolonial states on questions of secession and non-intervention. Within the Soviet Bloc, however, Soviet legal scholars and UN delegates advanced a theory of 'socialist self-determination' to account for their annexation of the Baltic states, military occupation of Eastern Europe, creation of the GDR and suppression of a popular uprising there in 1953, and interventions in Hungary (1956), Czechoslovakia (1968), and Afghanistan (1979). It derived from the premise that the USSR and its constituent republics had already exercised their right to self-determination by choosing to federate and advancing to the socialist stage of history. Similar principles applied to the nations of the Eastern Bloc, which had exercised their right to self-determination by becoming Peoples' Republics. When Nikita Khrushchev announced the Principles of Peaceful Coexistence at the twentieth Congress of the Communist Party of the Soviet Union in February 1956, he hoped to convince Western critics of Soviet rule in Eastern Europe and the Baltics of the legitimacy of their sovereignty.

Some Eastern Bloc leaders and legal theorists, while generally embracing the tenets of 'socialist self-determination', advanced distinctive visions which reflected their national priorities. East German legal scholars explicitly framed their self-determination claims in anticolonial terms as a defence of their sovereignty against West Germany's 'imperialistic' claim to represent all German peoples, as well as a realization of the human rights of East German citizens.[58] Czechoslovakia and Yugoslavia, both multi-ethnic states created out of the remains of the Austro-Hungarian Empire at the end of the First World War, advanced conceptions of self-determination reflecting the need to preserve national unity while acknowledging the rights of national minorities. Antonín Šnejdárek, a historian and director of the Czech Institute for International Politics and Economics, warned of the dangers of German agitation on behalf of Sudeten Germans, and compared Czechoslovakia to other small nations victimized by European empires. Yugoslav leader Josip Broz Tito advanced a vision of what he termed 'revolutionary self-determination' by which Serbs, Slovenes, and Croats subsumed their national interests in the name of preserving a federated Yugoslav state. 'The state unity of the Yugoslav peoples', Slovenian politician and Communist Party Member Edvard Kardelj-Sperans

---

Siad Barre' (23 February 1977); 'Soviet Foreign Ministry and CPSU CC International Department Background Report on the Somali-Ethiopian Conflict' (3 April 1978); 'Memorandum of Conversation between [SED] Comrade Friedel Trappen and Soviet Comrade R. A. Ulyanovsky in the CC of the CPSU' (11 May 1978).

[58] *The Soviet Union and the Right of Peoples and Nations to Self-Determination: A Contribution to the German Question* (Bonn: Federal Ministry for All-German Questions, 1962); Bernhard Graefrath, *Die Vereinten Nationen und die Menschenrechte* (Berlin: Deutscher Zentralverlag, 1956).

wrote in 1958, could only be maintained 'on the basis of recognition of the right to self-determination and full independence of all the peoples of Yugoslavia: the Serbs, Croats, Slovenes, Macedonians, and Montenegrins'. The only problem was that Yugoslavia's recognized nationals (which included Muslims) were scattered unevenly across its constituent republics. While adhering formally to the Leninist position that the right to national self-determination included the right to secession, Tito insisted that federation could preserve the rights of dispersed national minorities.[59] This commitment 'to federation as an answer to the 'national question' in multi-ethnic socialist states was enshrined in successive post-1945 constitutions which granted Yugoslavia's republics substantial autonomy but over time sharpened local identities, producing demands for independence and secession in the 1980s.[60]

Socialist self-determination was a concept riddled with contradictions. Did the right reside in the state, in the working class, or the nation? And what if a socialist state, having already exercised its right to self-determination, decided to take stances that conflicted with Soviet doctrine? A few months after Khrushchev's announcement of the Principles of Peaceful Coexistence Soviet tanks rolled into Budapest to crush the Hungarian revolution, demonstrating that peaceful coexistence was a mirage if Eastern Bloc states attempted an independent path to socialism.[61] Imre Nagy later reflected 'the core of Hungary's tragedy lies in the fact that socialism and the idea of national independence became opposed [...] This was the first time in Hungarian history that a war of liberation, fought for national independence, self-determination, sovereignty and equal rights, had been led by the working class'.[62] The invasion of Hungary prompted Soviet legal theorists like Vladimir Mikhailovich Shurshalov to begin arguing that in socialist states the principle of peaceful coexistence had been replaced 'by the higher, more profound and qualitatively new principle of socialist internationalism'. Accordingly, socialist states had a duty to assist other socialist states to preserve their independence and sovereignty if they pursued a path that might threaten the Socialist Bloc as a whole.[63]

Soviet officials applied a similar logic to justify the invasion of Czechoslovakia. Upon coming to power as leader of the Czechoslovakian Communist Party (KPC) in January 1968, Alexander Dubček oversaw a period of remarkable reform

---

[59] Antonín Snejdárek, *Self-Determination: Good Slogan in Bad Hands* (Prague: Orbis, 1961); quote from Gorana Ognjenović and Jasna Jozelić (eds.) *Titoism, Self-Determination, Nationalism, Cultural Memory* (New York: Palgrave Macmillan, 2016), 84–85.
[60] Jasna Dragović-Soso, 'Rethinking Yugoslavia: Serbian Intellectuals and the "National Question" in Historical Perspective', *Contemporary European History* 13, no. 2 (2004): 170–84.
[61] István Bibó, *Democracy, Revolution, Self-Determination: Selected Writings*, edited by Károly Nagy (Highland Lakes, NJ: Atlantic Research and Publications, 1991).
[62] Quoted in János M. Rainer 'The Development of Imre Nagy as a Politician and a Thinker', *Contemporary European History* 6, no. 3 (1997): 274.
[63] Socher, *The Soviet Doctrine on the Right to Self-Determination Revisited*, 14–56.

expressly framed as a realization of the country's right to self-determination and an intensification of its independence and sovereignty. Soviet and Eastern Bloc officials viewed these reforms as a counterrevolutionary plot. 'The anti-socialist forces in Czechoslovakia were in essence using talk about the right to self-determination to cover up demands for so-called neutrality and the withdrawal of the CSSR [Czechoslovakian Socialist Republic] from the socialist commonwealth', *Pravda* warned. 'But implementation of such "self-determination", i.e., Czechoslovakia's separation from the socialist commonwealth, would run counter to Czechoslovakia's fundamental interests and would harm the other socialist countries'. Soviet Premier Leonid Brezhnev expanded on what later became known as the Brezhnev Doctrine in a speech to the Fifth Congress of the Polish United Workers' Party on 13 November 1968. 'The sovereignty of each socialist country cannot be opposed to the interests of the world of socialism, of the world revolutionary movement', he declared. Czechoslovakia's attempts at what Khruschev called 'antisocialist' self-determination 'encroaches upon the vital interests of the peoples of these countries and conflicts, as the very root of it, with the right of these people to socialist self-determination'.[64]

The invasion of Czechoslovakia by Warsaw pact forces provoked a 'crisis of internationalism' and profound disillusionment with the Soviet commitment to self-determination that rippled throughout the socialist world but especially in Eastern Europe.[65] The Socialist International condemned the invasion as a betrayal of socialist principles.[66] Global South countries overwhelmingly opposed the invasion, as did the governments of Romania and Yugoslavia, while Western European communist parties began to distance themselves from Moscow and pursue reformist agendas.[67] Within the Soviet Union itself, dissidents slowly began speaking out against Brezhnev's calls for the assimilation of national identities into a new 'Soviet people', as did national groups abroad.[68] In response, Radio Liberty

[64] The Action Programme of the Communist Party of Czechoslovakia Adopted at the plenary session of the Central Committee of the Communist Party of Czechoslovakia on 5 April 1968, www.marxists.org/subject/czech/1968/action-programme.htm, accessed 1 June 2024; 'The International Obligations of Socialist Countries', *Pravda*, 25 September 1968, https://soviethistory.msu.edu/1968-2/crisis-in-czechoslovakia/crisis-in-czechoslovakia-texts/brezhnev-doctrine/; speech by First Secretary of the Soviet Union Leonid Brezhnev, 13 November 1968.

[65] Aurélie Dianara Andry, *Social Europe, the Road Not Taken: The Left and European Integration in the Long 1970s* (New York: Oxford University Press, 2022), 121; Mircea Munteanu, 'When the Levee Breaks: The Impact of the Sino-Soviet Split and the Invasion of Czechoslovakia on Romanian-Soviet Relations, 1967–1970', *Journal of Cold War Studies* 12, no. 1 (2010): 43–61.

[66] Julius Braunthal, *History of The International: World Socialism 1943–1968* (New York: Routledge, 2019), 460–506; Silvio Pons and Michele Di Donato, 'Reform Communism', in *The Cambridge History of Communism: Volume 3: Endgames? Late Communism in Global Perspective, 1968 to the Present*, edited by Juliane Fürst, Mark Selden, and Silvio Pons (Cambridge: Cambridge University Press, 2017), 178–202; John Connelly, *From Peoples into Nations: A History of Eastern Europe* (Princeton: Princeton University Press, 2020), 622–47.

[67] United Nations Library, s/8765, letter dated 22 August 1968 from the Permanent Representative of Yugoslavia addressed to the President of the Security Council.

[68] Boris Meissner, 'The Soviet Concept of Nation and the Right of National Self-Determination', *International Journal* 32, no. 1 (1976): 56–81; Peter G. Stercho, *Soviet Concept of National*

began beaming broadcasts on the nationality question into Soviet Bloc countries stressing Moscow's betrayal of the principle. Soviet officials and legal theorists such Grigory Tunkin continued to defend the invasion of Czechoslovakia as 'a logical extension' of the concept of 'socialist international law' and 'the legal prevention of inroads by capitalist influences into a socialist state'.[69] Few outside the Soviet Union were persuaded.

Soviet leaders and jurists continued to struggle to contain the contradictions in their vision of socialist international law and self-determination, which parted dramatically with the commitments to territorial sovereignty and non-intervention in the 1970 Friendly Relations Declaration.[70] When Soviet officials began negotiations with the Organization for Security and Cooperation in Europe (OSCE) in 1972 on a statement of common European principles, they rejected a European proposal to include 'the equal rights and self-determination of peoples', arguing that it only applied to colonial areas outside of Europe and that the socialist states of Eastern Europe had already exercised their rights to this end. Socialist self-determination was an act, not a process of liberal self-government. Western negotiators would not budge, and 'refused to accept any formulation that did not include human rights and self-determination'. Soviet officials eventually acceded. They and their Eastern Bloc allies were more concerned with gaining European acceptance of principles of non-intervention and the inviolability of frontiers. They believed that socialist self-determination represented a realization rather than a repudiation of human rights and did not seem to believe that critics could effectively criticize them on these grounds.[71] They were wrong. Principle VIII of the Helsinki Final Act defined self-determination as a continuing right of peoples 'to determine, when and as they wish, their internal and external political status, without external interference, and to pursue as they wish their political, economic, social and cultural development'.[72] As Helsinki Watch groups formed across Europe and the United States, they mobilized around the demand that Soviet Union allow the

---

Self-Determination: Theory and Reality from Lenin to Brezhnev (New York: The Ukrainian Congress Committee of America, 1979).

[69] Alan McDougall, *Youth Politics in East Germany: The Free German Youth Movement 1946–1968* (New York: Oxford University Press, 2004), 216; Wilson Center Digital Archive, Radio Liberty Broadcast Position Statement: The Nationality Question (17 April 1970); Bowring, 'The Soviets the Right to Self-Determination of the Colonized', 425; Grigory Tunkin, *Theory of International Law*, trans. William E. Butler (London: George Allen & Unwin, 1970), 498–99.

[70] Boris Meissner, 'The Right of Self-Determination after Helsinki and Its Significance for the Baltic Nations', *Case Western Reserve Journal of International Law* 13, no. 2 (1981): 375–84.

[71] Daniel Thomas, *The Helsinki Effect: International Norms, Human Rights, and the Demise of Communism* (Princeton, NJ: Princeton University Press, 2001), 58–62.

[72] Conference on Security and Cooperation in Europe Final Act, Helsinki 1975, https://www.osce.org/files/f/documents/5/c/39501.pdf, accessed 1 June 2024; Antonio Cassese, 'The Helsinki Declaration and Self-determination', in *Human Rights, International Law and the Helsinki Accord*, edited by Thomas Buergenthal (Allanheld: Osmun, 1977), 83–119.

peoples of Eastern Europe and the Baltic states to exercise their right to political self-determination in the form of free elections.[73]

The Helsinki Final Act provided opponents of Soviet rule with a powerful tool for critiquing its failure to allow self-determination for the Baltics and Eastern Europe. But these were still mostly European debates. The 1979 invasion of Afghanistan moved the Soviet vision of self-determination to the centre of global politics.[74] The Moscow-backed Marxist People's Democratic Party of Afghanistan (PDPA), which had come to power in an April 1978 coup that it characterized as a continuation of the decolonization process, initiated a broad range of reforms alongside a brutal campaign against its opponents. Over the course of 1979, Prime Minister Hafizullah Amin and other members of the PDPA repeatedly 'invited' Soviet intervention to bolster it against growing religious and regional rebellions against its rule. Soviet troops finally invaded on 27 December, but this was in order to overthrow Amin and install a new government that Soviet officials thought stood a better chance of survival. They would stay for the next ten years.

Soviet and Eastern Bloc officials framed the invasion of Afghanistan as a straightforward application of the Brezhnev Doctrine, drawing parallels to the interventions in Hungary and Czechoslovakia. Cuba and other pro-Soviet members of the Non-Aligned Movement likewise expressed support for the invasion as an example of socialist internationalism in defence of a beleaguered ally.[75] At the UN, however, the invasion provoked strong opposition not only from the US and European governments but also from a majority of UN member states in the Global South and Non-Aligned Movement, many of which had remained mute following the invasion of Czechoslovakia a decade earlier. 'Few Powers if any have identified so sympathetically with the aspirations of the peoples of Africa for liberation and self-determination as the Union of Soviet Socialist Republics', lamented Nigeria's UN Ambassador. As a result, 'No words [...] can therefore fully convey the deep sense of disappointment and disillusion which the Government

---

[73] *The CSCE and the End of the Cold War: Diplomacy, Societies and Human Rights, 1972–1990*, edited by Nicholas Badalassi and Sarah Snyder (New York: Berghahn Books, 2019); Sarah Snyder, *Human Rights Activism and the End of the Cold War: A Transnational History of the Helsinki Network* (Cambridge: Cambridge University Press, 2011); Eric Weitz, *A World Divided: The Global Struggle for Human Rights in the Age of Nation-States* (Princeton, NJ: Princeton University Press, 2019), 309–12.

[74] Elisabeth Leake, 'States, Nations, and Self-Determination: Afghanistan and Decolonization at the United Nations', *Journal of Global History* 17, no. 2 (2022): 1–20. On the broader global dimensions of the invasion, see Elisabeth Leake, *Afghan Crucible: The Soviet Invasion and the Making of Modern Afghanistan* (Oxford: Oxford University Press, 2022).

[75] Leake, 'States, Nations, and Self-Determination', 15; Wilson Center, Cold War International History Project, 'Soviet briefing on the need to counter-balance Yugoslav endeavors concerning the Afghan question in the non-aligned countries' (1980), cited in ibid.. Mongolia's representative defended the invasion, arguing that 'when the Afghan people, in defence of its right to self-determination and its revolutionary gains, requested a friendly country to render assistance and received much needed aid, all of a sudden, those forces turned into the defenders of the cause of self-determination for the Afghan people. That is clear evidence of the hypocrisy and double standards of those who have imposed the discussion of this question on the United Nations', A/ES-6/PV.5, record of meeting held on 12 January 1980.

and people of Nigeria felt when they heard the news of the Soviet armed intervention in Afghanistan'. Though the Soviet Union was able to veto a Security Council resolution condemning the invasion, it could not stop the General Assembly or the Human Rights Commission, which repeatedly called on it to withdraw from Afghanistan.[76]

The damage to the Soviet Union's vision of 'socialist self-determination' had been done. For nearly a quarter century after the founding of the UN, the Soviet Union had portrayed itself, not without reason, as the staunchest Great Power supporter of the right to self-determination in international politics. This was especially the case in the decolonizing world, where Soviet diplomatic and material backing for anticolonial movements had garnered widespread support and admiration, and extensive concern in Western capitals. But the contradictions of a conception of self-determination that rendered it a secondary priority to the strategic imperative of socialist internationalism were too much to bear.

Eastern European dissidents and their Western supporters continued to challenge the Soviet doctrine of 'socialist self-determination'. Across Europe and North America Helsinki Watch committees monitored the status of human rights in the Soviet Union and Eastern Europe, pressed governments to demand Soviet compliance with the Helsinki Final Act, and called for self-determination for the Baltic states and the socialist republics of the Eastern Bloc.[77] As they lobbied officials, conducted research, publicized their findings, passed resolutions, and engaged in acts of creative protest, Eastern European dissident and Helsinki Watch groups popularized self-determination as a grassroots language of solidarity. To cite one of innumerable examples, in 1985 Latvian, Lithuanian, and Estonian exiles from around the world gathered in Copenhagen under the auspices of the Baltic World Congress to hold a mock tribunal against the Soviet Union for its violations of human rights and international law, including the Helsinki Final Act. Afterwards, student activists boarded a 'Baltic Peace and Freedom Cruise' and sailed into international waters off the Baltic coast, where they passed resolutions endorsing the Helsinki Final Act and affirming the right of the Baltic peoples to self-determination in the form of free elections to determine their political status.[78]

---

[76] A/ES-6/PV.2, record of meeting held on 11 January 1980; E/CN.4/RES/3(XXXVI), UN Commission on Human Rights, 36th Session, Geneva. Resolution, 'The right of peoples to self-determination and its application to peoples under colonial or alien domination or foreign occupation: denial of the right to self-determination and other fundamental human rights of the people of Afghanistan as a consequence of the Soviet intervention in Afghanistan and its ensuing effects'. The resolution was adopted at the 1541st meeting on 14 February 1980; E/1980/13 and E/CN.4/1408. New York, *Commission on Human Rights: Report on the 36th session, 4 February–14 March 1980*.

[77] Daniel Thomas, *The Helsinki Effect: International Norms, Human Rights, and the Demise of Communism* (Princeton, NJ: Princeton University Press, 2001); Nicholas Badalassi and Sarah Snyder (eds.), *The CSCE and the End of the Cold War: Diplomacy, Societies and Human Rights, 1972–1990* (New York: Berghahn Books, 2019); Sarah Snyder, *Human Rights Activism and the End of the Cold War: A Transnational History of the Helsinki Network* (Cambridge: Cambridge University Press, 2011).

[78] Julian Isherwood, 'Preparations complete for Baltic tribunal', *United Press International* (24 July 1985).

At the UN and in other international forums, Western diplomats and legal scholars insisted with increasing frequency that meaningful self-determination was an ongoing process which required democratic self-government and respect for individual human rights. They were joined by leaders of other regional organizations like the Organization of African Unity, which in June 1981 proclaimed the African Charter on Human and Peoples' Rights, acknowledging that the right to self-determination had both collective and procedural dimensions.[79]

Through the mid-1980s, Soviet and Eastern Bloc officials clung to their belief in 'socialist self-determination' and human rights as a countervailing vision to the Helsinki movement, even as economic stagnation eroded their legitimacy. In late 1985 East German Ideology Minister Kurt Hager proposed that the socialist states develop their own 'Socialist Declaration of Human Rights', rooted in longstanding commitments to anticolonialism and social and economic rights. Two years later Warsaw Pact foreign ministers discussed a draft declaration which echoed the 1960 Declaration Against Colonialism and the 1966 Human Rights Covenants, stating that the 'peoples of the socialist states realize their right to self-determination through which they determine, free from exploitation and oppression, their economic, social and cultural development'. Discussion broke down, however, over an inability to agree on a common understanding of the role of human rights in the socialist project. The Declaration, in the end, was not a new vision but rather the last gasp of a dying one, which 'confirmed the exhaustion of socialist, revolutionary internationalism'.[80] 'Socialist self-determination' was disintegrating. But what would replace it?

---

[79] Miriam Bak McKenna, *Reckoning with Empire: Self-Determination in International Law* (Leiden: Brill Nijhoff, 2022), 132–35; S. Kwaw Nyameke Blay, 'Changing African Perspectives on the Right of Self-Determination in the Wake of the Banjul Charter on Human and Peoples' Rights', *Journal of African Law* 29, no. 2 (1985): 147–59; Richard N. Kiwanuka, 'The Meaning of 'People' in the African Charter on Human and Peoples' Rights', *American Journal of International Law* 82, no. 1 (1988): 80–101.

[80] Ned Richardson-Little, 'The Failure of the Socialist Declaration of Human Rights: Ideology, Legitimacy, and Elite Defection at the End of State Socialism,' *East Central Europe* 46, no. 2–3 (2019): 318–41, 329; Fritz Bartel, *The Triumph of Broken Promises: The End of the Cold War and the Rise of Neoliberalism* (Cambridge, MA: Harvard University Press, 2022).

4

Soviet Lawyers and Concepts of Aggression in International Law

Michelle Penn

Introduction

Initial Soviet approaches to international law replicated the general Bolshevik ideas of law. Evgeny Pashukanis, the Soviet Union's premier legal scholar, best exemplified the early Soviet legal approach, articulating the 'commodity theory of law', which argued that law, like a commodity, was a special type of superstructure to the economic base. As commodity relationships would disappear under Marxism, legal relationships based on property would also evaporate.[1] On the international level, this meant that the revolutionary Soviet state could not be bound by the international law of 'bourgeois' states. Not only was the Soviet state not limited by customary international law (i.e. international law based on state practices or customs) but they could also not make meaningful treaties or agreements with these states.

Only other socialist states were thus appropriate signatories to treaties and agreements with the Soviet state. However, Pashukanis' approach to international law collapsed, both due to Stalin's turn toward the appearance of law in the 1930s and the Great Terror. Pashukanis was accused of being a 'counter-revolutionary Trotskyist-Bukharinite parasite' and a 'fascist agent' by Andrei Vyshinsky—the infamous prosecutor of the Stalin show trials—and Pashukanis was subsequently executed without a trial.[2] Vyshinsky replaced Pashukanis at the top of the Soviet legal hierarchy and supported his own protégé, Aron Trainin, in rethinking the socialist position on the field of international law.[3]

---

[1] E. B. Pashukanis, *Obshchaia Teoriia Prava i Marksizm: Oput kritiki osnovnukh iuridicheskikh poniatii* (Sotsialisticheskoi akademii Moskva, 1924).

[2] Michael Head, 'The Rise and Fall of Evgeny Pashukanis and Stalinism', *Canadian Journal of Law and Jurisprudence* 17 (2004): 269–94, 275.

[3] Pashukanis, Vyshinsky, and Trainin had all been colleagues at Moscow State University. ARAN Fond 1711, opis 1, no. 8, l. 1–2. At that time, Vyshinsky was Trainin's direct supervisor at Moscow State University, where he was heavily involved in supervising Trainin's work and driving his research agenda. See ARAN f. 277, op. 3, d. 43 for an example of Vyshinsky's close involvement with events at the Institute and f. 1711, op. 1, no. 21, l. 1–2 for an example of Vyshinsky's oversight over Trainin. Vyshinsky steered Trainin toward researching the concept of complicity and international criminal law, and Trainin regularly acknowledged Vyshinsky's influence. ARAN f. 1711, op. 1, no. 21, l. 1–3. Additionally, Vyshinsky was known for trying to protect his subordinates, as when he 'categorically forbid' the arrest of his workers in the Procurator-General Office. Peter Solomon, *Soviet Criminal*

Michelle Penn, *Soviet Lawyers and Concepts of Aggression in International Law* In: *Socialism and International Law*. Edited by: Raluca Grosescu and Ned Richardson-Little, Oxford University Press. © Michelle Penn 2025.
DOI: 10.1093/9780198920205.003.0004

The approach of the USSR to international law regarding the concept of aggression and aggressive acts in the mid-twentieth century was paradoxically particularly Soviet and consistent with trends in international law from outside the Soviet bloc. Soviet lawyers, most notably Trainin, articulated a concept of crimes against peace that centred on the atrocities of Nazi Germany, but in which the aggression of the Soviet Union was not recognized as such. Though the Soviet portrayal of aggression was self-serving, the USSR greatly influenced the development of modern international criminal law (ICL) at the International Military Tribunal (IMT) at Nuremberg (1945–46). The IMT changed the organizing Soviet framework for ICL from crimes against peace to crimes against humanity (or alternatively, crimes against peace and humanity). At the same time, Soviet lawyers limited the application of crimes against humanity, genocide, and other developing concepts of international law to the pre-existence of aggression and crimes against peace. In this way, aggressive actions remained the bedrock of Soviet depictions and interpretations of ICL. As discussed in this chapter, this relative consistency with aggression is likely due, at least in part, to Soviet propaganda about the inherently peaceful nature of socialist states. This portrayal of the Soviet Union as innately peaceful meant that the concept of aggression in turn became both foundational to Soviet understandings of international law and of greater centrality than other international crimes.

This chapter begins with an exploration of Aron Trainin's concept of crimes against peace, which served as the standard Soviet framework for understanding ICL until the German invasion in 1941. After this date, Trainin's concept of crimes against peace moved from abstract legal concept to everyday reality, and the concept of crimes against peaceful civilians took precedence to reflect the ongoing occurrence of atrocities committed during war (rather than what was simply the threat of atrocities). With the IMT and the 1948 Genocide Convention, many crimes that Trainin had outlined as crimes against peaceful citizens or crimes against peace were re-articulated as crimes against humanity, war crimes, and genocide. Nonetheless, Trainin's concept of crimes against peace remained relevant in Soviet approaches to international law (as in the 1954 Draft Code for Crimes against Peace and Mankind), and in the general Soviet emphasis on the

Justice under Stalin (Cambridge: Cambridge University Press, 1996), 246. Trainin also likely benefited from a reputation for competence, as many supervisors took the opportunity of the Terror to rid themselves of incompetent employees. See ARAN f. 1711, op. 1, no. 20, l. 2–3 (overwhelmingly positive reviews of Trainin's performance by the Head of the Institute of Law). Trainin has received more attention in recent years, see e.g. Francine Hirsch, *Soviet Judgment: A New History of the International Military Tribunal After World War II* (Oxford: Oxford University Press, 2020); Valentyna Polunina, 'The Human Face of Soviet Justice? Aron Trainin and the Origins of the Soviet Doctrine of International Criminal Law', in *Stalin's Soviet Justice: 'Show' Trials, War Crimes Trials, and Nuremberg*, edited by David Crowe (London: Bloomsbury, 2019); Thomas Earl Porter, 'In Defense of Peace: Aron Trainin's Contributions to International Jurisprudence', *Genocide Studies and Prevention: An International Journal* 13, no. 1 (2019), 98–112, 98; Michelle Penn, 'Genocide is Fascism in Action: Aron Trainin and Soviet Portrayals of Genocide', *Journal of Genocide Research* 22, no. 1 (2020), 1–18.

need for war and aggression to exist as a legal basis in order to apply the concepts of genocide and crimes against humanity. This chapter traces the evolving articulations of these offences and concludes with their continuation into the 1960s Soviet understandings of international law, as portrayed in the later work of Soviet lawyer Pyotr Romashkin, who took over the academic mantle from Trainin on Soviet approaches to ICL in the 1950s, though he never rose to Trainin's level of international influence.

Aron Trainin and Soviet Engagement with Concepts of Aggression

Aron Trainin's first substantial publication in international law was the 1935 *Criminal Intervention: Movement towards the Unification of Criminal Law in Capitalist Countries*.[4] Trainin, like other international lawyers from around the world, recognized that international law had failed 'in the struggle with warlike aggression'.[5] In *Criminal Intervention*, Trainin criticized much of the capitalist world's international legal attempts to prevent war and its atrocities; in his next work, he would more fully outline the official Soviet approach to aggression and crimes against peace (as well as international law more broadly) that would remain dominant from the mid-1930s (when the Soviet Union turned towards engagement with capitalist countries in international law, and strongly increased their participation in treaties and international conventions with capitalist countries) to the Soviet Union's entry into the Second World War.

Crimes against peace were first fully outlined to the Soviet legal community in Trainin's 1937 book, *The Defence of Peace and Criminal Law*.[6] Trainin wrote the book during the lead-up to the Spanish Civil War in 1936, when the Soviet Union was the focus of Nazi Germany's anti-Bolshevik propaganda. The Soviet Union, surrounded by capitalist states since the 1917 Revolution, now saw even more aggressive anti-communist enemies gain power across Europe. In *Defence of Peace*, Trainin outlined the clash between the two main forces in the world: capitalism and socialism. Capitalism, according to Trainin and the Soviets, resulted in the 'preparation for war', while socialism represented 'the struggle for peace'.[7] According to Marxist–Leninist doctrine, capitalism inevitably led to fascism,[8]

---

[4] Aron Trainin, *Ugolovnaia interventsiia: dvizhenie po unifikatsii ugolovnogo zakonodatel'stva kapitalisticheskikh stran* (Criminal Intervention: Movement for the Unification of Criminal Legislation in Capitalist Countries) (Moscow: Gos. izd-vo Sovetskoe zakonodatel'stvo, 1935).

[5] Ibid., 19.

[6] Aron Trainin, *Zashchita mira i ugolovnyi zakon* (The Defence of Peace and Criminal Law) (Moscow: Urid.izd-vo NKU SSSR, 1937).

[7] Ibid., 7.

[8] Presenting fascism as the logical end result of capitalism was not unique to Soviet propaganda. Members of the Frankfurt School also made this argument. See, Theodore Adorno and Max Horkheimer, *Dialektik der Aufklärung* (Amsterdam: Querido Verla 1947).

which itself 'was war, war today and for days to come'.[9] Current events seemed to support Trainin and the Soviet fear of fascism as particularly aggressive: In 1931, Japan invaded Manchuria, to only mild international condemnation; in 1935, Italy invaded Ethiopia, again with little international protest. Trainin rightly declared that Italy, Japan, and Germany were preparing for war and the League of Nations was hopelessly unable to preserve peace. All of this aggressive behaviour was taking place despite the fact that the 1928 Kellogg–Briand Pact (whose signatories included not only the Soviet Union and other world powers but also Germany and fascist Italy) had, at least nominally, outlawed war.[10]

In order to combat the feebleness of international law in the face of aggression, Trainin outlined his conception of 'crimes against peace'. This included three different broad types of crimes against peace that provided the foundation for an international convention to fight aggression, which Trainin proposed in *Defence of Peace*.[11] The first type of crime against peace was 'aggressive actions' (*agressivnie deistviia*), which encompassed aggressive war, blockades, and the threat of aggression.[12] The second type was 'hostile actions' (*vrazhdebne deistviia*), which included offences like aggressive propaganda, terrorism, support for armed bandits, boycotts, and violations of international treaties designed to protect peace. 'Unfriendly actions' (*nepriiaznennie deistviia*), the third type of crime against peace, included actions like spreading false information or false documents regarding other states (essentially constituting any insulting actions designed to harm relations with other states).[13]

One of the stickiest issues regarding aggression in international law in the twentieth century was how to define aggression itself. The 1928 Kellogg–Briand Pact had outlawed war but did not actually attempt to define aggression—the lack of an actual definition, some argued, enabled powerful countries to exploit other countries.[14] Trainin's concept of 'aggressive actions', which drew heavily from what Soviet Foreign Minister Maxim Litvinov proposed at the 1933 London Conference for the Reduction and Limitation of Armaments in his definition of aggression ('Litvinov definition'), was generally in line with existing efforts in international

---

[9] Trainin, *Defence of Peace*, 7. Soviet thinkers were of course not alone in identifying fascism with war. See Walter Benjamin, *Selected Writings*, vol. 4, translated by Edmund Jephcott, edited by Howard Eiland and Michael W. Jennings (Cambridge, MA: Harvard University Press, 2003), 269.

[10] The Pact was a break in international law in that, rather than simply attempting to discourage war through sanctions, it declared war illegal. However, the Pact lacked any mechanisms to actually enforce the illegality of war.

[11] Trainin, *Defence of Peace* (1937), 49. Trainin states that 'there can be and must be an international convention created to combat crimes threatening peace. Unfortunately, on this issue, as well as the entire issue of criminal defence, very little attention has been paid to international criminology conferences and the existing criminal laws in capitalist countries.'

[12] Ibid., 112.

[13] Ibid., 113.

[14] See Kirsten Sellars, '*Crimes against Peace' and International Law* (Cambridge: Cambridge University Press, 2015), 270, recounting an Iranian official's suggestion that a clear definition of aggression in the 1930s could have prevented the exploitation of small countries.

law to deter war. It essentially saw aggression as a declaration of war, invasion of territory by foreign armed forces, attacking on foreign land, air and sea forces, territory, vessels, or aircraft; naval blockades of coasts or ports, and providing assistance to armed bandits intruding on the territory of another state (the armed bandits being a concession to Turkish concerns over Kurdish rebels).[15] Trainin's proposal had the virtue of being relatively specific and impartial, and had already been supported by a variety of states, including France, Poland, Turkey, and Persia at the 1933 London Conference.

Litvinov and Trainin's definition of aggressive actions was thus (relatively) specific when compared with earlier international efforts to ban aggression (efforts that failed to actually define aggression) such as the Kellogg–Briand Pact, and left Trainin with the task of defining the vaguer and more particularly socialist category of 'hostile actions' like aggressive propaganda. Trainin drew from contemporary events to identify propaganda (false statements designed to spark enmity in some way) that rose to the level of 'hostile actions', citing Nazi propaganda against communists and warning about 'wars between peoples (nations, or *narod*), wars between races, between religions, for mutual extermination',[16] a warning that was particularly dangerous given that new technology had been invented 'for the extermination of humanity'.[17] This aggressive propaganda was used by fascist states to 'manufacture militaristic ideas and attitudes' which 'intoxicate people' and to call for 'the destruction of the Soviet Union'.[18] Soviet attempts to ban 'aggressive propaganda' shared strong similarities with the work of some lawyers outside of the sphere of Soviet influence such as Romanian international lawyer Vespasian Pella, who had likewise argued not only the prohibition of public propaganda designed to support aggressive war but also a ban on the dissemination of false news designed to negatively influence international relations and attribute false acts to a state with the aim of portraying the state in a negative light.[19]

In Trainin's narrative, 'aggressive propaganda' could be distinguished from 'revolutionary propaganda', of the sort advocated by the Soviet Union and other socialist states, because aggressive propaganda called for 'the extermination of thousands upon thousands of civilians'. Such a narrative conveniently ignored the propaganda of the Stalinist Terror calling for the extermination of Soviet enemies and the atrocities committed under its auspices.[20] Taking the opposite position to Trainin, some Western scholars argued in favour of banning 'revolutionary propaganda'. The British émigré lawyer of Polish origin Hersch Lauterpacht claimed that

---

[15] Trainin, *Defence of Peace*, 119. For an overview of the London Conference, see Sellars, 'Crimes against Peace', 34–40.
[16] Trainin, quoting Litvinov, *Defence of Peace*, 125.
[17] Ibid., 123.
[18] Ibid., 123–25.
[19] Michael Kearney, *The Prohibition of Propaganda for War in International Law* (Oxford: Oxford University Press, 2007), 27.
[20] Ibid., 129.

'revolutionary propaganda' was illegal under international law. Without clearly defining propaganda, Lauterpacht argued that 'revolutionary propaganda' was a clear violation of a state's freedom from external interference.[21] Lauterpacht was not alone in his position, and with the growing concern over socialist revolutionaries in the 1920s and 1930s, some states attempted to ban such revolutionary propaganda, exemplified by efforts like the 1936 League of Nations Treaty 'The International Convention Concerning the Use of Broadcasting in the Cause of Peace', in which states such as Brazil, Chile, Estonia, Denmark, and France, among others, agreed to prohibit broadcasting for propaganda purposes, motivated in part by fear of 'fifth columns' and 'revolutionary propaganda'. Although the USSR also signed the treaty, it never ratified it.[22]

As with 'aggressive propaganda', Trainin classified 'terrorism' as another crime of 'hostile action'. Just like 'aggressive war', 'terrorism' was an offence that both Western and Soviet lawyers agreed should be prevented, but they differed in the details of its prohibition. Historically, the offence of terrorism had its origins in the concept of 'crimes constituting a common danger', first developed in the late 1920s.[23] The 1934 assassination of King Aleksander of Yugoslavia pressured the League of Nations to further develop the crime of terrorism, and the 1937 Convention for the Prevention and Punishment of Terrorism provided the standard definition of terrorism for many years—for both Western and Soviet lawyers—as 'criminal acts directed against a State and intended or calculated to create a state of terror in the minds of particular persons, or a group of persons or the general public'. Terrorism was thus determined by the aim of the terrorist to induce a state of terror, the state as the ostensible target, and the means used to induce terror, as opposed to particular political motives.[24]

Trainin's definition of terrorism was consistent with what was outlined in the 1937 Convention as far as its statist focus (the Soviet Union wanted to both prevent revolutions internally and ease the extraditions of White Russians from abroad).[25] However, it differed from the Convention in so far as the particularly Soviet interpretation focused on the political motives of the act (revolutionary communism), in opposition to the Convention's definition of terrorism which did not take political aims into account. Terrorism, as with aggressive propaganda, did not apply to socialist actions, as the Soviet view maintained that actions against capitalist states were 'revolutionary acts', rather than acts of terrorism. Many Western lawyers, of

---

[21] Hersch Lauterpacht, 'Revolutionary Propaganda by Governments', *Transactions of the Grotius Society* 13 (1927): 143–164.
[22] See Kearney, *Prohibition of Propaganda*, 22–33.
[23] Mark Lewis, *The Birth of the New Justice: The Internationalization of Crime and Punishment, 1919–1950* (Oxford: Oxford University Press, 2014), 123.
[24] Lewis, *Birth of the New Justice*, 123.
[25] Ibid., 144.

course, advocated for the prohibition of terrorism in order to prevent such revolutionary acts in addition to anticolonial acts against colonizing states.

It was all well and good for Trainin to outline these conceptual 'crimes against peace', but how were these prohibitions to be enforced in international law? Trainin called for both an international conference and national laws to prohibit crimes against peace.[26] For these offences to be truly criminal and not simply illegal, they needed to be punished.[27] One possible mechanism of prosecution could be an International Court on Crimes against Peace, which Trainin envisioned as the highest court of the League of Nations, 'to combat crimes encroaching on the peaceful coexistence of peoples'.[28] While Trainin's idea of international prosecutions excluded the punishment of Soviet states by capitalist states (and indeed wholly foreclosed prosecuting the Soviet state as it was ipso facto peaceful), it had origins in an earlier proposal by Vespasian Pella to criminalize and prosecute war in an international court, and, other than its socialist exception (a significant one), was broadly consistent with the positions of Western lawyers who advocated for such a court at the International Association of Penal Law.[29] Pella was one of the most influential proponents of criminalizing war (as well as terrorism) and prosecuting such crimes in an international court. His 1925 book *The Collective Criminality of State and the Criminal Law of the Future* argued international law was in the process of being 'fundamentally transformed', and that, while the laws of war used to exist, now 'war is a crime' and thus only 'the law of peace' remained.[30]

For Trainin, peaceful socialism, realized on the international stage by the Soviet Union, was the only solution to the problem of war. In accordance with this belief, a crime against the Soviet Union was thus by definition a crime against peace.[31] The mere incantation of the words Soviet or socialist meant that the Soviet Union was incapable of committing a crime against peace; such atrocities could only be committed by capitalist states. This socialist exceptionalism meant that the Soviet Union strongly advocated (at least in rhetoric) for state sovereignty and self-determination, an increasingly popular argument for colonized peoples.[32] In the 1930s, the global left increasingly identified as communist, with communist

---

[26] Trainin, *Defence of Peace*, 159.
[27] Without a mechanism for punishment, an action could be declared illegal in international law but not considered criminal.
[28] Trainin, *Defence of Peace*, 177.
[29] See Lewis, *Birth of the New Justice*, 106–10.
[30] Vespasian Pella, *La criminalité collective des États et le droit pénal de l'avenir* (Bucharest: Imprimerie de l'Etat, 1925), 10–11.
[31] Though this belief may seem ridiculous, it parallels the thinking of Western colonial legal figures, who defined themselves as civilized, and non-Western societies as uncivilized, in order to justify their colonial wars. See e.g. Antony Anghie, *Imperialism, Sovereignty and the Making of International Law* (Cambridge: Cambridge University Press, 2005).
[32] See John Hazard, *Communists and Their Law: A Search for the Common Core of the legal Systems of the Marxian Socialist States* (Chicago and London: University of Chicago Press, 1969), x–xi, for evidence of Soviet law as inspiration for colonized and formerly colonized peoples.

movements for national liberation in colonial Vietnam, Cambodia, and India, gaining in influence and popularity, as well as communist movements in China, Albania, Yugoslavia, and elsewhere growing in scope.[33] Communist leaders like Ho Chi Minh studied in the Soviet Union, and Ho's critiques of the international legal order echoed those of Trainin and other Soviet scholars.[34] Though many in Eastern Europe accused the Soviet Union of acting as an oppressive and exploitative imperial power, particularly after the Second World War, Soviet lawyers helped to articulate an alternative to imperial Western international law that was viewed as progressive by some colonized peoples. Acts that would otherwise be classified as international crimes were often not crimes when committed by colonized peoples, according to the Soviet view. Acts that might otherwise be considered terrorism could simply be claimed to be acts of self-defence if committed by colonized peoples against a colonizer.

The ideas put forth by Trainin were distinctly Soviet and socialist, but neither the themes nor the doctrines were wholly original. The Soviet lawyer's incantations of self-serving exceptionality had a long history in international law, deployed by states of all ideological orientations. The conflict between this exceptionality (or what is usually articulated as state sovereignty—the right of states to govern over their territory without outside intervention) and the desire for actual constraining norms in international law is a constant feature of international legal argumentation.[35] In this way, Trainin recreated the double standards of Western international legal thinking (such as the colonial clause, etc.) but with a distinctly socialist ideological slant. Trainin elided this contraction by maintaining that states, particularly socialist states, could reject international customs (for how can a socialist state be expected to behave the same as a capitalist state?)[36] but were obligated to

---

[33] See S. Neil MacFarlane, 'Successes and Failures in Soviet Policy toward Marxist Revolutions in the Third World', in *The USSR and Marxist Revolutions in the Third World*, edited by Mark Katz (Cambridge: Cambridge University Press, 1990); Galia Golan, *The Soviet Union and National Liberation Movements in the Third World* (Boston: Unwin Hyman, 1988); Odd Arne Westad, *The Global Cold War* (Cambridge: Cambridge University Press, 2007), especially 55.

[34] Quynh N. Pham and Maria Jose Mendez, 'Decolonial Designs: Jose Marti, Ho Chi Minh, and Global Entanglements', *Alternatives: Global, Local, Political* 40, no. 2 (2015): 156–73, 161. Pham and Mendez cite Hồ Chí Minh's *Toàn Tập*. While the USSR's ideas and positions certainly had a global reach through their support of socialism and liberation movements abroad, it can be difficult to draw a firm line from Soviet support for a position and similarities between Soviet views and those of Third World leaders and scholars. The USSR, of course, attempted to educate Third World elites according to Soviet economic and social models. See Andreas Hilger, 'Building a Socialist Elite', in *Elites and Decolonization in the Twentieth Century*, edited by Jost Dulffer and Marc Frey (London: Palgrave Macmillan, 2011).

[35] Martti Koskenniemi, *From Apology to Utopia: The Structure of International Legal Argument* (Cambridge: Cambridge University Press, 2005, originally published by Finnish Lawyers Publishing Company, 1989). See also Gerrit W. Gong, *The Standard of Civilization in International Society* (Oxford: Oxford University Press, 1984).

[36] To allow the Soviet Union to be judged by capitalist countries would 'allow a situation in which the Soviet Union could be accused before swarms of spectator capitalist countries'. Trainin, *Defence of Peace*, 109. In this situation, the socialist state would be 'violating the foundations of capitalist morality' and would become 'the object of punitive intervention'. Ibid., 109–10.

follow codified international law.[37] In this way, the 'sovereignty of the state remains unshakeable'.[38]

In spite of socialist exceptionality, by and large Soviet lawyers like Trainin were in step with general trends in international law. For example, the Soviet focus on the importance of both preventing war and actions that might lead to war in international law was part and parcel of the various ideological convictions of statesmen and lawyers in the 1930s.[39] This focus was unsurprising given both the horrors of the still recent Great War and the (largely accurate) perception that the contemporary world was divided into opposing aggressive forces.[40]

The Development of Modern ICL: Hitlerite Responsibility at the IMT

With the Nazi invasion of the Soviet Union and the subsequent Soviet entry into the Second World War, Soviet articulations of crimes against peace and aggression shifted from the theoretical to practical. With the realization of some of the worst fears of war, the Soviet focus on ICL moved from 'crimes against peace' (which was concerned with the *threat* and *danger* of aggression) to 'crimes against peaceful Soviet citizens' (which focused on the actual atrocities committed by invasion forces). Even as it was uncertain whether or not the Soviet Union would survive the war, Soviet leaders called for an international tribunal to bring Nazis to justice, knowing that reparations would be necessary to rebuild their destroyed cities.[41]

By December 1943, the first Soviet war crimes trials took place in Kharkov; in his 1944 book *Hitlerite Responsibility Under Criminal Law*,[42] written with the end of the war in sight, Trainin situated these trials in his new international legal framework, in which war and atrocities were not merely threatened (as in *The Defence of Peace*) but had actually taken place. Though the prosecutions of invaders had been articulated in vague terms by Soviet leadership and the press throughout the war (as 'crimes against peaceful Soviet citizens'), its specific articulation was made more pressing now that the end of the war was near. 'Crimes against peaceful citizens' (specifically 'peaceful Soviet citizens') were a large part of *Hitlerite Responsibility*, which would become Trainin's most well-known book, and was the only book of

---

[37] Ibid., 61.
[38] Ibid., 62. Soviet use of the concept of 'sovereignty' was arguably also somewhat exceptional. See Lauri Mälksoo, *Russian Approaches to International Law* (Oxford: Oxford University Press, 2015), 6 ('What the Bolsheviks eventually seem to have meant, was: peoples formerly part of the Russian Empire could have their sovereignty and self-determination *but only under the guidance of Moscow*'.)
[39] See Oona Hathaway and Scott Shapiro, *The Internationalists: How a Radical Plan to Outlaw War Remade the World* (New York: Simon & Schuster, 2017).
[40] See Aron Trainin, 'Vzryvaiushchie mir' (Exploding world) *Izvestiia* (15 April 1937), 2.
[41] Hirsch, *Soviet Judgment*, 4.
[42] Aron Trainin, *Hitlerite Responsibility under Criminal Law*, translated by Andrew Rothstein (London: Hutchinson & Co., 1945).

Trainin's intended to be read widely by the international legal community. It was rapidly translated into a number of languages, including English and French, to allow consumption by the Allies at the IMT, including Justice Robert Jackson, the US chief counsel.[43]

The IMT was established by the Allied victors—the USSR, Great Britain, the United States, and France—to reckon with Nazi atrocities committed during the war. There was much controversy over how the IMT would be conducted—the USSR had assumed that the IMT would be a carefully controlled show trial— exposing the full scope of Nazi crimes before sentencing the defendants to death. The United States, however, believed that IMT should provide the defendants with a real opportunity to refute the charges, with vastly different ideas about what evidence could be introduced and the rights of the defendants, lending an element of unpredictability to the trials. Moreover, the crimes charged were the result of substantial negotiations among the four Allied countries, with the Soviet Union the main proponent of charging the crime of aggressive war.

The IMT outlined four counts against the German defendants: conspiracy to wage aggressive war, crimes against peace, war crimes, and crimes against humanity. The contemporary distinctions in ICL thus found their articulation at the IMT, though all of the offences overlapped with portions of both Trainin's broader articulation of crimes against peace in 1937's *Defence of Peace* and his re-envisioning of these crimes in the 1944 *Hitlerite Responsibility*. Given this intersection with much of Trainin's work, it is unsurprising that he helped to represent the Soviet Union at the IMT. As Francine Hirsch has shown in her definitive exploration of the Soviet role at the IMT, Trainin and the Soviets played meaningful roles in the development of international law at the Tribunal.[44] Though Trainin's work was primarily influential among the Western Allies, it became so important in large part due to the advocacy of the United Nations (UN) War Crimes Commission's Czech representative Bohuslav Ečer, who praised it as 'one of the most creative and progressive contributions' to the punishment of war criminals.[45] Later, Trainin's work would play a similarly significant role at the IMT for the Far East—whose

---

[43] See Robert H. Jackson, *Report of Robert H. Jackson, United States Representative to the International Conference on Military Trials, London, 1945* (Washington DC, 1949), 99, 126, 299, 379, 416 (both Jackson and the British representative cite Trainin's work multiple times). See also Memorandum from the United Nations War Crimes Commission, 'Report Made by Dr. Ecer on Professor Trainin's Book', 11 November 1944. Rosenman Papers, War Crimes File. October 1944–November 1945 (Harry S. Truman Presidential Museum & Library).
[44] See generally Hirsch, *Soviet Judgment*.
[45] Memorandum from the UN War Crimes Commission, 'Report Made by Dr. Ecer'. See also Valentyna Polunina, 'The Absent Player: The Soviet Union and the Genesis of the Allied War Crimes Trials Program, 1941–1943', *Journal of the History of International Law (Revue d'histoire du droit international)* 24, no. 3 (2022): 354–72. Besides Trainin's influential role in prosecuting aggression at the IMT, he also advocated for the prosecution of German industrialists—very much a reflection of the Marxist belief that the state was representative of the bourgeoisie. While not the focus of his book, John Quigley also discussed some of Trainin's contributions to the concept of aggressive war in *Soviet Legal Innovation and the Law of the Western World* (Cambridge: Cambridge University Press, 2007), 156.

prosecutors and judges included not only Western Allies, but also lawyers and justices from India, China, and the Philippines—though both Trainin's influence and the IMT for the Far East would be ignored in the coming decades on the international stage.[46]

The articulation of both the conspiracy count and crimes against peace in particular reflected Soviet influence at the IMT. Trainin and the Soviets were strong advocates of the 'conspiracy' charge, Trainin having devoted a chapter of *Hitlerite Responsibility* to complicity, building off of his 1941 book on the subject.[47] Conspiracy has a long history in Soviet domestic law, and Trainin's own definition of the term drew from that used by Andrey Vyshinsky in the Moscow show trials.[48] These trials saw the prosecution of Stalin's perceived political enemies, including alleged 'Trotskyists', many of whom were accused of conspiring to commit crimes like assassinate Stalin, destroy the Soviet Union, and re-establish capitalism. (The aforementioned Pashukanis, alleged to be a 'Trotskyite saboteur', was also executed as a part of this conspiracy.) Conspiracy, in both the Moscow show trials and at Nuremberg, required that the participants be complicit in a common plan. To be 'complicit' in a conspiracy meant that numerous individuals were involved in a plan to commit a crime, but that all participants were responsible for the acts performed in accomplishment of their common plan.

As to the other offences the Nazi defendants would be tried for, Trainin divided ICL into two groups in *Hitlerite Responsibility*, one, crimes against peace and, two, crimes connected with aggressive war. The first group were of the sort outlined in his 1937 *The Defence of Peace*—aggressive war and actions that might lead to aggressive war. Because aggression 'directly breaks the peace, and forces war on the peoples' it is 'the most dangerous international crime'.[49]

The initial draft of the offence of 'crimes against peace' at the IMT was a cooperative effort between the Soviet Union and Great Britain, though the Soviet delegation called for extensive changes to later drafts, concentrating largely on the depiction of Nazi crimes (the Soviets were keen to avoid mentions of the German–Soviet Non-Aggression Pact), rather than the offence of crimes against peace itself.[50] The German–Soviet Non-Aggression Pact and subsequent Soviet invasion of Poland in cooperation with the Nazis in 1939, as well as the annexation of the Baltic states the following year, clearly contracted the Soviet narrative that socialist countries were inherently peaceful. The Soviets naturally tried to supress obvious conclusions about Soviet aggression at the IMT.[51]

---

[46] Kirsten Sellars, 'Treasonable Conspiracies at Paris, Moscow and Delhi', in *Trials for International Crimes in Asia*, edited by Kirsten Sellars (Cambridge: Cambridge University Press, 2015), 25–54.
[47] Trainin, *Hitlerite Responsibility*, 78–89. Trainin wrote about complicity in Soviet criminal law in Aron Trainin, *The Doctrine of Complicity* (*Ucheniye o souchastii*) (Moscow: Institiut prava AN SSSR/ Urid. Izd-vo NKU SSSR, 1941).
[48] Trainin, *Hitlerite Responsibility*, 84.
[49] Ibid., 37.
[50] Hirsch, *Soviet Judgement*, 80–84.
[51] Ibid., 249, 262, 264–68, 279–81, 291, 302, 305.

Trainin's work in *Hitlerite Responsibility* was key to persuading the Western Allies to prosecute the waging of war as a crime against peace at the IMT.[52] Besides crimes against peace, the second group of crimes Trainin outlined in *Hitlerite Responsibility* were crimes that resulted from the aggressive war itself. They comprised four types of offences: (i) crimes against prisoners of war and wounded and sick soldiers; (ii) banditry, or the destruction of towns; (iii) the destruction of cultural treasures; and (iv) crimes against 'peaceful civilians'.[53]

Trainin's offence of 'crimes against war prisoners and wounded and sick soldiers' reflects the concept of war crimes as outlined in the earliest Hague and Geneva Conventions in the nineteenth century, including prohibitions against killing or torturing wounded and captured soldiers.[54] War crimes had a long history that preceded the IMT, but Trainin and Soviet views of Nazi war crimes (as reflected both in the IMT negotiations and in *Hitlerite Responsibility*) were consistent with the views of the other powers at the IMT (the IMT definition of war crimes was congruent with Trainin's 'crimes against prisoners of war and wounded and sick soldiers'). It was the inclusion of war crimes committed by Soviet forces that instigated the most controversy at the IMT, rather than the general contours of the offence of war crimes itself.[55] In particular, the Soviet addition of the Katyn Forest Massacre to the IMT indictment as a war crime committed by Germany (when it was actually the Soviet secret police who had murdered 22,000 Polish prisoners of war) was breath-taking in its boldness.[56]

Trainin's concept of 'banditry' from *Hitlerite Responsibility*—exemplified by the destruction of dozens of towns of 'Russia, Ukraine, Byelorussia, Moldavia, the Karelo-Finnish Soviet Socialist Republic'[57]—and the concept of 'Plundering and Destruction of Cultural Treasures'—demonstrated by the Nazi destruction and plunder of '112 libraries, 4 museums, 54 theatres and cinemas' in the Moscow region alone[58]—found its conceptual home not as a specific crime against peace but as both a war crime and a newly articulated offence: 'crimes against humanity'.[59]

---

[52] Ibid., 36–42.
[53] Trainin, *Hitlerite Responsibility Under Criminal Law*, 45–46.
[54] Trainin concludes that in spite of these prohibitions, 'murders, tortures, ill-treatment and humiliation of war prisoners, sick and wounded, constitute the "everyday life" of the Hitlerite troops' and provides numerous examples of abuses inflicted on Red Army soldiers by Nazi Germany. Ibid., 47–50.
[55] Though the Allies agreed to prosecute war crimes, there was disagreement in the international community on this point, including the International Committee of the Red Cross, which advocated for a more limited and conservative position on prosecuting war crimes. Lewis, *Birth of the New Justice*, 238–39.
[56] Hirsch, *Soviet Judgement*, especially 86, 93, 100, 102 on the inclusion of Katyn in the indictment. For the defence's successful refutation of the charges, see ibid., 247–62, 270, 293–95.
[57] Trainin, *Hitlerite Responsibility*, 65.
[58] Ibid., 65–67.
[59] On crimes against cultural heritage, see also Nelly Bekus, Chapter 8 in this volume.

The Nuremberg Charter—the agreement between the Allied powers that set out the rules and procedures of the IMT—defined crimes against humanity as the following offences committed against civilians:

> murder, extermination, enslavement, deportation, and other inhumane acts committed against any civilian population, before or during the war, or persecutions on political, racial or religious grounds in execution of or in connection with any crime within the jurisdiction of the Tribunal.[60]

As with Trainin's crimes against peaceful citizens, crimes against humanity functioned as a broad concept to encompass atrocities committed against civilians during the war or in connection with its preparation.

Though the exact details of the decision to adopt the term 'crimes against humanity' are unknown, the term appears to have been suggested as an alternative to Trainin's concept of crimes against peaceful citizens from *Hitlerite Responsibility*.[61] 'Crimes against humanity', according to the Chief US Prosecutor Robert Jackson, had 'no specific content' and thus was apparently chosen in part as an uncontroversial term.[62] In addition to prosecuting war crimes, the Soviet and French representatives at the IMT were jointly responsible for prosecuting crimes against humanity, arguably the most significant legacy of the IMT in international law.[63] The Soviets undoubtedly conceptualized the offence similarly to Trainin's articulations of 'crimes against peaceful civilians', as the atrocities encompassed by crimes against humanity were largely the same, including murder, deportation, and robbery, outlined by Trainin in *Hitlerite Responsibility*.[64] The prosecution of crimes against humanity was also limited to atrocities committed 'in execution of or in connection with' another crime in the Tribunal's jurisdiction (such as in connection with waging of aggressive war). This limitation of a connection to the war further reflects Trainin's articulation of 'crimes against peaceable citizens'—because in the Soviet incantation, atrocities are only committed under international law as a result of fascist, capitalist aggression.

---

[60] Nuremberg Charter, 8 August 1945.

[61] See *Report of Robert H. Jackson*, 'Draft Showing Soviet and American Proposals in Parallel Columns', 169 and 'Revision of Definition of Crimes, Submitted by American Delegation, July 31, 1945', 395.

[62] The term 'crimes against humanity' was advocated by Justice Robert Jackson after meeting with Lauterpacht. David Luban has noted that the two men 'decided to leave their deliberations unrecorded, apparently to avoid courting controversy'. David Luban, 'A Theory of Crimes Against Humanity', *The Yale Journal of International Law* 29, no. 1 (2004):85–167, 86.

[63] See Jon Kevin Heller, *The Nuremberg Military Tribunals and the Origins of International Criminal Law* (Oxford: Oxford University Press, 2011). For the significance of crimes against humanity in international criminal law prosecutions, see Leila N. Sadat, 'Crimes Against Humanity in the Modern Age', *American Journal of International Law* 107, no. 1 (2013): 334–77.

[64] Trainin, *Hitlerite Responsibility Under Criminal Law*, 61–62.

While the prosecutions at the IMT differed in some significant ways from Trainin's vision in *Hitlerite Responsibility*, they also reflected his influence, as well as the broader Soviet influence, on the development of ICL. The innovations at the IMT informed Trainin's next substantial work, *A Study of Criminal Offences*, published in 1946.[65] Trainin presented an initial draft of this work in 1940 to his Institute of Law colleagues, focusing on domestic criminal law in both socialist and bourgeois countries.[66] With the IMT, Trainin merged this earlier writing on domestic Soviet criminal law with an analysis of the quickly changing field of ICL that he was instrumental in co-creating.

Rather than persist with his earlier framing, Trainin shifted in *A Study of Criminal Offences* to replicating the divisions of international crimes from the IMT: a narrowed understanding of crimes against peace, war crimes, and crimes against humanity.[67] He also duplicated the narrower definition of crimes against peace from the IMT, rejecting his previous iteration of crimes against peace as an expansive legal category that included offences like propaganda. His readiness to accept the IMT's narrower definitions underscored the significance of the IMT to socialist international law. Of course, Trainin continued to promote the role of the Soviet Union in the development of ICL, but in his account, the purpose behind international law was to end aggression and promote peace. Peace, according to Trainin, was, of course, only obtainable through communism.

Echoes of Crimes against Peace in the 1948 Genocide Convention and the 1954 Draft Code of Crimes against the Peace and Security of Mankind

One novel concept in international law that was not prosecuted at the IMT was genocide. The 1948 Genocide Convention was the result of both this omission and heavy lobbying by Raphael Lemkin (the man who coined the term itself). While the Soviet approach to the concept of genocide was initially oppositional, given that the atrocities of the Holocaust had first been encompassed by Trainin's concept of crimes against peace and peaceful civilians[68] (and later by crimes against humanity)—Soviet politicians and legal functionaries wanted, however,

---

[65] Trainin's book differs significantly from his draft of the same book, written before the war. Compare Aron Trainin, *Uchenie o Sostave Prestupleniia* (Moscow: Legal Publishing House of the USSR Ministry of Justice, 1946) and ARAN, f. N 1934, op. N1, d., 190, l.1–30.

[66] ARAN, f. N 1934, op. N1, d., 190, l.23.

[67] Trainin, *Uchenie o Sostave Prestupleniia*, 178.

[68] Trainin, *Hitlerite Responsibility*, 54–59. Trainin's depiction of 'crimes against peaceful Soviet citizens' drew from the Kharkov trials. Both the Kharkov court and the Extraordinary Commission (whose findings the Kharkov court relied on), used 'peaceful civilians' as the standard phrase to describe victims of Nazi atrocities. See USHMM RG 22.002M reel 8, 435 and 438.

to participate in defining genocide on the international stage.[69] As with crimes against peace and aggression, the Soviet approach to the concept of genocide was that it only applied to fascist (capitalist) states. Only fascist-Nazi states, through their inherent aggression, could commit genocide.[70] Though this severe limitation on the concept of genocide did not succeed, other Soviet attempts to reformulate Trainin's earlier expansive concepts of crimes against peace—and thus Trainin's continuing influence—were evident in various efforts at the UN. One such project in international law was the 1954 UN International Law Commission's Draft Code of Crimes against the Peace and Security of Mankind and the Nuremberg Principles. The Soviet Union had originally proposed what would become the 1954 Draft Code before the UN General Assembly—allegedly as an attempt to codify the principles of international law charted at the IMT. The 1954 Draft Code did a bit more than codify the Nuremberg Principles. For one, it embraced a slightly broader concept of crimes against peace than the relatively narrow understanding of aggression at the IMT. The 1954 International Law Commission's definition of 'crimes against peace' revealed many consistencies with Trainin's work, like prohibiting preparation for war, encouraging terrorist activities in other states, threats of war, and economic and political interventions or coercions.[71] The USSR was thus generally supportive of the 1954 Draft Code, as were many socialist states and non-aligned countries.[72]

While most of the state socialist countries in Eastern Europe followed the USSR in promoting the criminalization of aggression, those outside of the Soviet bloc (like Tito's Yugoslavia) favoured prohibiting aggression due to anxieties about possible Soviet interventions. Representatives and lawyers in other non-aligned countries, such as Iran and Egypt, recognized that the Soviet definition of aggression could have helped prevent their exploitation by Britain.[73] Various countries exploited by colonial powers championed the Soviet definition of aggression, but other Third World approaches to aggression differed substantially. For example, Indian jurist Radhabinod Pal—one of the judges on the IMT for the Far East—skewered the view advocated by the Soviets (and the Allies more generally) at the IMT that aggression was a crime under international law because it presumed

---

[69] See Anton Weiss-Wendt, *The Soviet Union and the Gutting of the Genocide Convention* (Madison, WI: University of Wisconsin Press, 2018) for an overview of the political machinations behind the Genocide Convention on the Soviet end. Though the Soviets wanted to limit genocide in important ways, in other ways they advocated a broad definition of genocide that included cultural genocide.
[70] Hirad Abtahi and Philippa Webb (eds.), *The Genocide Convention: The Travaux Préparatoires* (Leiden: Martinus Nijhoff, 2008), 697.
[71] See Article 2 of the Draft Code of Offences against the Peace and Security of Mankind (1954), defining offences against the peace and security of mankind. Though specific offences against peace and security were defined, aggression itself was not.
[72] Chile, for example, approved the 1954 Draft Code in its entirety. Third Report Relating to a Draft Code of Offences Against the Peace and Security of Mankind by J. Spiropoulos, Special Rapporteur, A/CN.4/85.
[73] Sellars, *'Crimes against Peace'*, 270.

that there was an international community able to resolve disputes (such as self-determination) without resorting to war.[74] While Trainin, Romashkin, and the Soviets defined aggression to exclude colonialist struggles, many Third World lawyers like Pal rejected any position that threatened to restrict major developments on the international stage, in part because of the recognition that both Soviet and American powers led to a loss of sovereignty for states within their spheres of influence.[75] Such disputes foreshadowed the conflict over the status of wars of national liberation in international law over the coming years, and the friction between the Eastern Bloc and postcolonial states over the centrality of anti-imperialism versus antifascism.

In spite of the influence of Trainin's work on the international stage, his position within the USSR changed quickly in the early 1950s. Beginning in 1948, the Soviet state and press began their campaign against 'cosmopolitans'. The anti-cosmopolitan campaign had clear antisemitic motivations and resulted in the firing and death of many Soviet Jews, whose perceived international connections (particularly after the creation of the state of Israel) were now considered suspect. Along with a fellow law professor, Mikhail Strogovich, Trainin was declared to be the leader of 'cosmopolitans' at Moscow State University.[76] His downfall was publicized in a January 1953 *Izvestiia* article charging that 'the monopoly position of some scholars', including Trainin, 'stinks of the suppression of dissenting views' and 'interferes with the proper growth of cadres'.[77] The bourgeois suppression of these views by Trainin led to the 'poor quality' of legal works. Trainin's work 'did not rise to the high scientific level' required by the Institute of Law, even though Soviet academic lawyers had a duty to 'respond with attention and care to the party' and produce work that was 'worthy of the great era of the building of communism'.[78]

These allegations of shoddy work were in sharp contrast with the tributes that Trainin's work had previously received. Besides the praise and international attention to his publications, Trainin had been celebrated for his leadership at the university and his mentorship of students only months before his firing.[79] However, Stalin's death in March 1953 shortly after Trainin's disgrace spared him what was likely to have been additional punishments and humiliations. All the same, the allegations led to a temporary halt in recognizing Trainin and his work in the Soviet

---

[74] Ibid., 236–37. Though Pal agreed with the Soviet position that colonization was inherently aggressive, he disagreed with the criminalization of aggression as he believed it would be applied to the benefit of imperialist powers.

[75] See Radhabinod Pal, 'Renunciation of Force in Inter-State Relations', *India Quarterly* 16, no. 4 (1960): 349–57, 356 (publication of a 16 February 1959 speech).

[76] Like Trainin, Strogovich was a well-known legal scholar, though he focused on domestic Soviet criminal law. See ARAN, f. 1839, op. 1, no. 4, 6, 10.

[77] 'Overcoming Lags in Jurisprudence', *Izvestiia*, 23 January 1953, 2–3. (Original title: 'Preodolet' otstavanie pravovoi nauki'.)

[78] Ibid.

[79] ARAN, f. 1711, op. 1, no. 5, l. 1–8.

legal arena. One notable example is Pyotr Romashkin's 1953 book *War Crimes of Imperialism*.[80] Just a few years earlier Romashkin and Trainin had coordinated the compilation and editing of *Documents and Materials on the Struggle against War Criminals and Warmongers* (1949).[81] At that time, Romashkin was working for the Council of Ministers of the Soviet Union. In 1952, Romashkin joined Trainin on the faculty at the Department of Law. (Romashkin would leave the faculty in 1958 to take over as director of the prestigious Institute of State and Law of the Russian Academy of Sciences, a role previously held by both Pashukanis and Vyshinsky). In spite of this prior working relationship, the fact that Trainin was the most influential Soviet scholar writing about aggression and crimes against peace, and the similarity in subject matter of *War Crimes of Imperialism* with Trainin's work in *Defence of Peace* and *Hitlerite Responsibility*, Romashkin never cites him in the book. This was undoubtedly because of the ongoing anti-cosmopolitan campaign. Stalin, rather than Trainin, is the most cited authority throughout *War Crimes of Imperialism*.[82] In this book, Romashkin follows Trainin, however, in invoking the incantation of the Soviet socialist state as 'peace-loving' and 'opposed to aggression by nature', a 'stronghold for peace and the defence of people'.[83] The task of Soviet lawyers, according to Romashkin, was to expose the 'apologists for imperialism' of their 'refusal to comply with the laws and customs of war'.[84]

Nevertheless, Romashkin's exploration of war crimes is more sweeping than war crimes as typically envisioned and articulated by Trainin after the IMT. Romashkin's 'war crimes of imperialism', is a broader portrayal, more analogous to Trainin's earlier work in the 1937 *Defence of Peace*. It is possible that Romashkin's portrayal of the same atrocities as Trainin as war crimes of imperialism was intended to be an alternative to the Soviet formulation of crimes against peace since the Soviet portrayal of the concept was closely associated with the recently disgraced Trainin. Romashkin's depiction of imperialist war crimes is expansive and covers actions typically covered by the concept of aggression—that is, arms build-ups, as well as starting or joining wars. For example, Romaskhin describes the struggle of the Soviet Union for disarmament: the 'Soviet state has no aggressive goals', and 'does not intervene in other countries',[85] in contrast to the imperialist states like America, England, and other countries from the 'aggressive bloc' who refused to support Soviet General Assembly resolutions on disarmament and

---

[80] Pyotr Romashkin, *Voennye prestupleniia imperializma* (War Crimes of Imperialism) (Moscow: Gos. izd-vo iūrid. lit-ry, 1953).

[81] *Dokumenty i materialy po voprosam bor'be s voennymi prestupnikami i podjigatelyami voyny* (Pyotr Romashkin & Aron Trainin, eds., Moscow: RIO VYUA, 1949).

[82] Though the book was published after Stalin's death, it was prior to Khrushchev's secret speech denouncing Stalin in 1956, and the subsequent Thaw. In lieu of citing Trainin, Romashkin cites one of Trainin's favorite non-Soviet scholars, Vespasian Pella.

[83] Romashkin, *War Crimes of Imperialism*, 3.

[84] Ibid., 22.

[85] Ibid., 59.

nuclear weapons.[86] Other actions that might have been classified by Trainin as acts of war or aggression, such as the involvement of the United States and Britain in the Russian Civil Wars (opposing the Bolsheviks), are called 'war crimes'.[87]

After Stalin's death, Trainin was rehabilitated, and in 1956 he published *The Defence of Peace and the Struggle with Crimes against Humanity*.[88] The book borrowed heavily from 1937's *Defence of Peace*, but incorporated the concept of 'crimes against humanity' as a notable idea in international law, as Trainin declared 'crimes against peace' to be the 'gravest crime against humanity'.[89] Aggression, war crimes, and genocide, were all subsumed under the concept of crimes against humanity.[90] At the same time, Trainin's version of 'crimes against humanity' was dependent upon the pre-existence of aggression, and thus the crimes of war and aggression still underlay all of ICL. Moreover, Trainin's later depiction of crimes against humanity as the organizing offence of ICL was not universal in postwar Soviet portrayals. For example, a 1952 *Izvestiia* article documenting the alleged crimes of the United States in Korea continued the wartime practice of classifying all international crimes under the general concept of 'aggressive war', or crimes against peace.[91]

In February 1957, Trainin suffered a heart attack and died in his adopted hometown of Moscow. His *Izvestiia* obituary described him as 'one of the first Soviet legal professors' and praised his work in the 'struggle against aggression'.[92] As I will show below, long after the deaths of both Stalin and Trainin, Pyotr Romashkin reverted to the more traditional (Trainin-influenced) articulation of crimes against peace in his later major work in international law, with the 1967 *Crimes against Peace and Humanity*.

Pyotr Romashkin's Crimes against Peace and Humanity

In his 1967 work *Crimes against Peace and Humanity*, Romashkin returned to a portrayal of Soviet ICL that more closely resembled Trainin's from before the Nuremberg Trials but adapted to the new Cold War environment.[93] Instead of

---

[86] Ibid., 62.
[87] Romashkin, *War Crimes of Imperialism*, 96.
[88] Aron Trainin, *Zashchita mira i bor'ba s prestupleniiami protiv chelovechestva* (The Defence of Peace and the Struggle with Crimes against Humanity) (Moscow: Izd-vo Akademii nauk SSSR, 1956).
[89] Trainin, citing Lenin referring to imperialist wars, *Sostav prestupleniia* (1951), 357.
[90] Trainin had used crimes against humanity as a foundational concept in international law in a chapter of an earlier book focused primarily on domestic Soviet law, see Trainin, *Sostav prestupleniia po sovetskomu ugolovnomu pravu* (Moscow: Gosurizdat, 1951).
[91] 'Doklad komissii Mezgdunarodnoi assotsiatsii uristov-demokratov o rassledovanii prestuplenii amerikanskikh agressorov v Koree', *Izvestiia*, 11 April 1952, 3. The article described genocide as the most serious crime against humanity (which was itself called a crime against peace).
[92] ARAN, f. 1711, op. 1, no. 24, l. 16 published as 'A.N. Trainin', *Izvestiia*, 10 February 1957, 10.
[93] Pyotr Romashkin, *Prestupleniya protiv mira i chelovechestva* (Crimes against Peace and Humanity) (Moscow: Наука, 1967).

focusing on Nazi Germany as the epitome of capitalism, Romashkin turned his focus to the capitalist West and their military alliances (such as NATO) as prime targets.

Trainin is one of the most heavily cited scholars in *Crimes against Peace and Humanity*, if not the most.[94] Following his rehabilitation and death, the similarities between Trainin's later work and Romashkin's are much more apparent than in *War Crimes of Imperialism*, with Romashkin's adhering to more traditional Soviet depictions of war crimes, crimes against humanity, and genocide. Moreover, by referring to 'crimes against peace and humanity', Romashkin emphasized the primacy of crimes against peace and aggression in Soviet international law (as well as echoing the 1954 Draft Code). That is, crimes against humanity are only committed as a result of crimes against peace. Without war, aggression, and crimes against peace (committed solely by capitalist states), such atrocities would not take place. Interestingly, the Soviet state broke with this traditional doctrine the following year by supporting the 1968 UN Convention on the Non-Applicability of Statutory Limitations to War Crimes and Crimes against Humanity, which severed crimes against humanity from the war.[95]

Romashkin does discuss some 'war crimes of imperialism' such as 'banditry'—what Trainin had originally referred to as a crime against peaceful civilians, but following Nuremberg, referred to as a war crime. Romashkin also discusses the propaganda of aggression—significant as such propaganda is the underlying cause of war[96]—and classifies aggression as the 'gravest crime against peace and humanity',[97] while genocide is declared the 'gravest crime against humanity'.[98]

Aggressive interventions by the capitalist/imperialist powers, such as the American war in Korea, long a focus of Romashkin's publications, as well as Trainin's later work, loomed large in *Crimes against Peace and Humanity*.[99] However, the issues that arguably featured most prominently in the book are, one, racism and, two, military alliances like NATO. Romashkin, like Trainin and other Soviet writers before him, emphasized the problem of racism in capitalist countries, particularly in the United States.[100] Accordingly, Jim Crow race laws in the

---

[94] There are cites or discussion of Trainin's work at ibid., 21, 26, 40, 41, 47, 48, 171, 174, 185, 210, 246, 251, 258.

[95] Raluca Grosescu, 'State Socialist Endeavours for the Non-Applicability of Statutory Limitations to International Crimes: Historical Roots and Current Implications', *Journal of the History of International Law* 21, no. 2 (2019): 239–69. The text of the 1968 UN Convention prohibited 'crimes against humanity whether committed in time of war or in time of peace.'

[96] Romashkin, *Crimes against Peace and Humanity*, 40.

[97] Ibid., 18.

[98] Ibid., 264.

[99] Romashkin published works such as Pyotr Romashkin, *The Heinous Crimes of the American Aggressors in Korea* (*Chudovishchnye prestupleniia amerikanskikh agressorov v Koree*) (Moscow: Gos. izd-vo polit. lit-ry, 1953) and Pyotr Romashkin, *On the Peaceful Resolution of the Korean Question* (*Za mirnoe razreshenie koreĭskogo voprosa*) (Moscow: Gos. izd-vo polit. lit-ry, 1954).

[100] Romashkin, *Crimes against Peace and Humanity*, 270.

US South and South African apartheid amounted to genocide and other crimes against humanity in both the Soviet portrayal and the portrayal of many Black American intellectuals, as in the 'We Charge Genocide' petition submitted to the UN, which featured the socialist W. E. B. Du Bois as a signatory. While the Soviet lawyers were motivated by the propaganda value of emphasizing racism in capitalist countries, Soviet indictments of Jim Crow racism did play a role in how racial equality was viewed, both in the United States and on the world stage.[101] In the Soviet view, racism was intertwined with aggression, genocide, and war, as it led to imperialist hierarchies, of which war and genocide were the logical result.[102] Besides racism, military alliances were another feature of capitalist countries that inevitably led to war and destruction.

In his overview of 'crimes against peace and humanity', Romashkin discusses the 'aggressive bloc' of NATO. Romashkin declared NATO and other military alliance organizations opposed to Soviet influence, along with their creation of military bases on foreign territories to be a 'new conspiracy of imperialists against peace'.[103] Romashkin dedicated a significant portion of *Crimes against Peace and Humanity* to the threat of NATO and the expansion of American military influence. In his section titled 'On the creation of an aggressive block and military bases on foreign territories', he refers to NATO as the central 'aggressive bloc' for the United States as a means to prepare for war against the Soviet Union and other socialist countries (though other organizations, like the Southeast Asia Treaty Organization (SEATO) and the Central Treaty Organization (CENTO), are also worth mentioning).[104] In Romashkin's portrayal, US military bases in foreign territories were 'one of the most important weapons of the aggressive policy of the imperialist blocs', designed to encircle the Soviet Union and their socialist allies.[105] Though the United States claimed to be helping these foreign governments, Romashkin asserts that behind this help was the desire to deprive these governments of their sovereignty and to 'enslave' them economically and politically.[106] This position was similar to that taken by many Third World scholars: that new European institutions continued to further both military and economic imperialism.[107] Although

---

[101] See Meredith L. Roman, *Opposing Jim Crow: African Americans and the Soviet Indictment of U.S. Racism, 1928–1937* (Lincoln, NB: University of Nebraska Press, 2012); Richard Lentz and Karla K. Gower, *The Opinions of Mankind: Racial Issues, Press, and Propaganda in the Cold War* (Columbia, MO: University of Missouri Press, 2011).

[102] Trainin, *Zashchita mira i bor'ba s prestupleniiami protiv chelovechestva*, 222. For the connections between anti-racism and international law in Soviet doctrines see also Bogdan Iacob, Chapter 7 and Raluca Grosescu, Chapter 10 in this volume.

[103] Romashkin, *Crimes against Peace and Humanity*, 319.

[104] Ibid., 299.

[105] Ibid., 307.

[106] Ibid., 308.

[107] Contemporary Third World Approach to International Law scholars continue to make this argument, see B. S. Chimni, 'International Institutions Today: An Imperial Global State in the Making', *European Journal of International Law* 15, no. 1 (2004): 1–37; Antony Anghie, 'Europe and International Law's Colonial Present', *Baltic Yearbook of International Law* 6, no. 1 (2006): 79–84; Antony Anghie,

there had been earlier friction over the exact definition of aggression in regards to anticolonial conflicts, on this point there was now clear agreement between the East and the South.

Likewise, decolonization movements could generally count on Soviet support for their position that colonization was itself a form of aggression, and thus their movements could claim self-defence against colonial repression as a defence against claims of aggression, war crimes, terrorism, and the like.[108] Though Third World support for the self-defence justification may have echoes of Trainin and Romashkin, Third World Approaches to International Law did not entirely map onto Romashkin's critique, and can be viewed as specific approaches that had similarities with the Soviet views on international law but clearly departed from them.

Conclusion

Soviet support for self-determination movements in much of the world continued long after the deaths of Trainin and Romashkin despite shifts in Soviet approaches to international law.[109] The USSR regularly advocated both for criminalizing aggression and carving out exceptions for self-determination, as when the Soviet Union and other socialist states argued in favour of limitations to international humanitarian law (arguing that international humanitarian law should not apply to the victims of aggressors in aggressive wars) in discussions for what would become Protocol 1 to the Geneva Conventions in 1977.[110]

Aggression continued to be a topic of discussion on the international stage, and in 1974 the General Assembly adopted Resolution 3314, the 'Definition of Aggression'. The Resolution defined aggression as 'the use of armed force by a State against the sovereignty, territorial integrity or political independence of another State, or in any other manner inconsistent with the Charter of the United Nations, as set out in this Definition'. While there were broad similarities with the 1933 Soviet proposal, the Resolution's definition of aggression was considerably

---

Imperialism, Sovereignty and the Making of International Law (Cambridge: Cambridge University Press, 2005)

[108] See Jochen von Bernstorf, 'The Battle for the Recognition of Wars of National Liberation', in *The Battle for International Law: South–North Perspectives on the Decolonization Era*, edited by Jochen von Bernstorff and Philipp Dann (Oxford: Oxford University Press, 2019), 64; see also Giovanni Mantilla, 'The Protagonism of the USSR and Socialist States in the Revision of International Humanitarian Law', *The Journal of the History of International Law* 21, no. 2 (2019): 181–211.

[109] See Bill Bowring, 'The Soviets and the Right to Self-Determination of the Colonized Contradictions of Soviet Diplomacy and Foreign Policy in the Era of Decolonization', in *The Battle for International Law*, edited by von Bernstorff and Dann.

[110] Giovanni Mantilla, 'The Origins and Evolution of the 1949 Geneva Conventions and the 1977 Additional Protocols', in *Do the Geneva Conventions Matter*, edited by Matthew Evangelista and Nina Tannenwald (Oxford: Oxford University Press, 2017), 62.

narrower than those proposed by Trainin and Romashkin. The Resolution also contained some notable loopholes, as it was a proposed and non-binding definition for the Security Council.[111] Nonetheless, the Resolution eventually prompted the UN International Law Commission to return to working on the Draft Code, and the International Law Commission finally adopted the Draft Code of Crimes against the Peace and Security of Mankind in 1996, which contained an article on aggression. As with the 1974 Resolution, the 1996 Draft Code was substantially narrower than that advocated by many Soviet lawyers, and it was largely ignored after its creation. However, the International Criminal Court (ICC) drew on it in drafting the crime of aggression.[112] Though the ICC's jurisdiction over the prosecution of aggression became effective in 2018, the crime of aggression at the ICC is extremely narrow, with many limitations, including one that allows the ratifying parties to opt out at any time.[113]

That the ICC's crime of aggression would be limited is unsurprising given the history of the offence. Soviet lawyers like Trainin and Romashkin articulated an approach to aggression that by definition excluded their state's own aggressive behaviour. At the same time, this self-serving definition of aggression was not unique to the Soviet Union. International law is built upon the contradiction between normative limitations on state behaviour and state sovereignty.[114] Ultimately, the self-serving approach of Soviet lawyers like Trainin and Romashkin to aggression is inherent to international law, including socialist international law.

---

[111] The definition provided specific examples of acts of aggression, including invasion by armed forces, bombardment, and blockade. It also stated that 'a war of aggression is a crime against peace', but it did not make such a statement for simple acts of aggression (like blockades), suggesting that these acts were not necessarily criminal.

[112] Rome Statute, Article 8 bis. The crime of aggression is defined by the ICC as 'the planning, preparation, initiation or execution, by a person in a position effectively to exercise control over or to direct the political or military action of a State, of an act of aggression which, by its character, gravity and scale, constitutes a manifest violation of the Charter of the United Nations' and gives specific examples of acts of aggression, including bombardments and blockades.

[113] See Alex Whiting, 'Crime of Aggression Activated at the ICC: Does it Matter?', *JustSecurity* (19 December 2017), www.justsecurity.org/49859/crime-aggression-activated-icc-matter/, accessed 26 September 2024 for an overview of the key limitations of the crime at the ICC.

[114] Koskenniemi, *From Apologia to Utopia*.

5
Decentring Marxism: The Poznań School and Socialist International Law in Eastern Europe after 1945

Jakub Szumski

Introduction

In a 1966 textbook on international law, the author intoned that 'universal international law consists of rules that apply to all states belonging to the international community'.[1] There were also regional international systems, with a geographically limited application, he continued. Soviet scholars have argued in favour of the 'so-called socialist international law'.[2] If such a thing existed at all, the author claimed, it was merely a form of East European geographical particularism. In fact, even the Soviet scholarship 'shows no interest in the development of particular international law or in the development of the so-called socialist international law'.[3] Surprisingly, considering its derisive tone, the author was Alfons Klafkowski, professor and Chair of International Law at Poznań University in Poland, which was at that time a socialist state and part of the Soviet-led Eastern Bloc.

Klafkowski presented socialist internationalism as a form of particularism, even though one of its core principles, as it emerged after the Bolshevik Revolution in 1917, was its purported universality. In contrast to its Western liberal counterparts, this universality determined the emancipatory potential of socialist international law to change relations between states, nations, and classes on a global scale. Klafkowski's intervention thus signalled a growing pluralization in the legal scholarship within the Eastern Bloc. Contrary the view that countries of the Soviet sphere of interest were ideologically monolithic, there were not only widespread disputes among the legal elites of Eastern Europe over the content of international law but also over the question of whether socialist international existed at all. How was that possible?

---

[1] Alfons Klafkowski, *Prawo Międzynarodowe Publiczne* (Panstwowe Wydawnictwo Naukowe, 1966), 25.
[2] Ibid., 26.
[3] Ibid., 27.

This chapter examines the project of international law in Eastern Europe and questions the philosophically socialist character of the discipline in state socialist regimes. It looks at international law in Eastern Bloc's countries as fields in search of defending their autonomy from other academic disciplines and political power,[4] and elucidates the fine-grained differences in international legal doctrine within particular schools and milieus. The chapter reveals how Marxist–Leninist doctrine—or rather the version introduced to Eastern Europe after 1945—was decentred and negotiated from within by drawing from pre-socialist national legal traditions and contemporaneous Western approaches. It follows the developments across the region but focuses on the Poznań School of International Law in Poland, which represented the clearest example of a philosophically non-socialist way of thinking about international law while still remaining part of the academic mainstream in a state socialist country.

During the Cold War, international law was not only a product of political, social, and economic structures,[5] it was also deeply rooted in the logics of national and international academic and legal traditions.[6] What was considered 'socialist', 'liberal', or identified simply as 'international law' without adjectives was never absolute nor fixed. This chapter analyses these various doctrinal positions in international law relationally—that is, by looking at how they were formulated against their perceived counterparts and within a network of power relations based on varying forms of capital, understood here as the resources and prestige that determined the position of particular actors in the hierarchy of the academic discipline.[7] The relationality of what was 'socialist' and 'liberal' is crucial. During the Cold War, although the Soviet scholarship never constructed a coherent international vision in a legal sense, it nonetheless claimed monopoly on the labelling of various ideas and concepts.

The chapter historicizes the impact of socialist internationalism in Eastern Europe and shows how its reception was dependent on both the national traditions

---

[4] Philip S. Gorski, 'Conclusion: Bourdieusian Theory and Historical Analysis: Maps, Mechanisms, and Methods', in *Bourdieu and Historical Analysis*, edited by Philip S. Gorski (Durham, NC: Duke University Press, 2020), 329; Mikael Rask Madsen, 'Reflexive Sociology of International Law: Pierre Bourdieu and the Globalization of Law', in *Research Handbook on the Sociology of International Law*, edited by Moshe Hirsch and Andrew Lang (Cheltenham: Edward Elgar, 2018), 189–207.

[5] Natasha Wheatley, 'Law and the Time of Angels: International Law's Method Wars and the Affective Life of Disciplines', *History and Theory* 60, no. 2 (2021): 311, 317.

[6] Anthea Roberts, *Is International Law International?* (Oxford: Oxford University Press, 2017), 2.

[7] This chapter recognizes two basic forms of capital: political and cultural. In the Polish context (and in the Eastern Bloc as a whole), individuals drew political capital from the support they received from the communist nomenklatura or from employment in the state apparatus. Cultural capital stemmed from one's academic credentials, family connections, support among dissident factions of the intelligentsia and/or the hierarchy of the Catholic Church, knowledge of foreign languages, and international recognition. John W. Mohr, 'Bourdieu's Relational Method in Theory and in Practice: From Fields and Capitals to Networks and Institutions (and Back Again)', in *Applying Relational Sociology: Relations, Networks, and Society*, edited by François Dépelteau and Christopher Powell (New York: Palgrave Macmillan, 2013), 101–35; Tomasz Zarycki, 'For a Relational Critical Discourse Analysis', *Stan Rzeczy* 12, no. 1 (2017): 322–23.

and trajectories of particular schools and milieus and the particular actors who engaged in this process.[8] By moving beyond the mere recovery of the 'contribution' of peripheral actors to the canon,[9] be it liberal or socialist, it reveals how the divisions and convergences between 'socialist' and other pre-existing visions of the law existed in practice: In short, the history and traditions of the individuals involved, often on the sub-national level, mattered. This historical context often went chronologically beyond the Cold War and is explored here through biographical vignettes, most detailed in the case of the representatives of the Poznań School.

The first part of the chapter explores the vulnerabilities of Marxist–Leninist international law and posits that it was a set of markers or litmus tests on key issues in the discipline, rather than a fixed doctrine. The second part introduces the Poznań School and situates it in the context of unsuccessful attempts to establish a Marxist–Leninist project of international law throughout Poland prior to 1956. The third part zooms out from Poznań to reveal how Marxism–Leninism was decentred after 1956 across the Eastern Bloc by examining different positions on the existence of socialist international law and its relationship to other versions of this body of law.

The Vulnerabilities of Socialist Internationalism

Broadly understood, the legal aspects of socialist internationalism as a project in the Soviet-controlled Eastern Europe consisted of two elements: First, it was a specific school of international legal scholarship inspired by Marxism–Leninism, which introduced a set of new norms. Second, it was a legal principle aimed at facilitating the conditions for new, improved relations between states. Both in form and substance, it was expected to be clearly distinguishable from older approaches, norms, and principles, as well as from counterparts derived from other ideologies.

Marxist–Leninist international law adopted core Marxist philosophical assumptions, including a materialist view of history, a focus on capitalism and class struggle, a critique of the universality of the discipline's claims, and anti-imperialism.[10] Its preferred method was the 'sociological-historical' approach, which, as Theodor Schweisfurth writes of East German legal theory, 'emphasize[s]

---

[8] Stefan Troebst, 'Eastern Europe's Imprint on Modern International Law', in *History and International Law*, edited by Annalisa Ciampi (Cheltenham: Edward Elgar, 2019), 22–42; Anne-Isabelle Richard, 'Between the League of Nations and Europe: Multiple Internationalisms and Interwar Dutch Civil Society', in *Shaping the International Relations of the Netherlands, 1815–2000* (London: Routledge, 2018), 97–116.

[9] See James Thuo Gathii's notion of 'contributionism' in discussing the role of peripheral regions in the development of international law. 'Africa', in *The Oxford Handbook of the History of International Law*, edited by Bardo Fassbender and Anne Peters (Oxford: Oxford University Press, 2012), 407–28.

[10] Susan Marks, 'Introduction', in *International Law on the Left: Re-Examining Marxist Legacies*, edited by Susan Marks (Cambridge: Cambridge University Press, 2008), 2–15.

interstate power relations under the viewpoint of transition from capitalism to socialism. It is constantly concerned with revealing the class interests behind the states' approaches to international law as well as their position with respect to norms of international law.'[11] New research on Soviet international law, without questioning the basic accuracy of such fixed characterizations, has challenged their usefulness and illuminated the roots of Soviet international legal thinking in earlier debates that vacillated between the establishment of a pragmatic legalist dictatorship and utopian visions of abolishing law altogether. Boris N. Mamlyuk calls the actual Soviet practice 'anti-formalist formalism',[12] wherein certain legal declarations produced no consequences at all, whereas others were non-negotiable. According to Anna Isaeva, Soviet doctrine was 'liquid'—modifiable and flexible when faced with difficulties.[13]

There were also certain doctrinal markers, aimed mostly at securing the Cold War foreign policy priorities of the Soviet Union. These markers included the claim that sovereign states were the main subjects of the law, the reduction of sources of law to only those norms (treaties and customs) which were agreed upon between states,[14] and the primacy of national over international law.[15] Although Soviet international law defined itself against 'formalism' and 'dogmatism', Soviet scholars also charged Western liberals like Hersch Lauterpacht or Philip Jessup—who claimed the supremacy of international law over national systems or advocated strengthening the role of international organizations and individuals—with 'idealism' and 'cosmopolitism', both of which supposedly threatened the sovereignty of small states.[16]

There is nothing revolutionary or socialist as such in these Soviet doctrinal positions. The effort to create a socialist international law encountered the same problems as many intellectual projects when seeking to formulate a coherent, normative alternative to traditional and liberal visions of international law. As Daniel Joyce writes, those who have attempted to criticize liberalism 'have sometimes themselves shared liberal and/or functionalist visions of the international order'. They also 'have tended to illuminate problems of power, indeterminacy,

---

[11] Theodor Schweisfurth, 'The Science of Public International Law in the German Democratic Republic', *German Yearbook of International Law* 50 (2007): 154.
[12] Boris N. Mamlyuk, 'The Cold War in Soviet International Legal Discourse', in *International Law and the Cold War*, edited by Gerry Simpson, Matthew Craven, and Sundhya Pahuja (Cambridge: Cambridge University Press, 2019), 352–53.
[13] Anna Isaeva, 'The Cold War and Its Impact on Soviet Legal Doctrine', *International Law and the Cold War*, edited by Gerry Simpson, Matthew Craven, and Sundhya Pahuja (Cambridge: Cambridge University Press, 2019), 266.
[14] Mamlyuk, 'The Cold War in Soviet International Legal Discourse', 369.
[15] Bill Bowring, 'Positivism versus Self-Determination: The Contradictions of Soviet International Law', in *International Law on the Left*, edited by Marks, 135–37.
[16] Iain Scobbie, 'Wicked Heresies or Legitimate Perspectives? Theory and International Law', in *International Law*, edited by Malcolm D. Evans (Oxford: Oxford University Press, 2006), 85; Kazimierz Grzybowski, 'Soviet Theory of International Law for the Seventies', *The American Journal of International Law* 77, no. 4 (1983): 870.

inequality, and hubris, but at the expense of a wider interest in normative concerns'.[17] If one removes the Marxist 'sociological-historical' method (which lost its monopolistic position even in Soviet scholarship as early as the late 1970s)[18] and the specific confrontational anti-capitalist, anti-imperial language, one can subsequently imagine a perfectly non-socialist scholar who argues for the same markers of international law as those of the socialist: positivism and a narrow catalogue of the sources of international law, some form of domestic law's primacy over international law, and a downplaying of the subjectivity of individuals and international organizations. This hypothetical scholar could be characterized as a conservative sovereigntist and would likely fit well within the boundaries of the international legal mainstream during the Cold War, be it liberal or socialist. The conservative sovereigntist position made sense for the USSR, which had long considered itself 'encircled' by international enemies. Since legal doctrinal positions were flexible, the decisive factor in defining socialist international law was a belief in the viability of socialist internationalism as a universal proposition and an alternative to other universalisms. But such beliefs were impossible to codify and enforce. As we will see, it was exactly this indeterminacy and liquidity that was utilized by Eastern European lawyers to follow their own idiosyncratic paths and enabled a convergence with non-socialist traditions. The indeterminacy and fluidity of doctrinal socialist international law—and the socialist internationalist project writ large—created a certain level of flexibility, but it also created a certain vulnerability.

The early documents of Bolshevik foreign policy called for urgency and militancy, promoting non-state subjects ('the working class') and transnational activity, in the belief that certain issues—such as class-based struggles—were too important to sacrifice in the name of respecting national sovereignty.[19] Through the chapter, this position will be referred to as revolutionary socialist internationalism. It assumed a global sphere of influence: Since capitalist and colonial exploitation operated beyond national borders, socialism needed to overrun national sovereignty to respond in kind.[20] The Cold War and the need to accommodate new satellite states in Eastern Europe witnessed the narrowing of this vision. This Cold War socialist internationalism was held up as an ideal of the commonwealth of states in the Eastern Bloc, organized in the Warsaw Pact and the Council for Mutual Economic Assistance (COMECON), and bound by bilateral treaties, which cooperated and

---

[17] Daniel Joyce, 'Liberal Internationalism', in *The Oxford Handbook of the Theory of International Law*, edited by Anne Orford and Florian Hoffmann (Oxford: Oxford University Press, 2016), 476.
[18] Grzybowski, 'Soviet Theory', 864.
[19] Jörn Leonhard, *Der überforderte Frieden: Versailles und die Welt 1918–1923* (Munich: C. H. Beck, 2018), 75–78; Kathryn Greenman, Anne Orford, Anne Saunders, and Ntina Tzouvala, 'International Law and Revolution: 1917 and Beyond', in *Revolutions in International Law: The Legacies of 1917*, edited by Anna Saunders, Kathryn Greenman, Ntina Tzouvala (Cambridge: Cambridge University Press, 2021), 1–11.
[20] Amer Lodhi, 'Soviet Concept of International Law and International Relations', *Pakistan Horizon* 28, no. 3 (1975): 29.

helped each other, going above and beyond 'standard' rights and obligations. In pursuit of this goal, new norms of international law were needed.[21] While the Truman and the Bush Doctrines of American liberal internationalism legitimized interventions and regime change abroad,[22] socialist internationalism was best known for the Brezhnev Doctrine, according to which the interests of the socialist community had precedent over formally understood national sovereignty. The Brezhnev Doctrine thus legitimated interventions by the USSR to prevent political change in socialist states.[23] The revolutionary socialist international order imagined a global sphere of influence rooted in a community of working-class forces pitted against capitalist and colonial exploitation beyond national borders—but this vision remained largely unrealised. By contrast, the narrow Cold War socialist internationalism was realized far more often in practice as the Soviet invasions of Hungary in 1956, Czechoslovakia in 1968, and Afghanistan in 1979 demonstrated. In its most brutal form, the Cold War variant of socialist internationalism created a zone where the 'normal' formal rules of international law did not apply, and its participants had absolutely no legal recourse against the socialist hegemon.[24] The underlying threat of Soviet violence at the heart of the project helps to explain the lack of enthusiasm of some Eastern Bloc authors towards the concept.

In the 1960s, the representatives of the Soviet Union and other socialist countries attempted to codify the basic tenets of socialist internationalism and elevate them to the level of binding international law. They put much effort into elaborating universally recognized principles of 'peaceful coexistence' between the Cold War blocs that included socialist elements in the final wording of an international legal declaration. This project culminated in 1970 with the signing of the Friendly Relations Declaration.[25] The tensions between the proposed socialist and the 'standard' international law came to an apex in the aftermath of the Warsaw Pacts military intervention in Czechoslovakia in 1968. Soviet representatives argued that their actions could not have been scrutinized from the perspective of 'standard' laws: sovereignty or the use of force meant something different in the socialist context.[26] These two events sparked debates around the Eastern Bloc on

---

[21] Lodhi, 'Soviet Concept of International Law', 31.
[22] 'President Harry S. Truman's Address before a Joint Session of Congress, March 12, 1947', https://avalon.law.yale.edu/20th_century/trudoc.asp, accessed 24 October 2023; 'National Security Strategy 2006. March 16, 2006', https://nssarchive.us/national-security-strategy-2006/, accessed 24 October 2023.
[23] Jakub Szumski, 'Leonid Brezhnev and Edward Gierek: The Making and Breaking of an Uneven Friendship', *The Soviet and Post-Soviet Review* 45, no. 3 (2018): 267.
[24] Grzybowski, 'Soviet Theory', 867.
[25] Alina Cherviatsova and Oleksandr Yarmysh, 'Soviet International Law: Between Slogans and Practice', *Journal of the History of International Law* 19, no. 2 (2017): 317; Samuel Moyn and Umut Özsu, 'The Historical Origins and Setting of the Friendly Relations Declaration', in *The UN Friendly Relations Declaration at 50: An Assessment of the Fundamental Principles of International Law*, edited by Jorge E. Viñuales (Cambridge: Cambridge University Press, 2020), 23–48.
[26] Sergei Kovalov, 'Document 31: Sovereignty and the International Duties of Socialist Countries', *Chronique de Politique Étrangère* 23, no. 1/2 (1970): 247; Philip Bergmann, *Self-Determination: The Case of Czechoslovakia 1968-1969* (Lugano-Bellinzona: Grassi, 1972), 130–35.

the meaning of socialist international law and whether it actually existed. These debates did not contribute to the strengthening of socialist internationalism as an intellectual project. To the contrary, the various interventions in this debate, elaborated in the third part of this chapter, serve as the main example of how the concept was decentred and its relevance waned in the legal scholarship of Eastern Europe.

The Poznań School and the Field of International Law in Poland

The Poznań School of International Law epitomized the vulnerabilities and contradictions of socialist law through its long tradition of legal scholarship and skilful, self-assured adaptation to Communist Party rule after 1945. During the nineteenth century, the city of Poznań and the surrounding region of Greater Poland (*Wielkopolska*) were a place where modern nationalism and political Catholicism were born in reaction to efforts to unify the Protestant German state—which ruled over Wielkopolska between 1793 and 1918—and to the emergence of political ideologies such as agrarianism, socialism, and Zionism. Poznań's elite culture was a mixture of assertiveness against and attraction towards Germany (which was seen as a centre of superior culture and civilization) and an anti-Jewish edge grounded in perceived cultural and economic vulnerability, and staunch Catholicism directed towards political goals.[27] During the Second Polish Republic (1918–39), Poznań was a financial and political base for the National Democrats (known as *Endecja*), a political movement that emerged in the late nineteenth century and advanced an ethnocentric notion of the nation beyond estate and class differences and postulated a reversal of social-economic hierarchies,[28] through which the Polish majority would gain the upper hand against the German and Jewish minorities. The National Democratic movement evolved into one of the leading political forces after 1918 and beyond. When Poland regained independence after more than a hundred years of partition between Austria, Germany, and Russia, and the city fell within its borders, the University of Poznań was founded in 1919. The university's goal was to solidify the Polish character of the region and educate future elites to serve in the bureaucracy of the newly sovereign country. This emphasis on ostensible Polish national character also meant that university

---

[27] Patryk Babiracki, 'A Tower of Tangled Histories: The Upper Silesia Tower in Poznań and the Making of an Unromantic Poland, 1911–1955', *Slavic Review* 79, no. 3 (2020): 569–70; Robert E. Alvis, *Religion and the Rise of Nationalism: A Profile of an East-Central European City* (Syracuse, NY: Syracuse University Press, 2005), 145–81.
[28] This is similar to how Fabian Baumann describes nineteenth-century Russian nationalism in the Ukrainian–Polish borderlands in Fabian Baumann, *Dynasty Divided: A Family History of Russian and Ukrainian Nationalism* (Ithaca, NY: Cornell University Press, 2023), 106–11.

administrators limited the number of Jewish students and, in 1937, excluded them fully from attending the university.[29]

Within the University of Poznań, the Poznań School of International Law traces its origins to 1923, when Bohdan Winiarski (1884–1969) became Chair of International Law.[30] Winiarski was born near Łomża in Eastern Poland and spent his teenage years involved in clandestine National Democratic youth groups. He studied law in Warsaw, Kraków, Paris and Heidelberg, witnessed the October Revolution in St. Petersburg, and—based on his academic credentials and the political capital he had amassed within the nationalist movement—served as a legal counsel in Paris for the Polish National Committee (aligned with the *Entente*) during the First World War, as well as at the Paris Peace Conference in 1919. In Poznań, Winiarski established himself as a prominent figure with domestic and international prestige through his positions as Chair of International Law and Member of the Polish Parliament, as well as his experience in international negotiations around the contentious consequences of the First World War.[31]

During the nineteenth century, Polish authors, deprived of their own national state, developed far-reaching theories about the self-determination of nations subjected to imperial rule.[32] In the newly established Polish state, Winiarski now changed course, highlighted state sovereignty, and used international legal arguments to defend the material interests of his country. In a 1934 monograph, he argued against the 1921 Convention and Statute on Freedom of Transit, which set up international governance over the river Vistula. Since only its estuary was in the territory of the Free City of Danzig, Winiarski considered the Vistula to be an exclusively Polish river; internationalizing the Vistula and allowing foreign commercial fleets free rein would weaken the national economic interest.[33] In his activity and academic work there was little trace of the lofty internationalism or cosmopolitanism of the discipline's first generation, as portrayed by Martti Koskenniemi in

---

[29] Maciej Michalski and Krzysztof Podemski, 'Antysemityzm na Uniwersytecie Poznańskim w latach 1919–1939: Wprowadzenie', in *Wyparte historie: antysemityzm na Uniwersytecie Poznańskim w latach 1919–1939*, edited by Maciej Michalski and Krzysztof Podemski (Poznań: Wydawnictwo Naukowe UAM, 2022).

[30] Tadeusz Gadkowski, 'Historia Katedry Prawa Międzynarodowego i Organizacji Międzynarodowych', in *Myśląc o Przyszłości Nie Zapominamy o Przeszłości: Księga Jubileuszowa: 100 Lat Wydziału Prawa i Administracji Uniwersytetu Im. Adama Mickiewicza w Poznaniu*, edited by Roman Budzinowski, Joanna Agnieszka Haberko, Katarzyna Elżbieta Kokocińska, Małgorzata Materniak-Pawłowska, Tomasz Nieborak (Poznań: Wydawnictwo Miejskie Posnania, 2019), 443.

[31] Krzysztof Skubiszewski, 'Bohdan Winiarski 1884-1969', *Ruch Prawniczy, Ekonomiczny i Socjologiczny* 1 (1970), 387–88.

[32] Rafał Tarnogórski, 'Za naszą i waszą wolność: polskie powstania XIX wieku a prawo międzynarodowe', in *Wbrew królewskim aliansom: Rosja, Europa i polska walka o niepodległość w XIX wieku*, edited by Łukasz Adamski and Sławomir Dębski (Warsaw: Centrum Polsko-Rosyjskiego Dialogu i Porozumienia, 2016), 148–49, 159.

[33] Jan Sandorski, 'Sylwetka profesora Bohdana Winiarskiego', in *Z kart historii polskiej nauki prawa międzynarodowego*, edited by Anna Przyborowska-Klimczak (Lublin: Wydawnictwo Uniwersytetu Marii Curie-Skłodowskiej, 2002), 83–84.

his now-classic *The Gentle Civilizer of Nations*.[34] Indeed, Winiarski's nationalism was by no means moderate: before the Second World War he was a fundamentalist Catholic, anti-communist and political antisemite. His antisemitism was grounded in an understanding of the Jewish middle classes as competition for the Polish majority, destroyers of traditional Catholic morals, a guiding spirit of the Bolshevik Revolution, and participants in a campaign to besmirch the Polish Republic internationally.[35] Winiarski's generation of nationalists was vocal in its opposition to 'total rule' practiced in the 1930s in Germany and Italy, and defended parliamentary democracy at home,[36] but they saw nothing wrong with the daily discrimination or 'economic warfare' against Jews. Since he saw the international realm as a stage to advance national and ethnic interests, Winiarski was an internationalist through and through. He was a member-correspondent of Institut de Droit International from 1927 onwards, which intellectually and practically facilitated the development of the discipline in Poland. When the Second World War broke out, Winiarski escaped occupied Poland and worked for the government-in-exile in London. After 1945, due to conflicts with fellow National Democrats, he reached an agreement with the new Soviet-backed Communist Party government to support his candidacy as a judge at the International Court of Justice (ICJ), which was accepted in 1946. He remained a judge of the Court until 1967.[37] He also officially remained Chair of International Law until 1949, continuing to exert his influence from The Hague by drawing on his networks and institutional position as an ICJ judge to support Poznań academics.

Following Winiarski, the next Chair of International Law was Alfons Klafkowski (1912–92), who appeared at the beginning of this chapter. Klafkowski was born in Poznań to a working-class family and joined the National Democrats while attending the University of Poznań. He had begun to prepare a dissertation under Winiarski, but these plans were hindered by the war. After 1945, Klafkowski began as an outsider whose academic credentials were questioned by Winiarski himself and his circle. At that moment, however, much like his estranged mentor, Klafkowski gained the backing of communist political actors, and without completing the ostensibly required *habilitation* degree, became professor and Chair of International Law in 1950, a position he held until he retired in 1982. Without applying Marxist methods in his work but by focusing, like Winiarski, on geopolitically contentious issues like the post-1945 Polish–German border, he gained much

---

[34] Martti Koskenniemi, *The Gentle Civilizer of Nations: The Rise and Fall of International Law, 1870–1960* (Cambridge: Cambridge University Press, 2002), 216.

[35] Stefan Meller, 'Bohdana Winiarskiego Świat Polityczny', *Studia Łomżyńskie* 12 (2001): 32–33; Sandorski, 'Sylwetka profesora Bohdana Winiarskiego', 78.

[36] John Connelly, *From Peoples into Nations: A History of Eastern Europe* (Princeton, NJ: Princeton University Press, 2020), 420.

[37] Jan Sandorski, *Bohdan Winiarski: prawo, polityka, sprawiedliwość* (Poznań: Wydawn. Poznańskie, 2004), 105. On Bohdan Winiarski's role in the 1966 South West Africa decision at the ICJ, see also Raluca Grosescu, Chapter 10 in this volume.

political capital and held positions in high state offices. Klafkowski is often considered the actual founder of the School in its Cold War iteration, as he protected it from political interference, supported academic mobility to Western Europe and the United States, and provided his students with academic appointments as well as diplomatic posts and positions in the state bureaucracy.[38]

The third—and probably internationally best known—representative of the School was Poznań-born Krzysztof Skubiszewski (1926–2010), whose extended bourgeois and land-owning family was also entangled in the networks of the National Democrats.[39] Skubiszewski earned his PhD in 1950 with a dissertation on the United Nations, which was de facto supervised by Winiarski, who was in The Hague at that time and with whom Skubiszewski corresponded until his mentor's death.[40] With the support of both Klafkowski close to home and Winiarski from afar, Skubiszewski took full advantage of Poland's post-1956 opening to the West and, among other stays abroad, earned a Master of Laws at Harvard Law School in 1959. Beginning in the late 1950s, Skubiszewski had become an international scholar, participating in the English, German, and French discourses and publishing not only on topics relating to Central and Eastern Europe[41] but also on the law of international organizations or the law of war.[42] In 1968, the Ministry of Higher Education denied Skubiszewski a full professorship at Poznań University; in 1973, he instead took up a research professorship at the Institute of State and Law at the Polish Academy of Sciences in Warsaw, where he remained until the end of communist rule.

Alfons Klafkowski and Krzysztof Skubiszewski—the core of the post-1945 Poznań School—were both rooted in that city and had links to the National Democratic movement, as well as to Winiarski and his methods of doing international law. If Klafkowski was an example of a pragmatic cooperation with political actors, Skubiszewski gained his prestige from his family's cultural capital and his international academic networks, and he seemed to disregard any contact with

---

[38] Gadkowski, 'Historia Katedry Prawa Międzynarodowego i Organizacji Międzynarodowych', 447.

[39] Jerzy Makarczyk, 'Introduction. Krzysztof Skubiszewski: His Professional and Public Activity', in *Theory of International Law at the Threshold of the 21st Century: Essays in Honour of Krzysztof Skubiszewski*, edited by Jerzy Makarczyk (The Hague: Kluwer Law International, 1996), 15.

[40] Patrycja Grzebyk, 'Organizacja Narodów Zjednoczonych w Działalności Naukowej i Praktycznej Krzysztofa Skubiszewskiego Oraz w Polityce Rzeczypospolitej Polskiej Po 2015 Roku', in *Dziedzictwo Krzysztofa Skubiszewskiego w Polityce Zagranicznej RP*, edited by Agnieszka Bieńczyk-Missala and Roman Kuźniar (Warsaw: Wydawnictwo Naukowe Scholar, 2020), 260–64; Jerzy Łukaszewski, 'Krzysztof Skubiszewski, 1926–2010. Człowiek - myśl - działanie - spuścizna', in *Krzysztof Skubiszewski - dyplomata i mąż stanu*, edited by Roman Kuźniar (Warsaw: Polski Instytut Spraw Międzynarodowych, 2011), 15; Jan Sandorski, 'Profesor Krzysztof Skubiszewski (1926–2010)', *Nauka* 1 (2010): 166.

[41] Tomasz Warczok and Tomasz Zarycki, *Gra peryferyjna: polska politologia w globalnym polu nauk społecznych* (Warsaw: Wydawnictwo Naukowe 'Scholar', 2016), 48–50; Roberts, *Is International Law International?*, 10.

[42] Krzysztof Skubiszewski, 'Enactment of Law by International Organizations', *British Yearbook of International Law* 41 (1966 1965), 198–274; Krystof Skubiszewski, 'Use of Force by States. Collective Security: Law of War and Neutrality', in *Manual of Public International Law*, edited by Max Sørensen (New York: St. Martin's Press, 1968).

the communist nomenklatura, which was likely a direct cause of his unsuccessful attempts to secure a professorship in Poznań. Klafkowski's strategy within the state socialist regime was effective in the short term, paving the way towards positions in high judicial and political offices. Skubiszewski's strategy, however, proved more beneficial in the long term: his political profile rose during the 1989 transition as his cultural credentials and contacts among the dissident intelligentsia and the Catholic hierarchy allowed him to assume the post of Foreign Minister between 1989 and 1993.

Despite these individual differences, it is important to underline the shared approach and methodological understanding of the Poznań School, which ignored Marxism as a philosophy and as a method but was at the same time perfectly reconcilable with the actual practice of international law in the Eastern Bloc. This approach to international law—which can be described as 'normative-dogmatic'[43]—did not negate international law's geopolitical implications and entanglements with historical contingency, but was organized in contrast to sociological, functionalist, realist, Marxist and economically situated approaches, and understood law as a self-sustained system to be researched with the use of its own categories. In his lecture notes, likely from the 1960s, Skubiszewski wrote that 'in terms of methodology, the science of the law of nations faces the same problems as other sciences on particular branches of law (legal-dogmatic sciences). [...] Explanations in this matter should be sought in works devoted to the theory of law in general, and not to international law.'[44] There was thus also only one, unique, normative-dogmatic method. The job of international lawyers was therefore, so claimed Klafkowski, to identify, systematize, and interpret legal norms.[45] For Tadeusz Gadkowski (1952–), a doctoral student of Klafkowski's and later Chair of International Law during the 2010s, the discipline solved concrete 'research problems' and contributed to its further development by regulating new spheres of life.[46] This normative-dogmatic method accommodated many subjects of study[47] and could encompass numerous positions in response to basic questions such as the relationship between international and municipal law or positivism versus broad sources of international law.

---

[43] Jan M. Smits, 'What Is Legal Doctrine?: On the Aims and Methods of Legal-Dogmatic Research', in *Rethinking Legal Scholarship: A Transatlantic Dialogue*, edited by Edward L. Rubin, Hans-W. Micklitz, and Rob van Gestel (Cambridge: Cambridge University Press, 2017), 210, Aleksander Peczenik, 'Empirical Foundations of Legal Dogmatics', Logique et Analyse 12, no. 45 (1969): 32.
[44] Instytut Zachodni Poznań, Archwium Osobiste Krzysztofa Skubiszewskiego, 132, Teoria, [no date].
[45] Tadeusz Gadkowski and Jerzy Tyranowski, *Alfons Klafkowski - prawnik internacjonalista* (Poznań: Wydawnictwo Poznańskie, 2004), 41–42.
[46] Tadeusz Gadkowski, *International Liability of the State for Nuclear Damage* (Poznań: Adam Mickiewicz University Press, 1989).
[47] Paweł Kwiatkowski, 'Poznańska Nauka Prawa Międzynarodowego Na Łamach "Ruchu Prawniczego, Ekonomicznego i Socjologicznego"', *Ruch Prawniczy, Ekonomiczny i Socjologiczny* 83, no. 2 (2021): 209–25.

Looking beyond Poznań, socialist Poland's experience with the discipline was generally one of continuity. The burgeoning autonomy of the discipline and its establishment as an independent field in the Republic of Poland after 1918 took place in a climate of international law as a classical academic discipline that insisted on the promotion of 'national interest'. The field of international law was made up of a small group of men who had established themselves during the interwar years and then gained recognition abroad as scholars, diplomats, or public servants of the Polish state. The future path of the discipline was not, however, preordained, since international lawyers—educated in the interwar years at Polish universities, especially in Lviv and Kraków—went on to work around the world in different traditions after 1945.[48] After the war, the chairs of international law at the three 'old' universities (Kraków, Poznań, and Warsaw) that remained on Polish territory were occupied by professors with pre-socialist pedigrees;[49] this was also the case in most newly created ones.[50] After 1945, university textbooks used before the war were re-issued, especially if the authors had survived the Second World War and continued to teach and engage in academic work in the country. New textbooks written by experienced scholars were published with different methodological approaches, but, with one exception which will be addressed below, none that identified themselves as socialist.[51]

An outlier was Warsaw. There—at the University of Warsaw and to a larger extent at the newly created state and Communist Party colleges where law, including international law, was taught—political actors could directly intervene and shape the discipline. At these institutions, radical lawyers, many of them Jewish, who had received their legal educations during the Second Republic, but who had been side-lined because of their communist activities, could rise through the political and academic ranks. The trajectories of these lawyers differed greatly from those

---

[48] See Natasha Wheatley's portrayal of Charles Henry (Karol) Alexandrowicz and Krystyna Marek, both alumni of Jagiellonian University in Kraków who went on to work in international law during the Cold War outside of Poland in Natasha Wheatley, *The Life and Death of States: Central Europe and the Transformation of Modern Sovereignty* (Princeton, NJ: Princeton University Press, 2023), 261–73.

[49] Lviv and Vilnius, together with their universities, fell to the territory of the Ukrainian and Lithuanian Soviet Republics after 1945, Bartłomiej Krzan, 'Karol Wolfke - profesor prawa międzynarodowego', in *Prawo międzynarodowe publiczne: studia i materiały. T. 2*, edited by Kinga Stasiak, Wojciech Szczepan Staszewski, and Anna Szarek-Zwijacz (Lublin: Towarzystwo Naukowe KUL, 2019), 156; Wojciech Matuszewski, 'Uniwersytet Jagielloński', in *Z kart historii polskiej nauki prawa międzynarodowego*, edited by Anna Przyborowska-Klimczak (Lublin: Wydawnictwo Uniwersytetu Marii Curie-Skłodowskiej, 2002), 119; Karol Karski, 'Uniwersytet Warszawski', in *Z kart historii polskiej nauki prawa międzynarodowego*, edited by Anna Przyborowska-Klimczak (Lublin: Wydawnictwo Uniwersytetu Marii Curie-Skłodowskiej, 2002), 137.

[50] Anna Jasińska and Izabela Skomerska-Muchowska, 'Uniwersytet Łódzki', in *Z kart historii polskiej nauki prawa międzynarodowego*, edited by Anna Przyborowska-Klimczak (Lublin: Wydawnictwo Uniwersytetu Marii Curie-Skłodowskiej, 2002); Wojciech Konaszczuk, 'Uniwersytet Marii Curie-Skłodowskiej', in *Z kart historii polskiej nauki prawa międzynarodowego*, edited by Anna Przyborowska-Klimczak (Lublin: Wydawnictwo Uniwersytetu Marii Curie-Skłodowskiej, 2002).

[51] Anna Przyborowska-Klimczak, 'Polskie podręczniki prawa międzynarodowego wydane w XX wieku', in *Z kart historii polskiej nauki prawa międzynarodowego*, edited by Anna Przyborowska-Klimczak (Lublin: Wydawnictwo Uniwersytetu Marii Curie-Skłodowskiej, 2002), 48–51.

in Poznań, since they saw the law not as a tool to advance the national interest or to serve an abstract 'international community' but as a response to the ethnic discrimination and social injustice they had encountered before the Second World War.[52] Their experiences were shaped by radical leftist university organizations, a clandestine Communist Party, exile, and time spent in jail as political prisoners. Nonetheless, these figures were very few in number, and most had only shifted to international law from other subdisciplines after the Second World War in response to the needs of the socialist state. Juliusz Katz-Suchy (1912–71) had studied law at Jan Kazimierz University in Lviv (then within Poland), but he did not graduate due to time spent in prisons for communist activities. After the Second World War, Katz-Suchy became a diplomat, an expert on international affairs and a professor of international law at the University of Warsaw.[53] Marian Muszkat (Marion Mushkat) (1909–95) was educated in Warsaw before completing a PhD in Nancy, France, during which time he was a member of various communist-affiliated youth and student organizations. After the German attack on the Soviet Union, Muszkat sought refuge behind the front, and returned to Poland as a political officer in the Polish Army formed in the USSR. After 1945, Muszkat remained in the military as a judge, oversaw the retribution against the enemies of the new regime, and was delegated to the Nuremberg Tribunal and the UN War Crimes Committee. He then taught at several newly established law schools that provided expediated training for the future cadre of the socialist judiciary, before finally settling as professor in the Chair of International Law in Warsaw.[54] Both Katz-Suchy and Muszkat can be understood as occupying positions at the opposite end of the field of international law to the Poznań lawyers. Politically socialized in the communist movement and with experience in political posts after the Second World War (Communist Party, diplomacy, military, and judiciary), they had been excluded—despite their credentials (Muszkat)—from interwar academic hierarchies and were now building a new Marxist–Leninist and anti-imperialist scholarship in international law, instead of continuing the normative-dogmatic work of older professors such as Bohdan Winiarski.

When Polish international scholars reflect on the history of their discipline, the introduction of socialist law—understood here as scholarship inspired by Marxism–Leninism and modelled after the work of Soviet politician, prosecutor, and legal academic Andrey Vyshinsky—is identified as a top–down 'Stalinization' forced onto the profession by the ruling Communist Party. In June 1950,

---

[52] See Łukasz Bertram's portrayal of activists of the radical leftist academic organization, ZNMS 'Życie' in interwar Poland, who after 1945 became part of Communist Poland's ruling elite; Łukasz Bertram, *Bunt, Podziemie, Władza: Polscy Komuniści i Ich Socjalizacja Polityczna Do Roku 1956* (Warsaw: Wydawnictwo Naukowe Scholar, 2022), 145–52.

[53] Karol Karski, 'Juliusz Katz-Suchy - dyplomata i profesor', *Polski Przegląd Dyplomatyczny* 37, no. 3 (2007): 125–34.

[54] Karol Karski, 'Marian Muszkat - profesor prawa i stosunków międzynarodowych', *Polski Przegląd Dyplomatyczny* 38, no. 4 (2007): 75–83.

international lawyers met at the Polish Institute of International Affairs, a think tank of the Foreign Ministry, to approve a resolution that condemned, in language identical to that applied to other academic disciplines, the existing 'idealist' scholarship which surrendered to 'cosmopolitanism, the ideological tool of American imperialism'.[55] The lawyers present also promised to follow Marxism–Leninism going forward.

In response, Marian Muszkat edited a new—socialist—textbook that was supposed to upend the existing academic hierarchies. The opening chapters, written by Muszkat himself, resolved all doctrinal issues according to the Soviet orthodoxy of the time. Employing wording and a line of reasoning very different from the normative-dogmatic tradition, yet eerily reminiscent of what Winiarski's claimed about the internationalization of Polish rivers and German power after the First World War, Muszkat argued that more international governance would simply bring about the hegemony of the United States. The most powerful state in the world system had the power to police international rules and to decide at will what behaviour was deemed illegal. The 'international community' did not exist, and by proposing greater internationalization, bourgeois lawyers provided cover for the domination of their state over weaker ones. 'For this purpose', wrote Muszkat, 'they are asking [...] to "strengthen" international law, to transform it into "world law", supra-state law, to create a centralized coercive centre independent of the will of states to guarantee the enforceability of this "law"'.[56] More international law would not actually provide smaller states with greater autonomy. To the contrary. This instance again reveals the persistence of the discipline's past and a hidden similarity between a Marxist and national-sovereigntist approach to international law, where even a Marxist author intending to break with national tradition comes to repeat it. Furthermore, this critical historical-sociological Marxist method was never consistently applied. The Muszkat textbook, apart from the statements quoted above, was in fact a dogmatic discussion of existing law with hardly any productive references to Marxism. This is not surprising, when we consider that among the contributors we find Klafkowski and Skubiszewski, together with Poznań's Bolesław Wiewióra (1926–63).[57] These authors could clearly not have shifted to practicing international law using Marxist–Leninist methods overnight—even under political pressure.

Although there was a great deal of compromise among academics, in the early 1950s, the Poznań School was widely criticized as too conservative and too focused

---

[55] Quoted in Przyborowska-Klimczak, 'Polskie podręczniki prawa międzynarodowego wydane w XX wieku', 55.

[56] Marian Muszkat, *Materiały Do Nauki Prawa Międzynarodowego: Dla 1 Semestru r. Akad. 1953–54. Cz. 1* (Warsaw: Uniwersytet Warszawski, 1953), 9.

[57] Jan Sandorski, *Nie Deptać Prawników: Wydział Prawa Uniwersytetu Im. Adama Mickiewicza w Poznaniu w Anegdocie* (Poznań: Wydawnictwo Poznańskie, 2011), 173–74; Przyborowska-Klimczak, 'Polskie podręczniki prawa międzynarodowego wydane w XX wieku', 55–56.

on static and literal readings of international law that obfuscated its political and adversarial character. Normative-dogmatic methods, wrote Muszkat in his textbook, 'say nothing about the genesis of [international] norms, about their substantive content, that is, about the relations that brought them to life, about the manner of their protection'.[58] Party officials responsible for research policies attempted to intervene in Poznań to balance the School's dogmatic tendencies; in 1953, two lawyers from outside Poznań were assigned by the Ministry of Higher Education to the faculty, but they both left in 1956.[59]

In 1957, four years after his scathing portrayal of the 'bourgeois legal sciences', Marian Muszkat—fearing an antisemitic backlash as well as reckoning for his actions as a military judge in political trials—left for Israel, where after many complications, he became law professor in Haifa, Jerusalem and Tel Aviv.[60] His Polish colleagues commented that, in Israel, Muszkat repurposed his old textbook by simply removing the Marxist phraseology.[61] Katz-Suchy was similarly forced to leave Poland after a purge among the communist elite during the antisemitic campaign of March 1968.[62] Just as the continuation of the normative-dogmatic approach reflected the personal biographies and legal traditions in which its practitioners were embedded, attempts to introduce Marxist methods and socialist internationalism as universal were similarly unsuccessful, in part due to the biographies of their advocates. Moreover, the period of Stalinization within the law was short. Lawyers are, as a rule, well positioned to portray their discipline as technical, and thus not prone to interpretation or paradigm shifts.[63] Professors maintained cohesion in their departments and saw their primary loyalty not to the state and its policies but to their professional and collegial ethos, favouring cultural over political capital.[64] The new socialist version of international law proved unviable, especially in practice. It also turned out that the more traditional approaches to law were very efficient in representing state interests in international relations and became a common language for political and academic elites, between whom figures like Klafkowski, with one foot in the academic and one in the political world, mediated. Any alternatives to the traditional way of looking at international law as symbolized by the Poznań School, any experimentation, realist approaches seeing law as a product of politics and economy, anti-imperialism, or Third World-ism was

---

[58] Muszkat, *Materiały Do Nauki Prawa Międzynarodowego: Dla 1 Semestru r. Akad. 1953–54. Cz. 1*, 5.
[59] Gadkowski, 'Historia Katedry Prawa Międzynarodowego i Organizacji Międzynarodowych', 449.
[60] Karski, 'Marian Muszkat - profesor prawa i stosunków międzynarodowych', 79–80.
[61] Archwium Instytutu Pamięci Narodowej, Warsaw, BU 00170/443, Notatka (stenogram rozmowy przeprowadzonej dnia 23.VI. z 'Alfą'), 23 June 1963, 154.
[62] Karski, 'Juliusz Katz-Suchy - dyplomata i profesor', 130.
[63] Madsen, 'Reflexive Sociology of International Law', 190.
[64] John Connelly, *Captive University: The Sovietization of East German, Czech and Polish Higher Education, 1945–1956* (Chapel Hill: University of North Carolina Press, 2000), 284; Agata Zysiak, *Punkty Za Pochodzenie: Powojenna Modernizacja i Uniwersytet w Robotniczym Mieście* (Kraków: Zakład Wydawniczy 'Nomos', 2016).

seen as tainted by the Stalinist era. Not only Marxist–Leninist methodology but also phraseology, were both considered a sign of alignment with the Communist Party nomenklatura and with the choice of political capital over professional solidarity.[65] While the nomenklatura controlled state and expert appointments, it had a very limited reach in academia, which maintained its own systems of power and status in Poland.

Today, the argument that the School lacked fidelity to Marxist–Leninist principles in the 1950s is considered a badge of honour by the Poznań's representatives,[66] since it reinforces the notion that while their critics were ideologues responding to political currents, they had succeeded in preserving the tradition of objective legal studies.[67] While Mikael Rask Madsen suggests that the meaning of 'the international' in law is constructed nationally,[68] the case of Poznań suggests that this delineation is less national than at the level of particular schools and milieus. Poznań's 'internationalism' was based on a conservative reading of international law, which was sceptical towards both socialist internationalism and more expansive regulations that threatened the status quo (e.g. systems that empowered individuals in the international realm). Certain positions and areas of study may have changed, but the general outlook and philosophy of the discipline, the normative-dogmatic method, and the expectation that the autonomy of the discipline, understood as distance from the socialist political project, be upheld remained. After the failure of socialist internationalism as an intellectual proposition, beginning roughly after 1956, conflicts in the discipline of international law began to look like those to be found everywhere, revolving more around material and academic resources than pitched ideological battles. Within the Poznań circle, when representatives characterized their opponents, they would almost never point to any methodological differences in their academic writing or attitude towards international law but rather to the lack of cultural capital (a lack of diligence, or of knowledge of the relevant literature, or foreign languages) and to their

---

[65] This retreat to the normative-dogmatic approach after the failed introduction of Marxism was visible in other branches of the law in Poland as well: Jarosław Kuisz, *Charakter Prawny Porozumień Sierpniowych 1980–1981* (Warsaw: Wydawnictwo 'Trio', 2009), 473–80; Maciej Kisilowski, 'The Middlemen: The Legal Profession, the Rule of Law, and Authoritarian Regimes', *Law & Social Inquiry* 40, no. 03 (2015): 700–22; Rafał Mańko, 'Weeds in the Gardens of Justice? The Survival of Hyperpositivism in Polish Legal Culture as a Symptom/Sinthome', *Pólemos* 7, no. 2 (2013): 207–33 ; Wojciech Zomerski, *W Kierunku Demokratycznej Nauki Prawa? Dogmatyka, Edukacja, Postanalityczność* (Warsaw: Wydawnictwo Naukowe Scholar, 2023), 104.

[66] Sandorski, 'Profesor Krzysztof Skubiszewski (1926 -2010)', 167; Paweł Wiliński, ed., *Wydział Prawa i Administracji Uniwersytetu im. Adama Mickiewicza* (Poznań: Wydział Prawa i Administracji UAM, 2004), 23.

[67] For similar examples from sociology, see Agata Zysiak, 'How Sociology Shaped Postwar Poland and How Stalinization Shaped Sociology', in *The Social Sciences in the Looking Glass*, edited by Didier Fassin and George Steinmetz (Durham, NC: Duke University Press, 2023), 190.

[68] Madsen, 'Reflexive Sociology of International Law', 193; see also Roberts, *Is International Law International?*, 3.

privileged positions garnered through the support of Communist Party and state authorities.[69]

What was Socialist International Law?

What was actually socialist international law in the context of the late Cold War? How was it different from its bourgeois counterpart? Was this distinction at all meaningful? The question as to when and how law was truly 'socialist' was already extremely difficult to reconcile in the domestic sphere; the international sphere added another layer of difficulty, including the necessary persistence of earlier pre-socialist norms and the parallel development of contemporaneous competing non-socialist norms.[70] In the 1979 edition of his textbook *Introduction to the State and Legal Sciences*, a Polish legal scholar from outside the discipline of international law and eclectic critic of dogmatic legal sciences, Stanisław Ehrlich (1907–97), argued that, before the Bolshevik Revolution of 1917, international law was certainly a bourgeois creation that served the interests of the capitalists. After the Revolution, however, a new—socialist—form of state emerged. Together with the Afro-Asian Bloc, which had emerged out of decolonization, these socialist states began to constitute a counterweight to the previously unchallenged domination of the capitalist ones. Bourgeois and socialist approaches thus competed for legitimacy against each other; international law was born out of this competition. 'In the current system of international relations, international law expresses compromises between states with opposing or different class structures, compromises centred on the preservation of peace.'[71] International law was, Ehrlich wrote, an 'inter-regime bridge' between different systems interested in maintaining peace. 'Thus', Ehrlich continued, 'while we can speak of capitalist or socialist law in domestic law, insisting on the class nature of modern international law would be meaningless'.[72] There was no place for separate socialist international law in this thinking, even as a regional sub-system.

In 1973, the authors of the first East German textbook on international law provided a different answer than their Polish colleague. To them, socialist international law clearly existed. Moreover, 'the socialist principles and norms of international

---

[69] Karol Marian Pospieszalski, '*To wszystko przeżyłem...*': *wspomnienia*, edited by Piotr Grzelczak, Bogumił Rudawski, and Maria Wagińska-Marzec (Poznań: Instytut Zachodni, 2019).
[70] The same issues plagued Cold War debates over human rights. 'Bourgeois' political rights were seen as the basis for social rights, but at the same time social rights were supposed to dialectically overcome their limitations: see Ned Richardson-Little, *The Human Rights Dictatorship: Socialism, Global Solidarity and Revolution in East Germany* (Cambridge: Cambridge University Press, 2020), 122–29.
[71] Stanisław Ehrlich, *Wstęp Do Nauki o Państwie i Prawie* (Warsaw: Państwowe Wydawnictwo Naukowe, 1979), 298.
[72] Ibid.

law represent a legal order of a higher type than democratic international law'.[73] For instance, if 'democratic international law'—their term for the positive international law valid for all states and based on the 'principle of peaceful coexistence'—guaranteed only the peaceful relations between states, then socialism offered more, the 'principle of brotherly friendship and all-round mutual assistance'.[74] Both ('socialist' and 'democratic') types of international law were, however, only temporary phenomena in the historical transition from capitalism to socialism. What law was needed once full socialism was achieved remained unclear.[75] So much for the future. What was actually enforceable was socialist international law in its narrow sense, namely the particular norms used by socialist states in their mutual and multilateral relations.[76] Applying their dialectical reasoning to this issue, the authors underline that the socialist character of these special norms, 'does not mean, however, that they contradict the generally binding principles of democratic international law [...] The socialist principles and norms of international law represent a qualitative development of the principles of democratic international law'.[77]

The different approaches visible in the distance between East German and Polish scholars were rooted in Soviet doctrine itself. During the 1960s, Grigorij Tunkin (1906–93), the most internationally recognized Soviet legal scholar of this period,[78] developed Khrushchev's ideas of 'peaceful coexistence'. Tunkin, discussing with more orthodox Marxist–Leninst views on law, claimed that international law, although part of the superstructure, was not dependent on the economic base in the same way as domestic legal systems were. Due to its roots in the consent of various sovereign states and the dynamic interactions between them, international law was thus to some extent detached from the historical process of class struggle.[79] At his most conciliatory, Tunkin wrote of the 'general international law common to the socialist and capitalist states' of which socialist countries were co-creators.[80] These positions did not remain unchallenged, with one counter-argument inspired by the work of Yevgeny Korovin (1892–1964), who opposed this accommodation to existing traditions and insisted that international law did indeed had a class character. Socialist international law existed (or should have existed), claimed Korovin, in both the stricter and wider sense, and stood as an

---

[73] Maria Bauer and Herbert Kröger (eds.), *Völkerrecht: Lehrbuch* (Berlin: Staatsverlag der DDR, 1973), 44.
[74] Ibid.
[75] Michael Stolleis, *Sozialistische Gesetzlichkeit. Staats- und Verwaltungsrechtswissenschaft in der DDR* (Munich: Beck, 2009), 158; Soviet authors were not certain either, see Cherviatsova and Yarmysh, 'Soviet International Law', 318.
[76] Bauer and Kröger, *Völkerrecht: Lehrbuch*, 45.
[77] Ibid., 44.
[78] Lodhi, 'Soviet Concept of International Law', 32; Bowring, 'Positivism versus Self-Determination', 133.
[79] Grigorij I. Tunkin, *Theory of International Law* (Cambridge, MA: Harvard University Press, 1974), 236, 241.
[80] Ibid., 233.

alternative to 'bourgeois' international law.[81] Soviet doctrine was fluid, and as long as these debates were considered important, doctrinal positions and their exact wording continued to be challenged and recalibrated. Legal scholars decentred socialist international law in the Eastern Bloc precisely by using this fluidity—for example, in order to make a specific point by quoting the more conciliatory pre-1970 Tunkin instead of the more conformational post-1970 Tunkin. Both the interventions by Stanisław Ehrlich and the East Germans mentioned above, despite their differences, were understood by their authors as being fully in accordance with Soviet scholarship and with Tunkin in particular. Ehrlich saw international law as a unified phenomenon that rested on a constant compromise between the two dominant approaches. The East German scholars, on the other hand, understood international law as a combination of 'socialist' and 'bourgeois' norms, wherein both maintained their separate status. Because of the indeterminacy and fluidity of the Soviet scholarship, these (and many other positions) were able to be formulated in the field, and then interpreted on the national level as belonging to the socialist mainstream.

The discipline of international law in East Germany was small, encompassing only around twenty full-time academics, including doctoral students, working at four universities and two research institutes.[82] East German scholars published only one proper, collectively authored textbook (the above-quoted *Völkerrecht: Lehrbuch* in two editions) on international law.[83] There was major discontinuity in the discipline after 1945 and the differences with Poland are clear. Those established lawyers who remained in the Soviet-occupied part of Germany and survived the personnel purges, which in the East German case were carried out also after 1956, attempted, together with younger academic elites, to build a new legal scholarship from scratch.[84] In light of the liberal alternative represented by their direct rival, the Federal Republic of Germany, academics from the German Democratic Republic had cause to theorize and codify the project of socialist internationalism with greater fervour than their neighbours in the Eastern Bloc.[85] The lawyers who shaped the new national legal field after 1945 identified with the interests of the state: Marxist methods were dominant, and their application was

---

[81] Francine Hirsch, *Soviet Judgment at Nuremberg: A New History of the International Military Tribunal after World War II* (Oxford: Oxford University Press, 2020), 407.
[82] Humboldt University in Berlin, Martin Luther University in Halle, Friedrich Schiller University in Jena, and Karl Marx University in Leipzig, as well as the Institute of the Theory of the State and Law at the East German Academy of Sciences and the Institute of International Relations at the Academy of State and Legal Sciences of the German Democratic Republic; Walter Poeggel, 'The Development of Teaching and Research in the Field of Public International Law at the Universities of the Former German Democratic Republic, *German Yearbook of International Law* 50 (2007): 139–40.
[83] Ibid., 140.
[84] Schweisfurth, 'The Science', 150; Stolleis, *Sozialistische Gesetzlichkeit. Staats- und Verwaltungsrechtswissenschaft in der DDR*, 31.
[85] Sebastian Gehrig, *Legal Entanglements: Law, Rights and the Battle for Legitimacy in Divided Germany, 1945–1989* (New York: Berghahn, 2021), 105–36.

understood as an act of emancipation from old formalist and normative-dogmatic traditions. Most prominent East German-educated international lawyers such as Bernhard Graefrath (1928–2006) and Hermann Klenner (1926–) never renounced their socialist credentials—even after 1990—and remained critical of the post-Cold War American-led liberal international order.[86] Nonetheless, East German doctrine, even at its most orthodox, was not immune to the influence of outside events and continued to evolve as time passed. Up to the 1960s, scholars underlined the autonomous character of socialist law. These attitudes weakened during the 1970s, when, as we have seen, East German scholars underlined the universal character of socialist internationalism but were forced to admit that it 'replaced' general norms only in relations between socialist states.[87] In the 1988 concise *Völkerrecht: Grundriß* (*International Law. A Basic Outline*), its authors—Edith Oeser (1930–2005) and Walter Poeggel (1929–2019)—downplayed the issue altogether and claimed that both systems were closely correlated.[88] This evolution was consistent with what legal historian Michael Stolleis has called the 'objectivization' (*Versachlichung*) of the discipline, which instead of deconstructing legal norms and institutions from a class standpoint, retreated into dogmatic reconstruction.[89]

In Czechoslovakia, despite the massive number of people who were ultimately purged after communists took power, non-socialist Antonín Hobza (1876–1954)[90] remained Chair of International Law at Charles University in Prague until he was succeeded by pre-Second World War diplomat Vladimír Outrata (1909–70). Czechoslovak authors analysed socialist law as a sub-system within the general international law,[91] which testifies to the continuity within the discipline of non-socialist visions of universality. After the crushing of the Prague Spring in 1968 many academics lost their jobs and went into exile, but during the 1970s, international law began to be researched and taught at four universities: in Bratislava, Brno, Košice, and Prague. Čestmír Čepelka (1927–2022) and Vladislav David (1927–2014), both from Brno University, worked on the crucial issue of sources of international law, where they combined normative-dogmatic and sociological approaches: Instead of the principle of 'consensus', promoted by the Soviet

---

[86] I rely here on the characterization of the discipline presented in Stolleis, *Sozialistische Gesetzlichkeit*. On Graefrath and Klenner, see Richardson-Little, *The Human Rights Dictatorship*.
[87] Schweisfurth, 'The Science', 163–67.
[88] Poeggel, 'The Development', 141.
[89] Stolleis, *Sozialistische Gesetzlichkeit*, 158.
[90] Veronika Bílková, 'Antonín Hobza - Naivní Snílek, Nebo Opatrný Realista?', *Právník* 155, no. 1 (2016): 93–104.
[91] Chrystel Papi, 'The Impact of Real Communism on the Development of International Law Scholarship in Europe Between 1945 and 1989 in Italy, Spain, and Czechoslovakia', Bachelor's degree thesis, Libera Università Internazionale degli Studi Sociali, Rome (2014), 58–60, https://tesi.luiss.it/15159/., accessed 3 September, 2024.

scholarship, which limited the applicability of customary law,[92] Čepelka and David proposed an approach that looked at how customary law functioned in the 'real behaviour of states' and adapted the catalogue of sources to such behaviours.[93] This original intervention into a fundamental question enabled the Czechoslovak field of international law to expand its autonomy—at least in relation to Soviet doctrinal markers. Čepelka and David, socialized and educated after 1945, considered themselves socialists, but they continued to explore the ambiguities and vulnerabilities of socialist internationalism as a rigid legal system.[94] If, in Poland, this decentring of socialist internationalism was attempted through the use of normative-dogmatic methods, then, in Czechoslovakia, it seems that a similar move was pursued through sociological means.

Romanian lawyers and experts, in their quest to distinguish themselves from Soviet scholarship, stressed the anti-imperialist and anticolonial elements of international law. Especially during the 1960s, they questioned the Eurocentric character of traditional international law, often interconnecting it with a strong emphasis on sovereignty.[95] Romanian legal scholar Edwin Glaser raised non-intervention in the domestic affairs of other countries as a rule of *jus cogens* which cannot be derogated by other principles or laws. In his historical and theoretical works, Glaser used non-intervention as a vehicle to openly (when it came to the West) or obliquely (when it came to the Soviet Union) critique imperial behaviour.[96] In terms of the possible existence of separate socialist international law, Glaser claimed that a plurality of legal systems—socialist and capitalist, as well as any others—would lead to 'legal nihilism'.[97] Later developments of the discipline in Romania were marked by contacts with the West and a convergence with non-socialist scholarship.

In the case of Hungary, a West German author underlined the major streams of the Habsburg tradition of international law, which were, however, destroyed by the communist rule. He argued, in 1976, that Hungarian lawyers had marked their autonomy by simply ignoring the issues of socialist internationalism as an alternative to standard international law.[98] Hungarian textbooks during the communist

---

[92] Grzybowski shows, however, that more expansive understandings of customs had been acceptable in the Soviet doctrine. It further testifies to the indeterminate nature and liquidity of Soviet approaches to international law. Grzybowski, 'Soviet Theory', 866–69.
[93] Šturma, 'The Internationalist Doctrine and Communism in Czechoslovakia (1945–1989)', in *Les Doctrines internationalistes durant les années du Communisme réel en Europe*, edited by Emmanuelle Jouannet-Tourme and Iulia Motoc (Paris: Société de législation comparée, 2012), 519–20.
[94] Ibid., 526.
[95] Robert Weiner, 'Romania and International Law at the United Nations', *The International and Comparative Law Quarterly* 32, no. 4 (1983): 1026.
[96] Ashby B. Crowder, 'Legacies of 1968: Autonomy and Repression in Ceaușescu's Romania, 1965–1989', Master of Arts thesis, Ohio University, Columbus OH (2007), 25.
[97] Weiner, 'Romania', 1028.
[98] Dietrich Frenzke, 'Die Entwicklung der Ungarischen Völkerrechtslehre nach dem Zweiten Weltkrieg', *Die Friedens-Warte* 59, no. 4 (1976): 318, 329.

period did not provide much elaboration on what the military intervention in this country in 1956 meant for international law, and tried to pay as little attention to the principle of socialist internationalism as possible. Only as late as 1976 was the intervention outrightly called a 'fraternal assistance', which supposedly exemplified the extended mutual obligations between socialist states.[99] Conversely, another author, writing about Bulgaria in 1982, underlined the lack of autonomy and the unclear position of the discipline in relation to neighbouring branches of law. He was likely exaggerating, but he went so far as to claim that Bulgaria had no traditions of international law scholarship to speak of and 'presently follow[s] to the extreme Soviet theory and practice'.[100]

To return now to the Poznań School. Like their Hungarian colleagues, the legal scholars in Poznań did not take sides in this debate in any substantive way. Socialist international law was considered a regional and technical system but without the status as something separate from standard international law.[101] Klafkowski's comments about the 'so-called socialist international law' quoted at the beginning reflect his lack of enthusiasm or commitment to the issue.[102] Indeed, Klafkowski – the Poznań academic with the closest ties to the Communist Party – distanced himself from the concept even in its most narrow definition in consecutive editions of his textbook.[103] In 1963 he wrote that international law 'is neither bourgeois, nor socialist. It is common and should remain common—and must remain common for all countries, all nations and all races'.[104] Skubiszewski would go even further. During a conference in Rome in 1981, he claimed that international law had 'European and Christian' roots. These roots were so strong and durable that even though international law had lost its exclusively European character, no other traditions had emerged to influence it. Moreover, despite the Cold War divide and the development of European communities in the Western part of the continent, regional international legal systems had not overshadowed international law as it was; 'nor, as far as the other side of Europe is concerned, has a separate socialist international law developed as a distinct system of norms'. In fact, according to Skubiszewski, 'at the present moment, European states, regardless of their system,

---

[99] Péter Kovács, 'L'Approche Marxiste dans l'enseignement du droit international entre 1945 et 1989. Le cas de la Hongrie', in *Les Doctrines internationalistes durant les années du Communisme réel en Europe*, edited by Emmanuelle Jouannet-Tourme and Iulia Motoc (Paris: Société de législation comparée, 2012), 440–41, 447–48.

[100] Ivan Sipkov, 'Public International Law of Bulgaria: Development and Status', *International Journal of Legal Information* 10, no. 6 (1982): 342.

[101] Kwiatkowski, 'Poznańska Nauka Prawa Międzynarodowego Na Łamach "Ruchu Prawniczego, Ekonomicznego i Socjologicznego"', 217.

[102] Klafkowski, *Prawo Międzynarodowe Publiczne*, 26.

[103] Gadkowski and Tyranowski, *Alfons Klafkowski—prawnik internacjonalista*, 39–40.

[104] Alfons Klafkowski, 'Współczesne Tendencje Rozwojowe Prawa Międzynarodowego', Ruch Prawniczy, Ekonomiczny i Socjologiczny 1, no. 25 (1963): 5.

are bound by a single, universal international law'.[105] In this statement, one can hear the echoes of nineteenth-century internationalism of German origin, which saw a common cultural unity of Europe and contacts between its 'civilized nations' as the source of international law.[106] Such a theory of international law's origins was hardly compatible, however, with two dominant internationalisms—socialist or liberal.

Conclusion

The project of socialist international law after 1945 oscillated between global, universalist ambitions (socialist internationalisms in the larger, revolutionary sense) and the pragmatic Soviet governance of the Eastern Bloc (in the stricter Cold War sense). The armed interventions in Hungary in 1956 and Czechoslovakia in 1968, as well as the discussions over the 1970 Friendly Relations Declaration, put the principle of socialist internationalism through a further stress test. Doctrinal positions on the status of socialist international law developed in the Soviet Union reflected not only the political context in which they were elaborated but also internal constellations within the discipline in each Eastern European country.

Across the Eastern Bloc, Soviet doctrine was followed, taken advantage of, decentred, or ignored. It was never determined at which point one could finally speak of a fully 'socialist' law or what that law was supposed to be. Soviet scholarship, however, remained one of the obligatory points of reference for any discussion within the discipline. As a result, legal scholars in the Eastern Bloc could draw from this indeterminacy and fluidity, by borrowing aspects of this doctrine when convenient, ignoring others, or intertwining them with pre-existing understandings of the law on an idiosyncratic basis. This allowed for a plurality of approaches that fit into the state socialist mainstream but were often not particularly socialist philosophically, methodologically, or doctrinally. In pursuit of greater autonomy for the discipline, particular schools and milieus consciously, if often implicitly, created their own visions of the 'international', wherein socialist internationalism constituted only one point of reference. Repeating the meandering Soviet line, associated, for better or worse, with the alignment to political actors such as Communist Party and state officials, meant losing this autonomy—the most precious of stakes. The Poznań School—where earlier normative-dogmatic traditions of doing international law were preserved and practiced throughout the Cold War and preferred over other approaches seen as imposed from the outside—constructed its

---

[105] Instytut Zachodni Poznań, Archiwum Osobiste Krzysztofa Skubiszewskiego, 1564, Komunikat (głos w dyskusji) przeznaczony dla sekcji instytucji prawnych konferencji organizowanej w Rzymie przez Uniwersytet Laterański i KUL (Tezy) [November 1981], no pages.
[106] Koskenniemi, *The Gentle Civilizer of Nations*, 223.

own vision of internationalism in explicit opposition to any socialist internationalism. During this period, every international law school in the region was grappling with the indeterminacy of Marxist–Leninist legal doctrine. Whereas East Germans invested in the separate and universal character of socialist international law, Czechoslovaks and Hungarians, also because of their experiences with Soviet military interventions, remained sceptical towards the concept. Poznań was thus only the utmost case of a pluralism present in Eastern Europe. Even in the Polish national context, Poznań represented the case most resistant to socialist internationalism, since during the Stalinist period, a more Marxist and anti-dogmatic international legal scholarship began to emerge.

Looking at specific groups of people in relation to each other, towards major categories and national, international, and global forces, not only reveals their diversity but also brings into question their fixed nature. Huge global projects with universalist pretences like socialism are never simply exported abroad; they are created and interpreted by particular actors in a particular context with particular positions and goals. As this chapter has shown, socialist international law and socialist internationalism were picked up, modified, or ignored, depending on concrete national considerations and global trends. Only through a fine-grained analysis can we understand their actual content, function, and meaning within this wider context.

Acknowledgements

This research was supported by the Volkswagen Foundation funded project "Towards Illiberal Constitutionalism in East Central Europe: Historical Analysis in Comparative and Transnational Perspectives". This article benefited greatly from feedback from Patryk Labuda, Daniel Ricardo Quiroga-Villamarín and Jiří Přibáň. I presented the main thesis of this paper in August 2023 at the Erasmus School of Law in Rotterdam. I would like to thank Michał Stambulski, as well as Alessandra Arcuri, Florin Coman Kund, Ioannis Kampourakis, Sanne Taekema and Stijn Voogt. Special thanks for their comments and support to Poznań University's Tadeusz Gadkowski and Paweł Kwiatkowski.

6
How China Came to Embrace International Institutions

Ryan Martínez Mitchell

Introduction

Ever since its founding in 1949, the People's Republic of China (PRC) has had an idiosyncratic relationship with international legal norms and institutions. Causes for the distinctive features of China's approaches to global governance are varied, but many can be traced to its unique and difficult path into the state-centric order dominated by the developed powers of the West. Other factors, increasingly, derive from its exceptional status as a geopolitical and economic superpower with an almost unparalleled global reach.

Given the centrality of international legal structures and processes to China's historical experience of foreign economic and political domination, studies of China's international relations tend to discuss these topics at length.[1] Meanwhile, the growing importance of China in the global order today, and its more confident activities in most spheres of regulation, have led to an expanding literature on its current emergence as a leading 'norm-maker', especially among scholars of international relations.[2] However, China's long-term trajectory of influence on the global legal order, and the formation of its stances, have been less frequently studied from the perspective of legal history. Above all, standard histories of international law in the West have tended to marginalize China's role as a participatory agent in its development over time. Only recently has the ongoing 'turn to history in international law' combined with a growing interest in non-Eurocentric approaches to the field to spur greater attention to this topic and its legacies.[3]

---

[1] Zheng Wang, *Never Forget National Humiliation: Historical Memory in Chinese Politics and Foreign Relations* (New York: Columbia University Press, 2014); David Scott, *China and the International System, 1840–1949: Power, Presence, and Perceptions in a Century of Humiliation* (Albany, NY: State University of New York Press, 2008).

[2] Yongjin Zhang, 'System, Empire and State in Chinese International Relations', *Review of International Studies* 27, no. 5 (2001): 43–63; Yaqing Qin, 'Why Is There No Chinese International Relations Theory?', *International Relations of the Asia-Pacific* 7, no. 3 (2007): 313–340; G. John Ikenberry, 'The Rise of China and the Future of the West-Can the Liberal System Survive?', *Foreign Affairs* 87, no. 1 (2008): 23.

[3] For important earlier studies analysing China's positions on international law, but which did not try to situate this topic in the history of international law more generally, see Jerome Alan Cohen and Hungdah Chiu, *People's China and International Law, Volume 1: A Documentary Study* (Princeton,

This chapter marks one contribution to these emerging efforts to properly situate China and its peoples in the history of international law.[4] It provides an overview of the shifting Chinese approaches to international law and especially its institutions, as they have figured in China's transition from 'semi-colonial' battleground for imperialist incursion, to third 'pole' of the Cold War, to central actor and (in the eyes of many today) rising hegemonic contender. As it shows, China's changing engagements with international law have often tended to centre on evolving valuations of the concept of state sovereignty.

While originally imported into the Chinese discursive context by foreign interlocutors representing imperialist powers, state sovereignty was by the early twentieth century reimbued by Chinese actors with associations of jurisdictional and policy autonomy. Throughout the Cold War, sovereignty as self-determination for oppressed peoples became the lodestone of official Chinese positions on international law, and of both a sceptical view of most Western forums and a resistance to what Beijing labelled as Soviet 'social imperialism'.[5] However, with the post-1970s shift to rapprochement with the West and China's embedding into the processes of globalization, sovereignty began to be viewed less absolutely, both in the economic realm and in other aspects of international legal regulation, including projects for regional order. Most recently, a more *á la carte* view of sovereignty has been reframed as the basis for a robust programme of institutional activity and indeed institution creation.[6] This global programme continues to emphasize state consent as a condition for legal obligation, but combines this with a strong interest in rulemaking, policy coordination, and the pursuit of common goods of development and security—especially where it also reinforces China's own status as a great power.

NJ: Princeton University Press, 2017); Hungdah Chiu, 'Chinese Views on the Sources of International Law', *Harvard International Law Journal* 28 (1987): 289.

[4] See Chen Yifeng, 'Bandung, China, and the Making of World Order in East Asia', in *Bandung, Global History, and International Law: Critical Pasts and Pending Futures*, edited by Luis Eslava, Michael Fakhri, and Vasuki Nesiah (Cambridge: Cambridge University Press, 2017): 177–95; Teemu Ruskola, 'The Dao of Mao: Sinocentric Socialism and the Politics of International Legal Theory', in *International Law and the Cold War*, edited by Matthew Craven, Sundhya Pahuja, Gerry Simpson, and Anna Saunders (Cambridge: Cambridge University Press, 2019): 376–96; Ryan Martínez Mitchell, *Recentering the World: China and the Transformation of International Law* (Cambridge: Cambridge University Press, 2022); see also Cai Congyan, Ignacio de la Rasilla, and Wang Jiangyu (eds.), *Histories of International Law in China: All Under Heaven?* (Oxford: Oxford University Press, forthcoming 2025).

[5] Suzanne Ogden, 'Sovereignty and International Law: The Perspective of the People's Republic of China', *NYU Journal of International Law and Politics* 7 (1974): 1.

[6] See e.g. Shahar Hameiri and Lee Jones, 'China Challenges Global Governance? Chinese International Development Finance and the AIIB', *International Affairs* 94, no. 3 (2018): 573–93; Hideo Ohashi, 'The Belt and Road Initiative (BRI) in the Context of China's Opening-Up Policy', *Journal of Contemporary East Asia Studies* 7, no. 2 (2018): 85–103.

International Law and the Discourse of State Sovereignty in China

The extensive treaty obligations placed on imperial China following the First and Second Opium Wars (1839–42 and 1856–60) involved the requirement to hand over administrative and judicial jurisdiction over a growing list of 'treaty ports', to provide access to Western merchants, missionaries, and vessels, and to both limit tariffs and duties to a specified schedule and hand over their collection to a foreign-administered bureaucracy.[7] These burdens were intensified beginning in the 1890s, as European states responded to a period of slowing economic growth and increased internecine rivalries by engaging in a new phase of last-ditch colonial expansion.[8] Japan's decision to emulate these policies of imperial expansion after decades of uncertainty regarding its relationship with its neighbour, culminating in the First Sino–Japanese War of 1894–95, cemented the sensibility of territorial crisis and revanchism in China that continues even today.[9] China's earliest international lawyers received their training at a time when ideas about international law and sovereignty were being imported in texts from the very states that were denying effective legal protection to China itself.[10]

Intertwined losses of territorial jurisdiction and policy autonomy in the nineteenth century led to efforts at recapture. By the turn of the twentieth century, Chinese officials and intellectuals actively sought to appropriate Western legal and political discourses as tools to reimagine and justify local state authority—a project that soon coalesced with new ideas of nationhood and self-determination.[11] The most important discursive trope was that of state sovereignty, rendered in Chinese as *zhuquan* (or 'the authority of the ruler'), which became the embodiment of these projects. Although traditionally a relational concept, the term as now used in diplomatic and international legal disputes between China and Japan or Western powers necessarily referred to a status and right that was exclusive and homogenous throughout state territory.[12]

The project of re-establishing *zhuquan* was to lay at the core of the efforts of successive regimes on the international stage and state-building within China's formal

---

[7] Stephen R. Platt, *Imperial Twilight: The Opium War and the End of China's Last Golden Age* (New York: Vintage, 2018); Stephen R. Halsey, *Quest for Power: European Imperialism and the Making of Chinese Statecraft* (Cambridge, MA: Harvard University Press, 2015); Hans Van de Ven, *Breaking with the Past: The Maritime Customs Service and the Global Origins of Modernity in China* (New York: Columbia University Press, 2014).

[8] Peter Zarrow, *After Empire: The Conceptual Transformation of the Chinese State, 1885–1924* (Stanford, CA: Stanford University Press, 2012).

[9] Yuanzhi Wang (ed.), *Jiaxu Gongdu Chaocun* (Taipei: Yinhang, 1959).

[10] Rune Svarverud, *International Law as World Order in Late Imperial China: Translation, Reception and Discourse, 1847–1911* (Leiden: Brill, 2007).

[11] Zhidong Zhang, *Quan Xue Pian* (Promotion of Learning) (Changsha: Liang Hu Shu Yuan, 1898); Yongle Zhang, *Jiu Bang Xin Zao: 1911–1917* (An Old State Remade: 1911–1917) (Beijing: Peking University Press, 2016).

[12] Stefan Kroll, *Normgenese durch Re-Interpretation: China und das europäische Völkerrecht im 19. und 20. Jahrhundert* (Baden-Baden: Nomos, 2012).

borders. At home, post-imperial governments dominated by warlords and then the quasi-democratic Nationalist Party of Sun Yat-sen and his more reactionary successor Chiang Kai-shek sought to exercise jurisdictional authority and to overturn Western-imposed treaty arrangements for extrajudicial jurisdiction, military incursions, and tariff controls. On the international stage, Chinese diplomats and international lawyers participated in major forums, from the Hague Conferences of 1899 and 1907 to the Paris Peace Conference of 1919 and its corollaries, to the major codification conferences of the 1920s and 1930s, solidifying an international law agenda premised on the equal rights of recognized sovereign states and the rejection of interstate coercion.[13]

This agenda saw gradual progress throughout the interwar period. This included the German loss of extraterritorial rights in China in 1919, and the Soviet Union's renunciation of such rights as first articulated by Lenin in the same year, though this was only confirmed over the course of a great deal of additional diplomatic wrangling through the end of the 1920s.[14] English, French, and American rights in China, however, were much slower to be abandoned. Extraterritorial jurisdiction for legal cases in the vast majority of foreign-run zones, as well as Western dictates over key domestic policies, would not be fully relinquished until well into the heat of the Second World War, as China quite suddenly transformed into a formal and theoretically equal ally of the United States, the United Kingdom, and the Soviet Union.[15] For China, this decisive shift came in the period between 1942 and 1943, as London and (especially) Washington decided on a policy of treating Chiang's Nationalist Government as at least formally a great power equal, including for the purposes of postwar planning; its inclusion as a UN Security Council permanent member, though not formalized until 1944, was effectively decided as of the previous year.[16]

In the meantime, the agenda of more fully asserting state sovereignty had become one of the most important common points linking the ruling Nationalist Party and the insurgent Chinese Communist Party, which had formed in 1921 and gone through several periods of crisis, internal conflict, and political reformation.[17] By the point when China sent a joint delegation to the 1945 San Francisco Conference founding the United Nations (UN), there was a shared agenda of asserting and consolidating Chinese *zhuquan* in part by promoting international

---

[13] Mitchell, *Recentering the World*, 98-144.
[14] Qihua Tang, 'The Sino-Soviet Conference, 1924–1927', *Journal of Modern Chinese History* 1, no. 2 (2007): 195–218.
[15] Ibid.
[16] This move was in part spurred by explicit concerns in Washington over Japan's appropriation of anticolonial rhetoric, as well as pointed Chinese references to the same issue, such as Chiang's assertion that Western postwar plans would 'lose all relevance' for East Asia if China were not included in making them. See ibid.
[17] Cf. Ishikawa Yoshihiro, *The Formation of the Chinese Communist Party* (New York: Columbia University Press, 2012); Patricia Stranahan, *Underground: The Shanghai Communist Party and the Politics of Survival, 1927–1937* (Lanham: Rowman & Littlefield, 1998).

legal organization, codification, restriction of the use of interstate coercion, and China's role as one of the great powers on the Security Council.[18] During the brief period after Japan's defeat, when the Nationalist Party and the Chinese Communist Party (CCP) sought to form a coalition government, UN-based promotion of international law was included as a pillar of their shared platform.[19]

The international lawyers of Nationalist China during the 1930s and 1940s were active in promoting the codification and development of international law, including through League of Nations-based efforts to coordinate sanctions against Japan for its acts of aggression,[20] strong advocacy during the Dumbarton Oaks conversations for the development of international law as a fundamental activity of the UN,[21] arguments in favour of a strong jurisdictional authority of the International Court of Justice (ICJ),[22] participation in the Tokyo Tribunal and development of a domestic war crimes tribunal regime,[23] and participation in the drafting of the Universal Declaration of Human Rights,[24] the Genocide Convention,[25] and other instruments. The UN International Law Commission, from its earliest stages, also embodied the advocacy and participation of Chinese jurists.[26]

---

[18] Wang Chonghui, 'Zhan Hou Shijie zhi Jiti Anquan: Zuori Zai Zhongguo Zhengzhixue Hui Nian Hui Jiangyan' (Postwar Collective Security: Yesterday's Address at the Annual Meeting of the China Political Science Association), *Da Gong Bao* (Chongqing), 7 July 1942.

[19] Mitchell, *Recentering the World*, 189-214.

[20] Yuen-li Liang, 'The Pact of Paris as Envisaged by Mr. Stimson: Its Significance in International Law', *China Law Review* 5 (1932): 198.

[21] Robert C. Hilderbrand, *Dumbarton Oaks: The Origins of the United Nations and the Search for Postwar Security* (Chapel Hill, NC: University of North Carolina Press, 2001), 229-244.

[22] See 'The Report of the Subcommittee on Article 36 (Compulsory Jurisdiction)', in *Documents of the United Nations Conference on International Organization, San Francisco, 1945*, vol. 14 (New York: UN Information Organizations, 1945), 286-87.

[23] Mei Ju-ao, *The Tokyo Trial Diaries of Mei Ju-ao* (Singapore: Springer, 2019); Anja Bihler, 'On a "Sacred Mission": Representing the Republic of China at the International Military Tribunal for the Far East', in *Transcultural Justice at the Tokyo Tribunal*, edited by Kerstin von Lingen (Leiden: Brill, 2018).

[24] Hans Ingvar Roth, *PC Chang and the Universal Declaration of Human Rights* (Philadelphia, PA: University of Pennsylvania Press, 2018).

[25] Chinese delegates at the 1948 meetings to draft the Genocide Convention were highly supportive of the initiative and made efforts towards contributing their own views on a broader notion of 'genocide'. This would encompass both drug trafficking (as both Britain and Japan had done with opium in Chinese areas under their military influence at various points) and a strong prohibition on cultural genocide (in line with Eastern European socialist approaches, as developed by Nelly Bekus, Chapter 8 in this volume), including via 'Prohibiting the use of the language and [/or] destroying systematically and by violence the libraries, museums, schools, historical monuments, places of worship or other cultural institutions and objects, of the group'. Hirad Abtahi and Philippa Webb (eds.), *The Genocide Convention: The Travaux Préparatoires* (Leiden: Martinus Nijhoff, 2008), 836.

[26] In particular, Liang Yunli (Yuen-li Liang), who would for decades serve as the Director of the UN Secretariat Division of Development and Codification of International Law, and thus the secretariat's main point of contact with the Commission, emerged as a leading early participant, organizer, and chronicler of codification efforts. Yuen-Li Liang, 'The General Assembly and the Progressive Development and Codification of International Law', *American Journal of International Law* 42, no. 1 (1948): 66-97; Yuen-Li Liang, 'Notes on Legal Questions Concerning the United Nations', *American Journal of International Law* 45, no. 3 (1951): 108; Yuen-Li Liang, 'Notes on Legal Questions Concerning the United Nations', *American Journal of International Law* 46, no. 1 (1952): 73-88.

At the same time, however, the international law profession in China, which remained small in size but had become a well-trained and internationally connected community of jurists by the end of the Second World War, was in a precarious political position. While few Chinese international lawyers were avowed Marxists, many found themselves to the left of a Nationalist Party that was turning towards increasingly dictatorial rule and had pursued ever-closer cooperation with Washington.[27] When relations between the two parties broke down in late 1945, leading to civil war and the eventual triumph of the Communist Party under Mao Zedong, a substantial portion of China's lawyers and other intellectuals and professionals decided to stay behind rather than join the Nationalist regime of Chiang Kai-shek in its flight to Taiwan. The writings of many of China's international lawyers during the period of civil war reflected a growing critique of US unilateralism as a force corroding the initially promising arrangements of the UN Charter.[28]

These views were largely consistent with the Communist Party's positions in the run-up to establishing the PRC. Indeed, future leader Mao Zedong's first significant publications in 1919 had been denunciations of the Treaty of Versailles and of Western failures to respect the principles of 'self-determination' with respect to China, as well as various other peoples including the Irish, Koreans, and Afghans.[29] He and other early leaders in the CCP had, from early on, combined patriotic / nationalist positions on matters of state sovereignty with a general critique of a capitalist world order that had, by then, proved itself to consistently reconfigure power relations in support of imperialist interests.

This impression was greatly reinforced when, in 1949, the US Truman administration intervened to preserve Taiwan as a bastion for the remaining Nationalist forces and decided not to accord recognition to the new Communist-led government.[30] From the very moment of its establishment in 1949, the PRC was met with an implacable US policy premised on the 'containment' of communist ideology that, in practical terms, meant the isolation of the new government, the sudden abrogation via an economic embargo of most of the trade upon which the Chinese economy had grown reliant, and, in Taiwan, an implicit existential threat in the form of a de facto US protectorate with aims to recapture the Mainland. In this environment, Washington came to be viewed as the new face of Western imperialism, denying China and other non-Western peoples their inherent *zhuquan*.

---

[27] Lloyd E. Eastman, *The Abortive Revolution: China Under Nationalist Rule, 1927–1937* (Cambridge, MA: Harvard University Press, 1990).

[28] Wang Tieya, 'Dulumenzhuyi yu Menluozhuyi' (The Truman Doctrine and the Monroe Doctrine), *Minzhu Luntan* 1, no. 9 (1947): 3–6; Zhou Ziya, *Meiguo Meizhou yu Shijie* (America, the Americas, and the World) (Shanghai: Shangwu Yinshuguan, 1946).

[29] Mao Zedong, 'Hao Ge Mingzu [sic] Zijue' (Some National Self-Determination!), *Xiangjiang Pinglun* 3 (14 July 1919); cf. Mark Mazower, *Governing the World: The History of an Idea, 1815 to the Present* (New York: Penguin, 2013).

[30] On the decisions underlying this choice, which were premised far less on legal niceties than on pure concerns of containment, see Paul J. Heer, *Mr. X and the Pacific: George F. Kennan and American Policy in East Asia* (Ithaca, NY: Cornell University Press, 2018), 97–105.

The Turn to Third World Engagement

During the early Cold War, the new regime found itself ostracized by the West based on the US policy of non-recognition. Its precarious role in international law led to an even more pronounced valuation of *zhuquan*, while also favouring a shift towards an agenda of both cooperation with the Soviet Union and, soon after, engagement with the Global South. The Chinese Communist Party's relations with Moscow had soured considerably during the 1930s and 1940s, as Stalin's favoured proxies in China lost internal power struggles. However, as Washington's containment policy took shape, it became clear that Beijing would have to 'lean to one side', as Mao put it in 1949.[31] The Sino–Soviet Treaty of Friendship, Alliance and Mutual Assistance on 14 February 1950, wrapping up Mao's two-month trip to Moscow, set the stage for a period of cooperation that, by the decade's end, collapsed into acrimony.

For the ruling Communist Party, the unresolved Chinese Civil War—which could not be 'concluded' because of the US naval intervention to defend the fleeing Guomindang regime in its outpost on Taiwan—bled naturally into the crisis of the Korean War. When Chinese troops crossed the Yalu River in October 1950 to assist North Korean forces against the US-led UN force invading from the south, this policy was framed as a direct response to 'American aggression' against the people of Korea, in line with Beijing and Moscow's interpretation of the conflict. All sides continued to insist upon their adherence to the UN Charter and to accuse the opposite Cold War bloc of violating Article 2 by engaging in prohibited uses of force constituting the crime of aggression.[32] From the Chinese perspective, these charges also went beyond the UN Charter text and were contiguous with a broader understanding of aggression (consistent with both CCP and Soviet positions after the Second World War), in which 'aggression' was to be viewed as a crime committed by anyone waging war against a just struggle by a people in pursuit of 'self-determination'.[33] Prominent Chinese international lawyers such as Chen Tiqiang criticized Washington's loose interpretations of UN norms governing the use of force and permitting intervention abroad.[34]

The arguments around *jus ad bellum* (i.e. the law on when it is legitimate to go to war) in Korea were complex and contestable, as leading international law scholars

---

[31] Mao Zedong, 'Lun Renmin Minzhu Zhuanzheng: Jinian Zhongguo Gongchandang Er Shi Ba Zhou Nian' (On the People's Democratic Dictatorship: In Commemoration of the 28th Annniversary of the Chinese Communist Party) (Beijing: Ren Min Chubanshe, 1949), 7–8.

[32] In this context, China was also officially branded as an 'aggressor' by a vote of the US-aligned General Assembly.

[33] See e.g. David E. Graham, 'The 1974 Diplomatic Conference on the Law of War: A Victory for Political Causes and a Return to the Just War Concept of the Eleventh Century', *Washington and Lee Law Review* 32, no. 1 (1975): 25.

[34] Chen Tiqiang, 'Shei Shi Guojifa de Pohuaizhe?' (Who Is Undermining International Law?), Shijie Zhishi 8 (1950): 7–8.

like Hans Kelsen were ready to admit: indeed, Washington's position justifying ostensible UN intervention relied upon multiple significant doctrinal innovations.[35] Meanwhile, with regards to *jus in bello* (the law regulating conduct during warfare), the situation was similarly contradictory. Neither the PRC nor the United States had ratified the Geneva Conventions of 1949 during the conflict, but both officially declared their intentions to apply the Conventions' principles.[36] In particular, the two sides sought to gain rhetorical and geopolitical advantage by accusing each other of mistreating prisoners of war and demonstrating their own 'humane' approaches.[37]

Against this backdrop, the conclusion of the Korean War in an uneasy armistice in July 1953 helped spur both Beijing and Washington to ratify the 1949 Geneva Conventions, to which they had already made extensive rhetorical commitments: Washington ratified in 1955 and Beijing in 1956. This moment of codification was, however, an outlier, as in other contexts Beijing mainly turned away from the delineation of new obligations and instead sought to promote consensus on the inherent, *zhuquan*-based rights of states against external intervention. The foundational moment for this agenda in international law was the 1955 Bandung Conference—at which China played a crucial role and the memory of which remains key to PRC diplomacy.[38]

The formation of the Bandung initiative took place against the context of the Korean War armistice, China's continued exclusion from the UN due to US opposition, and countervailing efforts by the two sides to win allies in Asia. In the search for stability and geopolitical support, Chinese premier Zhou Enlai engaged in extensive regional diplomacy, in particular focusing on China's southern neighbours. Extensive discussions with the Nehru government in India led to the preamble to the Agreement on Trade and Intercourse between Tibet Region of China and India, which was signed in Beijing on 29 April 1954 and incorporated a platform of 'five principles of peaceful coexistence' that included mutual respect for territorial

---

[35] Hans Kelsen, *The Law of the United Nations: A Critical Analysis of its Fundamental Problems: With Supplement* (Clark, New Jersey: The Lawbook Exchange Ltd., 2000), 934.

[36] Foreign Minister Zhou Enlai's Statement on China's Recognition of the 1949 Geneva Conventions (13 July 1952), *Zhonghua Renmin Gongheguo Dui Wai Guanxi Wenjian Ji, 1951–1953*, II (Beijing: Shijie Zhishi Chubanshe, 1957), 78–79.

[37] The United States accused Beijing of both traditional atrocities such as the physical mistreatment of prisoners of war and innovative violations such as 'brainwashing'. Beijing, meanwhile, promoted its own allegations against the United States, including the use of biological and entomological warfare, in violation of the 1925 Geneva Protocol banning poisonous gas and bacteriological methods of warfare (which have since been proven false). Geneva Conventions for the Protection of War Victims: Hearing Before the Committee on Foreign Relations, United States Senate, Eighty-fourth Congress, First Session (3 June 1955), 31–33; Jeffrey A. Lockwood, *Six-Legged Soldiers: Using Insects as Weapons of War* (Oxford: Oxford University Press, 2008), 164–66; Milton Leitenberg, 'China's False Allegations of the Use of Biological Weapons by the United States during the Korean War', Wilson Center, March 2016, www.wilsoncenter.org/publication/chinas-false-allegations-the-use-biological-weapons-the-uni ted-states-during-the-korean, accessed 1 October 2024.

[38] Yafeng Xia, 'New Scholarship and Directions in the Study of the Diplomatic History of the People's Republic of China', *The Chinese Historical Review* 14, no. 1 (2007): 114–40.

integrity and sovereignty, nonaggression, non-interference in internal affairs, equality and cooperation for mutual benefit, and peaceful coexistence. The principles were then incorporated into joint statements with both India and Burma.[39] From that point on, they would be treated as essential to China's positions on international law.[40]

The US-led founding of the Southeast Asian Treaty Organization (SEATO), a regional counterpart to NATO, occurred in February 1955.[41] Viewed in Beijing as an attempt at threat and encirclement, this development sparked intensified discussions about how China could go about winning recognition and support from its neighbours, despite their widely varying ideologies.[42] The previous year, the initiative for a conference of Asian and African states had already been formulated by the Asian neighbours with which Beijing's relations were warming, and in January 1955 officials of the Ministry of Foreign Affairs were already proposing that China should attend. This plan was endorsed by the Communist Party's Politburo in April, which framed China's vision for the meeting as a 'convention of peace' that would promote an agenda against aggression, militarism (e.g. SEATO and other such alliance arrangements), hegemony, racism, and colonialism. Beijing also opposed economic coercion, such as the embargo that had been placed on it by the United States.[43]

Zhou became one of the central figures at Bandung, and while staying faithful to the Politburo's instructions found ways to improve its appeal to China's partners at the forum. For example, while expressing China's opposition to SEATO, he was careful not to condition acceptance of a joint platform on other states renouncing the organization.[44] Indeed, it was the Nehru government of India, officially neutral in the Cold War, that expressed more open reservations about SEATO members (notably its rival Pakistan) joining the conference, while Zhou publicly qualified this as a 'defensive' posture that was not inherently threatening.[45] The final communiqué of the Bandung Conference incorporated Zhou and Nehru's Five Principles of Peaceful Coexistence, as well as additional affirmations of nonintervention, beneficial cooperation, and support for states' inherent rights to neutrality and non-alliance.[46]

---

[39] For an overview of this timeline, see Chen, 'Bandung, China, and the Making of World Order'.
[40] See e.g. Wen Jiabao, 'Carrying Forward the Five Principles of Peaceful Coexistence in the Promotion of Peace and Development', *Chinese Journal of International Law* 3 (2004): 363.
[41] Ronald C. Nairn, 'Seato: A Critique', *Pacific Affairs* 41, no. 1 (1968): 5–18.
[42] Chen, 'Bandung, China, and the Making of World Order'.
[43] Ibid.
[44] Ibid.
[45] See Vanja Hamzic, 'Pakistan's Cold War(s) and International Law', in *International Law and the Cold War*, edited by Matthew Craven, Sundhya Pahuja, Gerry Simpson, and Anna Saunders (Cambridge: Cambridge University Press, 2019): 447–66.
[46] A. Doak Barnett, 'Chou En-lai at Bandung: Chinese Communist diplomacy at the Asian-African Conference', *American Universities Field Staff* (1955): 1–15; A. Doak Barnett, 'Asia and Africa in Session: Random Notes on the Asian-African Conference', *American Universities Field Staff* (1955): 1–36.

Although Beijing had originally envisioned Bandung forming the basis for a permanent institution, this goal was soon abandoned due to exacerbated tensions with India over territorial disputes as well as more generally worsening regional and global Cold War conflicts.[47] These were also reflected in a rapidly worsening domestic environment in China for lawyers and other professionals. Although Chinese international lawyers continued to be involved in formulating Beijing's public positions on issues such as sovereignty over Taiwan and the 1956 Suez Crisis,[48] they were soon after targeted by the Maoist Anti-Rightist Campaign of 1957–59, during which members of the profession found themselves, and their views, for the most part marginalized in policy discourse.[49]

One pivotal event in this process was the conference held jointly by the Shanghai Society of Law and the East China Institute of Political Science and Law in February 1958, during which legal experts (representing those trained in the Republican period before 1949 and younger colleagues with post-1949, and thus 'revolutionary', educations) argued over questions such as whether international law was inherently divided between capitalist norms and those valid among the community of socialist states, whether there was instead a single, unified system for all states, or, alternatively, a mixture of particular norms (such as those that might be developed among socialist states) along with some universally valid principles.[50] Though the issue was not decided, the overall consensus tended to point in the direction of a mixed system, favouring a limited set of rules shared across ideological fronts.

One issue on which the positions of Chinese jurists became distinctive at this point was on the claims of national liberation movements to be recognized as subjects of international law alongside traditional nation-states.[51] In keeping with the principles of Third World solidarity and promoting decolonization that China had committed to at Bandung, some Chinese international lawyers argued that China should take the stance that suppression of uprisings in colonies should be regarded as an illegal 'war of open aggression banned by the law of nations', rather than as merely internal armed conflicts.[52] This view was taken to its extreme during the early phase of the Cultural Revolution, from 1966 to 1976, during which Maoist China embarked on a more adventurous phase of diplomatic and legal divergence.

---

[47] Chen Dunde, *A New Era: Zhou Enlai to Bandung* (Beijing: China Youth Press, 2013).

[48] Ch'en T'i-Ch'iang, 'Taiwan-A Chinese Territory', *Law in the Service of Peace: International Association of Democratic Lawyers*, no 5. (1956): 38–44.

[49] See Cohen and Chiu, *People's China and International Law*, Vol. I, 14-16, 28, 59.

[50] Ibid.

[51] See Athanassios Vamvoukos, 'Chinese and Soviet Attitudes toward International Law: A Comparative Approach', *Review of Socialist Law* 5, no. 2 (1979): 131.

[52] See ibid. (citing K'ung Meng, 'A Criticism of The Theories of Capitalist International Law on International Entities and the Recognition of States', *U.S. Joint Publications Research Service* 27, no. 3453 (June 1960): 33.

From Insurgent Legal Ordering to Institutional Integration

Although the split would not reach a crescendo until the second half of the decade, Beijing's international positions by 1960 had already sharply dissented from those of the Soviet Union under Nikita Khrushchev. The worsening relations with Moscow came as it pursued policies of de-Stalinization and 'peaceful coexistence' with the West, which came to be viewed in Beijing as 'revisionist' attempts to betray Marxism–Leninism in the name of Moscow's own goals of imperial expansion and hegemony within the socialist camp.[53] In a parallel with Beijing's relatively stronger support for the principle of sovereign equality and non-interference (as seen at Bandung and in its rejection of formal alliance arrangements like the Warsaw Pact), it now openly accused Moscow of violating 'the independent and equal status of fraternal parties', as a kind of intra-socialist norm violation.[54]

As Moscow removed its experts from China and undertook a range of other sanctions, Beijing doubled down on its positions. These included the promotion of ties with other non-Western states, and the promotion of its position as a partner for diplomacy and trade across ideological lines while, simultaneously, laying claim to a purer version of Marxism–Leninism that was less hegemonically inclined, and more supportive of revolutionaries abroad, than that of the Soviet Union.[55] In settings like the Tricontinental Conference of Solidarity of the Peoples of Africa, Asia and Latin America, held in Havana in January 1966, Chinese representatives sought to articulate a position of friendship and aid for non-Western and Global South peoples in general and for anticolonial movements in particular.[56]

These positions were intensely radicalized during the early period of the Cultural Revolution, during which Mao, who had been largely sidelined from day-to-day governance throughout the 1960s, launched a party-based political campaign to reassert his authority. Comprising, in essence, a coup against the current Communist Party establishment, the Cultural Revolution campaign mobilized the entire citizenry in a radical political praxis of denouncing, and often seizing, the apparatus of government at various levels throughout the country. Rising as Mao's lieutenant during the early phase of this movement, Marshall Lin Biao temporarily took Zhou Enlai's longstanding place as the voice of Chinese foreign policy, articulating a new stance of more active support for global revolution under the

---

[53] 'Peaceful Coexistence: Two Diametrically Opposed Policies: Comment on the Open Letter of the Central Committee of the Communist Party of the Soviet Union', *People's Daily* (12 December 1963). Text in English published by the Foreign Language Press, Beijing.
[54] See Editorial Departments of *People's Daily* and *Red Flag*, 'The Leaders of the CPSU Are the Greatest Splitters of Our Times', *People's Daily* (4 February 1964), in Cohen and Chiu, *People's China and International Law: Vol I*, 140-143.
[55] Huang Hua, *Qinli Yu Jianwen: Huang Hua Huiyi Lu* (Experience and Insights: Huang Hua's Memoir) (Beijing: Foreign Languages Press, 2008).
[56] Isaac Saney, 'Tricontinentalism, Anti-Imperialism and Third World Rebellion', in *Routledge Handbook of South–South Relations*, edited by Elena Fiddian-Qasmiyeh and Patricia Daley (London: Routledge, 2018), 1797.

banner of 'building rural base areas and using the countryside to encircle and finally capture the cities'—just the strategy that the CCP had used in its own domestic struggle for power, now to be translated onto the world stage.[57] Pledging unremitting support for North Vietnam in its struggle against US intervention, Lin called for a 'people's war' against both US imperialism, wherever it was to be found, and Soviet revisionism.[58]

For Lin and the radical activists of the early Cultural Revolution, existing international law was largely irrelevant to this project of armed struggle against imperialism and revisionism. Lin declared China the centre of global revolution, and Chinese engagements with many foreign states were halted, at least temporarily. Indeed, even embassy grounds within China itself were targeted by Red Guard groups. 'Bourgeois' professionals, international lawyers included, were excluded from all public or academic activities.[59] Meanwhile, within the broader socialist camp, Chinese–Soviet relations reached their nadir, particularly with the Soviet invasion of Czechoslovakia to suppress the Prague Spring in 1968, during which Beijing denounced Soviet leader Leonid Brezhnev as a 'red tsar' and labelled Soviet interventions against fellow socialist states as imperialist aggression in violation of Lenin's original support of the right to self-determination.[60] At the same time, China itself was engaging more comprehensively in policies of military aid to insurgent groups abroad that—under mainstream international law doctrine—would be viewed as potential acts of aggression against recognized sovereign states.[61]

Shortly after Lin's fall from power in mid-1971, Chinese policies domestically and abroad underwent another major shift. In October of that year, UN General Assembly Resolution 2758 officially confirmed UN membership for the PRC (and in turn the Nationalist government on Taiwan's loss of UN recognition and its seat on the Security Council).[62] This was achieved through a process of diplomacy that was greatly facilitated by the US Nixon administration's desire to capitalize on Sino–Soviet tensions and constrain Moscow's ability to achieve its international goals.

With entry into the UN and more widespread recognition as China's sole government under international law, Beijing was now finally able to also participate

---

[57] Lin Biao, *Long Live the Victory of People's War!: In Commemoration of the 20th Anniversary of Victory in the Chinese People's War of Resistance Against Japan* (Peking: Foreign Languages Press, 1965).
[58] Ibid.
[59] Mobo Gao, 'The Cultural Revolution: Class, Culture and Revolution' in *Handbook on Class and Social Stratification in China*, edited by Yingjie Guo (Cheltenham: Edward Elgar, 2016), 44-58.
[60] Ruskola, 'The Dao of Mao', 386; see also 'Lieningzhuyi, haishi shehui diguozhuyi?: Jinian weida Liening dansheng yi bai zhounian' (Leninism, or social imperialism?: Commemorating a century since the birth of the great Lenin), *People's Daily* (22 April 1970).
[61] Jodie Yuzhou Sun, 'Supplied Cash and Arms but Losing Anyway: Chinese Support of the Lumumbist Insurgencies in the Congo Crisis (1959–65)', *Cold War History* 22, no. 4 (2022): 459-78.
[62] Huang Huikang, 'China's Contribution to the International Rule of Law since the Restoration of its UN Seat 50 Years Ago', *Chinese Journal of International Law* 20, no. 3 (2021): 533-43.

on a wider basis in important legal settings, albeit in a tentative manner. For example, with respect to the 1977 Additional Protocols to the Geneva Conventions, PRC delegates only participated in the first session of the diplomatic conference that ran between 1974 and 1977, withdrawing amid controversy over the participation of the Vietcong/South Vietnamese Provisional Government, which was supported by many socialist and Third World states but opposed by the US and its allies. This issue also embodied a broader, ongoing disagreement with the West about the nature of aggression, which Chinese delegates continued to portray as essentially connected with 'unjust' actions to suppress peoples struggling for self-determination.[63] With the ultimate passage of Protocol I, the Third World position on the applicability of key norms of *jus in bello* to various forms of anticolonial 'internal' armed conflict finally became a recognized element of international humanitarian law.[64]

Meanwhile, in the context of the negotiations on the 1982 UN Convention on the Law of the Sea (UNCLOS), for which meetings had previously been held in 1958 and 1960, Beijing's representatives joined only as of the third conference in 1973, after its entry into the UN. Being awarded a membership on the UN Seabed Committee by a vote of the General Assembly in 1971, China became increasingly involved in legislative efforts surrounding maritime law issues. Calling for a more 'fair and reasonable marine order' for the Global South, Chinese delegates supported rules advanced by developing states, such as the common heritage of mankind principle with respect to deep seabed resources, articulated in UN General Assembly Resolution 2749 in 1970, which was also supported by Soviet-aligned states but opposed by the United States and several other Western powers. While this provision for a redistributive regime under UNCLOS was incorporated in the final text, it has had limited impact thus far due to ongoing 'engineering, financial, and regulatory issues' which make it difficult to economically exploit the deep seabed.[65] China would later ratify the Convention in 1996, and UNCLOS has become a core factor in its relations with regional neighbours.[66]

---

[63] 'Rineiwa Gongyue Waijiao Huiyi Xiu Hui Tongguo Di San Shijie Guojia Ti An, Guiding Fandui Zhimin Tongzhi, Waiguo Zhanling He Zhongzuzhuyi Zhengquan De Wuzhuang Douzheng, Ying Shou Rineiwa Gongyue De Falü Baohu' (The Geneva Conventions Diplomatic Conference Adjourns with Adoption of Third World States's Proposal that Armed Struggles Opposing Colonial Domination, Alien Occupation, and Racist Regimes Should Receive the Protection of the Geneva Conventions), *People's Daily* (31 March 1974); cf. Jessica Whyte, 'The "Dangerous Concept of the Just War": Decolonization, Wars of National Liberation, and the Additional Protocols to the Geneva Conventions', *Humanity: An International Journal of Human Rights, Humanitarianism, and Development* 9, no. 3 (2018): 313–41.
[64] On the development of this position at the conference, see Georges M. Abi-Saab, 'The Third World Intellectual in Praxis: Confrontation, Participation, or Operation Behind Enemy Lines?', *Third World Quarterly* 37 (2016): 1957.
[65] Aline Jaeckel, Jeff A. Ardron, and Kristina M. Gjerde, 'Sharing Benefits of the Common Heritage of Mankind—Is the Deep Seabed Mining Regime Ready?', *Marine Policy* 70 (2016): 198–204.
[66] Nong Hong, *UNCLOS and Ocean Dispute Settlement: Law and Politics in the South China Sea* (London: Routledge, 2012).

Following Mao's death in 1976 and the transition to Deng Xiaoping's policies of engagement and 'opening up' to Western capital, Chinese international law engagement gathered pace, though it continued to exhibit a disinclination for taking the lead in proposing new norms. As part of a raft of treaty signings and increased international law engagement beginning in 1979, Beijing signed and ratified the 1977 Geneva Protocols I and II in 1983, thus committing to a robust set of new obligations related to both international and non-international armed conflicts.[67]

In 1984, Ni Zhengyu, who had represented the Nationalist government at the Tokyo Tribunals but subsequently stayed in China after the communist victory, was appointed to the ICJ as the PRC's first judge on that body. Nearly 80 years old by the time he took up the position, Ni had over the previous decades engaged in international law consultation for Beijing related to the law of the sea and other topics. His political reliability and legal expertise made him an ideal candidate for a position intended to bolster official PRC state views but left some room for collegial innovation.[68] Ni's role at the ICJ would last until 1994, during which time he issued opinions on cases including the *Nicaragua v United States* case, decided in 1986, where the court held that the United States had violated international law and committed aggression against Nicaragua by supporting the Contra rebels against the Sandinistas and direct military actions such as the mining of the country's harbours. With respect to the various issues involved in that case touching on the law of armed conflict, Ni supported the majority opinion regarding the US violation of Article 2 of the UN Charter, but sought a stronger finding regarding the inapplicability of multilateral treaty-based reservations to ICJ jurisdiction, which the United States had cited along with collective self-defence as justifying its opposition to adjudication.[69] With his rejection of these positions, Ni closely represented Beijing's ongoing position opposing the US defence alliance system, which it had condemned as incompatible with the prohibition on the use of force contained in Article 2.

The fall of the Soviet Union and the apparent end of the Cold War spurred a renewed sense in Washington and its allied capitals that the international legal order could be developed to promote and entrench favoured liberal norms.[70] Among the most immediate consequences in international law was the resumption of the long-since abandoned project of international criminal law, which was soon embodied

---

[67] Cf. Huang Lie, 'Guoji Rendao Fa Gaishu' (Summary of International Humanitarian Law), *Huanqiu Falü Pinglun* 004 (2000): 70–81.

[68] In Ni's autobiography, notably, he refrains from criticizing even many of the extreme policies of the Cultural Revolution that were later generally disavowed such as re-education of intellectuals through manual labour. Ni instead recounts his own (relatively mild) experiences with such practices as having had a positive effect. Ni Zhengyu, *Danbo Congrong Li Haiya* (Simply and Calmly Established at The Hague) (Beijing: Beijing University Press, 2015), 134, 210.

[69] See *Nicaragua v United States*, 'Separate Opinion of Judge Ni Zhengyu' (27 June 1986).

[70] Cf. Harlan Grant Cohen, 'Multilateralism's Life Cycle', *American Journal of International Law* 112, no. 1 (2018): 47–66.

in the International Criminal Tribunals for Yugoslavia (ICTY, from 1993) and Rwanda (ICTR, from 1994). Chinese involvement in the ICTY and in the shared appellate mechanism for both tribunals would consist of the international lawyers Li Haopei, Wang Tieya, and Liu Daqun, with Li serving on the ICTY from 1994 to 1997; Wang from 1997 to 2000; and Liu from 2000. Like Ni, Li and Wang were old, pre-1949, stalwarts of China's international law community—their continued prominent activity was in part reflective of the fact that the extreme politics of the Mao era had severely stunted the growth of the international law field.

Like Ni at the ICJ, Li and Wang at the ICTY adopted positions tending to embody Beijing's commitments to existing principles of both *jus ad bellum* and *jus in bello* and were also interested in engaging with or contributing to progressive legal innovations. Wang, for example, ruled in favour of the outcome in the 1997 *Tadić* case, which weakened the test for attributing uses of force from an armed group abroad to a state actor, potentially allowing for broader liability for states intervening in armed conflicts.[71] This position was in line with the other members of the ICTY judiciary, but would have likely been seen as anathema as recently as the mid to late 1970s, as being in clear tension with Beijing's official positions (and material assistance) supporting 'armed revolutionary struggle' against oppressors of self-determination in various parts of the world.

By the late 1990s, Chinese lawyers, judges, and diplomats active in international law settings related to the law of war were frequently in favour of the establishment of increased liability norms and further development of mechanisms of jurisdiction for their enforcement. This extended to the plans for an International Criminal Court (ICC) that developed into the Rome Conference of 1998. Beijing would ultimately only express its support in principle for the ICC but opposition to the institution as it took shape at the conference. The latter was expressed by delegate Liu Daqun, who articulated Beijing's misgivings regarding what would become the Rome Statute's Article 12 provisions for ICC jurisdiction, one, without UN Security Council action; or, two, without consent of the defendant's state. This broad jurisdiction meant 'violating the sovereignty of State parties', Liu argued, and imposed 'greater obligations' on non-parties than parties.[72]

Despite such qualms, Beijing chose not to outright reject the ICC and continues to hold out the possibility of eventually joining it (presumably pending revisions to the Rome Statute). Its present position could be summed up as continued caution about restricting state autonomy combined with a conciliatory stance on conducting multilateral legal regulation via global institutions with clearly delimited authorizations based on state consent. This has, essentially, come to be the

---

[71] Cf. Antonio Cassese, 'The Nicaragua and Tadić Tests Revisited in Light of the ICJ Judgment on Genocide in Bosnia', *European Journal of International Law* 18, no. 4 (2007): 649–68.
[72] A/CONF.183/C.1/SR.42 UN Diplomatic Conference of Plenipotentiaries on the Establishment of an International Criminal Court, Rome, 15–17 June 1998.

Chinese approach across a number of realms, including maritime, environmental, and international economic law. In each of these areas, Chinese views increasingly embody what might be described as an idiosyncratic form of commitment to legal formalism as a way to reconcile state sovereignty and international norm development.

Neo-Statism, Formalism, and Twenty-First Century Global Governance

China's opposition to the ICC as an independent judicial organ with broad criminal jurisdiction for international criminal and human rights law violations was indicative of a gradual recovery of Beijing's prioritization of sovereignty in general within the new context of intensifying globalization. From the relatively comprehensive conciliatory engagement of the 1990s, which coincided with China's process of preparing for World Trade Organization (WTO) accession and other aspects of global trade integration, the early 2000s marked a shift towards a world of renewed geopolitical tensions.

The tasks of 'preserving' the autonomy of the state while also increasingly taking up a role as a great power norm-maker with a strong institutional role has been reflected in a number of domains. With respect to forums such as the UN Development Programme, which develop soft-law norms on a consensual basis and preclude centralized enforcement actions against norm violators, Beijing has been an enthusiastic participant. For example, it has embraced the framing and reporting of the UN Millennium Development Goals, and subsequently the Sustainable Development Goals, as models for coordinated cooperation in global affairs.[73] This marked a shift from the earlier rhetoric of the 1970s and 1980s, when Beijing articulated views about a 'right to development' with more redistributive implications.[74] The climate change-related commitments of the Paris Agreement have likewise been heavily endorsed in domestic and international settings.[75]

Regarding the use of force, the return of bloc-based conflicting interpretations was already in evidence by 1999 when China strongly condemned the NATO airstrike campaign in Kosovo, which it regarded as an illegal use of force, as well as during the US invasions of Afghanistan and Iraq in 2002 and 2003.[76] The sharp

---

[73] Cf. Wing Thye Woo, Shi Li, Ximing Yue, Harry Xiaoying Wu, and Xinpeng Xu, 'The Poverty Challenge for China in the New Millennium', Report to the Poverty Reduction Taskforce of the Millennium Development Goals Project of the United Nations (2004).

[74] Ryan Mitchell, 'The Emerging Chinese Model of Statist Human Rights', *American University International Law Review* 37 (2021): 617.

[75] See e.g. Robyn Eckersley, 'Rethinking Leadership: Understanding the Roles of the US and China in the Negotiation of the Paris Agreement', *European Journal of International Relations* 26, no. 4 (2020): 1178–202.

[76] Cf. David Shambaugh, 'China's Military Views the World: Ambivalent Security', *International Security* 24, no. 3 (1999): 52–79.

Chinese criticism of Washington on these *jus ad bellum* issues reflected a hardening of internal conversations in Beijing regarding the extent to which reconciliation with Western global governance should be pursued in tandem with economic 'reform and opening'.[77] Though a number of different viewpoints and policy positions were expressed, including within the Party leadership, the ultimate consensus clearly pointed towards a more selective approach. The first decade of the twenty-first century saw Beijing take a decided shift in engagement strategies towards UN-based and other explicitly multilateral state-oriented initiatives, and away from both autonomous international organizations as well as ad hoc frameworks dominated by Washington.

Thus, while avoiding any positive engagement with both the 'coalition of the willing' operations in the war on terror, as well as with the ICC, Beijing reiterated a relatively strict interpretation of prohibitions on the use of force in the kinetic realm. However, with regards to more innovative aspects of legal doctrine on the use of force, such as in the cyber realm or in the area of so-called 'grey zone' operations of informal maritime militias in contested sea zones, Beijing has adopted a much more lax approach, allowing for the exercise of its comparative advantages and the extension of its practical interests, for instance, by passing domestic legislation that legitimizes 'maritime militia' activities in disputed waters.[78] In other areas where existing positive legal doctrine does not specify state obligations, Beijing has tended to opt for a relatively conservative, gradualist, and state-centric set of interpretations, for example, seeking to ensure that international environmental law agreements avoid imposing strict principles of state liability for their contributions to the problem of climate change.

With regards to the limits of self-determination, for example, Beijing formulated the firm position in its 2009 submission to the ICJ regarding the *Kosovo* Advisory Opinion that there is no right for regions or peoples to unilaterally declare independence from host states on the basis of self-determination.[79] Similarly, it took the position that civil wars were not to be understood as giving rise to 'international armed conflict' without the explicit intervention of a foreign state.[80] These positions were expressed to the ICJ by Xue Hanqin, in the first oral argument by a PRC representative before an international tribunal. Shortly thereafter, Xue was nominated for her current position as China's judge on the court.

---

[77] Cf. Shiyan Sun, 'The Understanding and Interpretation of the ICCPR in the Context of China's Possible Ratification', *Chinese Journal of International Law* 6, no. 1 (2007): 17–42.

[78] Joseph L. Votel, Charles T. Cleveland, Charles T. Connett, and Will Irwin. 'Unconventional Warfare in the Gray Zone', *Joint Forces Quarterly* 80, no. 1 (2016): 101–09; Dan Efrony, and Yuval Shany, 'A Rule Book on the Shelf? Tallinn Manual 2.0 on Cyberoperations and Subsequent State Practice', *American Journal of International Law* 112, no. 4 (2018): 583–657.

[79] Written Statement of China, 17 April 2009, *Accordance with International Law of the Unilateral Declaration of Independence in Respect of Kosovo* (2009).

[80] Ibid.

In each of these respects, Chinese positions on contentious international law issues were coalescing further around a statist posture that viewed the stability of sovereign territory as the highest value. This implied both the strong rejection of any uses of force outside of the narrow bounds of UN Charter Article 2—indeed, taking such a position more clearly than ever—and also a rejection of international liability for the suppression of domestic 'insurgents', except to the extent of the Additional Protocol II of the 1977 Geneva Conventions, and not via the ICC or any international criminal process not vetted by the UN Security Council.

Regarding the doctrine of the 'Responsibility to Protect' (R2P), a notion advanced by Western states as a potential justification for intervention against states at risk of major human rights atrocities, Chinese delegates in 2000 were cautiously open to the notion, provided that any interventions were ordered and supervised by the UN Security Council.[81] However, the subsequent experiences of R2P in practice, particularly the NATO-led 2011 regime change operation in Libya, provided sufficient cause for Beijing to shift its policy towards outright rejection of R2P-based interventions into situations of internal civil conflict.[82] It was only after the 'failure' of the Libya example that Beijing's statism was fully expressed on the issue of R2P interventions, and thus came fully into line with its position on armed interventions more generally, as already earlier expressed in the *Kosovo* submissions of 2009.

In the realm of the law of armed conflict, then, China's official views have come to reconcile an acceptance of international norms, adjudicatory mechanisms, and regulatory institutions with a continued emphasis on the *zhuquan* of the (recognized) sovereign state. Where there have been conflicts between sovereigns that touch on China's own interests, meanwhile, it has tended to recur to principles and justifications that are seemingly connected with maintaining its great power status and corresponding grand strategy objectives. The firm insistence on Article 2, for example, has been challenged by Beijing's unwillingness to, fully and clearly, condemn Russia's military invasion of Ukraine since February 2022, in large part on the basis of alleged 'justified security concerns' stemming from NATO's potential expansion were it to accept Ukraine as a candidate member. The rejection of individual state uses of force in violation of Article 2 thus came into conflict with the rejection of the US alliance system, and with a 'realist' appraisal of other powers' relativization of Article 2.[83] Although China has not fully articulated its position

---

[81] See e.g. Tiewa Liu and Haibin Zhang, 'Debates in China about the Responsibility to Protect as a Developing International Norm: A General Assessment', *Conflict, Security & Development* 14, no. 4 (2014): 403–27.

[82] Ibid; see also Yang Yonghong, 'Lun Baohu Zeren Dui Libiya Zhi Shiyong' (On the Application of Responsibility to Protect to Libya), *Falü Pinglun* 2 (2012): 120–26.

[83] While not representing China's official position, ICJ Judge Xue Hanqin has articulated a similar view of the limits of the tribunal's ability to issue provisional measures regarding international armed conflicts where there is no clear jurisdictional grant of authority to do so. *Ukraine v Russian Federation*, 'Declaration of Judge Xue', 16 March 2022, Allegations of Genocide under the Convention on the Prevention and Punishment of the Crime of Genocide. ('It appears that the acts complained

on potential justifications for Russian use of force in Ukraine, several government publications have raised the concept of a 'security space' within which states might have interests that give rise to apparent rights of intervention.[84]

Chinese practice in another arena, that of the law of the sea, has also demonstrated the emerging mixture of state-centric and institution-embracing approaches. Typical in this regard has been China's engagement with adjudication and dispute resolution mechanisms in maritime law. A notable milestone was the September 2023 oral submission before the International Tribunal on the Law of the Sea (ITLOS) of Ma Xinmin, Director-General of the Department of Treaty and Law of the PRC Ministry of Foreign Affairs. This was only the second ever appearance by a representative of the PRC for an oral statement before an international tribunal (after Xue's at the ICJ in 2009).[85] China's oral and written interventions at the ITLOS were made with respect to the request by the Commission of Small Island States on Climate Change and International Law (COSIS) for an ITLOS advisory opinion on states' legal duties regarding climate change.[86] Beijing's position rejected broad advisory jurisdiction for the full ITLOS tribunal, as well as a classification of greenhouse gas emissions as 'pollution' under UNCLOS Article 192 et seq., and the notion that 'liability or compensation' could be applied to states for their contributions to climate change.[87]

Ma's oral remarks also emphasized the notion that climate change obligations under international law are fully embodied in the 1992 UN Framework Convention on Climate Change and the Paris Agreement of 2016. Expressing a conservative view of the development of legal norms by international tribunals, he denied that a body such as the ITLOS could act on its own initiative to strengthen protections for the environment, saying it could only do so with explicit consent

of by Ukraine namely Russia's recognition of the independence of the Luhansk and Donetsk regions of Ukraine and Russia's military operations in Ukraine cannot be directly addressed by the interpretation and application of the provisions of the Genocide Convention, as the issues they have raised are concerned with the questions of recognition and use of force in international law. They do not appear to be capable of falling within the scope of the Genocide Convention [...] Whether the Russian Federation may exercise self-defence, as it claims, under the circumstances is apparently not governed by the Genocide Convention.')

[84] See e.g. Li Zhiwei, 'Meiguo Ya Dui Wukelan Weiji Chengdan Zhuyao Zeren' (The United States Must Take Primary Responsibility for the Ukraine Crisis), *People's Daily* (21 April 2022).

[85] 'China Participates in an Oral Proceeding before the International Tribunal for the Law of the Sea for the First Time', Ministry of Foreign Affairs, People's Republic of China, 19 September 2023, www.mfa.gov.cn/eng/wjb/zzjg_663340/tyfls_665260/tfsxw_665262/202309/t20230919_11145482.html, accessed 1 October 2024.

[86] 'Written Statement of China', 15 June 2023, Request for an advisory opinion submitted by the commission of small island states on climate change and international law (2023).

[87] Ibid. These positions do not place China outside the spectrum of mainstream interpretations of the relevant international law frameworks. Indeed, several participants, such as India and the United Kingdom, resemble China in taking clear positions against advisory competence for the full tribunal. Others, including Japan and the European Union, expressed varying degrees of openness to ITLOS's accepting the request while diminishing the potential scope of the eventual opinion.

from states to the issuance of new norms.[88] A similarly state-centric interpretation was included in his verbal rejoinder to member states that cited the 2016 China–Philippines *South China Sea* Arbitration, which he described as having 'acted *ultra vires* [i.e. beyond the scope of appropriate authority], erred in fact finding, misinterpreted and perverted the law' by operating in violation of China's reservation over dispute resolution on issues of territorial sovereignty.[89] While this was a restatement of China's consistent position on the *South China Sea* arbitration, it also has direct implications for international environmental law, as the award included extensive discussion of Part XII of UNCLOS, relating to rules regarding pollution and harm to marine environments.[90]

Finally, on a more conceptual level, Ma also raised the spectre of 'the fragmentation of international law in relevant fields' that could result from the full tribunal of ITLOS using advisory competence to produce jurisprudence departing from existing climate change norms. This perspective also extends to efforts at pushing the boundaries of jurisdiction in other forums as well. Indeed, even in the context of the *Chagos* Advisory Opinion at the ICJ, China's written submission emphasized the need to 'uphold and respect the principle of consent when a purely bilateral dispute is involved' and, by implication, decline to exercise its advisory competence in advancing an agenda of decolonization.[91] Strikingly, then, even in a legal proceeding touching on core issues of anticolonialism, Beijing found itself eschewing the fiery rhetoric of its earlier eras demanding the self-determination of oppressed and colonized peoples. Instead, an emphasis on sovereign state *zhuquan*, as a quality of recognized and established powers, such as itself, took precedence.

These sometimes status quo-reinforcing stances, however, continue to be tempered by reiterations of longstanding views within the context of centralized institutions. Thus, despite its ambivalent intervention during the *Chagos* proceedings, subsequent to the Advisory Opinion being released Beijing voted along with the majority in the General Assembly calling upon the United Kingdom to comply.[92] In the later *Occupied Palestinian Territory* Advisory Opinion proceedings, meanwhile, China's official intervention provided a firm statement in support of self-determination of the Palestinian people. At the same time, China also pointed out its continued stance that there is no right to 'remedial secession' or 'remedial self-determination' under international law, as 'state sovereignty and territorial integrity constitutes a fundamental principle of international law which goes to the core of, and lays down the basis for, the contemporary international legal order.'[93]

---

[88] Statement of Ma Xinmin, 15 September 2023, ITLOS/PV.23/C31/10.
[89] Ibid.
[90] See e.g. Statement of Victoria Hallum, 15 September 2023, in ibid.
[91] 'Written Statement of China', 1 March 2018, Legal Consequences of the Separation of the Chagos Archipelago from Mauritius in 1965.
[92] United Nations General Assembly, Seventy-third Session, 83rd Plenary Meeting, A/73/PV.83, GA/12146 (22 May 2019).
[93] 'Written Statement of China', 25 July 2023, Legal Consequences Arising from the Policies and Practices of Israel in the Occupied Palestinian Territory, Including East Jerusalem.

Conclusion

Notions of both state sovereignty and international law were introduced into China alongside extensive Western interventions that compromised both self-determination and territorial integrity. From the turn of the twentieth century on, successive Chinese regimes spent many decades pursuing the realization of these substantive features of sovereignty, in part through the use of international legal argumentation as well as through the pursuit of cooperative relations with similarly positioned states. Alongside this approach, there also emerged critical discourses on international legal topics that saw China align itself closely with Global South agendas, albeit with sometimes conflicting notions as to its own role as a kind of great power.

Following the Cold War, an initial period of post-1989 convergence was followed by a renewed statist turn that foreclosed some of the more exotic new legal processes being pioneered by the still Western-centric international law community. More recently, meanwhile, Beijing has exhibited a turn once again to the opposite direction of increasingly active engagement with international norms and processes, and a vocal assertion of its views about the future of various global governance institutions and areas of law. The deepening of 'South-South' cooperation across various forums has now also become a project that is tied to China's own generation of new institutions, in particular in the realm of international development.

Beijing has, to be sure, maintained key aspects of its longstanding emphasis on state autonomy. It has done so in part via restrictive interpretations of tribunal jurisdiction, strict definitions of capacious legal concepts, and limits on the acceptable forums for legislating new rules. Yet China's developing stances also involve the pursuit of agency, and prestige, as a maker of international norms. Some 'disruptive' causes within international law, from the empowerment of the ICC to pierce the veil of immunity to the judicial generation of norms favouring small island states in the face of climate change, are seen as being in potential tension with its *zhuquan*. However, China's considerable recent investment in the legitimacy of 'international law with the UN at its core' suggests the intention to continue embracing and exploring the forms of multilateral, institutionalized, and legalistic global governance.

7
Health as a Human Right and Eastern European Anticolonialism

Bogdan C. Iacob

Introduction

During the Cold War, health as a human right was codified into international law through four cardinal documents. The Constitution of the World Health Organization (WHO, established in 1946) states that 'the enjoyment of the highest attainable standard of health is one of the fundamental rights of every human being without distinction of race, religion, political belief, economic or social condition'. The 1948 Universal Declaration of Human Rights (UDHR) does not list it as a right in its own right, but it stands as part of a series of economic and social rights in Article 25(1). Article 12 of the UN International Covenant on Economic, Social and Cultural Rights (ICESCR, adopted in 1966, entered into force in 1976) gives health as a human right a separate legal identity based on four tenets concerning child welfare, hygiene, disease prevention and control, and the creation of conditions for medical services to all. Lastly, the Alma-Ata Declaration issued by the WHO in 1978 'strongly reaffirms that health [...] is a fundamental human right'.[1] While other international documents, such as the Convention on the Elimination of All Forms of Discrimination Against Women (1979) and the Convention on the Rights of the Child (CRC) (1989), did include it, the WHO Constitution, the UDHR, the ICESCR and the Alma-Ata Declaration remain the fundamental landmarks for global debates on health as a human right. They circumscribe a timeframe, from the 1940s to the 1970s, that continues to be underexplored in the existing scholarship.

This chapter explores the contributions of state socialist regimes and their experts to the codification and implementation of health as a human right. Most of the literature assigns a peripheral role to Central and Eastern Europe in global debates. In the case of the UDHR, authors underline that the insertion of 'health' and 'medical care' in the document was not 'the product of communist ideology'.[2] While making passing reference to the Constitution of the USSR (1936), scholars

---

[1] WHO, 'Declaration of Alma Ata', https://cdn.who.int/media/docs/default-source/documents/almaata-declaration-en.pdf?sfvrsn=7b3c2167_2, accessed 19 May 2024.
[2] John Tobin, *The Right to Health in International Law* (Oxford: Oxford University Press, 2012), 15.

prefer to tie Article 25(1) to the history of social medicine, to Franklin Delano Roosevelt's 'New Deal' or his 1941 four freedoms speech, to the Beveridge report (1942), to constitutional efforts in Latin America (especially in Mexico and Chile), or interventions from recently decolonized countries such as India.[3] In terms of Article 12 of the ICESCR, interventions by Eastern European representatives are disconnected from the issues advocated for by the socialist camp and Yugoslavia at the WHO in the context of decolonization.[4] Moreover, the link between international law and health as a human right at the WHO is analysed either by focusing on decision-making at the level of the organization's secretariat or on the unwillingness of Western states, particularly the United States, to give a solid juridical foundation to this right.[5]

Furthermore, the end of the Cold War is widely considered one of the factors that sparked the resurgence of international advocacy for health as a human right. The end of ideological bipolarism allowed, in this view, for an increased focus on social and economic rights in postcolonial countries and the inclusion of health in their constitutions during the 1990s.[6] Such narrative overlooks the formative impact of the Cold War and decolonization upon the articulation of health as a human right. Eastern European socialist regimes often, but not always, found common ground with newly independent countries in Africa and Asia in their shared desire to advance health in international law as part of a vision of human rights in which political and civil as well as social and economic rights were interdependent and indivisible.[7]

The chapter follows two analytical paths to examine state socialist contributions to health as a human right. On the one hand, I contend, in support of Giovanni Mantilla's argument for socialist 'protagonism' concerning humanitarian law, that state socialist Europeans played an active role in shaping these deliberations.[8] Such

---

[3] Adam Gaffney, *To Heal Humankind: The Right to Health in History* (New York: Routledge, 2018), 101, 112–14.

[4] Benjamin Mason Meier, 'The Highest Attainable Standard: The World Health Organization, Global Health Governance, and the Contentious Politics of Human Rights', PhD dissertation, Columbia University (2009), 242.

[5] Benjamin Mason Meier, 'Global Health Governance and the Contentious Politics of Human Rights: Mainstreaming the Right to Health for Public Health Advancement', *Stanford Journal of International Law* 46, no. 1 (2010): 1–50.

[6] Colleen Flood and Aeyal Gross, 'Introduction: Marrying Human Rights and Health Care Systems: Contexts for a Power to Improve Access and Equity', in *The Right to Health at the Public/Private Divide: A Global Comparative Study*, edited by Colleen Flood and Aeyal Gross (Cambridge: Cambridge University Press, 2014), 2.

[7] Daniel Whelan, *Indivisible Human Right: A History* (Philadelphia, PA: University of Pennsylvania Press, 2010).

[8] Giovanni Mantilla, 'The Protagonism of the USSR and Socialist States in the Revision of International Humanitarian Law', *Journal of the History of International Law* 21, no. 2 (2019): 181–211. For the role of state socialism in developing international criminal and humanitarian law, see also Raluca Grosescu and Ned Richardson-Little, 'Revisiting State Socialist Approaches to International Criminal and Humanitarian Law: An Introduction', *Journal of the History of International Law* 21, no. 2 (2019): 161–80.

a role emerged not only through the drafting of international mechanisms such as the UDHR and the ICESCR, but also through the implementation at the WHO of the principles underlining health as a human right—as conceptualized by representatives from Central and Eastern Europe, and elsewhere. Although the UDHR and the ICESCR only partially fulfilled the agenda of state socialist countries in terms of this right, the 'leftover' components of their arguments were fulfilled at the WHO, where health as a human right became linked to decolonization and the ebb and flow of the Cold War. During the 1960s and the 1970s, state socialist experts at the WHO took on a global role in the conceptualization and enforcement of this right, tying it to other rights central to decolonization: self-determination, anti-racism, and the struggle for adequate living standards.

On the other hand, this chapter's intertwined exploration of international law and the politics of global health complicates the simplistic representation of human rights, particularly social-economic ones, as a struggle between East and West. While emphasizing the importance of Central and Eastern European interventions, I underline that the discussions about health as a human right were characterized by a diverse geography. Latin American (especially Chile and Uruguay) and non-aligned states (in particular Egypt and India) adopted positions at the United Nations (UN) and the WHO that reflected their traditions surrounding the relationship between medicine and the people, as well as the challenges they faced in the consolidation of national healthcare systems. The South–East relationship fluctuated between solidarity and dissonance on matters of self-determination and collective well-being.[9] Along the way, health as a human right turned into a vehicle for the ascendence of social justice concerns within the UN system, and particularly at the WHO.

Furthermore, just as European state socialists were not monolithic despite their close coordination, there was a diversity of positions in the West, which allowed for collaboration between communist and select capitalist countries. Experts from Norway, Sweden, and Denmark extolled interpretations of medicine (state duty for health to all, integration of curative and preventive medicine, socio-economic embedding of disease, etc.) that, to a large extent, overlapped with those from Central and Eastern Europe. It was a consequence of their traditions of linking communitarianism, social reform, and medicine, which, after the Second World War, converged in Nordic countries into the hegemonic concept of 'people's health'.[10] French representatives diverged from their state socialist counterparts in

---

[9] Paul Betts, 'Rights', in *Socialism Goes Global. The Soviet Union and Eastern Europe in the Age of Decolonisation*, edited by James Mark and Paul Betts (Cambridge: Cambridge University Press, 2022), 181.

[10] Sophy Bergenheim, Johan Edman, Johannes Kananen, and Merle Wessel, 'Conceptualising Public Health: An Introduction', in *Conceptualising Public Health: Historical and Contemporary Struggles over Key Concepts*, edited by Sophy Bergenheim, Johan Edman, Johannes Kananen, and Merle Wessel (London: Routledge, 2018), 8.

terms of anticolonialism, but not as much in terms of the formulation of health as a human right. State socialists were thus not protagonists in the sense of the uniqueness of their arguments but because of the resilience of their positions over three decades, which unwaveringly intertwined health with anticolonialism and anti-racism.

Health Anticolonialism in the Early Postwar Period

Beginning with the first World Health Assembly (WHA) in July 1948,[11] Central and Eastern European delegates argued that medicine, as an epistemic and policy field, should adopt 'a positive rather than defensive attitude', to quote Andrija Štampar, a Yugoslav reformer prominent in interwar and postwar health politics. By this, he meant that medicine should not focus only on 'the defence against certain diseases of international importance', but that the WHO treat 'health problems as problems of global importance' and that 'the community should be obliged to afford all its peoples health protection as complete as possible'.[12] This vision was embedded in the WHO Constitution, which defines health as 'a state of complete physical, mental and social well-being and not merely the absence of disease or infirmity', a formulation borrowed from Štampar's working paper on the basic principles of the WHO Constitution.[13] Furthermore, his address as president of the first WHA anticipated the debates about extending health as a human right to the entire world, including non-self-governing and trust territories (which existed under UN authority but were administered by Western empires), and newly independent countries. The principles of non-discrimination and self-determination attached to this right and extolled by Štampar became central arguments in global anticolonial health politics.

Štampar's position reflected the early prominence of experts from European state socialist regimes in connecting health as a human right and anticolonialism. He had played a decisive role in the creation of the WHO as a member of the Technical Preparatory Committee, which drafted the organization's Constitution (sixteen members, among them Marcin Kacprzak from Poland and Joseph Cančik from Czechoslovakia), and as chair of the Interim Commission that bridged the time until the WHO was operational.[14] His postwar visibility was a direct consequence of Eastern Europe's crucial role in the activities of the WHO's predecessor,

---

[11] The World Health Assembly is the legislative body of WHO, comprising representatives from each member state.

[12] WHO no. 13, First WHA, Plenary Meetings: Verbatim Records, Geneva, 24 June–24 July 1948, 30–31.

[13] WHO no. 1, Minutes of the Technical Preparatory Committee for the International Health Conference, Annex 9, Paris, 18 March–5 April 1946, 58.

[14] Marcos Cueto, Theodore Brown, and Elizabeth Fee, *The World Health Organization. A History* (Cambridge: Cambridge University Press, 2019), 43–44.

the League of Nations Health Organization (LNHO, created in 1921). The LNHO had been chaired until 1938 by Polish bacteriologist Ludwig Rajchman who, along with Štampar and other Central and Eastern European experts, had been instrumental in two sets of policies with long-term impact in global dynamics. The first was the linkage between social medicine and the idea of state-led health governance. Social medicine embedded disease into social-economic contexts, integrated preventive and curative practices, and focused on impoverished communities. By connecting it to the state, Central and Eastern European delegates at the LNHO sought international legitimacy for a vision of healthcare that covered their respective nations in their entirety. The second set of policies paired medical reforms in Europe, especially for underprivileged urban populations and rural communities, to those in Asia, Latin America and, to a lesser extent, in Africa.[15] In contrast to the postwar period, Central and Eastern Europeans did not challenge the imperial status-quo. However, state-building through medicine became entangled with the slow expansion and nativization of medical services in colonial territories. This association set the groundwork for the post-1945 solidarity between East and South on matters of self-determination via the establishment of national healthcare services.

The European Conference on Rural Hygiene held in Geneva in 1931 (initiated by Hungary and Republican Spain) and its follow-up, the Pan-Asian Conference on Rural Hygiene organized in 1937 in Bandung, Indonesia, placed social medicine and state-managed healthcare at the centre of global debates. There, Central and Eastern Europeans along with Western representatives (particularly those from Francophone and Scandinavian countries), as well as experts from Asia (where indigenous personnel was increasingly prominent, especially in India) and Latin America reached a consensus about health as a foundation of social life.[16] At the LNHO, international experts emphasized that 'governments determine[d] the conditions in which health services and healthy lives could flourish'.[17] The Soviet Union was part of these dynamics, with its delegates participating in LNHO programmes even before the 'first workers' state' joined the League of Nations in 1933. The Soviet experiment with centralized, government-funded, formally free access to healthcare fascinated medical elites in Europe, India, and Latin America. Even in the United States, the interest in so-called 'socialized medicine' triggered a grass-roots movement to bring about some form of federal provision of healthcare.

---

[15] Sunil Amrith, *Decolonizing International Health: India and Southeast Asia, 1930–65* (New York: Palgrave Macmillan, 2006).

[16] Bogdan C. Iacob, 'Health', in *Socialism Goes Global. The Soviet Union and Eastern Europe in the Age of Decolonisation*, edited by James Mark and Paul Betts (Cambridge: Cambridge University Press, 2022), 262–64. On the role interwar left-wing networks in the establishment of the UN system, see Sandrine Kott, *A World More Equal: An Internationalist Perspective on the Cold War* (New York: Columbia University Press, 2024).

[17] Iris Borowy, *Coming to Terms with World Health. The League of Nations Health Organisation 1921–1946* (Berlin: Peter Lang, 2009), 337–39.

Such lobbying was visible during the 'New Deal' and in the early postwar years, when the Wagner-Murray-Dingell Bill proposed a national medical and hospitalization programme, but was defeated because of red-baiting, in particular by the American Medical Association.[18]

While the WHO and its Constitution were the outcome of a prewar international consensus on the connection between social medicine and state-building, it also reflected the growing role of extra-European countries: the very idea of such a body originated with representatives from Brazil and China, both states having played a significant role at the LNHO. The definition of health as a human right in the WHO Constitution echoed the views of left-leaning Western experts, such as Norwegian Karl Evang, Belgian René Sand, and American Thomas Parran (Surgeon General of the United States, who, in 1948, was removed from office for his ideas). The idea of 'positive medicine' had been extolled during the sessions of the Technical Preparatory Committee not only by Štampar but also by Parran and Gregorio Bermann, the Argentinean representative.[19]

The drafters of the WHO Constitution also grappled with the issue of nondiscrimination and the relationship of the organization to existing colonial territories. On the first matter, the Sub-Committee on the Constitution's preamble, comprising Brock Chisholm (from Canada, the first director-general of the WHO), Szeming Sze (Republic of China), and Bermann, adapted a French proposal that equivocally linked health and the development of 'the rights of man [...] without distinction of race, sex, language or religion'. The final text unambiguously affirmed health as a fundamental human right that excluded any form of discrimination.[20] On the second topic, Sze and Štampar insisted that the WHO include 'all nations—Members of the United Nations, neutrals or others'. The Technical Preparatory Committee recommended that the future WHA 'consider the question of [the organization] providing services to trust territories, protectorates, colonies and other territories not eligible for separate membership in the United Nations'.[21] While this approach did not differ from previous LNHO practice, a coalition of Central and Eastern European and other states championing decolonization would use this provision to advance self-determination through the fulfilment of health as a human right in colonial territories, as shown below.

Once the Cold War took hold of the world during the 1950s, the idea of health as a human right premised on social medicine and state responsibility did not disappear. It was, however, eclipsed by ideological antagonism and the urgency of postwar reconstruction—which favoured less comprehensive medical policies,

---

[18] Anne-Emanuelle Birn and Theodore M. Brown (eds.), *Comrades in Health: U.S. Health Internationalists, Abroad and at Home* (New Brunswick, NJ: Rutgers University Press, 2013).
[19] WHO no. 1, Minutes of the Technical Preparatory Committee for the International Health Conference, 18.
[20] Ibid., 50, 61.
[21] Ibid., 70.

reliant on immunological innovations (e.g. antibiotics and DDT). Additionally, states (newly independent, such as India or Pakistan, or European ones) and empires worked with severely limited resources.[22] Even within the socialist camp, despite official claims of universal access, certain population categories (such as peasants refusing collectivization or people with disabilities) were not fully covered by free health services, while others, such us workers in heavy industry, had priority in the medical system.[23] Nevertheless, extensive welfare reforms held centre stage in Europe and Latin America. But the WHO increasingly focused on the control of infectious diseases in so-called 'underdeveloped countries' through technological means (pharmaceuticals, insecticides, and laboratory research) rather than addressing the broader local and global contexts fuelling such maladies.

Still, the debates during the first two WHAs reveal the resilience of the prewar consensus on medico-social approaches to national healthcare and its potential linkage to self-determination. Central and Eastern European delegates were quick to connect anticolonialism and the fulfilment of health as a human right; they were joined by decolonizing states. At the 1948 WHA, Rajkumari Amrit Kaur, the first minister of health in India, a leader of the independence and women's emancipation movements, said: 'a marked rise in the standard of the peoples of backward countries is an essential step towards the building of their national health on a sound foundation'.[24] Her intervention underlined the WHO's role in assisting decolonizing countries in the consolidation of their state medical systems. Central and Eastern Europeans went a step further: they envisaged their region and (formerly) colonial peoples as one space of suffering, and thus the primary terrain for WHO activities. The Soviet Deputy Minister of Health Nikolai Vinogradov argued that the organization should concentrate its activities on the needs of war-torn countries (referring to Central and Eastern Europe) as well as colonial and non-autonomous territories. In Vinogradov's view, national health services in these regions had similarly been obliterated by acts of aggression, equating the destruction wrought by Nazi Germany and Western empires.[25] The heavy burden of (re)construction in state socialist countries and newly independent ones was a foundation for solidarity between East and South.[26]

Stemming from these commonalities, state socialist representatives proposed policies at the WHO that were the medical equivalent of political

---

[22] James Gillespie, 'Europe, America, and the Space of International Health', in *Shifting Boundaries of Public Health: Europe in the Twentieth Century*, edited by Susan Gross Solomon, Lion Murard, and Patrick Zylberman (Rochester, NY: University of Rochester Press, 2008), 124.
[23] Michael Kaser, *Health Care in the Soviet Union and Eastern Europe* (London: Croom Helm, 1976); Maria Cristina Galmarini-Kabala, *The Right to Be Helped. Deviance, Entitlement, and the Soviet Moral Order* (DeKalb, IL: Northern Illinois University Press, 2016).
[24] WHO no. 13, First WHA, Plenary Meetings: Verbatim records, 32.
[25] Ibid, 40.
[26] Dora Vargha, 'Formalising Socialist International Health: From Aid to Diplomacy', paper presented at the conference 'Health and Socialism: Of Shortages and Solidarity' (Berlin, 9–10 October 2023).

self-determination: postcolonial states implementing preventive and curative programmes integrated into national health systems managed by local personnel. Colonial rule was deemed incapable of providing such a framework for medical self-governance. As Vinogradov argued, 'epidemics are due to poverty and colonial oppression, as well as the arbitrary exploitation of populations deprived of their rights, and the lack of effective organization of health services in colonial and non-autonomous territories'.[27] This merger between the failure of healthcare and colonialism tapped into a broader debate: the state's ability to create the institutional and legislative bedrock for, as one Brazilian delegate put it, 'the achievement of a standard of health and social welfare that is appropriate to human dignity'.[28] The remark echoed ongoing debates in his country as well as in Chile, Uruguay, and Mexico about bringing medical services under state control to expand their reach within the population.

At the WHO, Central and Eastern European and anticolonial voices converged on the idea that human dignity could not be achieved by empires, which were unable to ensure the well-being of their subject populations because of social, political, and racial discrimination. Such a state of affairs effectively made Western rule in Asia or Africa illegitimate. At the second WHA, the Bulgarian representative S. Stoyanoff accused the WHO of offering 'preferential aid to colonial powers' and thus absolving them of their 'supreme duty' towards the peoples that they 'oppressed and exploited'.[29] His intervention was in response to claims made by delegates from France and the United Kingdom about a sort of 'progressive imperialism',[30] which ostensibly brought development, healthcare included, to the colonies. Jacques Parisot stated in 1948 that 'the numerous peoples of [France's] overseas territories [...] have greatly benefited from the recent strides made in the field of health'.[31] Western empires sought to channel the consensus on social medicine and health governance into a renewal of the project of colonial administration rather than into self-determination, a trend that had its roots in the late 1930s.[32]

In this context, delegates from India, Egypt, and Ceylon—whose representatives fought to involve the Human Rights Commission in the evaluation of allegations of human rights abuses in non-self-governing territories—and representatives from Central and Eastern Europe envisaged health as a human right to be tied to medical self-rule and indigenous representation at the WHO. They argued that non-self-governing territories should have full decision-making

---

[27] WHO no. 13, First WHA, Plenary Meetings: Verbatim Records, 41.
[28] Ibid., 71.
[29] WHO, no. 21, 2nd WHA, Decisions and Resolution, Plenary Meetings: Verbatim Records, Rome, 13 June–2 July 1949, 100.
[30] Gillespie, 'Europe, America, and the Space of International Health', 125.
[31] WHO no. 13, First WHA, Plenary Meetings: Verbatim Records, 65.
[32] Tomoko Akami, 'Imperial Polities, Intercolonialism, and the Shaping of Global Governing Norms: Public Health Expert Networks in Asia and the League of Nations Health Organization, 1908–37', *Journal of Global History* 12, no. 1 (2017): 4–25.

powers and national representation in the regional offices of the organization. The idea had been first proposed by the Liberian delegate J. N. Togba, who also advocated for the participation of only African representatives in the WHO's regional committee for Africa.[33] Initially, colonial powers were reluctant to agree to the founding of such an institution, fearing the WHO's infringement upon their sovereignty over colonial territories, whereas state socialist delegates supported the pleas of Liberia, one of only two independent countries in Sub-Saharan Africa at the time. The WHO's African Regional Committee (AFRO) was created in the early 1950s as Western 'progressive imperialism' was unravelling. Empires turned to the WHO as a resource for low-cost assistance in disease control thus deflecting anticolonial criticism.[34] Until 1964, the chair of AFRO was the Portuguese malariologist Francisco Cambournac—epitomizing the resilience of colonial governance in the organization's programmes.[35] As decolonization swept across Africa, AFRO turned into a hub for critiques of racism as a paradigmatic violation of health as a human right.

Health as a Human Right in International Conventions

In parallel to the first WHA, in June 1948, the Soviet delegation advanced a set of basic proposals for inclusion in the UDHR. During the third session of the UN Human Rights Commission, Soviet legal experts presented a document that included extensive revisions to the initial draft of the Declaration, some of them targeting the text that became Article 25. The delegation proposed the inclusion of two clauses: 'everyone has the right to medical care and assistance in case of illness' and 'it is the duty of the state and society to take all necessary steps, including legislation, to ensure that everyone has a real opportunity of enjoying' this right.[36] Soviet delegates were not alone in their stance. The Chilean delegation advanced its own proposal that stated: 'the state must promote measures of public health and safety'. John Humphrey (Canada), the first director of the UN Division of Human Rights and the coordinating author of the UDHR, added the sentence 'everyone has the right to medical care' to the Chilean text.[37] Interventions from Eleanor Roosevelt, the former first lady and official representative of the United States to the UN, diluted the focus on 'the right to medical care' in favour of the

---

[33] WHO no. 13, First WHA, Plenary Meetings: Verbatim Records, 265.
[34] Jessica Pearson, *The Colonial Politics of Global Health: France and the United Nations in Postwar Africa* (Cambridge, MA: Harvard University Press, 2018), 159–72; Gillespie, 'Europe, America, and the Space of International Health', 132.
[35] Cueto, Brown, and Fee, *The World Health Organization*, 80.
[36] UN ECOSOC, E/800, Report of the Third Session of the Commission of Human Rights, 24 May–18 June 1948, 43.
[37] Johannes Morsink, *The Universal Declaration of Human Rights. Origins, Drafting, and Intent* (Philadelphia, PA: University of Pennsylvania Press, 1999), 192.

formulation 'the highest attainable standard'. The draft article was further transformed by the United Kingdom and India, whose representatives invoked the imperative of brevity to merge the right to healthcare with the rights to social security and the protection of mothers and children. Theirs would become the final form of Article 25 in the UDHR.[38]

Though Soviet lobbying succeed in preserving mentions of 'health' and 'medical care', health as a human right disappeared from the Declaration. Just as at the WHO, Central and Eastern European input during the early debates about the UDHR was tied to antifascism.[39] Soviet delegates presented their advocacy for provisions against racial discrimination in the UDHR as the continuation of the struggle against fascism.[40] For the Yugoslav delegate, Ljuba Radevanovic, the extension of the Declaration to 'any person belonging to the population of Trust and Non-Self-Governing Territories' reflected his country's emphasis on anti-discrimination as inherent to anti-imperialism.[41] State socialist anticolonialism was thus entangled with the extension of social-economic rights, particularly health, to colonial territories.

In 1947, the Soviet Union requested the addition of several questions to the questionnaire for the Trusteeship Council, the institution tasked by the UN with supervising the administration of trust territories (former German and Italian colonies), which represented a continuation of imperial rule by other means. Five of these questions pertained to health as a human right. They covered issues such as healthcare budgeting and infrastructure, access to medical care, number of physicians and nurses, and local medical personnel.[42] The debates over these topics represented a significant departure from prewar practice; the League of Nations had had no oversight powers over trust territories on matters of health. The Soviet queries reflected a wider Central and Eastern European advocacy that health as a human right could only be fulfilled by way of medical self-governance and full access, without any discrimination.

The idea of self-determination via health as a human right was reinforced by Soviet insistence on inserting the formulation 'the state's duty for legislative measures' in the UDHR.[43] Although René Cassin, the French representative and first chair of the left-wing International Association of Democratic Lawyers (for details see Raluca Grosescu's chapter), endorsed the move—signalling the early postwar

[38] Ibid., 194, 196.
[39] UN ECOSOC, E/800, Report of the Third Session of the Commission of Human Rights, 3, 38.
[40] Jessica Whyte, 'Human Rights, Revolution and the "Good Society." The Soviet Union and the Universal Declaration of Human Rights', in *Revolutions in International Law. The Legacies of 1917*, edited by Kathryn Greenman, Anne Orford, Anna Saunders, and Ntina Tzouvala (Cambridge: Cambridge University Press, 2021), 401–27.
[41] Morsink, *The Universal Declaration of Human Rights*, 98.
[42] UN ECOSOC, E/600, Report of the Commission on Human Rights. Second Session Geneva, 2 December–17 December 1947, 14.
[43] UN ECOSOC, E/800, Basic Proposals Advanced by the Soviet Delegation at the Third Session of the Commission of Human Rights, 43.

consensus surrounding universal healthcare reform. In contrast to the Soviets, he did not connect the idea of the welfare state to decolonization. Similarly, British representatives acknowledged the importance of the state in the provision of social-economic rights (i.e. health) but rejected the idea that such a guarantee could be inserted into an instrument of international law.[44] India was keen to avoid clear-cut references to state duties. The government in Delhi believed it did not have the resources to implement universal healthcare. Eleanor Roosevelt also rebuffed references to state obligations, arguing that such considerations were more pertinent to the deliberations on social-economic rights in the future International Bill of Rights.[45] The UDHR debate over 'legislative measures' with a view to the fulfilment of health as a human right would return in the deliberations over the ICESCR and at the WHO during the 1950s and 1960s.

The Central and Eastern European states represented at the UN in 1948 (the Belorussian Soviet Socialist Republic (SSR), the Ukrainian SSR, the USSR, Czechoslovakia, Poland, and Yugoslavia) abstained from the final vote on ratifying the UDHR, motivated by the Declaration's non-binding nature and the refusal of Western countries to condemn fascism and colonialism in the document. Nevertheless, Eastern European lobbying during the drafting prevented the inclusion of a colonial clause (see Sonja Dolinsek and Philippa Hetherington, Chapter 9 and Ned Richardson-Little, Chapter 11 in this volume). The UDHR's provisions applied to territories and peoples subject to Western imperialism—a development essential for decolonization. During the 1960s, as state socialist regimes reignited their anticolonial offensive within the UN system, the decision to abstain from signing the UDHR was swept under the rug.

Echoing their dissatisfaction with the UDHR, Central and Eastern European governments criticized the hegemony of the United States and Western colonial empires at the WHO. With Cold War tensions on the rise, by 1950, state socialist regimes withdrew from the organization, with the exception of Yugoslavia, which soon pursued a non-aligned path. They remained outside of the WHO until the end of the decade. Between 1951 and 1957, Western empires, and particularly the United States, shaped the organization into an instrument of ideological containment: the scourge of underdevelopment and the threat of communism became ideologically intertwined, while humanitarian crises in Asia and Africa were understood as security problems. Health was no longer an issue of human rights and comprehensive national medical services but of technical assistance targeting specific infectious diseases. Any discussion of racial discrimination in health disappeared.

---

[44] Brigit Toebes, *The Right to Health as a Human Right in International Law* (Antwerp: Intersentia, 1999), 36–40.

[45] UNOG Registry First Period 1946–1973, Box HR0007, SOA 317/1/01(1)C, Edward Lawson, 'First Draft for Y. Malik on the Declaration of Human Rights', 21 November 1948, 2.

Nevertheless, the first director-general of the WHO, Brock Chisholm, sought to involve the organization in the international codification of health as a human right. Chisholm had been a proponent of the pre-Second World War notion of a 'positive' definition of health that emphasized its social-economic contexts and state responsibility. His initiatives were frustrated by the overwhelming leverage of the United States over the WHO's activities. In 1953, Chisholm was replaced as director-general by Marcolino Gomes Candau, a Brazilian malariologist. Candau epitomized the organization's focus on technological interventions against specific infectious diseases at the expense of tackling global health disparities. He also extracted the WHO from the drafting of the international covenants on human rights.[46]

The change of leadership at the WHO did not eliminate the advocacy for national healthcare through the expansion of rural services in newly independent countries. Yugoslavia and India spearheaded this lobbying. During the 1950s, it found an institutional framework: the WHO Expert Committee on Public Health Administration, which included, among others, Karl Evang and Andrija Štampar. The Committee preserved the interwar consensus founded on social medicine and the establishment of state-funded networks of basic healthcare units. As shown below, this understanding of health as a comprehensive right rooted in community needs manifested both debates in the WHO Executive Board and the UN specialized committees. The phenomenon highlighted Yugoslavia's growing prominence in global humanitarianism: its experts distanced themselves from the centralized Soviet blueprint of healthcare and used self-managed socialism to connect to the development priorities of newly independent states.[47]

While Yugoslavia remained in the WHO, the Central and Eastern European countries who had withdrawn from the organization continued to impact discussions about health as a human right during the drafting of the ICESCR. Article 12 of the covenant was negotiated at the seventh (1951) and eighth (1952) sessions of the UN Human Rights Commission and at the eleventh General Assembly (late 1956 and early 1957). In the debates from the early 1950s, the idea of state interventionism in healthcare lingered—briefly pushing the United States and its allies into a minority position—before being set aside in the face of the challenges of state-building in the decolonizing world and Cold War geopolitics. The evaluations sent by some postcolonial governments to the UN with a view to the future ICESCR revealed their hesitation: India remarked that 'financially weak countries

---

[46] John Farley, *Brock Chisholm, the World Health Organization, and the Cold War* (Vancouver: University of British Columbia, 2008).

[47] Martin Gorsky and Christopher Sirrs, 'From "Planning" to "Systems Analysis": Health Services Strengthening at the World Health Organisation, 1952–1975', *Dynamis* 39, no.1 (2019): 205–33; Nicole Albrecht, 'Peasant Internationalism: Understanding Social Medicine Beyond Socialism', paper presented at the conference 'Health and Socialism: Of Shortages and Solidarity' (Berlin, 9–10 October 2023).

[...] will not be in a position to implement them.'[48] Yet, even for postcolonial countries fearful of the burden of state duties, social and economic rights, health among them, were not considered less important than civil and political rights. Instead, the issue was, as the Indian delegate remarked, 'creating a social order in which justice shall reign, in which inequalities shall be smoothed out'.[49]

During the 1951 meetings of the UN Human Rights Committee, the Soviet representative, Platon Morozov, returned to the principle rejected by the majority during the drafting of the UDHR: he reaffirmed that the new covenant should impose definite obligations on governments.[50] Soviet and Yugoslav representatives insisted on a broad definition of 'medical care' that included curative and preventive medicine and required access to services irrelevant of cost. The Yugoslav expert insisted on the decentralization of healthcare, a reflection of the country's distancing from the Soviet model.[51] Both delegates supported Mahmud Azmi Bey, an Egyptian legal expert, when he introduced an amendment that included the definition of health from the WHO Constitution. While in principle supportive of state involvement in the implementation of social-economic rights, the French delegate echoed US opposition to it, rejecting the notion of 'legislative measures' to guaranteeing health as a human right due to its potential applicability to the colonies. Nonetheless, backing from Chile, Uruguay, Sweden, Denmark, and the WHO director-general allowed the UN Committee to approve the most comprehensive formulation of health as a human right—one that included the duty of the state for implementation and the social-economic contextualization of illness.

A month later, during the eighth session of the WHO Executive Board, its members were called upon by Chisholm to evaluate the version of Article 12 discussed by the Human Rights Commission. The US representative, Henry van Zile Hyde, tried to eliminate 'legislative measures' from the provisions, contending that they were 'the least important' with a view to 'public health, sanitation, recreation and so forth'.[52] Though Hyde had the support of multiple delegates, including India, Pakistan, and Thailand, he was not able to obtain a majority. Despite the absence of state socialist countries (who had withdrawn from the organization in 1950; Yugoslavia was not a member of the Executive Board at the time), Swedish and Chilean representatives were able to expand the wording of Article 12. Chile had just legislated a National Health Service, effectively instituting universal coverage.[53]

---

[48] UNOG Registry First Period 1946-1973, Box HR0007, SOA 317/1/01(1)E, 'Views of the Government of India on the Draft International Covenant on Human Rights', [April] 1951, Comments from Governments, 1–2.
[49] Quoted in Whelan, *Indivisible Human Rights*, 131.
[50] UN General Assembly, Third Committee, A_C-3_SR-748, 11th Session, 748th Meeting, 31 January 1957, 335.
[51] Toebes, *The Right to Health*, 43–44.
[52] WHO, EB8/Min/9.Rev.1, Minutes of the Ninth Meeting, 7 June 1951, 7.
[53] Jadwiga Mooney, 'From Cold War Pressures to State Policy to Peoples' Health: Social Medicine and Socialized Medical Care in Chile', in *Peripheral Nerve. Health and Medicine in Cold War Latin*

Sweden was represented by Axel Höjer, who, similarly to his Central and Eastern European peers, had argued that 'a modern state must seek [...] the assurance of complete health to each and every one of its citizens'.[54] A relative majority decided to insert the formulation 'legislative and other measures' to signal that the achievement of health as a human right required not only juridical codification but also distinct policies and community action.[55] The ideas discussed at the WHO Expert Committee on Public Health Administration held central stage during the meeting of the Executive Board.

In 1952, at the eighth session of the UN Human Rights Commission, the situation shifted once again. Eleanor Roosevelt proposed six amendments that radically altered Article 12 of ICESCR, including the elimination of both 'legislative measures' and the definition of health from the WHO Constitution.[56] The Chileans and Uruguayians, both leaders in social medicine since the interwar years, resisted the initiative. They were backed by the Soviet and Polish delegates. Uruguay inserted two amendments to the US version of the article that effectively reverted it to its 1951 form by re-inserting 'legislative and other measures' and the WHO's definition of health.[57] India, Pakistan, and Lebanon supported the US intervention, arguing for the progressive realization of this right. The Swedish delegate sided with US, underlining the Cold War atmosphere at the UN Human Rights Commission as compared to the WHO Executive Board. The outcome was split: the terminology 'legislative measures' was eliminated (with Yugoslavia, the Ukrainian SSR, and the USSR along with Chile and Uruguay voting against; Pakistan and Egypt abstaining; the United Kingdom, France, the United States, Australia, Belgium, China, France, Greece, India, Lebanon, and Sweden voting for); Uruguay was able to maintain WHO's definition of health (with nine votes in favour, seven against, and two abstentions). This result showed the resilience of the social-economic contextualization of disease, despite the collapse of the consensus on state interventionism in healthcare.[58]

Central and Eastern European representatives were able to extend health as a human right to trust and non-self-governing territories, an element of their

---

America, edited by Anne-Emanuelle Birn and Raúl Necochea López (Durham, NC: Duke University Press, 2020), 187–210.

[54] Annika Berg and Teemu Ryymin, 'The People's Health, the Nation's Health, the World's Health', in *Conceptualising Public Health. Historical and Contemporary Struggles over Key Concepts*, edited by Sophy Bergenheim, Johan Edman, Johannes Kananen, and Merle Wessel (London: Routledge, 2018), 83.

[55] Bergenheim, Edman, Kananen, and Wessel, *Conceptualising Public Health*, 9.

[56] UN ECOSOC, E/CN.4/L.799/Rev.1, Commission on Human Rights, 8th session, 'United States of America: Revised Amendment to Article 25', 1–2. Article 12 of ICSECR had been initially numbered Article 25.

[57] UN ECOSOC, E/CN.4/L.109, Commission on Human Rights, 8th session, 'Uruguay: Amendment to the Revised Amendment Submitted by the United States of America', 1.

[58] UN ECOSOC, E/CN.4/SR.296, Commission on Human Rights, 8th Session, 15 May 1952, 8–9.

broader opposition to a colonial clause in the ICESCR. Article 12d, inserted in 1952 through the cooperation of Soviet, Polish, Yugoslav, Egyptian, and Chilean delegates, referred to 'the creation of conditions which would assure to all medical service in the event of sickness'.[59] State socialist delegates tapped into the growing support among postcolonial states for the linkage between the fulfilment of social and economic rights and self-determination. Arab states in particular (especially Saudi Arabia) used this connection to increase their criticism of Western powers. However, the relative majority's opposition to the terminology 'legislative measures' demonstrated that not only Cold War geopolitics but also the challenges of postcolonial state-building affected the drafting of international law premised on broad welfare goals. The same year, the leadership of the International Labour Organization failed to find sufficient support among Western and postcolonial states to craft a Social Security (Minimum Standards) Convention that would have imposed strict duties on governments in terms of comprehensive medical care and sickness benefits.[60]

In 1956–57, at the sessions of the UN Assembly's Third Committee, the fault lines of prior years remained. Romania, Yugoslavia, and the Soviet Union continued to insist, along with delegates from Iraq[61] and Chile, on a definition of health as a state duty for access to all. The same countries struggled to maintain the WHO's definition of health. Afghanistan and the Philippines proposed its elimination, yet another sign of not only Cold War alignments but also the global influence of a minimalist understanding of public health.[62] Echoing Andrija Štampar's presidential address at the 1948 WHA, Diaz Casanueva (Chile) insisted that health must be approached in a 'positive' manner, 'for medicine has ceased to be exclusively curative and had now also become preventive'.[63] As optimism about the eradication of infectious diseases via immunological innovations was on the rise, the arguments made by Casanueva and his Central and Eastern Europeans colleagues about the social-economic conditions for ill-health remained a minority position. In its final

[59] UN General Assembly, A/2910/Add.5, 10th session, Observations by the Government of the Federal People's Republic of Yugoslavia, 28 September 1955, 3–4.

[60] Just as the founders of the WHO formulated a broad vision for healthcare in 1946, two years earlier, the ILO (established in 1919) issued the Philadelphia Declaration that proclaimed: 'labor is not a commodity' and 'the extension of social security measures to provide [...] comprehensive medical care'. The ILO too failed to implement the ideals from this Declaration in international law, at least until the late 1960s. Martin Gorsky and Christopher Sirrs, 'Universal Health Coverage as a Global Public Health Goal: The Work of the International Labour Organisation, c.1925–2018', História, Ciências, Saúde 27, supl. (2020): 71–93; Christopher Sirrs, 'Promoting Health Protection Worldwide: The International Labour Organisation and Health Systems Financing, 1952–2012', International History Review 42, no. 2 (2020): 371–90.

[61] Iraq was represented at the Third Committee by Beida Afnan, an anticolonial advocate for women's rights. Roland Burke, Decolonization and the Evolution of International Human Rights (Philadelphia, PA: University of Pennsylvania Press, 2010), 41, 117.

[62] UN General Assembly, A/3525, 11th Session Report of the Third Committee, Draft International Covenants on Human Rights, 9 February 1957, 55.

[63] UN General Assembly, A-C-3-SR-746, 11th Session, Third Committee, 30 January 1957, 324–25.

form, Article 12 recognized 'the right of everyone to the enjoyment of the highest attainable standard of physical and mental health' and connected its implementation to four policy objectives that were reminiscent of the generous principles advocated for in the past.[64] Its direct connection to social-economic conditions of illness and state interventionism was, however, eliminated.

Health as Anticolonialism and Anti-Racism at the WHO

The drafting of international law instruments had a limited effect on the expansion of the anticolonial health internationalism. Only when state socialist regimes returned to the organization in the late 1950s was this vision of health as a human right again present at the WHO, further supported by newly decolonized countries that emerged from the massive wave of national liberation that gripped Africa in 1960. Western imperial powers and the United States increasingly found themselves on the defensive.

At the WHO, Central and Eastern European delegates reaffirmed the connection between the development of national health services for all and the elimination of discrimination, particularly racism. A year after the UN General Assembly passed the Declaration on the Granting of Independence to Colonial Countries and Peoples, the notion of self-determination through the fulfilment of health as a human right took on firmer form when the Soviet delegation submitted a draft resolution on the granting of independence to colonial countries and peoples and the tasks of the WHO during the 1961 WHA. It was accompanied by a memorandum that blamed hunger, epidemics, low life expectancy, and premature death in non-sovereign territories on colonial rule, and emphasized that in newly independent countries, swift progress had been made 'in the fields of economy, culture, general prosperity and, in particular, in the field of health'.[65] Represented by the all-union minister of health and those from the Uzbek and Tajik SSRs, the Soviet Union used the improvement in medical access in former 'backward' Central Asian republics, previously Tsarist colonies, to underline the link between socialism and the achievement of national healthcare services.[66] As a result, the Uzbek and Tajik SSRs served as showcases for countries in Africa and Asia.

The draft resolution and the memorandum caused much furore. The United States and (former) Western European empires (the Netherlands, Belgium, France, Portugal, and the United Kingdom) opposed any discussion of colonialism at the WHO, considering it a political issue reserved for the UN General

---

[64] UN General Assembly, A-C-3-SR-743, 11th Session, Third Committee, 28 January 1957, 313.
[65] WHO, A14/P&B/10, 14th WHA, Explanatory Memorandum and Draft Resolution submitted by the Government of the USSR, 19 January 1961, 1–7.
[66] WHO, no. 103, 13th WHA, Part II: Plenary Meetings: Verbatim Records, Geneva, 3–20 May 1960, 62.

Assembly. Colonial powers sought to show the achievements of imperial medicine, repeating arguments made at the first two WHAs.[67] However, a relative majority of delegates agreed with the principles behind the Soviet draft resolution and memorandum: racial discrimination and lack of independence prevented the fulfilment of health as a human right among colonial peoples. Ultimately, the Soviet document was reworked in order to maintain its general ideas without referring directly to colonialism. The new draft resolution was co-authored by Ghana, Cuba, Iraq, Mexico, New Zealand,[68] Poland, Saudi Arabia, the USSR, and the United Arab Republic, and approved as resolution WHA14.58. Ghana's authorship reflected the country's key role in shaping human rights politics during the 1960s, as well as Kwame Nkrumah's proclamation of a Ghanaian path to socialism, one, however, not bound to Soviet-style rule. The document proposed by Principal Medical Officer at the Ghanaian Ministry of Health J. N. Robertson, argued that self-determination was essential 'to social progress and better standards of life in larger freedom'. Echoing debates from the drafting of the UDHR and the ICESCR, it called for the development of national health services, and underlined the relationship between 'racial equality and non-discrimination' and the fulfilment of 'the fundamental right of every human being to health and health services'.[69]

Certain African countries were uneasy about the Central and Eastern European, particularly Soviet, propensity to tie anticolonialism, anti-racism, and health to Cold War objectives. Delegations who had more favourable positions towards the West were reluctant to issue a blanket condemnation of colonial health governance. Senegal and Gabon (who were members of the pro-Western Brazzaville group of African states) suggested that the all-out Soviet attack on colonialism (and thus implicitly on France) reflected a 'paternalism, so offensive to us, that people are trying to bring into Africa. We want neither colonialism nor paternalism; we are men like any others, equal to any others'.[70]

Such remarks targeted the Eastern European export of socialist development premised on assisting newly independent 'underdeveloped' peoples to overcome their 'backwardness'. Despite state socialist advocacy of health as a human right, their hierarchical relationship with the Global South produced its own 'white saviourism'. Moreover, as Central and Eastern European anti-racism and anti-apartheid militancy hit a crescendo during the 1960s, so too did racially motivated incidents targeting Asian and African students in socialist states. Between

---

[67] Intervention of L. P. Aujoulat (France) in WHO, no. 103, Part II: Plenary Meetings: Verbatim Records, 322.
[68] During the drafting of the UNHR, the representative of New Zealand considered 'oppression of colonial peoples intolerable'. Morsink, *The Universal Declaration of Human Rights*, 99. In 1938, New Zealand was the first liberal democracy to develop a National Health System based on tax-funded, universal health service. Gorsky and Sirrs, 'Universal Health Coverage', 75.
[69] WHO, no. 111, Part II: Plenary Meetings: Verbatim Records, New Delhi, 7–24 February 1961, 315.
[70] Dr Sar (Senegal) in WHO, no. 111, 14th WHA, part II: plenary meetings: verbatim records, 170. The Gabonese delegate accused the Soviets of treating 'Africans like children', 316.

1962 and 1965, the growing presence of 'Third World' students in Moscow, Prague, Sofia, Leipzig, or Bucharest became the background for local violent, discriminatory behaviour. African, Asian, and Latin American students organized anti-racist protests in these cities that were swiftly squashed by socialist authorities.[71] Throughout the Cold War, communist party-states branded racial discrimination as a phenomenon located outside their borders, in places where 'capitalism and imperialism reproduced it in the exploitative hunt for profit, whether in America, or Western resistance to liberation struggles in Africa and Asia'.[72] Central and Eastern Europeans presented themselves as 'better whites' who brought the benefits of a non-discriminatory socialist modernity to the postcolonial world. Yet, such assistance was premised on the superiority of state socialism over developmental models in the Global South. Even in the case non-aligned Yugoslavia, Čarna Brković points to 'a conditional antiracism' that combined anticolonial humanitarianism with discrimination against its decolonized partners for this new vision of the world.[73]

The idea of 'better whites' was reinforced in discussions over health as a human right at the WHO. As they had done in the late 1940s, state socialist representatives connected the plight of decolonizing peoples with the suffering inflected on Central and Eastern Europeans by Nazi Germany. After the 1961 resolution, African and state socialist delegates began a massive offensive against South Africa and the Portuguese empire, catalysed by the transformation of the WHO's African Regional Committee (AFRO) from a vehicle for imperial medicine into one for African emancipation. The arguments of delegates from Central and Eastern Europe, Liberia, and Egypt at the 1948 WHA had finally come to fruition. African experts began to use the committee to push against racism and colonialism, and place Africa's healthcare needs onto the WHO's agenda. In 1965, Alfred Comlan Quenum from Benin became chair of AFRO. A year earlier, African representatives issued a draft resolution calling for the suspension of South Africa's voting rights and the revision of the organization's constitution to allow the expulsion of a country from the WHO in cases of grievous violations to the human right to health; for South Africa, the crime was apartheid.[74]

In expressing their support for this initiative at the World Health Assemblies in 1964 and 1965, Czechoslovak, Yugoslav, and Soviet delegates invoked Nazi Germany's aggression against their peoples to show they were 'only too well aware of the meaning and effects of racism'.[75] Western countries, alongside Venezuela

---

[71] Bogdan C. Iacob, 'A Babel in Bucharest: "Third World" Students in Romania, 1960s–1980s', *Cahiers du monde russe* 63, no. 4 (2022): 669–90.

[72] James Mark, 'Race', in *Socialism Goes Global. The Soviet Union and Eastern Europe in the Age of Decolonisation*, edited by James Mark and Paul Betts, 219.

[73] Čarna Brković, 'Socialist Modernist Worldmaking: Yugoslav Interventions in the International Humanitarian Debates in the 1970s', *Humanity* (forthcoming 2024).

[74] WHO, no. 132, Executive Board, 33rd Session, part I: resolutions, annexes, Geneva, 14–24 January 1964, 59–61.

[75] WHO, no. 136, Part II: Plenary Meetings: Verbatim Records, Geneva, 3–20 March 1964, 442–43.

and Argentina, argued that anti-apartheid was not a topic for the WHO and warned that sanctions against South Africa would create a dangerous precedent.[76] They also sought to counter Central and Eastern European self-representations as 'better whites', by noting, for example, that 'racial discrimination is everywhere since the problem was world-wide [...] I [William Bauer (Canada)] did not think that any country should use the case in question to obscure that fact'.[77] As early as the 1961 WHA in New Delhi, Western and extra-European delegates accused the Soviet Union of implementing its own form of colonialism, in Europe and the world.[78]

Nevertheless, the lasting connection made by Central and Eastern European experts between the fulfilment of health as a human right, self-determination, and anti-racism overshadowed attempts to criticize the anti-democratic nature, paternalism, and racism of state socialism. The terms in which health as a human right were discussed during the 1960s reignited the issues raised but only partially codified in the UDHR and the ICESCR. For Central and Eastern European and African representatives, discrimination could be eliminated through the development of state-funded national healthcare services operated by indigenous personnel that integrated curative and preventive care for all. Voinea Marinescu, the Romanian minister of health, remarked that the absence of 'a close association [between] health and socioeconomic measures' and the exclusive focus on hygiene and epidemic control had internationally distorted the very idea of public health.[79] The debate about apartheid in 1964–65 was framed by socialist delegates at the WHO within a broader critique of global inequalities fostered by colonialism and Western hegemony.

South Africa's voting rights were subsequently suspended, but the country was not expelled from the organization. Some states, such as Norway, represented by Karl Evang, one of the founding fathers of the WHO, vociferously critiqued apartheid but remained wary of modifying the Constitution with a view to the expulsion of a member state, seeing it as a breach of the principle of universality.[80] Interestingly, the Central Committee of the Romanian Communist Party was similarly apprehensive about establishing a precedent through the exclusion of South Africa, in so far as it worried about its own autonomy within the socialist camp. At the 1965 WHA, the Romanian delegation was instructed not to make

---

[76] Ibid., 447, 450.
[77] Ibid., 452.
[78] WHO, no. 111, 14th WHA, Part II: Plenary Meetings: Verbatim Records, New Delhi, 7–24 February 1961, 321.
[79] WHO, no. 119, 15th WHA, Part II: Plenary Meetings: Verbatim Records Geneva, 8–25 February 1962, 80–81.
[80] WHO, no. 144, 18th WHA, Part II: Plenary Meetings: Verbatim Records, Geneva, 4–21 May 1965, 452–53. In 1961, invoking universality, Karl Evang supported a draft resolution that called for the membership of the People's Republic of China, the Democratic Republic of Vietnam and the Democratic People's Republic of Korea.

any statement on the matter, but to support the position of African countries if their resolution came to a vote.[81] The latter passed as WHA17.50, leading to the suspension of South Africa from the WHO and marking a watershed. Along with resolution WHA15.48 from 1961 (see above), the document confirmed the fusion between health, self-determination, and anti-racism. It revealed a new balance of power at the WHO: the West against a loose coalition of state socialist representatives and their allies in Africa, Asia, and Latin America.

The 1970s: A Revolution in Health

As anti-racism and anticolonialism reinforced Central and Eastern European 'protagonism' in global debates about health as a human right, state socialist regimes were able to push for a new consensus about national health services at the WHO. In the context of the failure of the global eradication of malaria, a programme heavily supported by the United States and the most widely touted WHO initiative since the mid-1950s, the socialist variant of epidemiological control integrated into state-managed basic health services accessible to all made headway on the organization's agenda. Building on experience on the ground in South America, Africa, and Asia, a new majority spearheaded by state socialist delegates became vocal about paring the struggle against disease with an embedding of health as a human right through state-engineered reforms. This development was part of the ascendence of social and economic rights as vehicles for the struggle against colonialism and racial discrimination, a phenomenon epitomized by the International Year of Human Rights in 1968.[82]

By the late 1960s, the comprehensive vision for health as a human right that had been articulated by Andrija Štampar in his presidential address at the first WHA in 1948 had returned to the forefront of global politics. The resurgence of both the socio-economic contexts of disease and the role of the state in medical access became official as state socialist countries were in a position to implement the principles lost in the drafting of the UDHR and the ICESCR at the WHO. During the 1970 WHA, the Soviet Union took the lead in proposing a draft resolution on basic principles for the development of national health services. The final document (resolution WHA23.61) passed with the support of Bulgaria, Cuba, Czechoslovakia, France, Hungary, Jamaica, Mongolia, Poland, Romania, and the United Kingdom—each of which either had a socialist health system or a national healthcare system that was predominantly under state control. Lastly, Jamaica was a state at the forefront of human rights advocacy during the 1960s. The resolution

---

[81] Arhivele Naționale Istorice Centrale, Comitetul Central al Partidului Comunist Român, Cancelarie, file no. 56, 19 April 1965, 75.
[82] Whelan, *Indivisible Human Rights*, 149.

argued, echoing debates during the drafting of the UDHR and the ICESCR, for 'the responsibility of the state and society for the protection of health of the population', 'the establishment of a nation-wide system of health services based on a general national plan', and 'the provision for the whole population of the country of the highest possible level of skilled, universally available preventive and curative medical care'.[83] The final resolution did not invoke the UDHR or the ICESCR, weakening the document's function as an international law instrument. The ICESCR had not yet entered into force, and the UDHR was likely deemed an unsatisfactory precedent in terms of enforcing health as a human right.

The main guidelines of resolution WHA23.61 were initially discussed among the participants at the 'Seminar on the Realization of Economic and Social Rights Contained in the Universal Declaration of Human Rights' organized in Warsaw in August 1967. A UN report underlined that the participants agreed on a minimum of healthcare provision, basically Article 12 of the ICESCR.[84] It also emphasized the need for the consolidation of national health services to overcome discrimination based on income, rural versus urban differences, and state budget capacities. This aspirational interpretation of health as a human right materialized in WHA23.61. Moreover, through WHA23.61, the WHO marked its involvement in the UN Decade for Action to Combat Racism and Racial Discrimination (1973–83). As part of the WHO's participation within the UN Decade, Bulgarian psychologist Assen Jablensky coordinated the organization's transcultural research project on mental health and apartheid.[85]

Resolution WHA23.61 signalled a new phase in Cold War dynamics at the WHO. Adopted at the height of détente in Europe, countries such as France and the United Kingdom, which had since the 1940s accepted the importance of state involvement in the fulfilment of health as a human right, were now less reluctant to internationalize this principle as they sought to move away from their colonial past. In addition, WHA23.61's focus on nationwide systems of health services that integrated preventive and curative medicine also constituted an implicit acknowledgement of the failure of WHO-USAID health planning programmes in Africa during the 1960s. The implementation of US-funded WHO plans in Gabon, Mali, Niger, Sierra Leone, and Liberia, with the goal of building up medical services through the expansion of specific disease programmes, had made little progress.[86] Central and Eastern European delegates, along with colleagues from Africa

---

[83] WHO, WHA23.61, Basic Principles for the Development of National Health Services, 1–2.

[84] 'The basic health law of a country should cover: maternal and child health care, nutrition, communicable diseases control, environmental sanitation, health education, mental health and occupation health services.' UN, Division of Human Rights, ST/TAO/HR/31, Seminar on the Realization of Economic and Social Rights Contained in the Universal Declaration of Human Rights, Warsaw, 15–28 August 1967, 19.

[85] Meier, *The Highest Attainable Standard*, 147–49.

[86] John Manton and Martin Gorsky, 'Health Planning in 1960s Africa: International Health Organisations and the Post-Colonial State', *Medical History* 62, no. 4 (2018): 425–48.

and Latin America, insisted on the prioritization of state-funded national health services without making it dependent on a focus on specific diseases (such as malaria).[87]

The pendulum of global politics had officially swung back to a capacious interpretation of health as a human right embedded in policymaking targeting multiple sectors of governance. During the debates over WHA23.61, Soviet Deputy Minister of Health Dmitry Venediktov[88] highlighted that the resolution advanced a notion of 'public health [...] as a whole immense complex of economic, social, political, medical, therapeutic, preventive and other measures which human society in any country and at any stage in its development uses to protect and continuously improve the health of each individual and of society'.[89] His intervention rebuked the US attempt to narrow the focus onto the medical profession rather than the whole range of health services.[90] The consensus reached during the 1970 WHA was ultimately possible because the majority of countries, regardless of ideological outlook, had embraced a collective understanding of health that favoured political decisions on the national and international implementation of social and economic rights.

Four years later, the WHO Executive Board issued a memorandum on 'Health Aspects of Human Rights in the Light of Developments in Biology and Medicine'. The document acknowledged the international entrenchment of health as a human right: namely 'the right to healthcare [...] legally enforceable in that a legal duty to provide such care can be created and applied to individuals and collectivities'.[91] The memorandum noted that state socialist countries had consolidated their constitutional provisions related to this right, exemplified by the new Constitution of the German Democratic Republic (GDR) promulgated in 1968. That same year, the International Year of Human Rights, Eastern European countries ratified the ICESCR. From the late 1960s until the early 1970s, the GDR, the USSR, Hungary, Poland, Bulgaria, and Czechoslovakia each drafted constitutional amendments or special laws that universalized access to health services. This national codification of international law ostensibly confirmed these states' pioneering role in the implementation of health as a human right. However, the global recession and subsequent severe economic crisis that hit these countries during the second half of

---

[87] WHO, WHA20.14, Malaria Eradication Program, 17 May 1967, 1–2.
[88] Dmitry Venediktov played a central role in the organization of the global conference on primary healthcare in Alma-Ata (see below). Anne-Emanuelle Birn and Nikolai Krementsov, '"Socialising" Primary Care? The Soviet Union, WHO and the 1978 Alma-Ata Conference', *BMJ Global Health* 3, Suppl. 3 (2018): 5, 8–10.
[89] WHO, no. 185, 23rd WHA, Part II: Plenary Meetings: Verbatim Records, Geneva 5–22, May 1970, 204.
[90] Ibid., 206.
[91] WHO, Executive Board, EB55/41, 'Health Aspects of Human Rights in the Light of Scientific and Technological Developments', 5 December 1974, 5.

the 1970s generated a growing chasm between the legal framework and the local reality of crumbling medical services.[92]

Nevertheless, by 1974, Central and Eastern Europeans had played a crucial role in the return of the 1930s and 1940s consensus on health as a human right embedded in social medicine and state intervention. One report issued by the WHO Executive Board acknowledged that 'the right [...] has to be considered in relation to a number of other rights, such as the right to food, clothing, and housing, and the right to freedom and privacy'.[93] The new reality was highlighted in a 1974 report by UN Special Rapporteur Manouchehr Ganji (Iran), who was in charge of the preparation of a comprehensive study on conditions of economic, social, and cultural rights,[94] which underlined the global consensus on the centrality of healthcare in welfare states (socialist or capitalist economies), while also noting the growing inequalities in the field between developed and 'less developed countries'.[95]

Contemporaries thus characterized the 1970s as 'a health revolution'.[96] International debates became tied to social justice ideals driven by both the sharpening conflict between North and South and criticism against the disparities, depersonalization, and overspecialization intrinsic to modern medicine. A new paradigm gained traction in the second half of the decade: primary healthcare. The key ideas behind it were: the focus on health technology reflective of the needs and possibilities of specific communities; opposition to medical elitism; health as tool for social-economic development; treatment for underprivileged people and regions; and community participation in medical care along with consideration of traditional medicine.[97] Devised specifically for postcolonial countries, it was also meant to democratize medical practice in the North. In 1978, the international conference on primary healthcare took place in Alma-Ata, the capital of then SSR of Kazakhstan. Some authors have argued that primary healthcare was not developed from the standpoint of human rights.[98] Their position overlooks the genealogy of the ideas promoted by the Declaration that framed health as a human right as embedded in social justice ideals and state action. Through the WHA resolutions discussed in this chapter, the right had evolved towards a collective meaning reflecting the revival of the welfare ideals from the 1940s.

---

[92] Kaser, *Health Care*, 270.
[93] WHO, EB55/41, 'Health Aspects', 6.
[94] In spring 1968, representatives from eighty-four states, four regional organizations, and fifty-seven non governmental organizations met in Tehran for the first UN International Conference on Human Rights.
[95] UN ECOSOC, E/CN.4/1131, Manouchehr Ganji, 'The Widening Gap: A Study of the Realization of Economic, Social and Cultural Rights', 18 January 1974, 6, 26.
[96] Meier, 'Global Health Governance', 39.
[97] Marcos Cueto, 'The Origins of Primary Health Care and Selective Primary Health Care', *America Journal of Public Health* 94, no. 11 (2004): 1867–68.
[98] Alison Lakin, 'The World Health Organization and the Right to Health', PhD dissertation, King's College, London (2010).

Despite their prominent role in the transformation of the international meaning of health as a human right, Central and Eastern European support for the Alma-Ata Declaration remained ambivalent.[99] While state socialist regimes publicly endorsed the document, behind the scenes, they criticized primary healthcare, considering it an outgrowth of the popularity of China's healthcare system tailored to low-income countries, which relied on 'barefoot doctors' and traditional medicine.[100] These Chinese policies drew on Mao Zedong's critique of socialist inequalities: it was a programme of training 'half-peasants, half-doctors' operating in cooperative medical service stations that offered curative and preventive care for agricultural collectives and linked these communities to urban facilities.[101] Realpolitik and a growing distance from the Global South tempered the willingness of Eastern Europeans to push for the consolidation of the Alma-Ata Declaration as an international law document during the 1980s.

In the final decade of the Cold War, state socialist lobbying for health as a human right turned increasingly hollow at home and at the WHO. Eastern European governments failed to live up to their self-proclaimed status as the right's champions. Health became a significant theme in dissident critiques of state socialism. In 1984, Charta 77 issued a statement condemning the 'deplorable condition of public health services' in Czechoslovakia.[102] Health as a human right had taken a road similar to other rights discourses developed in state socialist settings: it was 'internationalized and in turn re-domesticated by citizens seeking to challenge the state on its own terms through a complex interplay of the global and the local'.[103]

At the WHO, Central and Eastern Europeans wavered in their financial support at a time when the World Bank took over leadership in global health politics. Romania even stopped paying annual dues altogether, reducing its activity at the WHO to a minimum in the late 1980s.[104] There was scant opposition against a 1987 World Bank report that returned to the idea of public health as solely an activity targeting infectious diseases and argued that individual access to medical services was 'a private good'.[105] As most state socialist regimes struggled with massive foreign debt, their representatives had little to say about the structural adjustment

---

[99] Birn and Krementsov, '"Socialising" Primary Care?', 1–15; Walter Bruchhausen and Iris Borowy, 'Primary Health Care and Foreign Aid: A Tale of Two Germanys', *Journal of the History of Medicine and Allied Sciences* 79, no. 1 (2024): 85–86.

[100] Ministerul Sănătății, Direcția Coordonare și Control, Serviciul Relații Externe, file 8/1984, 'A 25-a Consfătuire a miniștrilor sănătății din țările socialiste, 20-22 martie Karlovy-Vary', 3.

[101] Xiaoping Fang, *Barefoot Doctors and Western Medicine in China* (Rochester, NY: University of Rochester Press, 2012).

[102] HU OSA (Open Society Archives) 300-30-7, Box 351, RAD Background Report/161, Sophia Miskiewicz, 'Health Services in Eastern Europe', 10 November 1986, 15–19.

[103] Ned Richardson-Little, Hella Dietz, and James Mark, 'New Perspectives on Socialism and Human Rights in East Central Europe since 1945', *East Central Europe* 46, no. 2–3 (2019): 172.

[104] WHO, WHA38.13, Members in arrears in the payment of their contributions to an extent which may invoke Article 7 of the Constitution, 14 May 1985, 1.

[105] Gorsky and Sirrs, 'Universal Health Coverage', 83.

programmes implemented by the World Bank in the Global South, which unleashed drastic cuts in health spending and a wave of privatization. The cardinal principles upon which health as a human right had ascended during the 1960s and the 1970s—state intervention and a capacious notion of public health—collapsed under the weight of neoliberal globalization and state socialist financial crises.

Conclusion

The participation of state socialist representatives in debates over health as a human right and their alliances with experts from Latin America or various newly independent countries mirrored the entanglement between the Cold War and decolonization. The pre-1945 consensus on social medicine and state duty to healthcare created solidarities that ran counter to East–West antagonisms. These principles, not fully present within the UDHR and the ICESCR, materialized in the later WHA resolutions. Central and Eastern European delegates at the WHO created a new global majority in favour of national health services available to all without any discrimination based on race, social status, gender, or religion.

This story is by no means teleological: for most of the 1950s, health as a human right was underdefined, fleshed out only during the 1960s. Though the 1970s brought a flurry of international activity in terms of the consolidation of this right, it once again experienced a downturn in the 1980s with the neoliberal sidelining of the WHO in favour of the World Bank. State socialist involvement in the promotion of health as a human right shows that the crafting of international law must be analysed at the juncture of multiple historical processes: the Cold War, decolonization, and globalization as well as entangled national and regional developments. Central and Eastern European interventions during the drafting of the UDHR and the ICESCR, as well as at the WHO, reveal the consolidating of health by making it interdependent with self-determination, critiques of racial discrimination, and the advocacy for adequate standards of living. This approach, combined with the growing profile of Central and Eastern Europe at the WHO, allowed experts from the region to spearhead global debates over health as a human right. The development of this right during the Cold War and decolonization set the foundation for its revitalization during the 2000s.

In August 2000, the Committee for Economic, Social and Cultural Rights (CESCR), created by the UN Economic and Social Council in 1986, issued General Comment 14 to clarify Article 12 of the ICESCR, which re-affirmed the central tenets advocated for by state socialists before 1989: the state's responsibility for the highest attainable standard of health; its embedding in social-economic contexts; and its interdependence with other human rights, 'beginning in preventive and curative health care and expansively encompassing underlying rights to food, housing, work, education, human dignity, life, non-discrimination, equality, prohibitions against torture, privacy, access to information, and the freedoms of association, assembly, and movement'.[106]

Reflecting the post-1989 liberal hegemony, the General Comment balanced collective and individual understandings of health as a human right. Yet, the tenets taken up since the late 1940s by state socialist experts at the WHO and the UN, in concert with delegates from Latin America, Africa, and social-democratic Europe, constituted the backbone of the CESCR's intervention. The robust support by Central and Eastern European representatives of health as a human right in combination with anti-racism and self-determination placed this right at the centre of debates about governance and emancipation—a conceptual legacy for the twentieth-first century.

Acknowledgements

This research was supported by the Romanian National Authority for Scientific Research and Innovation, CNCS-UEFISCDI, project number PN-III-P4-ID-PCE-2020-1337.

---

[106] Benjamin Mason Meier and Lawrence Gostin, 'Introduction: Global Health and Human Rights', in *Human Rights in Global Health: Rights-Based Governance for a Globalizing World*, edited by Benjamin Mason Meier and Lawrence Gostin (Oxford: Oxford University Press, 2018), 8, 24–25.

8
Protecting Culture Through International Law in the Postwar World

Nelly Bekus

Introduction

Histories of international cultural heritage protection have generally focused on the liberal European trajectories of heritage evolution in the twentieth century and tended to trace the Western roots of cultural globalization.[1] In recent years, however, the scholarship has begun to acknowledge the importance of non-Western perspectives on heritage and explore the role of actors from other world regions in shaping the global field of heritage protection.[2] Studies of diverse heritage regimes across the globe, however, have often remained confined to national frameworks that accentuate the linkages between national identities and cultural patrimonies, which in turn serve as important instruments in constituting and reasserting specific visions of a nation's histories, memories, and traditions.[3]

The rapid development of cultural heritage protection after the Second World War provided important instruments for the re-evaluation of the past under the new conditions arising from unprecedented global interdependence as multiple spheres of national life acquired a significant international dimension—the symptoms of which Glenda Sluga has called 'an apogee of internationalism in the age of nationalism'.[4] Alongside deepening economic integration, the establishment of various international organizations and the rise of international lawmaking, cultural internationalism became an important manifestation of interconnectedness and cooperation between countries and people.[5] The international protection of

---

[1] Kevin Walsh, *Representation of the Past: Museums and Heritage in the Postmodern World* (London: Routledge, 1992); Astrid Swenson, *The Rise of Heritage: Preserving the Past in France, Germany and England* (Cambridge: Cambridge University Press, 2013).
[2] Tim Winter, 'Beyond Eurocentrism? Heritage Conservation and the Politics of Difference', *International Journal of Heritage Studies* 20, no. 2 (2014): 12–137; Paul Betts and Corey Ross (eds.), *Modern Historical Preservation—Towards a Global Perspective* (Oxford: Oxford University Press, 2015).
[3] David Lowenthal, *The Heritage Crusade and the Spoils of History* (Cambridge: Cambridge University Press, 2012).
[4] Glenda Sluga, *Internationalism in the Age of Nationalism* (Philadelphia: University of Pennsylvania Press, 2013).
[5] Nelly Bekus and Kate Cowcher, 'Socialism, Heritage and Internationalism after 1945: The Second World and Beyond', *International Journal of Heritage Studies* 26, no. 12 (2020): 1123–31.

culture, in this context, also emerged as an important instrument in helping to further the agenda of 'governing the world'.[6] The legacy of the devastations of the Second World War prompted the rise of new initiatives committed to preserving cultural properties, whereby culture came to be seen as an integral part of society, identity, and human rights. Against this backdrop, the protection of cultural property and culture in a broader sense entered international law as a component of regulations governing the conduct of warfare.

The purpose of this chapter is to investigate the backstage discussions conducted in the process of preparing and drafting the relevant international documents and to reconstruct the motivations informing the positions of the socialist states and their contribution to the internal debates. Some of these countries, including Czechoslovakia, Poland, Yugoslavia, and the USSR, were victims of Nazi aggression and experienced the extensive destruction of cultural properties during the Second World as part of a racialized Nazi colonial project aimed at the obliteration of their culture, identity, and nationhood. As this chapter demonstrates, the position of socialist states on new legal tools for the protection of culture was informed by these experiences and the aspiration to secure the survival of national culture in future conflicts. At international venues, such as the United Nations (UN), these ideas morphed into socialist ideological agendas as other states ruled by the communist parties (with the support of the USSR) and certain Western countries that had experienced cultural losses during the Nazi occupation backed the proposals. In this way, Central and Eastern European countries like Bulgaria, Hungary, and Romania, all formerly allied with Nazi Germany, could reinvent themselves on the international stage through their association with progressive ideas endorsed by socialist doctrine. The contribution of socialist states was driven by strong opposition to racism and colonial policies, promotion of equality among nations, protection of minority rights, and defence of group cultural rights as opposed to the individual human rights that remained central to liberal conceptions.

This chapter begins with a discussion of the Nuremberg Trials and demonstrates how the limited consideration of the Polish and Czechoslovakian experience of the Nazi occupation was rectified through the establishment of separate, national, war crimes trials. It then considers the role played by socialist states in negotiating the UN Convention on the Prevention and Punishment of the Crime of Genocide in 1948. Integrating cultural genocide within the definition of the 'crime of crimes' advocated by socialist representatives addressed the experiences of many countries under Nazi rule, but the proposal came under attack for its potential to intervene in the domestic affairs and policies of Western states towards ethnic minorities and colonized people. Finally, the analysis moves to an examination of the drafting of the 1954 Hague Convention for the Protection of Cultural

---

[6] Lucia Allais, *Designs of Destruction: The Making of Monuments in the Twentieth Century* (Chicago, IL: University of Chicago Press, 2018), 14.

Property in the Event of Armed Conflict, focusing on the motives and arguments presented by the socialist countries. As this chapter demonstrates, the emergence of the Cold War and the rivalry between the great powers prevented the adoption of the most advanced measures to protect cultural properties, such as expanding the territorial reach of the Convention to colonies, prohibiting weapons of mass destruction, and removing the so-called 'military necessity clause', which provided a wide scope to excuse destructive tactics.

The chapter focuses on the first decade after the Second World War, when significant shifts occurred in world affairs, resulting from military actions such as the US aggression in Korea in 1950, the world's re-alignment of forces as the USSR approached nuclear capacity in 1949, and the admission of new non-aligned states to the UN in the mid-1950s. While the former accelerated the transition from an anti-Hitler coalition towards the new Cold War paradigm, placing the tensions between the great powers at the forefront of many debates, the latter highlighted the importance of decolonization, national liberation struggles, and the liquidation of colonialism in various spheres. In this context, socialist states emerged as key contributors to the development of the protection of cultural heritage in international law. Their agenda was formulated at the intersection of progressive ideas—antifascism, anti-racism, and anticolonialism—and a new era of realpolitik.[7]

The internationalization of heritage protection after the Second World War was linked to the nascent political agendas and foreign policies of the states involved. The devastation suffered by the USSR and other Eastern European countries fostered the perception of culture as inherently linked to national identity on the one hand, and international security and state sovereignty on the other hand.[8] In this context, the discourse regarding the protection of culture formed an important field within official state socialist cultural diplomacy in their numerous 'struggle for peace' initiatives.[9] The opposition between capitalist West and socialist East facilitated a growing awareness of the universal value of heritage, which required international protection and, paradoxically, created a demand for cultural engagement and cooperation between ideological rivals. The process of dealing with multiple challenges and drafting major international documents at that time revealed a complex interplay between what could be seen as 'selfish motives' and 'idealistic aspirations' in the creation of a new international order. The importance of culture,

---

[7] Raluca Grosescu and Richardson-Little, Ned, 'Revisiting State Socialist Approaches to International Criminal and Humanitarian Law: An Introduction', *Journal of the History of International Law* 21, no. 2 (2019): 163.

[8] Nelly Bekus, 'Transnational Circulation of Cultural Form: Multiple Agencies of Heritage Making', *International Journal of Heritage Studies* 26, no. 12 (2020):1148–65; Corinne Geering, 'Protecting the Heritage of Humanity in the Cold War: UNESCO, the Soviet Union and Sites of Universal Value, 1945–1970s', *International Journal of Heritage Studies* 26, no. 12 (2020): 1132–47.

[9] Corinne Geering, *Building a Common Past: World Heritage in Russia under Transformation 1965–2000* (Göttingen: Vandenhoeck & Ruprecht, 2019).

while inherently present in a wide range of discussions on various regulations and documents, was often overshadowed by other considerations.

Culture in the Context of War Crimes Prosecution after the Second World War

Two Eastern European countries, Czechoslovakia and Poland, endured the longest occupations by the Nazi regime after the former was annexed in 1938/39 (with some parts initially occupied by Hungary and Poland) and the latter was occupied after the German and Soviet invasions in 1939. The war waged by Nazi Germany in Eastern Europe was accompanied by cultural expansionism, including the Germanization of certain populations in some of the occupied countries, including Czechoslovakia and Western Poland. Poles and Czechs, however, were classified differently within Nazi racial ideology, with its notion of 'the relative national worth of Czechs' and 'national worthlessness of Poles'.[10] In practice, it meant that in Czechoslovakia, both land and people were to be Germanized, while in Poland, the Nazis were mainly interested in appropriating the land. In view of these differences, Nazi policy did not aim to destroy Czech cultural monuments due to their alleged cultural closeness to Germans, while the looting of artistic objects mainly involved Jewish property.[11] Polish national culture, by contrast, was seen by the Nazis as worthless, and their policy aimed to complete the erasure of Polish culture and encompassed the extensive plundering of art treasures and museum collections, as well as the destruction of cities, libraries, and archives. And yet, the conversion of Czechs into Germans essentially meant the destruction of Czech and Slovak national identity by cultivating its 'Aryan dimension' and diminishing the distinctiveness of Czech and Slovak culture. In effect, the Nazi policies were seen by Czechoslovakian elites as extremely damaging to their national cultures and traditions, reflected in the retribution decrees adopted by the postwar government.

Polish and Czechoslovak governments in exile began discussing the punishment for Nazi crimes long before the end of the War. Documenting cultural destruction and looting begun in Poland as early as the first days of occupation, when the government in exile published a book, *The German Invasion of Poland: Polish Black Book* (1939), followed by the 1941 volume *The German New Order in Poland*.[12] After the War, evidence of Nazi crimes collected by the Polish antifascist

---

[10] Alan E. Steinweis, 'German Cultural Imperialism in Czechoslovakia and Poland, 1938–1945', *The International History Review* 13, no. 3 (1991): 469

[11] Mass atrocities and destruction occurred in Czechoslovakia as retaliation for antifascist resistance, such as the case of Lidice, which was used as evidence at the Nuremberg Trials. The loss of cultural and historical monuments in Czechoslovakia occurred mainly during the liberation battle in 1945.

[12] *The German Invasion of Poland: Polish Black Book* (London: Hutchinson & Co, 1939).

underground movement was used by the government in exile and the state Commission to publicize the scale of Nazi crimes and the destruction of cultural properties in order to seek justice.[13] In 1942, the Czechoslovak government in exile and its Polish counterpart signed the 'Joint Czechoslovak-Polish Declaration on the punishment of crimes committed by Germans in occupied territories', publicly declaring their commitment to holding the Nazis accountable for their crimes.[14] Known as the 'St James Declaration' it was also signed by the United States and Great Britain in 1943 and formed the UN War Crimes Commission (UNWCC), comprising the nine governments in exile (including Czechoslovakia, Poland, Yugoslavia, and the Benelux countries, among others), Great Britain, the United States, China, Australia, and India.[15] The contribution of smaller nations united against Nazi Germany and Japan to developing legal questions relating to war crimes is often overlooked in the scholarship.[16] According to Telford Taylor, one of the American prosecutors during the Nuremberg Trials, the fact that the majority of the UNWCC's members represented shadow governments that might or might not be restored to power made the Commission politically weak.[17] Nonetheless, the debates that took place at the UNWCC surrounding the definition of crimes—such as crimes against humanity, the war of aggression, and crimes against minorities committed by a state against their own nationals—made an important contribution to the preparation of the Nuremberg and Tokyo Trials.

Two legal scholars and jurists from Czechoslovakia, Bohuslav Ečer and Egon Schwelb, played a leading role in drafting international norms on the capture and punishment of war criminals. Although the Soviet Union did not join the UNWCC, Ečer prepared the report based on Soviet jurist Aron Trainin's *Criminal Responsibility of the Hitlerites* and contributed to the dissemination of Trainin's ideas on the prosecution of war criminals among UNWCC members (see also Michelle Penn, Chapter 4 in this volume).[18] Ečer was the first to argue that Nazi leaders be tried for the crime of 'aggressive war', a charge that later became central to the Nuremberg Trials, during which he would lead the Czechoslovakian delegation.[19]

---

[13] Paul Betts, *Ruin and Renewal: Civilising Europe After the Second World War* (London: Profile Books, 2021), 233–34.
[14] Benjamin Frommer, *National Cleansing: Retribution against Nazi Collaborators in Postwar Czechoslovakia* (Cambridge: Cambridge University Press, 2005), 66.
[15] After the name of the location in London where the discussions were held.
[16] Kerstin von Lingen, 'Setting the Path for UNWCC: The Representation of European Exile Governments on LIA and Cambridge Commission, 1941–1944', *International Criminal Law Forum* 25, no. 1 (2014): 45–76.
[17] Telford Taylor, *The Anatomy of the Nuremberg Trials* (New York: Alfred A. Knopf, 1992), 26–27.
[18] Valentyna Polunina, 'The Absent Player: The Soviet Union and the Genesis of the Allied War Crimes Trials Program, 1941–1943', *Journal of the History of International Law (Revue d'histoire du droit international)* 24, no. 3 (2022): 354–72; Francine Hirsch, *Soviet Judgement at Nuremberg: A New History of the International Military Tribunal after World War II* (Oxford: Oxford University Press, 2020), 35–37.
[19] Arieh J. Kochavi, *Prelude to Nuremberg: Allied War Crimes Policy and the Question of Punishment* (Chapel Hill, NC: University of North Caroline Press, 1998), 97–100.

The Czechoslovakian national retribution trials began two months before the International Military Tribunal (IMT) at Nuremberg as a result of the 'Great Decree', signed in June 1945 by the re-established Czechoslovakian government, which outlined the punishment of Nazi criminals, traitors, and their accomplices. In response to the Nazi cultural policy of Germanization, the Decree introduced criminal responsibility for 'crimes against the state', which, among others, included 'the intent to subvert the moral, national, or state consciousness of the Czech people'.[20] This idea was further reiterated in the Decree 'On the Punishment of Certain Offences against National Honour' (1945), which introduced punishment for 'unbecoming behaviour insulting to the national sentiments of the Czech and Slovak people'.[21] Although criticized for its vagueness and lack of clear definitions, the decrees nonetheless served as a legal foundation for both prosecuting those who engaged in Germanization policies during the occupation and legitimizing the postwar national cleansing and mass deportation of ethnic Germans. As Benjamin Frommer demonstrates, despite various elements that went against traditional Western jurisprudence (such as its retroactivity, the ban on appeals, and summary executions), the Czechoslovakian retribution decrees were not introduced in response to Soviet pressure but originated in a draft prepared on behalf of the government in exile by a group of Czech legal scholars based in London who had been delegated to the UNWCC and the Nuremberg Tribunal.[22]

In the Nuremberg indictments, the destruction of culture was mentioned only a handful of times. Thus, Part Three (On War Crimes) had a section on looting and destruction of works of art. The indictment referred to looted museums in France, Belgium, Norway, the Netherlands, and Luxemburg. In the so-called 'Eastern countries', the examples used in the text came only from the Soviet Union and Czechoslovakia.[23] While mass destruction was illustrated through the cases of Oradour-sur-Glane in France, Lidice in Czechoslovakia, and a list of cities in the Soviet Union, paradoxically, no examples from Poland were mentioned.[24] The proceedings were designed to ensure that only the violent acts of selected German perpetrators would be assessed and punished. No effort was made to address the predicates of their violence, or its wider implications, including those associated with the destruction of culture and identity.[25]

Soviet legal scholar Aron Trainin, who was involved in the Nuremberg Trials, proposed a classification of different types of crimes resulting from war, which

---

[20] See Appendix I in Frommer, *National Cleansing*, 348–63.
[21] Ibid., 348–63.
[22] Ibid., 93.
[23] Nuremberg Trial Proceedings Vol. 1. Indictment: Count Three. *The Avalon Project: Documents in Law, History and Diplomacy*, https://avalon.law.yale.edu/imt/count3.asp, accessed 12 September 2024.
[24] 'The Polish indictment' (160 manuscript pages) was added to the evidence materials, but nothing was included in the texts of indictment.
[25] James Mark and Phil Clark, 'Not Nuremberg—Histories of Alternative Criminalisation Paradigms 1945–2021: Introduction to the Dossier', *Humanities* (forthcoming, 2024).

included the destruction and plundering of cultural treasures. In his book, *Hitlerite Responsibility under Criminal Law*, he elucidated this concept through the example of the Nazi destruction and plunder of libraries, museums, theatres, and cinemas in the Moscow region, as well as the plundering of historical and cultural treasures and cultural infrastructure in Belarus and Ukraine.[26] National cultural properties were described by Trainin as 'assets' belonging to the whole of humanity, which would later be echoed in the idea of culture as a universal value that underpinned and informed the discussions on the protection of culture in the 1954 Hague Convention.

The Polish representatives actively lobbied both the Soviets and the American occupation authorities for the right to establish their own Office of Prosecution at Nuremberg, stressing the magnitude of Nazi destruction in Poland. This request was, however, rejected, and the role of the Polish delegation was ultimately limited to providing evidence to the IMT, examining pertinent documents, and questioning individuals suspected of having committed crimes on Polish soil.[27] According to Gabriel Finder and Alexander Prusin, the Western allies were sceptical of Poland's victim status and wondered whether it was now acting as a victimizer, in light of concerns about postwar Polish antisemitism, exemplified by anti-Jewish riots, and the mass expulsion of ethnic Germans.[28]

In the Polish national context, the first legislative initiatives for the prosecution of the destruction of culture were advanced in 1944. The Decree 'Concerning the punishment of fascist-Hitlerite' became the foundation for several war crimes trials.[29] In 1945, a new paragraph was added to the Decree to cover the destruction of monuments of national culture, museums, galleries, and libraries. Both during the Nuremberg Trials themselves and the major trials of leading Nazis in Polish national courts, all those convicted with reference to the destruction of culture, be it the looting of cultural goods or their destruction, were sentenced to death. At Nuremberg, the indictments of several individuals contained reference to crimes associated with the destruction of culture, including those of Wilhelm Keitel and Alfred Jodl (both responsible for destruction and looting), Hermann Goering (who stole the most valuable pieces of art for his private collection), Alfred Rosenberg (responsible for looting cultural goods across Europe, but especially in Western Europe), and Hans Frank. Paradoxically, even the official indictment against Hans

---

[26] Aron Trainin, *Ugolovnaia otvetstvennost' gitlerovtsev (Hitlerite Responsibility under Criminal Law)* (Moscow: IUrid. izd-vo, 1944), 65–67.
[27] Tadeusz Cyprian and Jerzy Sawicki, *Przed Trybunałem Świata: Refleksje, Wspomnienia, Dokumenty*, vols. I and II (Warsaw: Książka i Wiedza, 1962).
[28] Gabriel N. Finder and Alexander V. Prusin, *Justice Behind the Iron Curtain* (Toronto: University of Toronto Press, 2018), 55.
[29] Decree of 31 August 1944 'Concerning the punishment of fascist-Hitlerite criminals guilty of murder and ill-treatment of [the] civilian population and prisoners of war, and the punishment of traitors to the Polish Nation', in *Law Reports of Trials of War Criminals*, United Nations War Crimes Commission (New York: Wm. S. Hein, 1997).

Frank—the head of the General Government in Nazi-occupied Poland—did not adequately address the 'sufferings of the Polish nation'.[30]

In Poland, three trials held under the auspices of the Polish Supreme National Tribunal (SNT) included a reference to crimes against national culture in their indictments, namely those of Artur Greiser, Josef Buhler, and Ludwig Fischer. Greiser was the first person to ever be convicted of waging aggressive war (1946), and his prosecution and judgment incorporated Raphael Lemkin's wholistic understanding of genocide, which included cultural aspects.[31] As we shall see, Polish, Czechoslovakian, and Soviet representatives advocated for the integration of this conception of genocide into the 1948 UN Convention on Genocide, but their efforts proved unsuccessful. However, in Poland, during Josef Buhler's trial, the prosecution was able to accuse Buhler and the German government of actions aimed 'at the extermination of the Polish intellectual classes', 'the destruction of the cultural values, and of the Polish nation' put in effect

> by the closing of all secondary, non-technical schools, and of universities, theatres, museums, public libraries and scientific institutes, [...] the exclusion of Polish language, history and geography from the syllabus of all primary and technical schools, [...] pillage and exportation to Germany of Polish property in general, and that of Polish scientific and cultural institutions in particular.[32]

The Polish Tribunal did not attract as much publicity and international attention as expected, despite the fact that the trial of Ludwig Fischer in 1946–47 had been attended by international observers, including Telford Taylor.[33] In each of these instances, however, the cases of mass murder committed by the accused superseded the crime against culture, and it remains unclear whether these culture-related crimes affected their final sentences.

Legal scholars Leora Bilsky and Rachel Klagsbrun have argued that the prominence of cultural genocide at the SNT was intended to stress the crimes against the Polish nation, whereas a narrow focus on physical genocide would have implied the centrality of Jewish victimhood. It should be noted, however, that while some trials, like those discussed above, did indeed emphasize cultural genocide and crimes against the Polish national culture, other SNT trials integrated the Holocaust as an

---

[30] Alexander V. Prusin, 'Poland's Nuremberg: The Seven Court Cases of the Supreme National tribunal, 1946–1948', *Holocaust and Genocide Studies* 24, no. 1 (2010): 4.

[31] Mark A. Drubl, '"Germans are the Lords and Poles are the Servants": The Trial of Arthur Greiser in Poland, 1946', in *Hidden Histories of War Crimes Trials*, edited by Kevin Heller and Gerry Simpson (Oxford: Oxford Academic, 2014), 411–29.

[32] UN War Crimes Commission, 'Law-Reports of Trials of War Criminals', vol. XIV (London: HMSO, 1949), 45, https://phdn.org/archives/www.ess.uwe.ac.uk/WCC/buhler1.htm. accessed 12 September 2024.

[33] Patrycja Grzebyk, 'The Role of the Polish Supreme National Tribunal in the Development of Principles of International Criminal Law', in *Historical Origins of International Criminal Law*, vol. 2, edited by Morten Bergsmo, Cheah Wui Ling, and Yi Ping (Torkel Opsahl: Academic EPublisher, 2014).

inseparable element of the Nazi war against Polish citizens. As Gabriel Finder and Alexander Prusin demonstrated, in the trials of Amon Goth, commandant of the Kraków-Płaszów concentration camp, Auschwitz Commandant Rudolf Höss, and members of his camp's administration, the crimes against Polish Jews were a central issue.[34] Furthermore, the Polish delegation at Nuremberg advocated for both ethnic Poles and Polish Jews as Polish citizens, despite the fact that the Nuremberg Trials took place as anti-Jewish animus and violence in Poland were at their peak. In this sense, the Polish delegation at the IMT did as much as any other state entity to represent Jews as a distinct group that had suffered at the hands of the Nazis. However, most of Polish society did not share in this advocacy, denying the recognition that the Jews were equal citizens of Poland.[35]

The prosecution of Nazi criminals in the countries where the crimes had been committed also necessarily involved the extradition of Nazi criminals to these states. In the context of growing ideological hostilities and distrust towards socialist governments, the extradition of the accused from the British and American occupation zones to Poland and Czechoslovakia often proved problematic. The extradition and prosecution of criminals for the destruction of culture appeared even less likely than for comparatively more prominent crimes such as aggressive war. For the socialist states, the extradition of war criminals would have indicated a tacit international recognition of the validity of their civilian criminal justice system.[36] In practice, a number of charge files submitted by the Polish War Crimes Office to the UNWCC contained detailed information on the destruction of cultural heritage, and the majority of these files accused specific individuals of specific war crimes. But from 1945 to 1947, most requests for the extradition of Germans accused of 'committing crimes against Polish culture' were rejected or ignored by the American authorities in Germany and Austria.[37]

Ultimately, only in one case was an individual put on trial in Poland for looting art—Wilhelm Ernst von Palézieux, who was extradited from the French-occupied zone. He had succeeded Kajetan Mühlmann in the office 'In Charge of Old Art' in 1943 while also working as an art adviser to the governor-general of Poland, Hans Frank. In 1948, Palézieux received a sentence of five years imprisonment for 'taking part in plundering and exportation of works of culture and art accumulated in Poland through the centuries-long work of its generations'.[38] While the punishment appeared to be somewhat symbolic, the indictment was significant as the

---

[34] Finder and Prusin, *Justice Behind the Iron Curtain*, 126.
[35] Ibid., 99.
[36] Louisa Marie McClintock, 'Projects of Punishment in Postwar Poland: War Criminals, Collaborators, Traitors, and the (Re)construction of the Nation', PhD thesis, University of Chicago, Department of Sociology (2015), 59.
[37] Michael Fleming, *In the Shadow of the Holocaust: Poland, the United Nations War Crimes Commission, and the Search for Justice* (Cambridge: Cambridge University Press, 2022), 254.
[38] Wyrok Sądu Okręgowego w Krakowie z 10 July 1948. See Stanisław Nahlik, *Grabież Dzieł Sztuki* (Wrocław-Kraków: Zakład Narodowy im. Ossolińskich, 1958), 319.

only case in the history of postwar trials in Poland in which the crime and the sentence were exclusively linked to the looting of cultural property during the War. Paradoxically, however, the sentence considered the looting and export of stolen cultural property, while the destruction of cultural property did not appear as a separate charge.

The Polish trials had broader international significance, establishing a precedent for the punishment of Nazi criminals for plundering and looting art. Furthermore, they were the first to deploy not only the concept of cultural genocide in the prosecution of crimes committed on Polish territory but also the terminology of 'genocide' in indictments of Nazi criminals.[39] Ultimately, the Czech and Slovakian experience of cultural denigration in the process of Germanization and the Polish experience of cultural loss and the struggle over the inclusion of culture in postwar justice shaped the positions of both countries in discussions on the drafts of the 1948 Genocide Convention and the 1954 Hague Convention.

Cultural Genocide: A Rejected International Law Project

One of the first indications of the emergence of a different approach to culture in international humanitarian law became visible in the heated debates surrounding the concept of cultural genocide in the Convention on the Prevention of Genocide. In this context, the ways in which various countries reflected on the experience of the Second World War shaped their understanding of what required protection and how culture was positioned within that definition.

For Raphael Lemkin, the cultural aspect was at the centre of the concept of genocide—a term he coined. In his *Axis Rule in Occupied Europe*, Lemkin argued for a broader understanding of genocide, which not only encompassed the immediate destruction of a nation through mass killings but also a coordinated plan of actions aimed at the destruction of the essential foundations of the life of national groups, with the intent to annihilate those groups.[40] This definition was introduced in the initial drafts of the UN Genocide Convention and, as late as April 1948, the idea of cultural genocide was still being discussed at the meetings of the UN Ad Hoc Committee, which included China, France, Lebanon, Poland, the Soviet Union, the United States, and Venezuela. At that point, Article III (cultural genocide) of the Draft included:

---

[39] The American Tribunal also deployed 'genocide', but it was cited as the 'prime illustration' of a crime against humanity. See Mathew Lippman, 'The Convention on the Prevention and Punishment of the Crime of Genocide: Fifty Years Later', *Arizona Journal of International and Comparative Law* 15, no. 2 (1998): 415–514.

[40] Raphael Lemkin, *Axis Rule in Occupied Europe. Laws of Occupation, Analysis of Government, Proposals for redress* (Washington DC: Carnegie Endowment for International Peace, 1944), 79

any deliberate act committed with the intent to destroy the language, religion or culture of a national, racial or religious group on grounds of the national or racial origins or the religious belief of its members such as prohibiting the use of the language of the group and destroying or preventing the use of libraries, museums, schools, places of worship or other cultural institutions of the group.[41]

In the version of the Genocide Convention that was eventually codified, however, most of the references to cultural genocide were removed, except for the 'forcible transfer of children of the group to another group'.[42]

The dynamics of the debate revealed the interplay between the 'self-centred interests' and the 'idealistic aspiration' of the participating states. Indeed, countries that had experienced what they considered to be cultural genocide during the Second World War, including Poland, Czechoslovakia, the Soviet Union, sought to incorporate this category in the Convention claiming that 'the destruction of the group' could be achieved by the destruction of the culture of this group.[43] In the preparation of one draft that interpreted cultural genocide as a loss of cultural rights, Poland and the USSR were joined by China, Lebanon, and Venezuela.[44] In contrast, the head of the US delegation and Chair of the Ad Hoc Committee John Maktos stressed that the General Assembly resolution on genocide had been inspired by the systemic massacre of Jews by Nazi authorities, which should thus be reflected in the legal concept: as such, the definition of the crime should be limited to barbarous acts committed against individuals.[45]

The draft Convention did, however, initially include crimes that were committed not only in the context of war but also in peacetime—likely as a critique of both Nuremberg and Tokyo trials for focusing on prosecuting crimes against humanity that were directly connected to inter-state aggression, thus preventing postwar criminal justice from being used as a tool by anticolonial activists to prosecute colonial crimes.[46] The United States, France, and the Netherlands, rejected the inclusion of cultural genocide on the grounds that it would invite the risk of political interference in the domestic affairs of states concerning the protection of minorities.[47] In response to the growing decolonization movement in Asia and

---

[41] Ad Hoc Committee Draft, Second Draft of the Genocide Convention Prepared by the Ad Hoc Committee of the Economic and Social Council (ECOSOC), meeting between 5 April 1948 and 10 May 1948, UN Doc E/AC.25/SR.1 to 28.
[42] UN General Assembly Resolution 260, Convention on the Prevention and Punishment of the Crime of Genocide, 9 December 1948 (UN Doc A/RES/260(III))
[43] Abtahi Hirad and Philippa Webb (eds.), *The Genocide Convention: The Travaux Préparatoires* (Leiden: Martinus Nijhoff, 2008), 19, 1516.
[44] Ibid., 892.
[45] Ibid., 727.
[46] Boyd van Dijk, *Preparing for War: The Making of the 1949 Geneva Conventions* (Oxford: Oxford Academic), 264; Milinda Banerjee, 'India's "Subaltern Elites" and the Tokyo Trial', in *Transcultural Justice at the Tokyo Tribunal*, edited by Kerstin von Lingen (Leiden: Brill, 2018), 262–83.
[47] Hirad and Webb, *The Genocide Convention*, 521.

Africa, the treatment of non-white and colonial peoples had emerged as a major issue in international affairs, bringing American discrimination against African Americans and the European mistreatment of colonial peoples into the spotlight.[48] As early as 1946, American civil rights activists led by Dr W. E. B. Du Bois campaigned at the UN to address racism in the United States and attempted to submit a petition—'We Charge Genocide'—that accused the United States of genocidal policies against African Americans. 'We Charge Genocide' never received a formal hearing at the UN nor any official response from US policymakers. In the context of the Cold War, these claims were dismissed by the US government as communist propaganda, while campaigners faced political persecution for acting against the interests of their state.[49]

Notably, Raphael Lemkin's position on colonization, proved less radical. He was an enthusiastic advocate of 'good colonialism' as a form of civilizational progress for Indigenous people but condemned its brutal forms.[50] Representatives from socialist states, in contrast, repeatedly stressed the issue of racism as a foundational factor in the cultural genocide that characterized colonial policies. The experiences of Nazi racial policies were thus translated into the language of socialist ideological warfare against Western racism and colonialism. The Czechoslovak representative emphasized that his country understood that the genocide of its Jewish population and the cultural genocide of the Czechs and Slovaks were both driven by the ideas of racial superiority, and that, despite the defeat of Nazism, racial discrimination still persisted in various parts of the world.[51] The Polish delegation emphasized that the inclusion of cultural genocide in the Convention would have a far-reaching beneficial effect especially in so far as 'colonial and dependent peoples were concerned' as 'colonial peoples were always in danger from the metropolitan states whether in the direct physical form or in the form of cultural genocide'.[52] The Yugoslav delegation was even more direct in pointing out that the crime of genocide was still being committed under the pretext of 'police measures' in colonial wars against oppressed peoples fighting for their freedom.[53] Among the countries from the developing world that supported the idea of cultural genocide were Pakistan, China, Venezuela, Egypt, Ethiopia, Syria, and Ecuador.[54]

One of the reasons for the eventual decision to exclude the cultural aspects of genocide from the Convention was the notion that cultural genocide could

---

[48] Charles H. Martin, 'Internationalizing "The American Dilemma": The Civil Rights Congress and 1951 Genocide Petition to the United Nations', *Journal of American Ethnic History* 16, no. 4 (1997): 35–61.
[49] Benjamin Meiches, 'The Charge of Genocide: Racial Hierarchy, Political Discourse, and the Evolution of International Institutions', *International Political Sociology* 13, no. 1 (2019): 20–36.
[50] Dominik J. Schaller, 'Raphael Lemkin's View on European Colonial Rule in Africa: Between Condemnation and Admiration', *Journal of Genocide Research* 7, no. 4 (2005): 536
[51] Hirad and Webb, *The Genocide Convention*, 19, 1322, 1517.
[52] Ibid., 1232, 2076.
[53] Ibid., 1296
[54] Ibid., 1518.

be qualified as a human rights violation that, as suggested by the French delegate, could be directly addressed in the Universal Declaration of Human Rights (UDHR) which was being drafted concomitantly to the Genocide Convention.[55] The timeline of the Genocide Convention and UDHR, however, reveals that the delegations participating in the Sixth Committee who called the issue of cultural genocide 'a human rights issue' to be addressed by the Third Committee working on the UDHR draft, understood that the latter was unlikely to give the matter serious consideration: The Declaration was adopted by the General Assembly one day after the adoption of the Genocide Convention at the same UN General Assembly in December 1948.[56]

Culture was, however, one of the factors shaping the development of the concept of human rights during the discussions on the draft UDHR, as many non-Western countries as well as Yugoslavia and the Soviet Union raised the issue of cultural differences rooted in traditions, customs, and religions. The fragment on the protection of the cultural survival of ethnic minorities also appeared in the initial drafts of the Declaration. Ultimately, however, it was excluded from the UDHR, as the protection of individual human rights took precedence.[57] The only brief reference to culture in the UDHR is in Article 27, which states that 'Everyone has the right freely to participate in the cultural life of the community, to enjoy the arts and to share in scientific advancement and its benefits'. While this article did introduce the idea that culture was an aspect of human rights, it did not elucidate the specific relationship between individuals, communities, and nations and did not clarify how conflicts among these three entities could or should be resolved. Furthermore, while it recognized that culture should be acknowledged as an essential component of human rights, since the concept of culture and heritage insists that individual identities be respected and protected, it failed to recognize culture as part of group identity and group rights in equal measure.[58] The wider emphasis on individual human rights in the UDHR can be read as an indication of the success of liberal individualist thinking in the battle over the definition of human rights in need of protection. It separated the human rights of individuals from what would later be known as 'second-generation' social, cultural, and economic rights, which emerged in international debates in the 1960s.[59] In a similar fashion, the Genocide Convention ultimately restricted the definition of genocide

---

[55] Marco Odello, 'Genocide and Culture: Revising their Relationship 70 years after Genocide Convention', in *The Concept of Genocide in International Criminal Law*, edited by Marco Odello and Piotr Łubiński (Abingdon: Routledge, 2020), 242; Hirad and Webb, *The Genocide Convention*, 1510.

[56] William A. Schabas, *Genocide in International Law* (Cambridge: Cambridge University Press), 214.

[57] Odello, 'Genocide and Culture', 245.

[58] Helaine Silverman and D. Fairchild Ruggles (eds.), *Cultural Heritage and Human Rights* (New York: Springer, 2007), 5.

[59] Monique Deveaux, 'Normative Liberal Theory and the Bifurcation of Human Rights', *Ethics & Global Politics* 2, no. 3 (2009): 171–91.

to acts of biological and physical destruction and followed the line of the American delegation that the crime of genocide was an act committed against an individual.[60] It narrowed the list of protected groups to national, ethnic, racial, and religious communities, while excluding cultural, linguistic, and political groups.[61]

Some of the ideas that were sidelined during the discussions on cultural genocide would eventually re-emerge in the aftermath of decolonization. Scholars have argued that this reckoning with the colonial past in the territories of former colonial empires was a return to the 'unfinished project' of international law started by Lemkin in the 1940s.[62] The rise of Indigenous activism in the 1970s and early 1980s sparked a new discussion around cultural genocide, which was now framed as interconnecting the discourse of human rights with that of the cultural rights of groups. The Working Group on Indigenous Populations, for example, was established at the UN in 1982 as a subsidiary body of the Sub-Commission on the Promotion and Protection of Human Rights. In the following decades, the protection of the culture and cultural rights of ethnic minorities and Indigenous peoples was addressed in several UN documents, namely the Declaration on the Rights of Persons Belonging to National or Ethnic, Religious and Linguistic Minorities (1992) and the Declaration of the Rights of Indigenous Peoples (2007), which was rejected by the same countries that voted against cultural genocide in 1948, including Australia, Canada, New Zealand, and the United States. The acknowledgement of the criminality of the destruction of culture would take a different path, appearing in various international treaties as early as the 1954 Hague Convention, discussed below.

The 1954 Hague Convention for the Protection of Cultural Property in the Event of Armed Conflict

The 1954 Hague Convention became the first international legal document to regulate the protection of cultural heritage in the event of armed conflict. Adopted at a point when wartime alliances had effectively vanished, to be replaced by the new Cold War conflict, delegates felt encouraged to take steps towards the articulation of rules for the protection of culture in the case of a new war. The socialist states—most of them members of the UN, but not all part of UNESCO in 1954—were invited to participate in drafting the Convention in The Hague from 21 April to 14 May. The discussions were attended by a wide

---

[60] Abtahi and Webb, *Genocide Convention*, 890.
[61] Anton Weiss-Wendt, *The Soviet Union and the Gutting of the UN Genocide Convention* (Madison: University of Wisconsin Press, 2017), 98.
[62] Hannah Schreiber, 'Cultural Genocide—Culturecide: An Unfinished or Rejected Project of International Law?', in *Culture(s) in International Relations*, edited by Grażyna Michałowska and Hannah Schreiber (Frankfurt am Main: Peter Lang, 2017), 319–46.

range of officials, including not only diplomats and lawyers but also military officials, representatives of cultural institutions and museums, and conservation experts from fifty-six different states.[63] Among the socialist countries, Poland and the Soviet Union played the most active roles: Soviet representatives, alongside other major powers, were included in all committees and working groups; Polish representatives sat on the drafting committee, the legal committee (together with Romania), and one of the working groups (together with Romania and Czechoslovakia). To demonstrate the maximalist aspirations of socialist countries in their desire to secure the best protection possible for cultural goods in the case of future conflicts, it is useful here to highlight three themes discussed at the conference in The Hague in 1954: the equality of all cultures of mankind and territorial extension of the Convention, the prohibition of nuclear weapons, and the introduction of the military necessity clause. By tracing the positions of socialist delegations, the convergence between the grievances in the aftermath of cultural losses experienced during the Second World War converged, and the socialist ideological battle against racism and colonialism and the geopolitical 'struggle for peace' in the context of the Cold War becomes visible.[64]

Some formulations codified in the Introduction of the Convention were truly revolutionary: The idea of the 'universal value of cultural property' for the first time acknowledged the equal value of cultures produced by different nations. The Soviet delegate Vladimir Semyonovich Kemenov stressed that cultural monuments both 'in the East' and 'the West' required protection, as their destruction 'affects mankind as a whole'.[65] The Soviet delegation proposed a paragraph in the preamble to the Convention that stated: 'Being convinced that damage to cultural property belonging to any people whatsoever means damage to the cultural heritage of all mankind, since each people makes its contribution to the culture of the world.'[66] The purpose of this statement was to address the existing inequality between the value assigned to European cultures and those of non-white people, a putative hierarchy that was still widely accepted, even if only implicitly. In this context, the contempt demonstrated by Nazi Germans towards the culture of Poland, Czechoslovakia, and the nations of the Soviet Union reiterated the contempt of Western empires towards the cultures of colonized peoples.[67] By recognizing the equal status and value of all cultures in the text of the 1954 Convention,

---

[63] Poland and Czechoslovakia joined UNESCO in 1946, Hungary in 1948, the Soviet Union in 1954, and Bulgaria and Romania in 1956. With the exception of Bulgaria, all took part in the conference.

[64] Other themes discussed at the conference included the definition of cultural property, the notion of special protection, international control, punishments for violations of the Convention, and restitution, among others.

[65] Fifth Plenary meeting, in *Records of the Conference Convened by the United Nations Education, Scientific, and Cultural Organization held at the Hague from 21 April to 14 May 1954* (The Hague: Staatsdrukkerij—en Uitgeverijbedrijf, 1961), 118.

[66] Working Documents, *Records of the Conference*, 272.

[67] Nahlik, 346.

socialist delegations drew on their experiences to push forward an anti-racial and anticolonial agenda and to call for a re-evaluation of the hierarchies of cultures dominated by the cultures of Western Europeans. Many non-Western delegates, including Iran and India, expressed appreciation for the universal character of the Convention and saw it as a form of recognition of the value their cultural civilizations.[68] It is noteworthy that the representative from Romania, a country that had allied with the Axis during the Second World War and was complicit in the mass murder of Jewish people, went a step further to underline that the principle of the universal value of culture should also be applied within nation-states: the artistic heritage of Romania had been the work not only of Romanians 'but [also] of those ancient people who inhabit the territory'.[69]

This problem of (in)equality among different cultures was raised again during the debate on 'the territorial extension of the Convention' (Article 35). The Soviet delegation proposed that the provisions of the Convention should be equally applicable to the metropolitan territories of signatory states and 'to all non-self-governing and trust territories or colonies, administered or governed by such states', which would reinforce the idea of the universal value of all cultures and the importance of their protection recognized by the Convention.[70] The delegations of Yugoslavia and Romania supported this addition as corresponding to the Convention's spirit of equality of all cultures of the world as expressed in the preamble. By emphasizing that the Convention was humanitarian in nature, and that the text had been approved by the Commission for Human Rights at the fifth session of the UN General Assembly, the Soviets also highlighted the connection between the cultural identity of groups and the human rights of all nations, which had previously been addressed in the discussions on cultural genocide during the drafting of the Genocide Convention but failed to gain wider recognition.

The socialist position was strongly opposed by those countries with existing colonies, such as Great Britain, France, and Belgium, who argued against universal applicability as a matter of democratic constitutional procedure since it would infringe upon the independence of certain territories. Introducing the clause thus risked the non-ratification of the Convention by many countries.[71] The position of the United States on this point was not driven by the opposition to colonialism but by Cold War hostilities, which prevented the American delegation from supporting the anticolonial cause.[72] (For the role of Eastern European countries in removing the colonial clause in international law, see Sonja Dolinsek and Philippa

---

[68] Fifth Plenary meeting, *Records of the Conference*, 120, 122.
[69] Ibid., 121.
[70] Working Documents, *Records of the Conference*, 392.
[71] Twentieth Meeting, Plenary session, *Records of the Conference*, 284.
[72] Mary Ann Heiss, 'Privileging the Cold War over Decolonisation: the US Emphasis on Political Rights', in *Decolonization, Self-Determination and the Rise of Global Human Rights Politics*, edited by Dirk Moses, Marco Duranty, and Roland Burke (Cambridge: Cambridge University Press, 2020), 132–50.

Hetherington, Chapter 9 in this volume). In its final version, the article states that Any High Contracting Party *may* declare that the Convention 'shall extend to all or any of the territories of which a High Contracting Party is responsible' but is not obliged to do so. The solution was presented as a compromise, but in effect, this formulation left the final decision on the Convention's territorial applicability to the individual states.

As the discussions on the Convention draft at The Hague reveal, heritage became embedded in the ideological warfare over the 'struggle for peace', which could be seen both as a continuation of postwar discourses and a reflection on the possibility of a new war. Soviet experts maintained their understanding of heritage as an issue of international security and criticized UNESCO for neglecting culture's social and political dimensions. The radicalism of many Soviet proposals, often supported by other socialist states that argued that the Convention should go beyond simply acknowledging that cultural properties were at risk in case of war, stemmed from their conviction that the cultural heritage of humanity could only be protected if another world war was prevented.[73] It was necessary, they insisted, to categorically condemn at a minimum the most dangerous weapons such as atomic and hydrogen weapons of mass destruction to secure the fate of cultural properties.

Both the Western and Socialist blocs maintained that their positions were informed by their version of realism. While the Western countries stated that their aim was to ensure that the Convention could be implemented in the context of war without affecting military operability and outcomes, the socialist states declared that their aim was to limit the chances of new wars or at least to reduce their damaging effects. In the words of Soviet delegate V. Kemenov, realism would mean acknowledging that:

> the new arms could not be ignored and steps for the protection of cultural property could not be elaborated without the undertaking not to use them. [...] It must not be forgotten that all the works of the Conference would be deprived of any practical sense unless the use of atomic weapons was forbidden, for they destroyed everything, wiped out towns, whole regions.[74]

This position was also supported by Romanian delegate Alexandru Lazareanu and Belarusian representative Pavel Lutorowich as a way to widen the scope of the

---

[73] In their comments on their collaboration with UNESCO in 1960–61, the USSR National Commission for UNESCO reported that 'some 1,200 cultural monuments of world interest on Soviet soil' had been damaged by Nazi Germany during the War., UNESCO Archives, Collaboration of the USSR with UNESCO 1961–1962X07.21(470) AR, Relations with U.S.S.R.—Annual Reports, 16.
[74] Twenty-First Meeting, Main Commission, in *Records of the Conference Convened by the United Nations Education, Scientific, and Cultural Organization held at the Hague from 21 April to 14 May 1954* (The Hague: Staatsdrukkerij—en Uitgeverijbedrijf, 1961), 264.

Convention.[75] Stanislaw Lorentz, a Polish delegate, raised the issue at the plenary session, pointing out that the Convention would be unable to sufficiently protect cultural property against atomic, hydrogen, and other weapons of mass destruction as their use had not been formally prohibited. In his view, 'if the Conference, in adopting the Convention, were not to affirm that the use of atomic weapons meant the destruction of culture, it would not have fulfilled its task'.[76] Major Western powers, however, opposed the inclusion of this reference to weapons of mass destruction, arguing that it made the Convention impracticable.[77]

Ultimately, however, the only trace of this heated discussion on ensuring the protection of cultural heritage in the face of weapons of mass destruction to remain in the text of the Convention is a statement that there are dangers for cultural properties associated with the development of military technology. Two delegations—the Turkish and the Irish—moved to call the Soviet draft containing the prohibition of weapons of mass destruction as out of order. They argued that the delegations participating in the conference were not competent to make decisions on weapons of mass destruction and that the technical limitation of armaments was beyond the Convention's scope.[78] Only socialist states—Poland, Czechoslovakia, Hungary, Romania, the USSR, Ukraine, and Belarus—voted against the motion, twenty-two countries voted in favour, and thirteen abstained.[79] The countries that abstained without explanation were an eclectic ideological and geopolitical mix, including India, Indonesia, Iran, Iraq, Libya, El Salvador, Syria, Italy, Switzerland and the Netherlands, and socialist Yugoslavia. The French representative, Brichet, confirmed that France agreed with the spirit of the Soviet resolution but believed that this was not a matter directly concerning the Convention. Instead, he pointed to a special committee established by the UN Security Council made up of the four great powers and Canada that was meeting at that moment in London to consider the issue of atomic weapons.[80] Within the context of the Cold War, France's sympathies with the Soviet proposal were seen as a betrayal by other Western powers. In his confidential note to the government, the British delegate commented on the French position as 'disappointing' in its readiness 'to go more than halfway to meet the Russian pseudo-idealism'.[81] The French justification for voting in favour of the out-of-order motion was, however, supported by the delegates of Israel, Italy, and the Netherlands. Ultimately, while the socialist countries aimed to widen the scope of the Convention by including the prohibition on nuclear weapons, most countries were not convinced by this maximalist approach and opted to support a

---

[75] Ibid., 265.
[76] Eleventh Plenary Session, in *Records of the Conference*, 291.
[77] 'Brief for United Kingdom Delegation' ED 157/227 The National Archives.
[78] Ibid., 264.
[79] Eleventh Plenary Session, in *Records of the Conference*, 291–92.
[80] Twenty-First Meeting, Main Commission, in *Records of the Conference*, 265.
[81] 'Note by Chairman of Working the Party', the Hague Conference 21 April–14 May 1954, ED 157/227 The National Archives.

narrower scope of the Convention, refraining from intervention in what they considered technical aspects of future military conflicts.

The concept of 'military necessity', which permits measures considered indispensable to accomplishing a legitimate military purpose and are not otherwise prohibited by international humanitarian law, became yet another point of contention between different understandings of realism in relation to the protection of culture. Socialist delegations were at the forefront of this discussion, arguing against the inclusion of the military necessity clause by insisting that it was incompatible with the spirit of the Convention. Lorentz reminded the delegates that his country had suffered frightful losses during the recent wars, when the Royal Palace of Warsaw, the Warsaw Cathedral, and a large number of Roman and Gothic churches had been bombed and destroyed. Yet if the generals had been asked to account for their actions in every case, they would have answered that there was an imperative military necessity.[82] He compared the clause to a 'patent of impunity' for military commanders—whenever barbaric destruction of cultural properties had taken place, military commanders would subsequently use the argument of military necessity.[83] Similarly, Lazareanu questioned the value of the Convention and its ability to protect if the exceptionalism of military necessity could be applied at any moment.[84]

The American and British delegations stood as the major proponents for military necessity as an exculpatory argument for the destruction of cultural heritage during armed conflict, supported by Italy, the Netherlands, Australia, the Philippines, Israel, and Turkey. The representative of the US Army, Colonel W. W. Perham, argued that ignoring military factors would lead to a failure of the entire conference, and the British delegate praised the sincerity of the American position as 'military necessity existed whether or not a definition could be found'.[85] Indeed, according to many supporters of the clause, such an approach was needed in order to make the Convention 'military operable' and to allow for the training of military personnel to safeguard and protect cultural property.[86] Representative of the Netherlands asserted that:

> military authorities should respect monuments of high cultural value, but during a battle, military necessity might require the destruction of cultural property for the reason that the lives of thousands of solders might depend on it and in

---

[82] Fifth Meeting, Main Commission, in *Records of the Conference*, 152.
[83] Fourth Meeting, Main Commission, in *Records of the Conference*, 145.
[84] The Roerich Pact is the inter-American treaty on the protection of Artistic and Scientific Institutions and Historical Monuments signed in Washington by twenty-one American states, including the United States, in 1935.
[85] Fourth Meeting, Main Commission, in *Records of the Conference*, 146.
[86] Third Meeting, Main Commission, in *Records of the Conference*, 141.

such event, no military leader would hesitate. It was absolutely necessary to be realistic.[87]

Other countries such as Italy agreed that military necessity should be taken into account, but suggested that it was possible to provide a strict definition of the cases in which it could be invoked.[88] The Cuban delegate mentioned cases where human life was at stake, and the French, Chinese, and Spanish delegates insisted that military necessity could only be claimed in very rare cases.[89] Essentially, the discussion revealed the extent to which a new war appeared possible for each of the delegations present. In the Irish representative's words, 'it was simply impossible to close one's eyes to the unmistakable possibility of war in the world today'.[90] The argument surrounding the practicality of the military necessity clause ultimately proved more convincing, and the final vote on the motion by the Soviet, Greek, and Ecuadorian delegation to remove the military necessity clause ended with twenty opposed, seven in favour, and fourteen abstentions.[91]

The inclusion of the military necessity clause became one of the most significant concessions to the interests of states and geopolitical realities in the Convention, which was otherwise considered a major success of postwar cultural internationalism. However, every country participating in the discussion envisioned these interests in the context of their own pressing conditions. Thus, Israel supported the military necessity clause so as not to limit its freedom to defend itself.[92] Notably, the concept of armed conflict discussed at The Hague includes international and domestic struggles and applies to wars of national liberation, which was not the case in the 1949 Geneva Conventions.[93] The conflict surrounding the military necessity clause reiterated the irreconcilable opposition between the idea of 'cultural property of all humankind' and the national interests of states in the context of potential military conflict. The only victory achieved by the socialist states on this front was the exclusion of any reference to military necessity from the preamble, which was supported by the majority of states and only opposed by Great Britain, Australia, Turkey, and Cuba.[94]

---

[87] Fourth Meeting, Main Commission, in *Records of the Conference*, 145.
[88] Ibid., 142–43.
[89] Fifth Meeting, Main Commission, in *Records of the Conference*, 151.
[90] Ibid., 148.
[91] In favour: Byelorussian SSR, Czechoslovakia, Hungary, Poland, Romania, San Marino, Ukrainian SSR, and USSR. Against: Australia, Belgium, China, China, Denmark, El Salvador, France Greece, India, Ireland, Israel, Italy, Japan, Netherlands, Norway, Philippines, Spain, Sweden, Switzerland, Turkey, United Kingdom, and United States.
    Abstentions: German Federal Republic, Holy See, Indonesia, Iran, Iraq, Libya, Monaco, and Yugoslavia. Absent: Ecuador, Egypt, Lebanon, Luxemburg, Nicaragua, Peru, Portugal, and Syria.
[92] Fifth Meeting, Main Commission, in *Records of the Conference*, 151.
[93] Roger O'Keefe, 'The Meaning of "Cultural Property" under the 1954 Hague Convention', *Netherlands International Law Review* 46, no. 1 (1999): 26–56.
[94] Twelfth Meeting, Main Commission, in *Records of the Conference*, 200.

Conclusion

The first decade after the Second World War saw the beginning of a long-term process of (re)constituting culture and cultural property as a subject of international politics and law. The experience of the cultural losses that certain socialist states suffered under the Nazi occupation shaped their enthusiastic and maximalist approach to new initiatives for the protection of culture in the context of armed conflict. Eastern European governments in exile had already begun working on legislation to prosecute crimes committed against their nations during the War and made important contributions at the UNWCC to discussions on the definition of the crimes taking place—crimes against humanity, the war of aggression, and crimes against minorities committed by a state, among others. Ultimately, however, the evidence collected by Poland and Czechoslovakia played a limited role in the Nuremberg Trials, which came to be dominated by the major powers.

Poland and Czechoslovakia introduced the crime of destruction of culture, be that physical obliteration or cultural denigration, into national legislation after the War, and later joined forces with the Soviet Union in a joint attempt to integrate the idea of cultural genocide into the 1948 UN Genocide Convention. This idea mirrored Lemkin's original definition of genocide, a concept coined to capture both the Jewish and ethnic Polish suffering during the War. Both Czechoslovakian and Polish delegations claimed to have experienced cultural genocide during the occupation and aimed to integrate this experience into the legal codification of the concept in the Genocide Convention. The failure of this initiative, however, made evident that the variety of discriminatory practices engaged in by various Western countries towards their own populations could be reinterpreted as cases of cultural genocide. This possibility sparked the vociferous opposition of those countries to this concept as it would risk interference in their domestic policies. Furthermore, attempts to relegate and reinterpret cultural genocide as a human rights issue proved equally futile as the emerging international discourse of human rights came to be dominated by a focus on individual human rights rather than group rights, as can be seen in the cases of cultural genocide claimed by Eastern European countries. These debates were informed by the racialized policies experienced by some socialist states under Nazi occupation, which were translated into the language of anti-racism and anticolonialism that they used as a main driver of their agenda in the international arena.

The active role played by socialist states in drafting the 1954 Hague Convention further demonstrates how their interest in ensuring the protection of their national cultures in the event of a new war became aligned with the promotion of socialist ideology. The very notion of the cultural property of all nations as inherently, universally, valuable and the property of all humankind in the Convention's preamble indicated an important shift away from existing cultural hierarchies embedded in the international order that reiterated the patterns of Western European thinking.

Conversely, the participation in these discussions by countries previously aligned with the Nazis was informed by their desire to reinvent themselves as international actors acting in defence of a progressive agenda aimed at fighting colonialism and racism and siding with maximalist aspirations to prevent future wars.

Heated discussions across the Iron Curtain on multiple issues, from the territorial extension of the Convention to the prohibition of nuclear weapons, and the military necessity clause, revealed the extent to which the protection of cultural property during armed conflicts became simultaneously a projection of conflicting interests and created the basis for joint initiatives. Ironically, however, despite the fact that compromise on the most contested issues was achieved by accepting the arguments of the Western powers, decades would pass before either the United States or Great Britain ratified the Convention (in 2009 and 2017, respectively). The countries of the Socialist Bloc, on the other hand, despite having suffered defeat in most of their initiatives to ensure the greatest possible protection for culture, ratified the Convention within the space of a few short years. As this chapter has demonstrated, developing a new regime for the protection of culture reiterated the major tensions emerging in the new international order of the Cold War, but it also served as a foundation for common initiatives between the East, West, and South. While the importance of the protection of cultural properties in future conflicts was recognized by all members of the international community, enmity between ideological rivals prevented the adoption of the most advanced measures to protect culture.

Acknowledgements

This research was supported by the Romanian National Authority for Scientific Research and Innovation, CNCS-UEFISCDI, project number PN-III-P4-ID-PCE-2020-1337.

9
Socialist Internationalism and Decolonizing Moralities in the UN Anti-Trafficking Regime, 1947–54

Sonja Dolinsek and Philippa Hetherington

Introduction

On 11 August 1954, the Union of Soviet Socialist Republics (USSR) acceded to the 1949 United Nations (UN) Convention on the Suppression of the Traffic in Persons and the Exploitation of the Prostitution of Others (1949 UN Convention), which had opened for signature at Lake Success on 21 March 1950.[1] The USSR, whose delegation to the UN Economic and Social Council (ECOSOC) had firmly supported the Convention in its draft stages, prefaced its accession with the declaration that: 'In the Soviet Union the social conditions which give rise to the offences covered by the convention have been eliminated.'[2] In characteristic doublespeak, the USSR's accession simultaneously supported the Convention and the international legal attempt to suppress prostitution globally, and denied that the social problems addressed by the Convention existed in areas under its jurisdiction. Embedded within this claim was the implicit assertion of the moral superiority of Soviet-style socialism, which had supposedly eradicated social 'problems' including commercial sex. By evoking a selfless commitment to the international importance of eradicating prostitution, the Soviet delegation positioned itself as the vanguard of social reform on a global scale.

Socialist countries in Eastern Europe played a crucial role in successfully shaping and passing the 1949 UN Convention. In the evolving taxonomies of international law, the 1949 Convention fell somewhere between pre-1945 conceptualizations of international criminal law (ICL) and international humanitarian

---

[1] UN Treaty Series (vol. 96, 1951), 271.
[2] 'Declarations and Reservations to the Convention for the Suppression of the Traffic in Persons and of the Exploitation of Others, Lake Success, New York, 21 March 1950', in ibid., 349. This declaration was also expressed by the delegations of Ukraine and Belarus. The Convention and accompanying Soviet reservations were published in the USSR in Ministerstvo inostrannykh Del SSSR, *Sbornik deistvuiushchikh dogovorov, soglashenii i konventsii, zakliuchennykh SSSR s inostrannymi gosudarstvami: Vypusk XVI* (Moscow: Gosudarstvennoe Izadatel'stvo Politicheskoi Literatury, 1957), 280–90.

law (IHL), best described as international law targeting transnational crime.[3] Later Soviet commentators would refer to this category as 'crimes of an international nature', to differentiate from state-driven atrocities.[4]

The Convention's home in the ECOSOC also highlighted the perceived humanitarian or social welfare exigencies of suppressing 'the exploitation of the prostitution of others'. But why was this Convention important to the Soviet Union and its Eastern European allies if it purportedly addressed a problem which did not exist in areas under their own jurisdiction? What may it tell us about the Convention—and about the ways both prostitution and the traffic in persons were conceptualized in the postwar world—that the eventual form and content bore their imprint? And what can we glean about the specificities of state socialist approaches to international law from this case study?

This chapter answers these questions by first examining the Convention's genealogy and the history of its genesis in the late 1940s. It then considers the ways in which socialist understandings of prostitution, its causes and potential 'solutions', were embedded within the responses of the Soviet, Ukrainian, and Czechoslovak delegations. Finally, the chapter turns to the little-known history of the Soviet delegation's successful effort to remove the colonial clause from the Convention and in so doing to claim a moral victory on behalf of socialism and anti-imperialism against capitalism. Examining the discussions on the Convention, the chapter focuses in particular on the Soviet approach, with reference to the differing position of fellow socialist state, Czechoslovakia.

We argue that the negotiations around the 1949 Convention were marked by ideological tensions, but these did not focus on the social desirability of suppressing prostitution, about which there was remarkable agreement. Rather, the Soviet Union and its allies saw the enforcement elements of the Convention as the key source of political contention between socialist and Western states. Focusing on these, socialist delegates as well as delegates from recently decolonized states put questions of sovereignty and jurisdiction at the heart of an ostensibly uncontroversial social policy debate. This was particularly evident in the debates over the inclusion of the so-called colonial clause, which allowed imperial powers to decide whether or not the Convention would extend to colonies, rather than guaranteeing automatic application to them. After Soviet and recently decolonized delegates successfully argued for the colonial clause's deletion, both France and

---

[3] On the dialogic relationship between conceptualizations of 'international' and 'transnational' crime in a Soviet context, see Philippa Hetherington, 'The Highest Guardian of the Child: International Criminology and the Russian Fight Against Transnational Obscenity, 1885–1925', *Russian History* 43, no. 3–4 (2016): 275–310.

[4] Gennady Esakov, 'International Criminal Law and Russia: From Nuremberg Passion to The Hague Prejudice', *Europe–Asia Studies* 69, no. 8 (2017): 1188; Karpets, I. I., *Prestupleniia mezh- dunarodnogo kharaktera* (Moscow: Iuridicheskaia Literatura, 1979), 31–53; Karpets discusses 'trafficking in women' specifically at 173–77, criticizing the 1949 Convention for focusing on prostitution to the detriment of a specific clause on *trafficking* for prostitution.

Great Britain voted against the Convention and refused to ratify it.[5] For the Soviet delegates, the oppressive or liberatory potential of the Convention resided less in substantive policy questions regarding the best way to end prostitution, about which they largely agreed with the 'capitalist' delegations, and more in the extent to which it did or did not advance an anti-imperial cause.[6] In highlighting these dynamics, our approach follows recent scholars in arguing that socialist states took international law 'seriously', despite the classical Marxist position that it was just a tool of the oppressing classes.[7] Their behaviour at the UN was not merely an effort to disrupt Western nations' foreign policy aims but also an effort to forge an alternative way of using and viewing the international legal system.

A Genealogy of Law Against Human Trafficking for Prostitution

The 1949 UN Convention was the fifth in a series of international anti- trafficking agreements that began with the 1904 International Agreement for the Suppression of 'White Slave Traffic'.[8] This agreement was signed by, among others, the Russian Empire, France, and the United Kingdom and it addressed trafficking as a problem of cross-border recruitment and 'procuring' of minors for prostitution. It explicitly

---

[5] For recent work on international law and empire, see Martti Koskenniemi, Walter Rech, and Manuel Jimenez Fonseca (eds.). *International Law and Empire: Historical Explorations* (Oxford: Oxford University Press, 2017). For a more recent study on the negotiations of the 1949 Convention with a focus on the British and French positions, see Sonja Dolinsek, 'Tensions of abolitionism during the negotiation of the 1949 "Convention for the Suppression of the Traffic in Persons and of the Exploitation of the Prostitution of Others"', *European Review of History: Revue européenne d'histoire* 29, no. 2 (2022): 223-248.

[6] It goes without saying that Soviet rhetorical opposition to imperialism did not include any self-reflection on Moscow's own, arguably imperial, relationship to Eastern Europe, Central Asia, or the Caucasus.

[7] Jennifer Amos, 'Embracing and Contesting: The Soviet Union and the Universal Declaration of Human Rights, 1948-1958', in *Human Rights in the Twentieth Century*, edited by Stefan Ludwig Hoffmann (Cambridge: Cambridge University Press, 2010), 147-65; Francine Hirsch, 'The Soviets at Nuremberg: International Law, Propaganda and the Making of the Postwar Order', American Historical Review 113, no. 3 (2008): 704-05; Bill Bowring, *Law, Rights and Ideology: Landmarks in the Destiny of a Great Power* (New York: Routledge, 2013), 77-96; Lauri Malksoo, *Russian Approaches to International Law* (Oxford: Oxford University Press, 2015), 42-71; Paul Betts, 'Socialism, Social Rights and Human Rights: The Case of East Germany', Humanity 3, no. 3 (2012): 407-26; Ned Richardson-Little, *The Human Rights Dictatorship: Socialism, Dissent, and Revolution in East Germany* (Cambridge: Cambridge University Press, 2019).

[8] There is a rich literature on the emergence of the 'white slavery' panic in Western Europe and North America at the *fin-de-siècle*; see especially Elisa Camiscioli, *Reproducing the French Race: Immigration, Intimacy and Embodiment in the Early Twentieth Century* (Durham, NC: Duke University Press, 2006); Jean-Michel Chaumont, *Le mythe de la traite des blanches: Enquête sur la fabrication d'un fléau* (Paris: La Découverte, 2009); Brian Donovan, *White Slave Crusades: Race, Gender and Anti-Vice Activism, 1887-1917* (Urbana-Champaign, IL: University of Illinois Press, 2006); Donna Guy, *Sex and Danger in Buenos Aires: Prostitution, Family and Nation in Argentina* (Lincoln, NE: University of Nebraska Press, 1991); Stephanie Limoncelli, *The Politics of Trafficking: The First International Movement to Combat the Sexual Exploitation of Women* (Stanford, CA: Stanford University Press, 2010); Judith R. Walkowitz, *City of Dreadful Delight: Narratives of Sexual Danger in Late Victorian London* (Chicago, IL: University of Chicago Press, 1992).

refrained from any discussion of national legislation on prostitution within a state's borders.[9] This agreement, and a later 1910 Convention extending it, were then taken up in the interwar period by the League of Nations' Traffic in Women and Children Committee, in which prostitution-regulationist states such as France held significant sway. The language of two League of Nations Conventions from 1921 and 1933 continued to focus only on the transnational recruitment and transportation of women for prostitution purposes, albeit they raised (1921) and then abolished (1933) the age limit at which it was considered women could consent to sex work abroad. They also introduced calls for more intensive surveillance of borders and migrant sex workers than those invoked by the earlier 1904 and 1910 agreements.[10] The League's anti-trafficking initiatives were a key pillar of what was known as the Social Section—that unit of the League dedicated to formulating international agreements to address 'social problems' as part of the broader efforts to buttress world peace.[11] Of particular relevance was the negotiation between 1930 and 1937 of the so-called Draft Convention for Suppressing the Exploitation of the Prostitution of Others (1937 Draft Convention), which was finalized in 1937 but never officially adopted due to the war.

In the postwar UN, the issue of 'social questions' was taken up by the ECOSOC.[12] On 29 March 1947, ECOSOC adopted Resolution 43 (IV) on Social Questions, which included—among other things—a section on the Suppression of the Traffic in Women and Children.[13] The resolution instructed the secretary-general to transfer the 'functions formerly exercised by the League of Nations' to the UN as well as to reassess and amend the 1937 Draft Convention before submitting it to governments and subsequently to the ECOSOC for approval. Thus, when the UN Social Defence section started working on the new draft, it did not start from scratch.[14]

---

[9] On the 1904 agreement and the 1910 Convention, see Allain, Jean. 'White Slave Traffic in International Law', *Journal of Trafficking and Human Exploitation* 1, no. 1 (2017): 1–40.

[10] On the League's 1921 'International Convention for the Suppression of the Traffic in Women and Children' and 1933 'International Convention for the Suppression of the Traffic in Women of the Full Age', see Stephen Legg, '"The Life of Individuals as well as of Nations": International Law and the League of Nations' Anti-Trafficking Governmentalities', *Leiden Journal of International Law* 25, no. 3 (2012): 647–64; Jessica Pliley, 'Claims to Protection: The Rise and Fall of Feminist Abolitionism in the League of Nations' Committee on the Traffic in Women and Children, 1919–1936', Journal of Women's History 22, no. 4 (2010): 90–113; Ashwini Tambe, 'Climate, Race Science and the Age of Consent in the League of Nations', *Theory, Culture and Society*, 28, no. 2 (2001): 109–30.

[11] On the League's social programmes, see Magaly Rodríguez García, Davide Rodogno, and Liat Kozma, *The League of Nations' Work on Social Issues: Visions, Endeavours and Experiments* (Geneva: UN Publications, 2016); Magaly Rodríguez García, 'La Société des Nations face à la traite des femmes et au travail sexuel à l'échelle mondiale', *Le Mouvement Social* 4, no. 241 (2012): 105–25.

[12] On background to the founding of the ECOSOC and its Social Commission, see Maurice Milhaud, 'Social Commission', *World Affairs* 110, no. 4 (1947): 245–51.

[13] UN Economic and Social Council, ECOSOC Resolution 43 (IV) on Social Questions, document E/437, 29 March 1947.

[14] Anja P. Jakobi, *Common Goods and Evils: The Formation of Global Crime Governance* (New York: Oxford University Press, 2013), 70–71.

The overall process leading to the final version of the 1949 UN Convention can be subdivided into three phases.[15] The first phase started before 1945 and can be found in the origins of the 1937 Draft Convention on which the UN's Social Defence section based its new draft. Since 1930, the League's Legal Sub-Committee of the Advisory Committee on Traffic in Women and Children had been discussing the institutionalization of the offence of 'pimping' as an international crime.[16] These efforts formed part of a broader push to unify criminal law that had been gaining pace within the League since the late 1920s.[17] Specifically, the Sub-Committee aimed at eradicating both the traffic in women and prostitution itself by explicitly targeting third parties and intermediaries in the sex trade: the so-called *souteneurs*.[18] However, reaching a common definition of the crime was no easy task. By 1937, the working parties agreed on the formula of the 'exploitation of the prostitution of others' to capture the crime committed by whomever:

> in order to gratify the passions of another and for the purposes of gain, procures, entices or leads away by whatever means, even with their con- sent, a person of either sex of full age for the purpose of exploiting that person's prostitution.[19]

The 1937 Draft Convention was the starting point of the new UN 1949 Convention. The negotiation process at the UN took nearly three years and included a number of ECOSOC Resolutions and two drafts from the Social Defence section in cooperation with the department of Legal Affairs.[20] During a first, non-public phase (1947–48), member states as well as Non-Governmental Organizations (NGOs) with consultative status were invited to offer comments on both drafts. It was only after this that the second draft was discussed in what may be described as a limited international public sphere in the Social Commission (May

---

[15] A full legal and historical account of the complex and lengthy process of negotiating the 1937 Draft Convention or the 1949 UN Convention has yet to be written and is beyond the scope of this chapter.

[16] Legal Sub-Committee, CTFE/CJ 1930–1936, CTFE/CJ/2nd session/PV 1933, CTFE/CS 1935–1936. Research on the Legal Sub-Committee is still rare. For a general overview see Magaly Rodríguez García, 'The League of Nations and the Moral Recruitment of Women', *International Review of Social History* 57, no. s20 (2012): 97–128, 113–19.

[17] See Mark Lewis, *The Birth of the New Justice: The Internationalization of Crime and Punishment, 1919–1950* (Oxford: Oxford University Press, 2014). From 1933, the advice of the International Association for the Unification of Penal and its Secretary General, Vespasian Pella, would be offered to the Sub-Committee. Vespasian Pella later became a delegate to the Legal Sub-Committee for Romania, and after 1945 to the 'Social Defence' section at the UN. League of Nations Archives, Social Section, Sub-Section on Traffic in Women and Children, Box R. 4664.

[18] Preliminary Draft International Convention of the punishment of persons who live on the immoral earnings of women, League of Nations Archives, CTFE/CJ/1.

[19] UN Division of Social Activities, Draft Convention of 1937 for Suppressing the Exploitation of the Prostitution of Others. Memorandum by the Secretary-General, E/574, UN Archives New York, Branch Registries, *Volume III—Convention for the Suppression of Traffic in Persons and Obscene Publications*, Box S-0441-1163, File 218/03/03, Article 1, 6.

[20] The Social Defence section was led by Polish-British criminologist Leon Radzinowicz, who reflected on the experience in his memoir: Leon Radzinowicz, *Adventures in Criminology* (London: Routledge, 1999), 380–87.

1949), the ECOSOC (July 1949), the Third and Sixth Committee of the General Assembly, and the Plenary Session of the General Assembly in the last quarter of 1949. It was during these sessions that the state socialist members of the UN attempted to mould the Convention at the level of both form and content.

Beside the internationalization of the individual crime of 'pimping', the second non-public phase saw the successful introduction of a regulation-abolitionist approach to prostitution into the Convention. When the UN Convention was circulated to member states in September 1947, its stated goal was to follow the 1937 draft in widening the scope of previous agreements to include the 'protection of persons of full age of either sex against being exploited for immoral purposes by a third party, *even with their consent* and *even without being taken abroad*' (emphasis added).[21] Compared to the Conventions of 1904, 1910, 1921, and 1933, the new text greatly expanded its reach into the national domain by requiring governments to repeal the regulation of prostitution and to create a criminal law framework targeting third parties. Beyond these criminal law provisions, the first draft targeted prostitutes themselves. Even though the direct criminalization of selling of sex was never explicitly on the table, Article 4 of the first draft criminalized prostitutes soliciting in public. The comment to this Article somewhat sheepishly acknowledged the contradictions between the punitive and rehabilitative aims of the Convention. It stated that while 'the draft convention does not intend to make the act or prostitution itself a punishable offense [...] it seems desirable to protect society, especially young persons, against accosting in the streets and other public places'.[22]

The proposed UN Convention also evinced a notably carceral approach to the 'social welfare' of women selling sex. Article 17(2) of the first draft specified that 'a specialized social service' should 'communicate to the Secretary-General of the UN information concerning effective methods which are used or contemplated for the social treatment of individual prostitutes or persons living on the verge of prostitution'.[23] This Article was followed by an unusually long comment laying out preventive, protective and rehabilitative measures, including some with a coercive character.[24] According to the vision of the Social Defence section, these rehabilitative measures were to be embedded in a system of doctors, psychiatrists, social workers, and 'women police'. This approach fit with the 'social defence' take on crime with its focus on the protection of society through the prevention of individual deviancy.[25] According to the later chief of the section, Manuel Lopez-Rey,

---

[21] UN Draft Convention of 1937, E/574.
[22] Ibid., 8–9.
[23] Ibid., 15.
[24] Ibid.
[25] Adolphe Delierneux, 'The United Nations in the Field of Prevention of Crime and Treatment of Offenders', in *Current Approaches to Delinquency: Yearbook 1949*, edited by National Probation and Parole Association (New York: National Probation and Parole Association, 1949), 248–58.

the focus on the prevention of individual crime targeted 'habitual crime', which included prostitution and 'related matters'.[26] Against this backdrop, the legal and social status of the prostitute remained contested. She or he was framed as both victim and potential agent of deviance against which society needed to be protected. While some elements of the first UN draft betrayed a carceral vision of the path to ending prostitution, other aspects were more grounded in the philanthropic and social reform genealogy of international approaches to prostitution since the nineteenth century. Article 14 mandated that signatory states provide 'free medical care for venereal diseases (VD) insofar as their national resources permit'.[27] The guarantee of free medical care addressed both the general public health issue of preventing VD in the wake of the mandated abolition of regulated prostitution and the need for prostitutes' 'physical rehabilitation'. According to the abolitionist framework, the treatment of VD was supposed to be provided free of charge and confidentially, guaranteeing both the protection of public health and the rights of prostitutes or persons with VD.

The first draft reveals the extent to which 'trafficking', always conceptualized as a crime at the intersection of forced migration and forced prostitution, had become a category through which prostitution could be debated more broadly in the postwar period. Throughout the 1930s and the 1940s, the 'solutions' proposed to trafficking had gradually shifted away from regulating transnational migration, which had dominated the discussion since the 1890s, to the suppression of commercial sex in general. While the substance and norms of a global approach to domestic prostitution laws were still contested, all delegations at the UN spoke with remarkable uniformity on their shared condemnation of prostitution as a manifestation of undesirable sexuality and undesirable labour.

Socialist States Confront the Convention for the International Suppression of Prostitution

At first, the Convention did not garner the interest of many governments; of the fifty-seven UN member states only fifteen replied to the first draft with suggestions and amendments, which were circulated in November 1948.[28] The newly socialist state of Czechoslovakia, whose communist government had been installed after a coup in February 1948, was one of the few that did. The first draft was deemed 'acceptable', because it 'conforms, for the most part, with the Czechoslovak

---

[26] Manuel Lopez-Rey, 'First U.N. Congress on the Prevention of Crime and the Treatment of Offenders', *Journal of Criminal Law and Criminology* 47, no. 5 (1957): 526–38.
[27] UN Draft Convention of 1937, E/574.
[28] UN Economic and Social Council, Observations submitted by Governments and Non-Governmental Organizations with respect to the revision of the 1937 Draft Convention Suppressing the Exploitation of the Prostitution of Others, 18 November 1948, E/1072/Annex 2.

regulations'.[29] Comments on single provisions were limited to Article 12 concerning international police cooperation. The Czechoslovak government favoured the creation of so-called 'criminal centres', which would directly communicate with each other in the 'international fight for the suppression of crime'.[30] This was not a new idea; indeed, in the interwar period much of the League of Nations' Traffic in Women Committee's energies had been devoted to calls for greater cooperation between police forces within signatory states to the 1921 and 1933 Conventions.[31] The International Criminal Police Commission (renamed Interpol in 1956) had played an increasingly prominent role in League discussions from the 1930s, sitting on the League Sub-Committee tasked with drafting what would become the 1937 Draft Convention from 1935.[32] Thus, when the Czechoslovak government argued that the Convention 'should express the principle of cooperation between the UN and the International Criminal Police Commission', it was laying a claim for a continuation of a carceral approach to the suppression of prostitution promoted by the international community since the interwar period.[33] On the question of specific conformity with Czechoslovak law the delegation remained silent. Perhaps this was because the Czechoslovak position was itself in flux at the time; it was not until 1950 that the communist government would produce its first socialist penal code, which criminalized pimping and brothel-keeping. Prostitution would, however, not be criminalized directly but come to be classed as a form of 'parasitism' in a 1956 amendment to the code.[34]

Other respondents to the 1947 draft were less reticent on substantive legal issues, and controversy soon arose over the question of relative culpability of those involved in the sex trade, especially the question of the social and legal status of the prostitute within the new framework. At heart was the following: Who should be penalized, the prostitute or the intermediaries (pimps, procurers, and brothel owners)? Over the course of the nineteenth and early twentieth centuries, increasingly influential abolitionist voices had argued that prostitutes themselves should not be blamed or punished for the 'crime' of prostitution.[35] However, the first draft

---

[29] Ibid., E/1072/Annex 2, 2.

[30] Ibid., 37.

[31] Mathieu Deflem, *Policing World Society: Historical Foundations of International Police Cooperation* (Oxford: Oxford University Press, 2002), 82. For some of the 'on-the-ground' implications of these calls for police cooperation, see David Petruccelli, 'Pimps, Prostitutes and Policewomen: The Polish Women Police and the International Campaign Against the Traffic in Women and Children between the World Wars', *Contemporary European History* 24, no. 3 (2015): 333–50.

[32] League of Nations, *Traffic in Women and Children. Report of the Work of its Fourteenth Session* (Geneva) 21 May 1935, C.227.1935.IV, 3. On the International Criminal Police Commission, see David Petruccelli, 'Banknotes from the Underground: Counterfeiting and the International Order in Interwar Europe', *Journal of Contemporary History* 51, no. 3 (2016): 507–30.

[33] UN Observations 1948, E/1072/Annex 2, 37.

[34] Barbara Havelková, 'Blaming all Women: On Regulation of Prostitution in State Socialist Czechoslovakia', *Oxford Legal Studies* 36, no. 1 (2016): 165–91, 171. The citation for the 1950 Czech Criminal Code is Act No. 86/1950 Coll, and the 1956 amendment is Act No. 63/1956 Coll, section 188a.

[35] Julia Laite, 'The Association for Moral and Social Hygiene: abolitionism and prostitution law in Britain (1915–1959)', *Women's History Review* 17, no. 2 (2008): 207–23; or for a comparative study on

proposed both the criminalization of third-party involvement in prostitution *and* of solicitation for commercial sex by individuals.[36] It was not a surprise that NGOs, such as the International Abolitionist Federation, expressed outrage at this draft, given the risk that women selling sex could be punished for keeping a brothel or soliciting.[37] These NGOs ensured that the negative implications for prostitutes in the first draft were duly noted by the UN Secretariat.[38]

In the light of the comments by both governments and NGOs, the Social Defence section drafted a revised second draft, whose reach was broadened to explicitly incorporate the provisions of all the previous anti-trafficking agreements, while abandoning the punishment of solicitation.[39] Just before the revised second draft was discussed in the Social Commission in May 1949, new observations by the Czechoslovak government signed by the Czech government's chief UN representative, Dr Vladimir Houdek, were sent to the Secretariat.[40] He took issue with the abandonment of soliciting as a crime, arguing that the newer 'provisions [...] do not quite tally with the regulation of Czechoslovak penal legislation'.[41] Houdek's comment helped to clarify the Czechoslovak delegation's understanding of the Convention, which he thought should indeed target prostitution per se. In line with socialist thought, he argued that efforts to prevent prostitution should focus on the improvement of socio-economic conditions.[42] However, he also called for 'repressive' means to end prostitution, which included 'enrolment for labour and re-education of women prostitutes' as well as 'curative treatment' conducted

---

the abolition of regulated prostitution in France, Germany, and Italy, see Malte König, *Der Staat als Zuhälter: Die Abschaffung der reglementierten Prostitution in Deutschland, Frankreich und Italien im 20. Jahrhunderts* (Berlin: Walter De Gruyter, 2016); on abolitionism, see also Judith R. Walkowitz, *Prostitution and Victorian Society. Women, Class and the State* (Cambridge: Cambridge University Press, 1980), 90–147.

[36] UN Draft Convention of 1937, E/574, 8.
[37] UN Observations 1948, E/1072/Annex 2, 21–22. The exact wording of Article 2 presented in draft E/574 was: 'Each of the High Contracting Parties further agrees to declare all houses or places of prostitution to be public nuisances and to provide for the punishment of any person who keeps or manages a building or place or a part thereof for the purpose of prostitution or being the owner thereof knowingly rents the said building or place or a part thereof for that purpose. / It shall be a punishable offense to finance or take part in the financing of a house or place of prostitution.' UN Draft Convention of 1937, 8.
[38] Ibid., E/574, 14–15; UN Observations 1948, E/1072/Annex 2, 45. Our interpretation of the NGOs' position is based not only on E/1072/Annex 2 but also on the bulk of archival records on NGOs' feedback to the first draft. See UN Archives New York, *Volume III*, Box S-0441-1163.
[39] The second draft was finalized in document E/1072, which also became the working draft in the Fourth Session of the Social Commission in May 1949 and was first circulated in December 1948, see UN Economic and Social Council, Draft Convention for the Suppression of the Traffic in Persons and of the Exploitation of the Prostitution of Others, E/1072, 23 December 1948.
[40] On Houdek's appointment to the UN immediately after the 1948 coup in Czechoslovakia, see 'Czech Coup Before Council', *United Nations News: Report on the United Nations and Its Related Agencies* (New York: Woodrow Wilson Foundation, 1948), 25.
[41] UN Division of Social Activities, 'Letter by Dr Vladimír Houdek, Permanent Delegation of Czechoslovakia to the United Nations, to Trygve Lie', 6 May 1949, UN Archives New York, *Volume III*, Box S-0441-1163, File 218/04/01.
[42] Ibid.

'simultaneously with the fight against VD' (a principle embedded within his support for compulsory treatment of disease).[43] Houdek defended 'the principle of compulsory treatment of VD', which he saw as the 'responsibility of the individual toward the whole community' and opposed the regulation-abolitionist idea of free, voluntary, and confidential treatment as 'gratis treatment of VD'.[44] This position, however, remained a rare instance of socialist support for a practice associated with prostitution regulation. More in line with the usual socialist antipathy to regulation was the response of the Soviet delegate during one of the sessions of the Social Commission in May 1949. Echoing abolitionism, the Soviet representative Aleksandr Borisov stressed how 'free treatment of VD' was necessary and 'constituted an important stage in the rehabilitation of prostitutes'. His amendment to introduce free services was, however, rejected.[45] Contrary to later claims that prostitution did not exist in Czechoslovakia, the focus on repressive measures as well as on international police cooperation in criminal matters points to the fact that prostitution or trafficking were not perceived to be gone from one day to the next. As Barbara Havelková has recently argued, prostitution policy in early state socialist Czechoslovakia, while surrounded by a discourse of class struggle, largely continued the abolitionist position that had been pursued during the interwar years. The language of 'enrolment for labour' presaged a shift that was concretized in the new 1956 Czechoslovak penal code towards classifying prostitution as a form of work shirking and thus 'parasitism', whereby prostitutes were to be condemned for failing to take their places as productive members of Czechoslovak society.[46] In contrast to Houdek's tacit acknowledgement that there was still the need for a 'struggle against prostitution', by 1949 the Soviet Union was claiming that the problem of prostitution and, by implication, the traffic in persons had been successfully abolished in the Soviet Bloc. The claim that prostitution had been 'eradicated' in the USSR had been the official position of the Soviet state since the early 1930s, when the supposed achievement of full female employment was meant to have removed any economic incentive to selling sex.[47] This claim was predicated on the long history of Marxist interpretations of prostitution, which framed commercial sex as a response to economic deprivation. According to this argument elaborated in the nineteenth century by Engels and August Bebel and in the early twentieth by Clara Zetkin and Aleksandra Kollontai, women in prostitution were victims of economic and social oppression and could only be 'saved' by a socialist

---

[43] Ibid.
[44] Ibid.
[45] UN Economic and Social Council, Social Commission, Fourth Session, Summary Record of the Seventy-Fourth Meeting, 5 May 1949, E/CN.5/Sr 74, 14.
[46] Havelková, 'Blaming all Women', 171.
[47] On attempts to reform Soviet prostitutes through labour, see Frances Bernstein, 'Prostitutes and Proletarians: The Soviet Labor Clinic as Revolutionary Laboratory', in *The Human Tradition in Modern Russia*, edited by William Husband (Wilmington, DE: Scholarly Resources Inc, 2000).

revolution.[48] At the same time, soon after the Bolshevik revolution, figures such as Kollontai began to talk uneasily of the threat of prostitution as a form of work shirking, decrying those women who continued to sell sex even when offered the option of 'productive labour' by the state. 'And what', Kollontai asked rhetorically, 'is the professional prostitute? She is a person whose energy is not used for the collective; a person who lives off others, by taking from the rations of others'.[49] With the declaration of the First Five Year Plan in 1928, the narrow space available to frame prostitutes as victims of capitalism disappeared. The NKVD, which had been quietly rounding up women as 'professional prostitutes' and sending them to labour camps since 1924, began to include them in mass sweeps of 'socially harmful elements'.[50] Women selling sex fell into the millions-strong category of victims of Stalinist terror.

Thus, when the Soviet delegate to the Third Committee of the 1949 General Assembly, Vasilii Zonov, asserted that 'better social and working conditions had long eradicated prostitution from his country', he was articulating a claim on the international stage that had been made domestically for two decades.[51] This stance largely excluded the Soviet delegation from debates about substantive issues and practical questions about how to deal with third parties, infrastructure (brothels), and prostitutes. There were, however, a few exceptions to the Soviet lack of engagement into matters of substance. For example, at various points during the negotiation of Article 1 and its definition of the 'exploitation of the prostitution of others' ('pimping'), the long-standing definitional controversy arose again over whether the goal of profiting from someone else's sexual labour ('motives of gain') was the defining element of this crime. While the British position was that a simple encouragement or mediation of prostitution should not be liable to punishment but only profiting from such encouragement, a number of NGOs, ranging from women's and religious organizations to the International Criminal Police Organization, opposed the retention of the 'purpose of gain' in Article 1, as did the Unites States and all socialist countries. The reasons they offered were not just based on legal

---

[48] Classic articulations include Friedrich Engels, *The Origin of the Family, Private Property and the State* (London: Penguin, 2010, originally published 1884); August Bebel, *Women and Socialism* (New York: Socialist Literature Co, 1910, originally published 1879); Clara Zetkin, *Die Arbeiterinnen und Frauenfrage der Gegenwart* (Berlin: Berliner Bolts-Tribüne, 1889); Aleksandra Kollontai, *Sotsial'nie osnovy zhenskogo voprosa* (Saint Petersburg: Znanie, 1909).

[49] Aleksandra Kollontai, 'Prostitution and Ways of Fighting it', in *Selected Writings of Alexandra Kollontai*, edited by Alix Holt (London: Allison and Busny, 1977, originally published 1921).

[50] On prostitutes as 'social parasites' and 'socially harmful elements', see *Gosudarstvennyi Arkhiv Rossiiskoi Federatsii*, hereafter GARF, Fond r-393, Opis' 1a, Delo 202, 1926, 'Rezoliutsii soveshchaniia Narodnykh Komissarov Vnutrennikh Del Soiznykh i Avtonomnykh respub- likh o bor'be s sotsial'nym paratsitizmam, strukture i metodakh raboty organov NKVD v tsentre i na mestakh i vzaimootnosheniiakh s drugimi vedomstvami i dr', ll. 3–3(ob) (Rezoliutsiia o bor'be s sotsial'nym parazitizmom); GARF f. A390, op. 21, d. 1, 'Narkomtrud, Komissiia po izucheniiu i ulucheniiu zhenskogo truda: Materialy o bor'be s prostitutsiei', 1923–28, ll. 52–53.

[51] UN General Assembly, Fourth Session 1949, Official Records, Third Committee (Social, Humanitarian and Cultural), 242nd Meeting, 5 October 1949, 40.

considerations but also ideas about civilizational progress that was supposedly inherent in the condemnation and criminalization of prostitution. In particular, delegates argued that criminal law should indeed target morally reprehensible behaviour. In his contribution during the 263rd plenary meeting of the General Assembly, the Soviet delegate Aleksandr Paniushkin supported the deletion of 'motives of gain' based on the moral condemnation of all parties involved in prostitution, including the prostitute as, he argued, 'prostitution was a profession incompatible with the elementary principles of morality and a crime offensive to public decency'.[52] The discussion of Article 1 reveals a conception of the role of criminal law that would go beyond the criminalization of exploitative practices. It was intended to police sexual behaviour that was considered to be morally and socially reprehensible (such as the act of selling sex).[53]

In their condemnation not just of trafficking but of prostitution itself, a variety of governments involved in the drafting of the 1949 UN Convention found a common political ground in a world that was increasingly divided. While the Cold War conflict became visible in assertions of countries such as the Soviet Union that prostitution did not exist on their territory because they had abolished the social conditions (poverty and unemployment) causing it, these conflict lines were neutralized in the shared critique of prostitution. This critique was framed in moral terms across the political spectrum, and bolstered (rather than challenged) a shift in the focus of opprobrium from prostitution to prostitutes in the Soviet Union, United States, and France. This Cold War consensus was all the more remarkable given the ultimate unworkability of the document the delegates produced. The near-global abolition of state-regulated prostitution during the twentieth century and especially after 1949 did not make prostitution, nor human trafficking, disappear. Instead, the social organization of commercial sex slowly adapted itself to conditions of increasing criminalization. The persistence of paid sex thus elicited myriad localized state and social reactions ranging from highly repressive approaches to limited toleration combined with informal strategies of spatial segregation, but it also, since the 1970s, increased opposition against abolition, especially by prostitutes' rights groups.[54]

---

[52] UN General Assembly, Fourth Session 1949, Official Records, 263rd Plenary Meeting, 2 December 1949, 461–62.

[53] UN General Assembly, Fourth Session 1949, Official Records, Sixth Committee, 205th Meeting, 25 November 1949, 428–29.

[54] Gail Pheterson, *A Vindication of the Rights of Whores: International Struggle for Prostitutes Rights* (Seattle, WA: Seal Press, 1989).

Consensus Breaks Down: The Debate over the Colonial Clause

Despite disputes over the clauses such as that concerning the compulsory treatment for VD or the 'motives of gain' wording, delegations across the emerging Cold War divide shared a moralistic commitment to eradicating prostitution, through carceral measures directed at prostitutes if necessary. Turning to issues of enforcement and jurisdiction surrounding the Convention, however, we can trace major splits between the socialist and newly decolonized states on the one hand, and the former imperial powers (and their allies) on the other. In these debates, socialist and newly decolonized delegations successfully connected the moral condemnation of prostitution to a moral condemnation of colonialism, conceptually linking sexual deviance and the evils of empire. Analysis of the 1949 UN Convention reveals that the issue of jurisdiction was a key lever for the cultivation of a 'socialist approach' to international law.

At heart was the issue of the Convention's enforceability and its applicability (or not) to non-self-governing territories. Initially, the Soviet delegation was closely involved in discussions on whether matters relating to the Convention should be settled in the International Court of Justice (ICJ) or by arbitration, as well as questions relating to extradition or international police cooperation.[55] Discussions of these aspects paled in comparison, however, to the extensive discussion on the issue of the so-called colonial clauses. All the prewar international anti-trafficking instruments contained articles that allowed a party state to sign on for, or exclude, any or all of its colonies—a so-called colonial clause.[56] By the post-Second World War period, critics contended that such clauses 'advanced the proposition that colonial territories were not valid, independent actors, and that in international law their existence was solely a function of the colonial relationship'.[57] This was articulated in the context of a broader push to make colonial powers accountable for the development of self-government in territories under their control from the early days of the UN. Chapter XI of the UN Charter dealt with non-self-governing territories, with Article 73 committing administering powers 'to ensure, with due respect for the culture of the peoples concerned, their political, economic, social,

---

[55] The Soviet Union was long an opponent of including clauses on the arbitration of cases in the ICJ, a position it only abandoned with Perestroika in 1989; see Theodor Schweisfurth, 'The Acceptance by the Soviet Union of the Compulsory Jurisdiction of the ICJ for Six Human Rights Conventions', *European Journal of International Law* 2, No. 1 (1990): 110–17.

[56] There is little scholarship on the colonial clauses, despite their importance to nineteenth- and early twentieth-century treaties, including the 1904 International Agreement and 1910 Convention. The British government reserved the right to adhere to or withdraw from the anti-trafficking agreements on the part of its colonies from the very first (1904) agreement, as correspondence between the Home Office and the Foreign Office attests; see The National Archives (TNA), FO 83/2199, 16 May 1904 Landsdowne to Monson. See also Article II of the International Convention for the Suppression of the White Slave Traffic (1910).

[57] Christopher N. J. Roberts, *The Contentious History of the International Bill of Human Rights* (New York: Cambridge University Press, 2014), 130.

and educational advancement' as well as 'to take due account of the political aspirations of the peoples, and to assist them in the progressive development of their free political institutions'.[58] From the outset, delegations from recently decolonized states in Africa and Asia were vociferous in their insistence on international accountability to ensure that colonial powers be held to these responsibilities.[59] In the rapidly changing context of the postwar world, their efforts ensured that questions of self-determination were embedded in the very foundation of the postwar international legal regime, setting the stage for the first debates over the colonial clauses.

Colonial clauses were not confined to the anti-trafficking treaties—they were also present in the League anti-narcotics agreements and in the Genocide Convention, among other instruments.[60] But it was the case of the anti-trafficking treaties which gave the Soviet delegation the first opportunity to announce its staunch opposition to such clauses and thus to the international legal approach of colonial powers. In October 1947, the Soviet delegation successfully proposed a resolution to the Third Committee of the UN General Assembly calling on it to delete all colonial clauses as part of the adoption of the anti-trafficking treaties by the UN.[61] Predictably, the British delegation made a countermove, calling for an amendment to reinsert these provisions.[62] In the immediate postwar period, Britain's Colonial Office remained insistent on the presence of colonial clauses, claiming that these provisions facilitated the consolidation of local autonomy in non-self-governing territories (to use the UN's preferred term for colonial territories).[63] Former British colonies in the General Assembly, however, fervently and loudly disagreed, expressing support for the original Soviet resolution. Mr Pirzada, the delegate for the (very) newly independent Pakistan, declaring that 'if this amendment is passed, it will provide a loophole for the reactionary elements in the colonies'.[64] Furthermore, Pirzada asserted that any attempt to retain colonial clauses would undermine the very universal claims of the UN project more

---

[58] For Article 73 of the UN Charter, see http://www.un.org/en/sections/un-charter/un-charter-full-text/, accessed 10 July 2018.

[59] See Yassin El-Ayouty, *The United Nations and Decolonization: The Role of Afro-Asia* (The Hague: Martinus Nijhoff, 1971), especially 29–66 'The Declaration Regarding Non-Self-Governing Territories and the Concepts of International Responsibility for Colonial Administration'.

[60] See Article XII of the Convention on the Prevention and Punishment of the Crime of Genocide (1948) and Article 8 of the Protocol Bringing Under International Control Drugs Outside the Scope of the Convention of 13 July 1931 for Limiting the Manufacture and Regulating the Distribution of Narcotic Drugs (1946). Domestic Soviet commentary on the Genocide Convention highlighted critique of the colonial clause; see S. Volodin, 'Konventsiia o preduprezhdenii prestupleniia genotsida i nakazanii za nego', Sovetskoe Gousdarstvo i Pravo 7 (1954): 125–28.

[61] UN General Assembly, Ninety-Seventh Plenary Meeting, Second General Assembly, 20 October 1947, 351.

[62] Ibid., 354.

[63] A. W. Brian Simpson, *Human Rights and the End of Empire: Britain and the Genesis of the European Convention* (Oxford: Oxford University Press, 2011), 288–89.

[64] UN General Assembly, Ninety-Seventh Plenary Meeting 1947, 354.

broadly, as by allowing imperial powers to pick and choose the colonies to which UN conventions applied they had the potential to exclude some subjects from the protections supposedly offered by international law.[65] In the light of opposition from both Socialist Bloc and recently decolonized states, the British amendment was rejected by the General Assembly, thus setting the scene for the decisive refusal of colonial clauses by the UN a year later when the revivified anti-trafficking Convention came up for discussion.[66] By the end of 1948, the second draft Convention for the Suppression of Traffic in Persons was open for commentary in the ECOSOC's Social Commission. In the fourth session of the Commission in May 1949, the Soviet representative, Aleksandr Borisov, registered objections to multiple proposed amendments, including the British attempt to remove the words 'for the purposes of gain' from the definition of pimping and a French attempt to allow for (limited) state regulation of prostitution.[67] But most important for the Soviets at this point was their opposition to the continued inclusion of the colonial clause (Article 27). Such a clause, Borisov declared, 'might lead to the uncontrolled expansion of the traffic in persons and the exploitation of prostitution in the very territories most predisposed thereto', as trafficking (he implied) was more likely to occur in the oppressed colonies, which had been denied the social and economic progress experienced by the metropole.[68] Mobilizing a discourse of cultural developmentalism, Borisov suggested that imperialism had imposed a moral backwardness on colonies that the 1949 Convention promised to rectify. In this way, he discursively linked the postwar language of global moral reform to the critique of empire, in language that would prove influential in the coming debates about the Convention's final form.

The United Kingdom and France opposed this argument, arguing that in fact the colonial clauses allowed them to consult with their non-self-governing territories, to give them the option to accede or not to the Convention even when they did not have self-government.[69] However, the Soviet delegations stood their ground, ensuring that the issue of the colonial clause would come up in the Third Committee's discussions about the draft text before the Convention came before the General Assembly. The Soviet intervention highlights the extent to which it perceived the 1949 UN Convention as having a humanitarian aim (despite the fact that it was technically framed within an inchoate body of transnational criminal law). In their representation, a colonial clause opened the door to a refusal of colonial powers to extend social benefits to the colonies. The debates over the colonial

[65] Ibid.
[66] UN Resolution of the General Assembly, UN Doc A/519. 1947, 32–39; UN General Assembly, Ninety-Seventh Plenary Meeting 1947, 355.
[67] UN Economic and Social Council, Report of the Fourth Session of the Social Commission to the Economic and Social Council, E/1359; E/CN.5/152, 31 May 1949, 5–7.
[68] Ibid., 7.
[69] Ibid., 8.

clauses, and the tussle between the United Kingdom and France on the one side, and the Soviet and decolonized bloc on the other, came to a head at the 264th Plenary Meeting of the General Assembly in December 1949, which was tasked with finalizing the Convention's text. In the final meeting of the Third Committee, prior to putting the draft convention before the General Assembly, the delegate of the Ukrainian Soviet Socialist Republic (SSR) put forward an amendment that declared that, in the wording of the Convention, 'The word State shall include all the colonies and Trust Territories of a State signatory acceding to the convention, and all Territories for which such State in internationally responsible.'[70] Thus the goal was not only to remove the offending Article 27 but also to ensure that imperial states signed on behalf of non-self-governing territories in relation to every article in the Convention. This amendment could not but raise the ire of said imperial states, especially the United Kingdom. The subsequent discussion in the General Assembly on 2 December 1949 opened with a declaration by UK delegate Gerard Corley-Smith, who announced his country's staunch opposition to this amendment. In doing so, he deplored the positions of

> delegations such as those of the Ukrainian SSR and Poland, who had tried to infer in the Third Committee that the United Kingdom was a totalitarian, imperialistic Power, which kept its colonial territories in subjugations and which did not wish to apply to convention to its territories because it had no desire to improve social standards in those territories.[71]

Suggesting that the Socialist Bloc had not only tried to interfere with but also to smear the United Kingdom, Corley-Smith stated categorically that were the General Assembly to approve a version of the Convention without the colonial clause, the United Kingdom could not accede to it.[72]

Labelling the United Kingdom hypocritical, the Pakistani delegate, Ahmed Shah Bokhari, mobilized the language of morality to link the 'moral crime' of prostitution with the immorality of colonialism, declaring that 'so long as the metropolitan powers clung to those vast congregations of peoples and to those vast territories, to

---

[70] UN Economic and Social Council, Fourth Session. Third Committee, Item 62. Draft Convention for the Suppression of the Traffic in Persons and of the Exploitation of the Prostitution of Others. Ukrainian Soviet Social Republic Amendments to Articles 23, 24 and 27. A/C.3/L.10, 30 September 1949. It is important to note that the status of the delegations of both the Ukrainian SSR and Belorussian SSR were different to that of the other Socialist Bloc countries, as both were federative units of the USSR but nonetheless had their own foreign ministries and own delegations. On the 'flexible' concept of sovereignty in the Soviet Union and the effect of this concept on the relationship between Soviet delegations at the UN, see Sabine Dullin and Etienne Forestier-Peyrat, 'Flexible Sovereignties of the Revolutionary State: Soviet Republics Enter World Politics', *Journal of the History of International Law* 19, no. 2 (2017): 178–99.

[71] UN General Assembly, Two-Hundred and Sixty-Fourth Plenary Meeting, Fourth General Assembly, A/PV.264, 2 December 1949, 467.

[72] Ibid., 468.

which they had no moral right even though they might be trying in their own way to do good, all their actions would be full of contradictions and difficulties'.[73] The removal of the colonial clause was a way to highlight the fundamental incompatibility of colonialism and the progressive social policies of the UN, as typified, in Bokhari's view, by the attack on trafficking and prostitution.

As the author of the key amendment removing the colonial clause, the Ukrainian delegate pronounced wearily that colonial powers clearly 'did not intend to combat seriously that social evil which was incompatible with the dignity of the human person', and were only 'taking refuge in legal quibbles' because they would like the traffic in persons to continue in their colonies.[74] By speaking simultaneously of the immorality of colonialism and the moral fight against prostitution, the socialist and decolonized delegates suggested that the anticolonial fight relied upon the moral uplift of colonies and their populations, and that the fight against prostitution was a key part of this struggle. That they did so in language which set aside claims for legal autonomy in favour of calls for the extension of international social programmes, speaks to the evolving nature of socialist and anticolonial activism in the context of the new UN, and of the postwar international legal landscape.

In the end, in December 1949, the postcolonial and Socialist Bloc argument won the day. The Ukrainian amendment was carried and entered the final text of the Convention, thus ensuring that it applied automatically to all constituent parts of a signatory state, and none could be excluded from it. When the ECOSOC produced a final Convention draft for the General Assembly to vote on in 1949, it lacked any colonial applicability clause.[75] When the time came to vote on the text during the fourth General Assembly on 2 December, the issue of colonial clauses contributed to the decision of Britain and France to vote 'No' (the only 'No' votes) and of the United States to abstain. The USSR, Belorussian, and Ukrainian delegations, alongside former colonial possessions including Burma, Cuba, Egypt, India, Iraq, Pakistan, and Syria and fellow state socialist delegations such as Czechoslovakia and Poland, contributed to the resounding 'Yes' vote.[76]

The October 1947 and December 1949 attacks on the colonial clause, spearheaded by the Soviet and Ukrainian delegations, preceded those which have been noted by historians as part of the 1947–50 debates over the Universal Declaration on Human Rights and the International Covenant on Human Rights; indeed they arguably provided the template for the later controversy.[77] In December

---

[73] Ibid., 470.
[74] Ibid., 469.
[75] Ibid., 472.
[76] Ultimately, thirty-five member states voted Yes, two voted No, while there were fifteen abstentions. Voting Record for UN Resolution A/Res/317(IV), 2 December 1949, via UN Bibliographic Information System Voting Record Search, https://digitallibrary.un.org/record/670744?ln=en, accessed 30 September 2024. It is worth noting that France later signed on to the Convention in 1960; Britain and the United States never signed.
[77] Roland Burke, Decolonization and the Evolution of International Human Rights (Philadelphia, PA: University of Pennsylvania Press, 2010), 40–41.

1947, two months after the initial discussion of the colonial clause and the 1949 Convention, the Soviet Union argued in the second session of the Commission on Human Rights that 'colonial dependencies should be explicitly included as beneficiaries of any human rights document'.[78] The issue of deleting the colonial clause also came up with regard to the drafting of the 1946 Protocol amending the 1931 Narcotics Convention as well as the 1948 UN Genocide Convention, although without success.[79] The Soviet and postcolonial bloc's deletion of the colonial clause in the 1949 Convention was thus the first of its kind in the postwar era. It prompted what Christopher Roberts called the UN's subsequent 'bright-line rule' on colonial clauses, that in the absence of a colonial clause any convention would automatically 'apply to all territories for which the Contracting States had international responsibility'.[80] Just as Hartley Shawcross, the British representative at the October 1947 meeting of the General Assembly, fearfully prophesied, the deletion of the colonial clauses from the 1949 UN Convention was used to bolster the anticolonial position in later multilateral treaties concerning cross-border crime or human rights.[81] Later, during the drafting of the International Covenants on Human Rights, the Soviet Union clashed again with Great Britain over exactly this issue, with the latter attempting to insert a clause allowing it to exclude colonies from the Covenants.[82] In the 1950 General Assembly, representatives of newly independent states including India and Syria excoriated the British position (which was supported by France and the United States) and praised that of the USSR.[83] In the end, the colonial clauses were definitively defeated, heralding the dawn of the anticolonial bloc within the UN.

Conclusion

As this chapter has shown, a closer look at the negotiations of the 1949 UN Convention reveals contested and often contradictory ideas about the goals of this instrument and the ways they were to be achieved. Tensions initially emerged with regard to the status of the prostitute in societies without regulated prostitution, including socialist countries. Based on the assumption that both prostitution and the prostitute had disappeared with the introduction of socialism, the socialist stance on prostitution created a double bind. As a non-existent problem, it could not be

---

[78] Roberts, *The Contentious History*, 128.
[79] See Letter from Mr Alan Renouf in the Legal Department to Mr Finn K. Tennfjord of the Social Activities Division, 5 July 1949, in UN-NY, File No.: LEG 2184/4/01, C/38/9/12/47.
[80] Roberts, *The Contentious History*, 130. Interestingly, while Roberts notes these discussions, he does not note their embeddedness within debates about the Convention on the Suppression of the Traffic.
[81] UN General Assemby, Ninety-Seventh Plenary Meeting 1947, 351.
[82] Roberts, *The Contentious History*.
[83] Ibid., 146, 149.

publicly discussed or debated without questioning the ideological pillars of the socialist stance on prostitution, and, possibly, socialism itself.

By shifting focus to the colonial clauses, the Soviet delegation was able to turn the apparently uncontroversial goal of protecting women from forced prostitution into a major ideological win for the socialist and anticolonial camp at the UN. What is more, by pointing out that in the Soviet Union, and many of the former colonies that stood with it, prostitution was criminalized or 'liquidated', the Soviet delegates were able to forge a discursive link between the moral outrage against colonialism and the moral outrage against prostitution and trafficking in women.[84] That they were able to do this despite a broad agreement across the emerging Cold War divides about the general immorality and criminality of prostitution speaks to evolving political and legal strategies within the UN. Faced with agreement on substantive issues, the Soviet delegations turned to questions of enforceability, and in particular questions of sovereignty and statehood in the applicability of international law. With these issues, they found a wedge with which to open up a (tense) debate on colonialism, decolonization, and the rights of non-self-governing territories.

The existing historiography on the Soviet Union, decolonization, and the Cold War at the UN largely presents the debates on colonialism as a development that emerged under Nikita Khrushchev, tied to the shift to the Third World within the Soviet Union itself.[85] As our analysis of the 1949 UN Convention deliberations shows, however, the Soviet delegation at the UN saw international law as a forum through which to critique imperialism, and to foster alliances against Western states, as early as 1947. This was a period in which Soviet diplomats and jurists were experiencing a 'mania' for international law, in the wake of their key role in the Nuremberg trials and involvement in the UN's International Law Commission.[86] Their engagement with the form and substance of the 1949 Convention was thus not merely an attempt to obstruct for the sake of obstruction (as similar involvement in the Genocide Convention has been rather tendentiously framed by one historian).[87] Instead, it represented an effort to use international law to propose an alternative vision of the new global political system, just as the British, French, and US delegates did.

---

[84] The liquidation of prostitution in Egypt was e.g. a key claim made by the Egyptian delegate at the aforementioned 2 December 1949 meeting of the General Assembly, A/PV.264, 468.

[85] On the Soviet role in discussions about decolonization at the UN under Khrushchev, see Ilya Gaiduk, *Divided Together: The United States, the Soviet Union, and the United Nations, 1945–1965* (Stanford, CA: Stanford University Press, 2013); Alessandro Iandolo, 'Beyond the Shoe: Rethinking Khrushchev at the Fifteenth Session of the United Nations General Assembly', *Diplomatic History*, 41, no. 1 (2017): 128–54.

[86] Hirsch, 'The Soviets at Nuremberg'. See Francine Hirsch, *Soviet Judgment at Nuremberg: A Cold War Story* (Oxford: Oxford University Press, 2020).

[87] See Anton Weiss-Wendt, *The Soviet Union and the Gutting of the UN Genocide Convention* (Madison, WI: University of Wisconsin Press, 2017).

The 1949 UN Convention has often been misunderstood by both legal scholars and activists as a human rights document.[88] Rather than human rights, however, this chapter has shown that a concern with the internationalization of criminal law and the creation of a global approach to commercial sex was the driving force behind the Convention. Further, it was not questions of content alone that determined the debates surrounding the Convention or the decision by, for example, Britain to not ratify it. Arguments about jurisdiction, in particular regarding the colonial clauses, were entangled with the birth pangs of the UN, and the newly decolonized world. The 1949 UN Convention was embedded in the particular historical moment of the early Cold War, something that should be acknowledged by those anti-trafficking activists who call for its revivification today.

---

[88] See e.g. Laura Reanda, 'Prostitution as a Human Rights Question: Problems and Prospects of United Nations Action', *Human Rights Quarterly* 13, no. 2 (1991): 202–28.

10
State Socialist Contributions to the Criminalization of Apartheid

Raluca Grosescu

Introduction

At the end of the Second World War, and particularly after the mid-1950s, anti-racism, anti-apartheid, and anticolonialism emerged as central issues on the United Nations' (UN) agenda. This chapter examines how and why Eastern European and African socialist governments and legal experts took the lead in criminalizing apartheid as a major international crime and denouncing the Western reluctance to move away from the colonial order and its so-called civilizational mission. It first demonstrates how socialist internationalism—in its different and often conflicting Marxist–Leninist and pan-African forms—laid the ideological foundation for anticolonial human rights politics, which connected the struggle against racial discrimination to self-determination, anti-imperialism, and anti-capitalism.

It then emphasizes how Eastern European and African socialists shepherd the adoption of three international instruments which outlawed apartheid as an international crime during the Cold War: the 1968 UN Convention on the Non-Applicability of War Crimes and Crimes against Humanity; the 1973 UN Convention on the Suppression and Punishment of the Crime of Apartheid; and the 1977 Addition Protocol I to the 1949 Geneva Conventions. Beside criminalizing apartheid, these instruments generated other legal innovations. They imposed the non-applicability of statutory limitations to major international crimes, proposed a prosecution regime based on universal jurisdiction, recognized wars of national liberation as international armed conflicts, and initiated the first debates on the criminalization of multinational corporations' complicity in mass crimes and political repression.

Finally, the chapter analyses the anti-apartheid engagements of the International Association of Democratic Lawyers (IADL), a global professional association largely funded by the Soviet Union and its Eastern European allies. Starting in the mid-1950s, this organization became a hub for leftist lawyers from across the world—including Western Europe. The IADL facilitated a wide-ranging transnational mobilization of socialist jurists and produced a far more radical anti-apartheid discourse than liberal experts in the West did. This discourse went beyond condemning political repression and racial discrimination in South Africa as violations of the rule of law and connected the anti-apartheid cause to the denunciation of colonialism as a whole and the recognition of wars of national liberation as international armed conflicts.

In contrast to the current scholarship on the criminalization of apartheid, this chapter moves beyond the legal analysis of specific international instruments and their relevance after the demise of South Africa's apartheid regime.[1] It focuses instead on the political history of a variety of interconnected legal mobilizations—including governmental initiatives at the UN, judicial engagements at the International Court of Justice (ICJ), and the transnational activism of professional legal associations. In so doing, it provides an alternative to two dominant narratives that have either tied the denunciation of apartheid to Third World/Non-Aligned activism (often seen as monolithic, despite ideological divisions)[2] or Eurocentrically emphasized the centrality of transnational human rights mobilizations led by Western non-governmental organizations.[3] The chapter demonstrates that making apartheid a major international crime originated in socialist ideology and agency from Africa and Eastern Europe, although countries and experts from other world regions and with non-socialist orientations endorsed these efforts. This account also complements an emergent literature on the role of the Eastern socialist camp in the anti-apartheid solidarity movement and the consolidation of UN discourses against racial discrimination,[4] by examining the global socialist cooperation to ban apartheid through international criminal and humanitarian law. The chapter avoids, however, a linear and triumphalist narrative: it highlights relations of both cooperation and conflict between various socialisms across the

---

[1] See M. Cherif Bassiouni and Daniel H. Derby, 'Final Report on the Establishment of an International Criminal Court for the Implementation of the Apartheid Convention and Other Relevant International Instruments', *Hofstra Law Review* 9, no. 2 (1981): 532–92; Ariel Bultz, 'Redefining Apartheid in International Criminal Law, *Criminal Law Forum*, 24 (2013): 205–33; Carola Lingaas, 'The Crime against Humanity of Apartheid in a Post-Apartheid World', *Oslo Law Review* 2, no. 2 (2015): 86–115; Paul Eden, 'The Practices of Apartheid as a War Crime: A Critical Analysis', *Yearbook of International Humanitarian Law* 16, no. 1 (2015): 89–117.

[2] See, for instance, the contributions on apartheid and national liberations movements in Jochen von Bernstorff and Phillip Dann (eds.), *The Battle for International Law: South–North Perspectives on the Decolonization Era* (Oxford: Oxford University Press, 2019).

[3] Audie Klotz, *Norms in International Relations: The Struggle against Apartheid* (New York: Cornell University Press, 1995); Robert Harvey, *The Fall of Apartheid. The Inside Story from Smuts to Mbeki* (New York: Palgrave, 2001); Rob Skinner, 'Humanitarianism and Human Rights in Global Anti-Apartheid', in *A Global History of Anti-Apartheid. 'Forward to Freedom' in South Africa*, edited by Anna Konieczna and Rob Skinner (Cham: Palgrave Macmillan, 2019), 33–65; Lorenzo Ferrari, 'Anti-Apartheid Goes to Brussels: Forms of Transnational Cooperation Between the Anti-Apartheid Movements and the European Community Countries: 1977–1992', in *A Global History*, edited by Konieczna and Skinner, 239–64.

[4] Sebastian Gehrig, 'Reaching Out to the Third World: East Germany's Anti-Apartheid and Socialist Human Rights Campaign', *German History* 36 no. 4 (2018): 574–97; Paul Betts, James Mark, Idesbald Goddeeris, and Kim Christiaens. 'Race, Socialism and Solidarity: Anti-Apartheid in Eastern Europe', in *A Global History*, edited by Konieczna and Skinner, 151–99; Sebastian Gehrig, James Mark, Paul Betts, Kim Christiaens, and Idesbald Goddeeris 'Eastern Bloc, Human Rights and the Global Fights Against Apartheid', *East Central Europe*, 46 no. 2–3 (2019): 290–317.

world, as well as moments of disruption in the socialist legal solidarity against apartheid and racial discrimination.

State Socialist Engagements with Apartheid and Self-Determination

Socialist denunciations of racial discrimination and its extreme incarnation in the apartheid regime began immediately after the end of the Second World War and amplified during the decolonization process in Africa, from the mid-1950s to the mid-1970s. For Eastern European governments, this was a matter of both principles and realpolitik. On the one hand, in contrast to the Wilsonian theory of self-determination, which had a basis in racial thinking and was designed mainly for so-called 'civilized nations', Bolshevik ideology envisaged self-determination as a right equally applicable to colonized, non-white, non-European peoples.[5] Anti-racism, anti-imperialism, and anti-capitalism were interconnected concepts in the Soviet doctrine of self-determination, which provided a theoretical foundation for national liberation movements across the globe.[6] On the other hand, anti-apartheid and anti-discrimination were instrumental for Eastern European governments to conflate capitalism and racism, to attack the West for its racial and segregationist policies in the colonies and the US South, assert comparative superiority of Soviet legality, and advance their socialist model in the Third World. Eastern European governments and experts systematically lobbied international organizations against colonialism and racism, provided financial support and military training for national liberation movements, and secured humanitarian aid for South African and Namibian refugees.[7]

Beginning in the mid-1950s, newly decolonized countries in Africa, particularly those adopting a socialist outlook (such as Egypt under Gamal Abdel Nasser, Ghana under Kwame Nkrumah, Guinea under Ahmed Sékou Touré, and Tanzania under Julius Nyerere), joined their Eastern European counterparts in condemning colonialism and apartheid at the international level and supporting national liberation movements, including the African National Congress in South Africa and the South West Africa People's Organisation (SWAPO) in Namibia. While the 1955 Bandung Conference highlighted the legitimacy of the right to self-determination, it did not engage directly with apartheid. It was the birth of newly independent African states with socialist orientations that brought anti-apartheid at the core

---

[5] Vladimir I. Lenin, 'The Right of Nations to Self-determination', in *V.I. Lenin: Collected Works*, vol 20 (Moscow: Progress, 1972), 393–454.

[6] Robert Knox and Ntina Tzouvala, 'Looking Eastwards. The Bolshevik Theory of Imperialism and International Law', in *Revolutions in International Law: The Legacies of 1917*, edited by Kathryn Greenman, Anne Orford, Anna Saunders, and Ntina Tzouvala (Cambridge: Cambridge University Press, 2021), 32–33; see also Bradley Simpson, Chapter 3 in this volume.

[7] Betts et al., 'Race, Socialism and Solidarity'.

of the Afro-Asian Bloc's militancy at the UN.[8] During the 1950s and 1960s, anticolonialism, pan-Africanism, and African socialism converged, generating mutually consolidating imaginaries. Left-leaning states played a central role in the struggle to achieve liberation for the entire continent and end both apartheid and white minority rule in the Portuguese colonies and southern Africa. Like their Eastern European counterparts, African socialists aimed to conflate capitalism and imperialism and legitimize an alternative political and economic model, even if certain African socialist governments did not renounce Western investment. As Priya Lal remarked, 'the countries where the most ambitious African socialist programmes were implemented also exhibited the deepest commitment to supporting anti-apartheid and ongoing liberation struggles. This common investment in anticolonial activism reflected and reinforced a shared commitment to the ideals of African socialism.'[9] First, Accra, Conakry, and Algiers, and later, Dar es Salaam became Meccas of liberation movements.[10]

Although understood in different ways, socialist internationalism—in the form of Marxism-Leninism or pan-African socialism—informed the first anticolonial and anti-apartheid discourses and actions at a global level. In terms of international law, during the negotiations of the 1948 Universal Declaration of Human Rights, the USSR campaigned to remove references to 'civilized nations' and assured the application of the Declaration in the colonies.[11] The same happened with the 1949 UN Convention for the Suppression of the Traffic in Persons and of the Exploitation of the Prostitution of Others, which was the first international convention to remove the 'colonial clause'.[12] The Soviet Union was inconsistent in its theory and practice of self-determination, as evinced by the annexation of the Baltic states and the invasion of Hungary and Czechoslovakia in 1956 and 1968.[13] However, the USSR pushed for the inclusion of a reference to 'self-determination' in the preamble of the UN Charter and the 1948 Universal Declaration and put the adoption of the Declaration on the Granting of Independence to Colonial Countries and Peoples by the General Assembly on the UN agenda in 1960.

---

[8] The 1955 Bandung Declaration mentions the right to self-determination nine times, and denounces racial segregation in South Africa, but specifically in connection to the Indian and Pakistani communities. Apartheid itself is, however, never mentioned.

[9] Priya Lal, *African Socialism in Postcolonial Tanzania: Between the Village and the World* (Cambridge: Cambridge University Press, 2015), 41. See also the chapters on Algeria, Ghana, and Tanzania in *The Road to Democracy in South Africa: Vol 5, African Solidarity Part 1*, edited by Sifiso Ndlovu (Pretoria: Unisa Press, 2013).

[10] Arnold J. Tumu and Joel Das Neves Tembre (eds.), *Southern African Liberation Struggles: Contemporaneous Documents* (Dar es Salaam: Mkuki na Nyota, 2014); Jeffrey James Byrne, *Mecca of Revolution: Algeria, Decolonization and the Third World Order* (Oxford: Oxford University Press, 2016).

[11] Jessica Whyte, 'Human Rights, Revolution and the "Good Society": The Soviet Union and the Universal Declaration of Human Rights', *Revolutions*, edited by Greenman et al., 421–22.

[12] See Sonja Dolinsek and Philippa Hetherington, Chapter 9 in this volume.

[13] Lauri Mälksoo, 'The Soviet Approach to the Right of Peoples to Self-determination: Russia's Farewell to jus publicum europaeum', *Journal of the History of International Law* 19, no. 2 (2017): 200–18.

Eastern European states were also instrumental in the adoption of the UN Convention on the Elimination of all Forms of Racial Discrimination (CERD) in 1965. They campaigned together with African and Asian governments to condemn apartheid as part of this international instrument, although they also made sure to eliminate discrimination on religious grounds, due to their atheist ideology and the antisemitism of their regimes in the 1960s.[14] Eastern Europeans not only lobbied for the prohibition of policies of racial discrimination but also for the condemnation of propaganda and incitement to racial discrimination into CERD—an aspect that fuelled the opposition of Western states (particularly the United States and the United Kingdom), who saw it as an infringement on the freedom of speech. Moreover, in 1966, in response to various African proposals, backed by the Eastern Bloc, UN Generally Assembly Resolutions 2184 (XXI) and 2202 (XXI) condemned apartheid as a crime against humanity. However, these texts did not have binding force and did not reflect on apartheid in legal terms.

Despite this coalition at the UN, Eastern European doctrines and international initiatives came along with a 'paternalistic vision of a socialist civilizing mission to aid benighted African blacks stuck in backwardness'.[15] Socialist African leaders often criticized this outlook, even as they made common cause with Eastern European countries at international organizations. Moreover, while Eastern European anti-racist commitments presented racial discrimination as a phenomenon located exclusively in the capitalist world, African socialists connected it to white oppression against Black people and often saw the Soviet Union as a new potential colonizer in Africa. Conversely, both Eastern European and African socialist regimes avoided any self-reflection on racial and ethnic discrimination in their own countries (such as against Jews and Roma people in Eastern Europe or against national minorities in African countries). As did their Eastern European counterparts, African socialists used the anti-apartheid cause to divert international attention from authoritarian practices at home. After independence, many of these new governments established dictatorial political systems. They joined Western colonial powers and the USSR in using human rights as a diplomatic 'weapon' at the UN, while infringing on human rights in their own societies.[16]

---

[14] Ofra Friesel, 'Race versus Religion in the Making of the International Convention Against Racial Discrimination, 1965', *Law and History Review* 32, no. 2 (2014): 351–83.

[15] James Mark, 'Race', in *Socialism Goes Global: The Soviet Union and Eastern Europe in the Age of Decolonization*, edited by James Mark and Paul Betts (Oxford: Oxford University Press, 2021), 227. See also Bogdan Iacob, Chapter 7 in this volume.

[16] Jochen von Bernstorff and Philipp Dann, 'Introduction', in *The Battle for International Law: South–North Perspectives on the Decolonization Era*, edited by Jochen von Bernstorff and Phillip Dann (Oxford: Oxford University Press, 2019), 19.

Outliers at the ICJ

The story of Eastern European–African anti-racist solidarity also had its juridical outliers. There were exceptional legal moments when jurists from the Eastern Bloc did not stand for the anti-apartheid and the anticolonial cause and instead sided with Western states. One example was the rulings of the ICJ in the *South West Africa* cases, a decision that continued the colonial tradition of international law and the reluctance to advance human rights, anti-apartheid, and anti-racial discrimination.[17] In 1960, Ethiopia and Liberia challenged the legality of South Africa's administration over the mandated territory of South West Africa at the ICJ. They contended that South Africa had violated its obligations under the League of Nations Mandate by, inter alia, introducing apartheid, establishing military bases in South West Africa, and refusing to submit reports on human rights or transmit petitions on rights violations to the UN. Ethiopia and Liberia argued that, as former members of the League of Nations, they were entitled to address the ICJ (which took over from the Permanent Court of International Justice in 1946) if a mandated territory was not ruled in the interests of the indigenous population, according to League of Nations' provisions.

In 1962, the ICJ ruled with a narrow majority of eight to seven that the complaint was legitimate and that the Court had jurisdiction over the case. The judges who opposed the decision came from contemporary and former colonial powers (the United Kingdom, France, the Netherlands) and Australia, but were surprisingly backed by the Polish representative, Bohdan Winiarski. In contrast, the US justice, Philip Jessup, stood with judges from the Third World, as did Soviet judge Vladimir Koretsky.[18] In 1966, the ICJ was supposed to decide upon the substantive part of the case, but the British and Australian judges once again raised questions regarding jurisdiction. Given that the composition of the Court had changed from 1962 to 1966 in favour of the colonial powers, the ICJ refused to address the merits of the dispute, arguing that Ethiopia and Liberia did not have any legal right or interest to present claims concerning South Africa's mandate. Once again, Winiarski supported this position. Jessup wrote a fierce dissenting opinion. He argued that apartheid amounted to a universal crime: based on the UN Charter and other international instruments, not only Ethiopia and Liberia but any UN member could in fact address the ICJ on South Africa's occupation of

---

[17] For detailed analyses of these cases, see Victor Kattan, '"There was an elephant in the court room": Reflections on the Role of Judge Sir Percy Spender (1897–1985) in the South-West Africa Cases (1960–1966) after Half a Century', *Leiden Journal of International Law* 31, no. 1 (2018): 147–70; Ryan M. Irwin, 'Apartheid on Trial: South-West Africa and the International Court of Justice', *The International History Review* 32, no. 4 (2010): 619–42.

[18] For the ruling and dissenting opinions, see https://www.icj-cij.org/en/case/47/judgments, accessed 31 March 2024.

(modern-day) Namibia. He specifically underlined the *erga omnes* (universal) obligations of states concerning fundamental human rights.[19]

The biography of the two judges might stand as an explanation for these decisions, which went against the general political outlooks of their governments and reflected different ideological commitments than the dominant East–West and North–South divides that characterized the 1960s. Born in 1884, Winiarski studied law in Kraków, Paris, and Heidelberg. He was a legal adviser to the Polish delegation at the Paris Peace Conference in 1919, where Poland requested— among other things—colonial territories in Africa. During the interwar period, he served in various positions at the League of Nations and taught international law at the University at Poznań. He was also member of parliament for the nationalist and antisemitic National Party (1928–35). Winiarski himself displayed antisemitic and racist positions in political and academic forums.[20] In 1946, he was elected as a judge at the ICJ, serving as its president from 1961 to 1964.[21] Despite representing socialist Poland, Winiarski's opinions were often closer to those of Western judges. Due to his educational and professional background and his experience at the League of Nations, he understood colonial Mandates through a Western lens and had a restrictive approach to national sovereignty and the competence of the ICJ.[22] The Eurocentric and positivist interpretation of international law he acquired during his studies and career, as well as his antisemitic stances during the interwar period may likely have influenced his vote.

By contrast, Philip C. Jessup had a left–liberal American legal trajectory. Born in 1897, Jessup graduated in 1924 from Yale University's Law School and received his PhD in 1927 from Columbia University. In the 1940s, he served in several roles at the UN, including as US representative at the General Assembly and the UN Committee on the Codification of International Law. In 1950, Jessup was attacked by Senator Joseph McCarthy, who accused him of sharing an affinity with communist causes. Although he was cleared of all accusations, the allegation prevented his nomination as representative to the UN in 1951 and as a member of the International Law Commission in 1955. Jessup spent most of the 1950s at Columbia University and working as a consultant for Rockefeller Foundation, on whose behalf he advised the governments of newly independent states in matters of international law. His friends described him as 'ambassador-at-large' of newly independent countries or territories engaged in decolonization.[23] Jessup was

---

[19] For Philip Jessup's 1966 dissenting opinion, see https://www.icj-cij.org/public/files/case-related/47/047-19660718-JUD-01-07-EN.pdf, accessed 31 March 2024.

[20] Stefan Meller, 'Bohdana Winiarskiego świat polityczny', *Studia Łomżyńskie* 12 (2011): 31–36.

[21] For Winiarski's biography and the Poznan School's Eurocentric vision of international law, see Jakub Szumski, Chapter 5 in this volume and Krzysztof Skubiszewski, 'Sir Hersch Lauterpacht and Poland's Judges at the International Court: Judge Bohdan Winiarski', *International Community Law Review* 3, no. 1–2 (2011): 87–91.

[22] Ibid., 1–14.

[23] For Jessup's biography, see Alan Brouder, 'Philip C. Jessup: The Original Transnational Lawyer', *Beiträge zum Transnationalen Wirtschaftsrecht* 50 (2006): 7–14.

a proponent of liberal internationalism and institutionalism as an alternative to realism in international law, arguing thus for the importance of 'ideas' and not only 'realpolitik' in international relations. In 1961, shortly after John F. Kennedy became president, Jessup was elected as a judge at the ICJ, where he served until 1970.

Winiarski's and Jessup's decisions in the *South-West Africa* cases reflected positions that transcended the East–West and South–North divide that characterized the 1960s. Their education, political experience, and ways of understanding international law underpinned their rulings, which departed from the politics of their governments. They reflect a larger heterogeny with both socialist and non-socialist positions, as certain Eastern European experts did not always support anti-racist internationalism and, in Winiarski's case, endorsed a 'conservative thought reminiscent of imperialism', and a 'a white man's court for a white man's international legal order'.[24]

Apartheid as a Major International Crime

African, Asian, and Eastern European efforts to outlaw apartheid became even more vocal after the 1966 ICJ ruling. Not only did they revoke South Africa's mandate over South West Africa in the General Assembly in October 1966 but they now seized any opportunity to make apartheid a major international crime.

Apartheid as a Crime against Humanity and the Imprescriptibility of Major International Crimes

Apartheid was incorporated in international criminal law (ICL) for the first time in the 1968 UN Convention on the Non-Applicability of Statutory Limitations for War Crimes and Crimes against Humanity (the 1968 UN Convention). This Convention was put on the UN agenda by Poland in 1965 to continue the prosecution of Nazi crimes.[25] The year 1968 marked the expiration of the statutory limitations for murder in the criminal code of the Federal Republic of Germany and several other countries where former Nazi criminals had taken refuge. The

---

[24] Ingo Venzke, 'The International Court of Justice During the Battle for International Law, (1955–1975). Colonial Imprints and Possibilities for Change', in *The Battle for International Law*, edited by von Bernstorff and Dann, 248–49, 256.

[25] For the role of state socialist countries in the adoption of this Convention, see Raluca Grosescu, 'State Socialist Endeavors for the Non-Applicability of Statutory Limitations to International Crimes: Historical Roots and Current Implications', *Journal of the History of International Law* 21, no. 3 (2019): 239–69. For the drafting process, see Robert H. Miller, 'The Convention on the Non-Applicability of Statutory Limitations to War Crimes and Crimes against Humanity', *The American Journal of International Law* 65, no. 3 (1971): 476–501; Natan Lerner, 'The Convention on the Non-Applicability of Statutory Limitations to War Crimes', *Israel Law Review* 4 (1969): 512–32.

Polish government, backed by France, proposed that the crimes defined in the Nuremberg Charter and committed by the Axis powers during the Second World War should not be subject to a statute of limitation and should be judged irrespective the lapse of time.[26]

The Afro-Asian Bloc at the UN criticized the proposal as too Eurocentric and focused on the European trauma of the Second World War. For African representatives in particular, apartheid and colonialism were ongoing crimes against humanity of greater importance than those committed in the past by the Nazis.[27] They asked to expand the definition of crimes against humanity beyond the Nuremberg definition to include present and future crimes perpetrated not only during wars but also in time of peace, and to cover episodes of mass repression on their respective continents. Arab countries succeeded (with the support of Eastern European and African governments) to introduce 'eviction by armed attack and occupation'—a category coined to encompass the alleged crimes against humanity committed by Israel in the Palestinian territories. For their part, African states were keen to introduce 'inhuman acts' resulting from a policy of apartheid. They underlined that ICL had not yet concerned itself with apartheid and racial oppression more generally. The Nuremberg category of crimes against humanity was limited to the existence or the preparation of a war of aggression. In its turn, the 1948 Genocide Convention included only crimes committed with the intent to eliminate a group, not crimes perpetrated with the intent to exploit or ensure the supremacy of one group over another.[28] Tanzania, which under Julius Nyerere epitomized African (non-Soviet style) socialism and anticolonialism, was among the most vocal proponents of this approach. Its representatives argued that African states were 'neutral as far as crimes committed by European against European during the Second World War were concerned', and that the current convention should include crimes 'that are now happening in countries like South Africa, Southern Rhodesia, and the Portuguese Territories of Apartheid'.[29]

Conversely, South Africa, Great Britain, Portugal, and the United States insisted on the elimination of any reference to apartheid. Many Western states had not yet critically engaged with apartheid and continued to be Cold War allies of South Africa and Rhodesia. Indeed, South Africa, benefiting from American investment, was still the cornerstone of US policy in the region. From a legal standpoint, Western representatives argued that a UN criminal law text should not deal with a political issue such as apartheid. Moreover, the Western argument went, it was not necessary to single out apartheid, given that the Nuremberg categories already covered inhuman acts against civilian populations. In the words of the UK

---

[26] Grosescu, 'State Socialist Endeavors'.
[27] UN Doc A/C3/SR/1547, 473.
[28] UN Doc A/C3/SR/1548, 479.
[29] Ibid.

representative, such a specification would have implied that 'inhuman acts committed as a consequence of a policy of apartheid are worse than an identical act committed elsewhere',[30] and—even worse—than Nazi crimes that were not specifically named.[31] For its part, Norway argued that 'inhuman acts of apartheid' was too imprecise a category to be included in an ICL convention. Following this critique, the UK delegate advanced a more general proposal to eliminate the statutory limitation for 'war crimes of grave nature and crimes against humanity as defined in international law'.[32] This phrasing avoided the direct criminalization of apartheid and posed a problem for civil law countries, where customary law was not a developed doctrine and who relied instead on written texts.[33] The Soviet representative noted this issue, arguing that 'since the principles of international law were subject to different interpretations, it was important to specify what crimes were meant'.[34] Moreover, Kenyan delegates stated that it was not enough to refer to international law in general, since 'the law which had been formulated in the past by developed countries did not take into account the present-day realities which were of the highest importance for the young countries'.[35] This opinion was a clear position against universality as a Western messianic project and a reflection on the negotiated character of law according to different political and economic realities.

In response to Norway's comment that inhuman acts that resulted from apartheid were not clearly defined, the Tanzanian representative answered that the wording was similar to the one used in the Nuremberg definition of crimes against humanity, which had already been accepted in international law. Apartheid acts in South Africa, ranging from 'genocide, deportation, economic and social exploitation of the indigenous populations and their wasting away by scientific experimentation, were the contemporary manifestations of crimes against humanity'.[36] The United Arab Republic, Czechoslovakia, and the Soviet Union backed Tanzania highlighted that various resolutions of the UN General Assembly had already condemned apartheid as a crime against humanity and the current convention would only confirm an already accepted principle. France and the United States refuted this argument. In their view, state policies could not be equated with international crimes. Moreover, the UN General Assembly resolutions were not legally binding and did not deal with crimes against humanity in a legal sense; such documents amounted to solely moral and political condemnations.[37]

---

[30] Bundesarchiv DP 3/1876/1968, unnumbered.
[31] Lerner, 'The Convention', 525.
[32] UN Doc A/C3/SR/1564/Rev 1.
[33] Socialist countries understood the formation of *jus cogens* mainly through multilateral treaties, while Western countries (particularly common law countries) saw it as the accumulation of state practice and *opines juris*. Grigore Geamannu, '"Jus Cogens", in dreptul internațional contemporan', *Revista de Studii Internaționale* 1–2 (1967): 85–100.
[34] UN Doc A/C3/SR/1566, 5.
[35] Ibid., 3.
[36] Miller, 'The Convention', 498.
[37] Ibid., 497–98.

Nevertheless, the voting coalition of African, Asian, and Eastern European states guaranteed the inclusion of the category of 'inhuman acts resulting for a policy of apartheid', a consequence of these countries' common anti-imperialist and anti-racist agendas against Western interests in Africa and Asia. The Convention expanded the definition of crimes against humanity as codified in the Nuremberg Charter by including genocide, eviction by armed attack or occupation, and inhuman acts resulting from the policy of apartheid. These crimes were also disconnected from the existence of war, they were not subject to statutory limitations and could be judged (retroactively) irrespective of when they were committed.[38]

The inclusion of this retroactive effect and the enlarged definition of crimes against humanity led many states to abstain from the final vote. The Convention was adopted in November 1968, but less than half of UN members voted in favour. Australia, Portugal, South Africa, the United Kingdom, and the United States voted against, while other Western and almost all Latin American states abstained.[39] The Convention entered into force in 1970, but only twenty-seven states ratified it during the Cold War, most of them from Eastern European. It is notable, however, that most African countries that ratified the Convention in the early years of its existence were not socialist, with the exception of Guinea and Cameroon. Tanzania, which was very active in the negotiation process, never signed the document. One plausible explanation for the lack of ratification by African socialist regimes was their general distrust of international law, which they perceived as Eurocentric. More research is needed to fully understand the motives behind this disengagement.

Until April 2024, the Convention remains marginal on the global stage, with only fifty-six ratifications (including the State of Palestine), and it is barely mentioned in the ICL literature. However, the Convention was employed after 1989 to overcome impunity for political crimes committed in various world regions, including post-socialist Eastern Europe.[40] Also, the introduction of 'inhuman acts resulting from the policy of apartheid'—although not clearly defined—contributed to the anticolonial and anti-racist struggle and prefigured the adoption of the 1973 Convention on the Suppression and Punishment of the Crime of Apartheid (the Apartheid Convention).

---

[38] Article I of the 1968 UN Convention on the Non-Applicability of Statutory Limitations to War Crimes and Crimes against Humanity.
[39] Miller, 'The Convention', 477–78.
[40] Raluca Grosescu, Justice and Memory after Dictatorship: Latin America, Central Eastern Europe and the Fragmentation of international Criminal Law (Oxford: Oxford University Press, 2024), ch 2.

The 1973 Apartheid Convention: Universal Jurisdiction and Attempts at Criminalizing Economic Cooperation with South Africa

Beginning in 1971, the USSR and Guinea—which conducted systematic political oppression and marginalization of national minorities under Sékou Touré—were crucial players in placing the Apartheid Convention on the UN agenda. Nigeria, the most vocal non-socialist anti-apartheid country in Africa, joined the initiative and became co-sponsor in 1972. The Commission on Human Rights established a working group composed of Bulgaria, Chile, Ecuador, Egypt, India, the Philippines, Senegal, the USSR, and Zaire to consider the draft. Diplomats from the United Kingdom and the United States opposed the initiative as anti-Western 'Soviet propaganda'. They refused to take part in the debates and were instructed by their governments to delay the drafting process.[41] In their view, the purpose of the Soviets was again to attack the West, to prevent debate on the Convention against Religious Intolerance, underplay accusations of antisemitism on their territory, and evade the establishment of a High Commissioner for Human Rights.[42] From the Western camp, only Austria (a neutral country) and the Netherlands (a liberal champion of human rights at the time) participated in the working group, but only as observers.[43]

Heated debates arose around two points: the definition of the crime, which aimed to criminalize any form of involvement (including foreign investment) in the repressive apartheid rule; and the prosecution regime, based on universal jurisdiction. The Convention incorporated a wide category of criminalized acts of varying gravity. It brought together elements from the 1948 Genocide Convention, such as 'infliction of serious bodily or mental harm' and 'conditions to cause the physical destruction of a racial group in whole or in part', and from the 1945 Nuremberg Charter, such as enslavement and persecution on racial grounds. It also echoed the 1965 CERD, by condemning any exclusion from political, social, economic, and cultural life based on racial premises and criminalizing acts of propaganda and incitement to apartheid.[44]

Western delegations opposed this definition as being too broad and vague and including acts which did not amount to crimes against humanity. American representative Clarence Clyde Ferguson Jr contended, 'we cannot [...] accept that apartheid can in this manner be made a crime against humanity. Crimes against humanity are so grave in nature that they must be meticulously and strictly

---

[41] British National Archives, Foreign Office and Foreign and Commonwealth Office records (BNA, FCO), File UM49/8/1973, unnumbered, 'Discussions of Racial Discrimination by UN (Convention on Apartheid)'.
[42] Ibid.
[43] Ibid.
[44] Bassiouni and Derby, 'Final Report'.

elaborated under existing international law.'[45] The British representative, Sir Anthony Parsons, also argued that crimes against humanity had 'specific legal meaning in international law, related to Nazi crimes [and the existence of a war of aggression], which we do not consider applicable to apartheid'.[46] Such positions revealed Eurocentric and conservative visions of ICL, confined to the Second World War and the Nuremberg trials. But Western criticism also had political motives, since countries such as the United States, the United Kingdom, France, West Germany, and Australia were allies of South Africa and did not entirely disassociate themselves from the apartheid regime. They claimed that the Convention was in fact directed towards the policies of a specific government (South Africa)—'an unacceptable basis upon which to formulate international law', according to British diplomats, who argued that the UN should not be used to isolate Pretoria and 'hinder trade, diplomatic and cultural relations with South Africa'.[47]

Moreover, from the perspective of various Western countries, the Genocide Convention and the CERD already covered legal provisions sufficient to fight apartheid: a separate anti-apartheid convention was superfluous.[48] Their argument was misleading: the Genocide Convention only covered acts intended to destroy a group, while the CERD referred to the responsibility of states to protect against racial discrimination. In contrast, the Apartheid Convention condemned the supremacy of one racial group over another, and sanctioned individual guilt (not state policies) under criminal law. Moreover, as the Haitian representative pointed out during final negotiations: despite 'the monumental importance of the CERD', many governments maintained their policies of racial discrimination and racial segregation based on white supremacy. The Apartheid Convention was needed to correct this 'savage behaviour'.[49]

The Convention also went beyond South Africa to include 'similar policies and practices of racial segregation and discrimination as practiced in southern Africa'.[50] Egypt proposed this expansion to make the Convention applicable to what Arab

---

[45] UNALIL, Convention on the Suppression and Punishment of the Crime of Apartheid, New York, Section 'Audio', Twenty-Eighth Session of the General Assembly, 2185th Plenary Meeting, 30 November 1973, Statement by Mr Ferguson (the United States of America): Explanation of vote, https://legal.un.org/avl/ha/cspca/audio 3.1.html, accessed 14 March 2024.

[46] BNA, FCO, File UM49/8/1973, unnumbered, 'Discussions of Racial Discrimination by UN (Convention on Apartheid)'.

[47] Ibid.

[48] UNALIL, Convention on the Suppression and Punishment of the Crime of Apartheid, New York, Section 'Audio', Twenty-Eighth Session of the General Assembly, Third Committee, 2008th Meeting, 26 October 1973, Statement by Mr Pardos (Spain): Explanation of vote, https://legal.un.org/avl/ha/cspca/audio_2.2.html, accessed 14 March 2024.

[49] UNALIL, Convention on the Suppression and Punishment of the Crime of Apartheid, New York, Section 'Audio', Twenty-Eighth Session of the General Assembly, 2185th Plenary Meeting, 30 November 1973, Statement by Mr Verret (Haiti): Explanation of vote, https://legal.un.org/avl/ha/cspca/audio_3.1.html, accessed 14 March 2024.

[50] Articles I and III of the International Convention on the Suppression and Punishment of the Crime of Apartheid.

countries considered a policy of apartheid imposed by Israel in the Palestinian territories after 1967. The Egyptian government was also successful in criminalizing the denial of the 'right of return' to one's own country, and the right to a nationality—acts specifically targeting Israeli policies in Palestine.[51] Arab countries used any opportunity to equate apartheid and Zionism and denounce the close relations between South Africa and Israel. The expansion beyond southern Africa worried various delegations, particularly from countries that practiced racial segregation or discrimination against local populations. In the words of the Australian representative, 'the concept of apartheid was being widened to such an extent that [...] the variety of ways in which the definition might be applied should be a matter of concern for any country whose population included a racial minority group'.[52]

Another contentious issue was the Eastern European Bloc's proposal to criminalize (as in the case of the CERD) not only policies of apartheid but also propaganda and incitement. Article III of the Convention sanctioned those who 'directly commit, participate in, incite or conspire' and those who 'abet, encourage, or cooperate in the commission of the crime of apartheid'.[53] Western states, but also Argentina and Chile, opposed this provision. They argued that it went against freedom of expression, and that it was so wide that it could apply to almost any form of cooperation with South Africa, including economic exchanges.[54] In fact, condemning Western investments in South Africa was a key issue for both Eastern European and African socialist states. It was a means to connect capitalism, racism, and imperialism and thereby promote an alternative political and economic model, even if certain African socialist governments did not renounce Western investment in their country. Also, African leaders, such as Nkrumah and Nyerere, systematically opposed theories of 'constructive engagement' that would supposedly democratize South Africa in the long run. They called instead for a full Western divestment from South Africa, with Nyerere arguing, for instance, in 1975 that 'investors in South Africa are participants in it [apartheid] however far distant they may live, and however non-racial they may be in their personal relationships. Opponents of apartheid, and of racialism as a state doctrine, have no honest choice but to isolate South Africa'.[55]

---

[51] Archives of the Romanian Ministry of Foreign Affairs (AMAE), File 5412/1973, 'Convenția Privind Eliminarea și Repimarea Crimei de Apartheid'.

[52] Quoted by Hercules Booysen, 'Convention on the Crime of Apartheid', *South African Yearbook of International Law* 2 (1976): 57.

[53] Article III of the 1973 Apartheid Convention.

[54] BNA, FCO, File UM49/8/1973, unnumbered, 'Discussions of Racial Discrimination by UN (Convention on Apartheid)'.

[55] Julius Nyerere, 'Some Aspects of Liberation', Speech Given during a State Visit to Britain at Oxford University', 19 November 1975, in *Freedom, Non-Alignment and South–South Cooperation. A Selection of Speeches 1974–1999* (Dar es Salaam: Oxford University Press, 2011), 77-78.

British diplomats reported to the Ministry of Foreign Affairs in London that criminalizing business with South Africa also went against Eastern European interests, since these states still had economic relations with South Africa.[56] This was also true for certain African countries such as Kenya and Zambia, which took a far less militant and radical stance against apartheid and the white settler domination in Portuguese colonies. Nevertheless, for other southern African states such as Tanzania, and for various liberation movements such as FRELIMO (Frente de Libertação de Moçambique) in Mozambique and MPLA (Movimento Popular de Libertação de Angola) in Angola, outlawing business with Pretoria was not only a fundamental element in ending apartheid but also in curtailing South Africa's economic and military influence in the region.[57]

The draft convention also demanded a new international prosecution regime. Article IV called for measures to bring to trial responsible persons 'whether or not they reside in the territory of the State in which the acts are committed or are nationals of that State or of some other State or are stateless persons'. Article V stipulated that the alleged perpetrators 'may be tried by a competent tribunal of any State Party to the Convention which may acquire jurisdiction over the person of the accused or by an international penal tribunal' whose jurisdiction was accepted by state parties.[58] These provisions were proposed by African states (particularly Nigeria, Ghana, and Tanzania) and, according to British diplomats, were initially met with reluctance from Eastern European countries, since they went against their principles of strong state sovereignty.[59]

For the first time, an international convention proposed the principle of universal jurisdiction—meaning that any citizen participating in, inciting, or encouraging apartheid could be prosecuted for these acts in any state that ratified the Convention. This was a radical change in comparison to previous ICL instruments, which restricted jurisdiction to the states in which the crimes had been perpetrated or to an international tribunal established by the UN. Proposals to introduce a diplomatic immunity clause were also rejected—again a radical departure from the status quo, criticized by certain Western and South African experts.[60]

The US representative, Clarence Clyde Ferguson Jr, expressed wider Western concerns during the final debate on the draft convention on 30 November 1973. He underlined that, in the absence of UN control over national courts, prosecutions based on universal jurisdiction could be politically instrumentalized by various states. Efforts to protect human rights, Ferguson continued, which 'ignore the rule

---

[56] BNA, FCO, File UM49/8/1973, unnumbered, 'Discussions of Racial Discrimination by UN (Convention on Apartheid)'.
[57] T. V. Sathyamurthy, 'Tanzania's Non-Aligned Role in International Relations', *India Quarterly* 37, no. 1 (1981): 7–9.
[58] Articles IV and V of the 1973 Apartheid Convention.
[59] BNA, FCO, File UM49/8/1973, unnumbered, 'Discussions of Racial Discrimination by UN (Convention on Apartheid)'.
[60] Booysen, 'Convention', 65.

of law can only lead to chaos'.[61] Only an international tribunal with clearly defined regulations was appropriate for prosecuting apartheid. The same concerns were expressed by British diplomats who worried that British nationals could be judged abroad for encouraging apartheid (including through investments and arms trade to South Africa). The United Kingdom thus had to block or at least delay the adoption of the Convention.[62]

The introduction of universal jurisdiction was also at odds with the Eastern European socialist doctrines on sovereignty. While actively involved in international lawmaking, Eastern European governments took every precaution to prevent the creation of a global system of justice that could override their own state prerogatives. This led to a staunch opposition against supranational courts (including the ICJ's oversight capacity over conventions). During the negotiations of the Apartheid Convention, Romanian legal experts warned that even though the crime of apartheid could not occur in socialist countries due to their progressive sociopolitical systems, universal jurisdiction (particularly when applied to state officials) was in contradiction with the principle of diplomatic immunity.[63] Moreover, they worried that criminal responsibility for legal entities could extend to states, a principle that departed from the classical international law doctrine which defended state sovereignty.[64] Nevertheless, Eastern Europeans finally agreed to support universal jurisdiction because they did not envisage the Apartheid Convention as applicable to them. As self-declared pioneers in the struggle against apartheid, they saw the instrument as designed only to target racist regimes in Africa and the Western states and individuals who supported such state entities.[65] This ideological interpretation provincialized the substance of the principle of universal jurisdiction, despite its formal adoption in the Apartheid Convention.

The Convention was adopted in November 1973 through a voting alliance between the Afro-Asian Bloc and the Eastern European camp. South Africa, the United States, the United Kingdom, and Portugal voted against, and twenty-six states abstained, most of them from the Global North. Even the Scandinavian countries, which had officially condemned the apartheid regime and organized

---

[61] United Nations, Audiovisual Library of International Law (UNALIL), Convention on the Suppression and Punishment of the Crime of Apartheid, New York, Section 'Audio', Twenty-Eighth Session of the General Assembly, 2185th Plenary Meeting, 30 November 1973, Statement by Mr Ferguson (the United States of America): Explanation of vote, https://legal.un.org/avl/ha/cspca/audio_3.1.html, accessed 14 March 2024.
[62] BNA, FCO, File UM49/8/1973, unnumbered, 'Discussions of Racial Discrimination by UN (Convention on Apartheid)'.
[63] AMAE, File 5412/1973, unnumbered, 'Convenția Privind Eliminarea și Repimarea Crimei de Apartheid'.
[64] Ibid.
[65] Grigore Geamanu, *Dreptul penal internațional si infracțiunile internaționale* (Bucharest: Editura Academiei Republicii Socialiste România, 1977), 165–67.

various pro-decolonization and anti-apartheid conferences in the 1970s,[66] refused to vote in favour. They criticized the potential criminalizing of foreign investors (including North European ones) doing business with South Africa. According to British diplomats, even countries that voted in favour thought the instrument would be inapplicable, due to the broadness and imprecision of its scope.[67]

The Convention entered into force in 1976, after 20 countries ratified it. Nine were Eastern European (Hungary, Bulgaria, USSR, Belarus, Ukraine, Poland, Czechoslovakia, East Germany, and Yugoslavia) and eight were Asian or African socialist states (Tanzania, Guinea, Libya, Somalia, Benin, Mongolia, Iraq, and Syria). Cameroon, Qatar, and Ecuador were the only non-socialist countries to contribute to ratification. Bulgaria and Hungary were also the first states in the world to criminalize apartheid in their penal codes in 1975 and 1978 respectively. However, this was only a sign of moral and political support for the global anti-apartheid cause and not a tool to prosecute discriminatory policies at home.[68] While the Convention produced the most radical reading of race in international law, it remained a controversial instrument and has, until today, not been ratified by any country in the West. In 2024, 109 out 193 UN members adopted it, but scholars remain split on whether this is an 'authoritative document', given its rejection by Western states and the lack of any judicial application since 1973.[69]

Apartheid as a War Crime and the Recognition of Wars of National Liberation as International Conflicts

The 1970s marked the intensification of political repression in South Africa and the acceleration of wars of liberation in the Portuguese colonies and of anti-apartheid activism across the world. Within this context, the negotiation of the 1977 Additional Protocol I to the 1949 Geneva Conventions once again centred apartheid on the ICL agenda and reproduced the longstanding tensions between the Western political and legal discourses and those in the Third World and the Eastern European camp. In 1976, during the Diplomatic Conference on the Reaffirmation and Development of International Humanitarian Law Applicable in Armed Conflicts organized with the aim of supplementing existing international

---

[66] For instance, in 1973, Norway provided 80,000 USD to host the International Conference of Experts for the Support of Victims of Colonialism and Apartheid in Southern Africa, organized by the UN in collaboration with the Organisation of African Unity. 5337/1973, 'Conferința internațională de experți pentru sprijinirea victimelor coloniasmului din Africa Australă, Oslo, 9–14 aprilie 1973'.
[67] BNA, FCO, File UM49/8/1973, unnumbered, 'Discussions of Racial Discrimination by UN (Convention on Apartheid)'.
[68] Mark, 'Race'.
[69] For these debates, see Christopher Keith Hall, 'Crimes Against Humanity', in *Commentary on the Rome Statute of the International Criminal Court: Observers' Notes, Article by Article*, edited by O. Triffterer (Munich: C. H. Beck, Hart, Nomos, 2008), 159; Bultz, 'Redefining Apartheid'.

humanitarian law (1974-77), Tanzania, Mongolia (both socialist countries), and Uganda, introduced an amendment to the draft list of grave breaches to add crimes such as outrages upon personal dignity, especially inhuman acts and degrading treatment generated by apartheid. The aim was to emphasize that the practice of apartheid not only involved crimes against humanity but also dangerous war crimes.[70] The Soviet Union, the Byelorussian Soviet Socialist Republic, the Ukrainian Soviet Republic, Yugoslavia, and Vietnam had put forward similar proposals in 1974 and 1975, though without formal amendments. This position would also be maintained by most African states in August 1977, during the World Conference on Action against Apartheid organized in Lagos, by the UN and the Organisation of African Unity.[71]

Due to Pretoria's military campaign in Angola (1975-76), its refusal to withdraw from Namibia, and its economic support for white minority rule in Rhodesia, many African states began to see South Africa not only as a racist oppressive regime but also as a source of military destabilization. As a leading member of the Frontline States (a coalition of African countries from the 1960s to the early 1990s committed to ending apartheid), Tanzania was particularly preoccupied by this issue.[72] As far as Uganda was concerned, anti-apartheid had always been on the country's international agenda, but it was now a way to distract from Idi Amin's campaigns—from 1972 onward—to ethnic cleanse various minority groups and to expropriate and expel Ugandan citizens of Asian origin. Despite Nyerere's condemnation of Amin's policies in international forums, the two states aligned to criminalize apartheid as a war crime. Eastern European countries backed the proposal.

After long negotiations, the list of 'grave breaches' (that ultimately became Article 85 of AP I) included 'practices of apartheid and other inhuman and degrading practices involving outrages upon personal dignity, based on racial discrimination'.[73] As in the case of the 1968 UN Convention, Western delegations, such as Austria and Finland, criticized the inclusion of 'practices of apartheid' as too vague and difficult to transpose into national criminal codes. Australia, which had not yet cut diplomatic ties with South Africa, argued that 'the introduction of political ideologies, hateful as they might be, into the system of grave breaches was not to reaffirm and develop humanitarian law but to distort it'.[74] Additionally, British diplomats criticized the creation of a war crime aimed at one state (South Africa), noting that Article 27 of the Fourth Geneva Convention already required respect for protected persons without distinction based on race, religion, or political opinion. British diplomat Gerald Draper noted that 'the practices of apartheid,

---

[70] Eden, 'The Practices'.
[71] AMAE, File 3987/1977, 'Conferința mondială împotriva apartheid Lagos 22-26 August 1977'.
[72] Sathyamurthy, 'Tanzania's Non-Aligned Role', 10-11.
[73] Article 85 of the 1977 Additional Protocol I to the 1949 Geneva Conventions.
[74] Eden, 'The Practices'.

however morally defective, are not acts in any way linked with armed conflict. Placing them in the Protocol will not make them so.'[75]

During the drafting process, the Ugandan representative agreed that apartheid was not necessarily a crime produced by war. Nevertheless, he added that apartheid had generated wars and that recognizing it as a grave breach would be a preventative measure likely to decrease the risk of war.[76] Tanzanian leaders denounced the fact that Pretoria, in its quest to maintain its influence on southern Africa, had invaded Angola and had armed paramilitary groups to fight against the legitimate governments of Mozambique and Zimbabwe. Such initiatives had fuelled wars in the region and had led to the perpetration of war crimes. According to the Tanzanian government, the apartheid regime represented an existential threat not only to Frontline states but also to the entirety of southern Africa.[77] The voting alliance between African, Asian, and the Eastern Bloc finally assured the insertion of apartheid as a war crime in the 1977 Additional Protocol I, even though such categorization is highly problematic[78]

Nonetheless, most countries did not ratify the Protocol until the mid-1990s, particularly because it recognized wars of national liberation and armed struggle against racism, colonialism, and apartheid as international conflicts, and imposed the status of prisoners of war (POWs) on combatants involved in such wars. In this sense, Eastern European and African socialist governments succeeded in including not only armed conflicts in which peoples are fighting against colonial domination and alien occupation but also those against racist regimes.[79] The aim was to legitimize the armed struggle against apartheid in South Africa, as well as the Palestinian cause.[80]

In contrast, many Western countries opposed giving 'freedom fighters' POW status as maximalist and dangerous. For a long period of time, former imperial powers refused to acknowledge anticolonial struggles as 'armed conflict', labelling them 'terrorism' or 'disturbances'. Western views on the matter changed over time, as Scandinavian opinions increasingly diverged from British and American positions. However, a general Western concern about a flexible definition of 'armed conflicts' and 'freedom fighters' lingered, as well as concern about the alleged entanglement between decolonization struggles with two current geopolitically sensitive conflicts (Palestine and South Africa).[81] Moreover, other issues were now

[75] Gerald Draper, 'The Modern Pattern of War Criminality', *Israel Yearbook on Human Rights*, 6 (1976): 42–43.
[76] Eden, 'The Practices'.
[77] Nyerere, 'Some Aspects', 77–78.
[78] Giovanni Mantilla, 'The Protagonism of the USSR and Socialist States in the Revision of International Humanitarian Law', *Journal of the History of International Law* 21, no. 3 (2019): 194.
[79] Giovanni Mantilla, *Lawmaking Under Pressure: International Humanitarian Law and Internal Armed Conflicts* (Ithaca: Cornel University Press), 146–47.
[80] Jochen von Bernstorff, 'The Battle for the Recognition of Wars of National Liberation', in *The Battle for International Law*, edited by von Bernstorff and Dann, 57.
[81] Ibid., 61.

at stake. British diplomats, for instance, worried about granting freedom fighters POW status, fearing that this clause would apply to the Irish Republican Army.[82] Spanish representatives also went to great lengths to exclude debates on claims to self-determination made by the Canary Islands Independence Movement.[83] As Mantilla points out, without Eastern European support, the coalition of Global South countries would not have had gathered enough votes to obtain the super-majority necessary for the recognition of wars of national liberation as international conflicts and, subsequently, for granting the status of POW to freedom fighters.[84] However, until today, only parts of the Protocol, not including the criminalization of apartheid, are widely recognized.

Legal Professional Associations against Apartheid

Socialist governmental efforts to criminalize apartheid were complemented by transnational mobilizations of socialist lawyers and legal experts who campaigned across the world against imperialism and racism and emphasized the legitimacy of anticolonial struggles. This section illustrates these transnational commitments through the example of the IADL, the most prominent global association of leftist lawyers and legal experts during the Cold War. Its anti-racist and anticolonial engagements can be understood in the context of the competing discourses and tactics deployed by a liberal and Western-dominated association of lawyers: the International Commission of Jurists (CIJ).[85] In contrast to liberal approaches to fighting apartheid through technical legal assistance for political prisoners and the denunciation of political repression and racial segregation in South Africa as infringement of the rule of law, the IADL connected anti-apartheid to a radical condemnation of colonialism as a whole and to the necessity of recognizing wars of national liberation as international armed conflicts.

The IADL was established in Paris in 1946 and gathered together European (many of them former participants in the antifascist resistance during the Second World War) and American jurists with the goal of fighting the legacies of fascism and advancing an international order based on human rights, peace, and the ban of nuclear weapons. Soon after its creation, the IADL became caught in the Cold War divide, and many of its members embraced a socialist agenda influenced by the Soviet Union. Starting in 1949, most Western liberal and conservative lawyers resigned, and only those with socialist and communist views remained. However, in the 1950s, the association rapidly expanded its membership in the

---

[82] Mantilla, *Lawmaking*, 147.
[83] AMAE, File 3987/1977, 'Conferința mondială împotriva apartheid Lagos 22–26 August 1977'.
[84] Mantilla, 'The Protagonism', 194.
[85] The official acronyms of the International Commission of Jurists and the International Court of Justice overlap. In order to minimize confusion, I use the French abbreviation of the Commission (CIJ).

Global South, and IADL national sections were established across Asia, Africa, and Latin America. The IADL assumed an overtly militant, socialist mission and understood law as a means to advance radical politics at the national and international level.[86] While largely funded by Moscow, the IADL was nevertheless a platform of dialogue between lawyers from across the world with their diverse socialist imaginaries, from radical Algerian socialists to more moderate scholars in Western Europe.

The CIJ was created in 1952 through a covert CIA operation to counter the IADL.[87] Unaware of the CIA connection, many Western jurists joined the CIJ to advance the consolidation of liberal rule of law and oppose the Eastern European socialist system. In the 1950s, the CIJ focused on documenting political crimes in Eastern Europe, although it also recorded human rights abuses of the fascist regimes in Spain and Portugal. The role of the CIA became public in 1967, leading to a crisis and the reorganization of the Association's agenda and a new focus on the Global South. The Association, however, continued to promote a liberal agenda of human rights based on the struggle against violations of civil and politic rights and the consolidation of the rule of law.

Both the IADL and the CIJ campaigned against apartheid, but with different approaches. Starting in 1949, the IADL's congresses connected apartheid and racist policies in the US South with European colonialism and American imperialism and promoted the right to self-determination. In 1949, the IADL established a permanent committee on the affairs of colonial, semicolonial, and dependent nations—led by African lawyers. A position of vice president was reserved for a representative of a colonial or dependent territory. As early as the 1950s, the Association provided legal assistance to political prisoners in South Africa and sponsored campaigns against decolonization, anti-imperialism, and anti-apartheid.[88] IADL sections in Europe supported liberation movements and offered their leaders venues to defend their cause. For instance, in the 1970s, Paulette Pierson-Mathy and Jean Salmon, two prominent Belgian socialist legal scholars and IADL members, wrote extensively on the illegality of apartheid, racism, and colonialism, and the need to recognize anticolonial wars of liberation as international conflicts. In the 1970s, with financial support from Eastern and Southern socialist countries (Yugoslavia, Romania, and Egypt), Pierson-Mathy

---

[86] The IADL activity reports and publications are available at the International Institute of Social History (IISH) in Amsterdam, Archival Fund ARCH04747, uncatalogued. The archives of the Belgian Association of Democratic Lawyers (BADL), held in Brussels at the Centre des Archives du Communisme en Bélgique (CArCOB), are another important source for tracing IADL activity. For a critique of the IADL in its early years, see A. J. M. van Dal, 'Under False Colours. A Report of the Character of the International Association of Democratic Lawyers', (1955), https://www.icj.org/wp-content/uploads/1955/11/IADL-thematic-report-1955-eng.pdf, accessed 24 March 2024.
[87] For the ICJ's history, see Howard B. Tolley Jr, *The International Commission of Jurists: Global Advocates for Human Rights* (Philadelphia, PA: Pennsylvania University Press, 1994).
[88] See the IADL annual reports at IISH, Archival Fund ARCH04747, uncatalogued.

invited leaders of liberation movements, such as Agostinho Neto (Angola) or Sam Nujoma (Namibia), to campaign in Belgium and France.[89] The IADL organized numerous conferences against apartheid and was thus an important partner for African liberation movements across both Eastern and Western Europe.[90]

In the first decade of its existence, the CIJ also denounced apartheid and racial discrimination but disconnected them from the colonial issue. At the first CIJ African conference, organized in 1961 in Lagos, CIJ President Vivian Bose (India) rejected proposals for the recognition of colonized peoples' right to independence and dismissed the idea of investigating racial discrimination in Britain's territories in southern Africa.[91] The Lagos conference and its Declaration (the Law of Lagos) focused primarily on procedural democracy, sidelining the right to self-determination and the struggle against racial discrimination, despite their crucial importance for African societies. During the 1960s, the CIJ issued critical reports on racial laws, violations of due process, and harassment of lawyers in South Africa. However, in contrast to the IADL, which systematically denounced racist minority rule in South Africa and the Portuguese colonies, the CIJ engaged in soft diplomacy with Pretoria and Lisbon to improve the legal conditions of Black people.[92]

During the 1970s, as the CIJ's agenda shifted to prioritizing human rights in the Global South, its new general secretary, Niall MacDermot, found common ground with the IADL to collaborate on topics such as development, postcolonial economic independence, and racism.[93] In the 1970s, the IADL and the CIJ participated together in various international conferences and affirmed their support for liberation movements. However, while the CIJ published reports on South Africa's human rights violations (including massacres, racial segregation, torture, and unfair trials), it never fully affirmed its support for the African National Congress nor militated for the recognition of anticolonial liberation movements under humanitarian law.[94] This approach reflected a more general attitude of Western scholars regarding wars of liberation. While they did not usually question the legitimacy of specific armed struggles against colonialism, they insisted on defining them as internal conflicts.[95]

In contrast, the IADL was much more vocal, lobbying for the adoption of the 1973 Apartheid Convention, the criminalization of Western corporations doing business with South Africa, and the extension of the Geneva Conventions to national liberation movements.[96] In 1978, an IADL conference on The Struggle

---

[89] (CArCOB), IADL Archival Fund, uncatalogued, '1971 BADL Annual Report'.
[90] See the IADL annual reports at IISH, Archival Fund ARCH04747, uncatalogued.
[91] Tolley Jr, *The International Commission*, 72.
[92] Ibid., 115–16.
[93] Ibid., 196.
[94] See, for instance, the ICJ reports from 1970 to 1980, www.icj.org/category/publications/reports, accessed 14 February 2023.
[95] Von Bernstorff, 'The Battle for the Recognition', 63.
[96] See the IADL annual reports at IISH, Archival Fund ARCH04747, uncatalogued.

against Racism and Apartheid organized in Baku issued a declaration on the legality of armed struggle for decolonization in Africa and called for the immediate ratification of the 1977 Additional Protocol I. The Conference also condemned Western investments in South Africa and NATO's indirect support for Pretoria.[97] While most participants came from Eastern Europe, prominent Western lawyers connected to the IADL also participated, among them Richard Harvey from the Haldane Society of Socialist Lawyers (United Kingdom), South African law professor Asmal Kader, founder of the Irish and British Anti-Apartheid Movements, as well as of British Irish Rights Watch, and Paulette Pierson-Mathy from the Belgian IADL branch.[98] These scholars and activists were united by their socialist outlook on world politics, as well as by their commitment to anticolonialism and anti-apartheid, and their support of liberation movements. Moreover, in the 1970s and 1980s, prominent IADL members such as Gerhard Stuby (West Germany), Amar Bentoumi (Algeria), and Robert Charvin (France) took positions against the equation of liberation movements with terrorism—an argument put forward by many Western states during the negotiations of the 1977 Additional Protocol I. They contended that such an equivalence was Western propaganda aimed at continuing a colonial order based on illegal occupation, political repression, and racial segregation, particularly in South Africa and Israel.[99] During the Cold War, the Soviet-backed IADL was thus a more radical proponent of anti-apartheid, decolonization, and anti-imperialism than the CIJ, which took a more conservative approach, based on a supposed 'apolitical' defence of civil rights and legal proceduralism, thus avoiding direct critique of Western colonial practices.

Conclusion

During the Cold War, African and Eastern socialist governments were the most active proponents of criminalizing apartheid under ICL. The three international conventions which codified apartheid as a crime against humanity and a war crime were put on the UN agenda by state socialist countries from Europe and Africa. They challenged the Western reluctance to move away from the colonial order, outlaw apartheid, and legalize national liberation movements under international humanitarian law. They also made radical interventions in ICL, including the non-applicability of statutory limitations to war crimes and crimes against humanity,

---

[97] Vyanko Vekilov, 'The Democratic Lawyers Condemn the Racial Discrimination and Apartheid', *Mezhdunarodni Otnosheniya* 1 (1979): 91–93. Reports on the Baku conference are available at CArCOB, IADL Archival Fund, uncatalogued.
[98] Ibid.
[99] The positions of these lawyers are best reflected in Hans Koechler (ed.), 'Terrorism and National Liberation: Proceedings of the International Conference Question of Terrorism', Special Issue of *Studies in International Relations*, vol XIII (1988).

the recognition of a prosecution regime based on universal jurisdiction, and the acknowledgement of wars of national liberation as international armed conflicts. Nevertheless, these ICL instruments remained peripheral and contested, pointing to the resilience of Western-centric hierarchies in international law. As a global professional association, with substantial national branches across the world, the IADL also played a crucial role in the struggle against apartheid. The association was an important platform for collaboration between Eastern, Western, and Global South socialist lawyers who understood anti-apartheid as intrinsically connected to a radical fight against imperialism and colonialism. In contrast to liberal approaches against apartheid (based on the denunciation of violations of civil and political rights and on technical legal assistance to political prisoners in South Africa), the IADL engaged in direct political support for the African National Congress and for liberation movements across Africa. Criminalizing apartheid and legalizing wars of national liberation under international law were thus two interconnected causes for the IADL.

The legacy of these efforts remains ambivalent. On the one hand, the three international instruments criminalizing apartheid were dismissed by the Western world at worst as Soviet propaganda or at best as maximalist texts without any potential applicability. No individual was ever tried for inhuman acts committed during the apartheid regime. The negotiated transition in South Africa entailed a model of dealing with the past based on pardon and truth-telling that avoided criminal prosecutions. While apartheid was included as a crime against humanity in the 1998 Rome Statute of the International Criminal Court, it is uncertain to what extent practices similar to apartheid might be put on trial in the present or future. Various activists and researchers have acknowledged apartheid-like policies against Palestinians in Israel or defined the *songbun* social system in North Korea as a form of apartheid. Others have, however, strongly disagreed.[100]

On the other hand, due to its retroactive effect and the disconnection of the category of crimes against humanity from the existence of war, the 1968 UN Convention was instrumental in putting former communist and right-wing military officials in Eastern Europe and Latin America respectively on trial.[101] The Apartheid Convention was often quoted as an example for the international recognition of the principle of universal jurisdiction by human rights activists and judges involved in extraterritorial prosecutions of crimes against humanity. Finally, the 1977 Additional Protocol I gave freedom fighters POW status and legitimized their anticolonial struggle. Socialist initiatives for the criminalization of apartheid thus had broad implications for the international order, even if their legal contributions were not always immediately effective as legal tools. Crucial aspects of

---

[100] For these debates, see Bultz, 'Redefining Apartheid'; Lingaas, 'The Crime against Humanity of Apartheid'.
[101] Grosescu, 'State Socialist Endeavors'.

cosmopolitan international law of the twentieth century—including anti-racism and anti-apartheid—were thus inescapably shaped by state socialist agency, even if the histories of these engagements remain largely forgotten.

Acknowledgements

This research was supported by the Romanian National Authority for Scientific Research and Innovation, CNCS-UEFISCDI, project number PN-III-P4-ID-PCE-2020-1337.

11
Terrorists, Revolutionaries, and Migrants: Cold War Conflicts and Convergences over International Air Hijacking Law

Ned Richardson-Little

Introduction

In 1978, two East German citizens forcibly diverted LOT Polish Airlines flight 165 to land at West Berlin's Tempelhof Airport. Seeking asylum in West Germany, Detlev Tiede and Ingrid Ruske had inadvertently landed the plane in a legal grey zone: Berlin was technically under four-power occupation by the United States, the United Kingdom, France, and the USSR and they had touched down in the American-occupied sector. Rather than being tried for hijacking in front of a West German court, the pair was charged by the specially convened United States Court for Berlin. Against the objections of the prosecutor and the US State Department, the presiding American Judge Herbert Jay Stern provided the defendants with a jury trial, dismissing the charges against Ruske as she had not been read her rights in accordance with US constitutional protections. Eventually, Tiede was convicted of hostage-taking, but only sentenced to time already served.

In Judge Stern's memoir of the events and the film adaptation that followed (in which he was heroically portrayed by actor Martin Sheen), this was a triumph of freedom over state socialist tyranny.[1] But from a diplomatic and legal perspective, it was a fiasco.[2] Despite the Cold War, the United States and the Eastern Bloc had, for nearly a decade, actually been productively cooperating to make airplane hijacking an international crime that could not be excused by political motivations. The years 1968–1972 witnessed a global proliferation in airplane diversions with 326 hijacking attempts (successful and unsuccessful) around the world—twenty-two

---

[1] Herbert J. Stern, *Judgment in Berlin: The True Story of a Plane Hijacking, a Cold War Trial, and the American Judge Who Fought for Justice* (London: Palgrave Macmillan, 1984). For the film adaptation, see *Judgment in Berlin* (Director: Leo Penn, 1988).
[2] Andreas F. Lowenfeld, 'Hijacking, Freedom, and the "American Way"', *Michigan Law Review* 83, no. 4 (1985): 1000–15.

of which took place in the Eastern Bloc.[3] For Eastern Bloc states, preventing illicit emigration via hijacked aircraft was a priority as part of their wider programme to restrict their citizens from departing to the West without the state's permission. The most iconic symbol of this was the Berlin Wall in East Germany; but the Soviet Union and the rest of the bloc not only sought to prevent emigration, but also compel the return of all defectors and irregular migrants who managed to reach the non-socialist world.[4] Although these restrictions on emigration generated protests from their American rivals, such policies actually dovetailed with US-led efforts to create a global migration regime to allow only selective entry to the West.[5]

In the field of international law, Eastern Bloc states had always upheld the sanctity of state sovereignty and insisted on non-intervention in internal affairs. Yet when it came to the hijacking of aircraft, these positions became a liability for domestic security and the protection of their own restrictive migration regime. So instead, they worked with the West towards criminalizing airplane diversions and ensuring the mutual prosecution and extradition of hijackers. Although the competition over the access and reach of civil aviation was an important element in the globalization of the Cold War, the Soviet Union and the United States were nonetheless able to find common ground when both states found themselves facing a wave of civilian airliner hijackings.[6] Contrary to the popular image of the Cold War as a period of hiatus for the production of international law, the genesis of legal tools to combat hijacking emerged directly from conflicts over freedom of movement between the socialist and capitalist world.[7]

But the question of hijacking was hardly only a problem of migration and jurisdiction, and it rapidly spiralled into other realms of law and politics. At first, the

[3] Robert T. Holden, 'The Contagiousness of Aircraft Hijacking', *American Journal of Sociology* 91, no. 4 (1986): 874–904.

[4] For a survey of the many forms of migration from the Eastern Bloc, see Anna Mazurkiewicz, *East Central European Migrations During the Cold War: A Handbook* (Berlin: de Gruyter, 2019). On the global efforts of the Soviet Union to prevent and return emigrants, see Erik R. Scott, *Defectors: How the Illicit Flight of Soviet Citizens Built the Borders of the Cold War World* (Oxford: Oxford University Press, 2023).

[5] On the restriction of migration to the West in a long-term perspective, see Adam M. McKeown, *Melancholy Order: Asian Migration and the Globalization of Borders* (New York: Columbia University Press, 2008).

[6] The literature on civil aviation and the Cold War focusses on the competition over flight routes and customers, not the problem of hijacking. See Jeffrey Engel, *Cold War at 30,000 Feet: The Anglo-American Fight for Aviation Supremacy* (Cambridge, MA: Harvard University Press, 2007); Robert Gruner, *Interflug und DDR-Außenpolitik: Die Luftfahrt als diplomatisches Instrument* (Hamburg: Diplomica, 2009); Jenifer van Vleck, *Empire of the Air: Aviation and the American Ascendancy* (Cambridge, MA: Harvard University Press, 2013); Peter Švík, 'East–West Relations in the Civil Aviation Sector between 1945 and 1963', *Journal of Transatlantic Studies* 13, no. 3 (2015): 263–78; Phil Tiemeyer, 'Launching a Nonaligned Airline: JAT Yugoslav Airways between East, West, and South, 1947–1962', *Diplomatic History* 41, no. 1 (2017): 78–103; Peter Švík, *Civil Aviation and the Globalization of the Cold War* (Berlin: De Gruyter: 2020).

[7] For a powerful critique of the hiatus historiography, see Matthew Craven, Sundhya Pahuja, and Gerry Simpson, 'Reading and Unreading a Historiography of Hiatus', in *International Law and the Cold War*, edited by Matthew Craven, Sundhya Pahuja, and Gerry Simpson (Cambridge: Cambridge University Press, 2019), 1–24.

Eastern Bloc and Global South states were able to work together stripping air law of its colonial vestiges—both in terms of how agreements would be interpreted regarding airstrips on external territories and the question of who was allowed to take part in negotiations. In the late 1960s, however, far-left revolutionaries and national liberation movements began hijacking flights to advance specific political agendas, particularly the cause of Palestinian statehood. The use of hijacking by national liberation movements opened a rift between Eastern Bloc states and the Global South, particularly radical socialist states in Africa. While the Eastern Bloc viewed hijacking as an intolerable crime that had to be met with mandatory prosecution in the state where the plane landed or extradition to the country where the hijacked flight originated, socialist states beyond the Soviet sphere prioritized the legal protection of national liberation movements and the sovereign rights of states to provide asylum. The international legal compromise over how to deal with hijackers—namely obligatory prosecution or extradition—developed from an agreement between East and West, tempered by the influence of the Global South, which became increasingly militant in defending the right of a state to exercise political discretion as to the treatment of hijackers.

The turbulent history of air hijacking complicates both the framing that the Global South advanced its goals due to the Cold War deadlock between East and West and the idea that the Eastern Bloc and the Global South were close allies until 1989.[8] In the academic literature, the role of the Eastern Bloc in promoting harsh punishment for 'aerial pirates' has been gradually forgotten over time and in its place a myth has arisen of the Soviets as secret masterminds of hijacking as a tactic of terror. The legal literature of the 1970s is replete with discussions of the Soviet and Eastern Bloc role in the creation of hijacking law.[9] By the 1980s, this had shifted as the US administration under President Ronald Reagan accused the Soviet Union of acting as a global sponsor of terrorism, which worked to erase consciousness of Eastern Bloc enthusiasm for the harsh punishment of hijackers.[10]

---

[8] See, respectively, Nehal Bhuta, 'Preface' and Martti Koskenniemi, 'Epilogue' in Jochen von Bernstorff and Philipp Dann (eds.), *The Battle for International Law: South-North Perspectives on the Decolonization Era* (Oxford: Oxford University Press, 2019), vi, 452.

[9] For example: 'the two governments that for different reasons were most concerned with the hijacking problem in 1970—[were] those of the United States and of the Soviet Union', Oliver J. Lissitzyn, Andreas Lowenfeld, and Alona Evans, 'International Control of Aerial Hijacking: The Role of Values and Interests', *American Journal of International Law* 65, no. 4 (1971): 82. Other examples include Amir Rafat, 'Control of Aircraft Hijacking: The Law of International Civil Aviation', *World Affairs* 134, no. 2 (1971): 143–56; Edward McWhinney, *Aerial Piracy and International Law* (Leiden: Martinus Nijhoff, 1971); Gary Horlick, 'The Public and Private International Response to Aircraft Hijacking', *Vanderbilt Journal of Transnational Law* 6, no. 1 (1972): 144; Peter van Krieken, 'Hijacking and Asylum: Some Remarks on the Hijacking Problem and its Repression, with Respect to the Law on Asylum', *Nederlands Tijdschrift Voor Internationaal Recht* 22, no. 1 (1975): 3–30.

[10] John F. Murphy and Donald R. Brady, 'The Soviet Union and International Terrorism', *The International Lawyer* 16 (1982): 139. For a comprehensive re-evaluation of this subject, see Adrian Hänni, Thomas Riegler, and Przemyslaw Gasztold, *Terrorism in the Cold War: State Support in Eastern Europe and the Soviet Sphere of Influence* (London: Bloomsbury, 2022).

By 1987, it had become general knowledge in anglophone scholarship that 'an intractable difference of interest between the Western democracies on the one hand and radical Third World and socialist states on the other existed with regard to the issue of international terrorism'.[11] Since the 1990s, the socialist states along with the Global South have been omitted from the history of the hijacking conventions or depicted as subordinate to the United States and the West, which obviously took the lead in the fight against terrorism.[12] In popular discourse, this has been encouraged by War on Terror era myth-making that it was the Soviet KGB that had secretly masterminded Palestinian hijackings and the use of airplane diversion as a terror tactic around the globe.[13] This chapter seeks to correct this erasure and demonstrate the decisive role of the Eastern Bloc in the genesis of anti-hijacking law in the 1960s and 1970s, and to examine how its development was halted in large part due to the split in the socialist world between North and South in response to the rise of terrorism during the Cold War.

The Emergence of Hijacking and the Decolonization of Air Law

In 1951, pilot Ivo Kacic diverted a JAT Yugoslav Airways flight from Ljubljana to Belgrade to land in Zurich, Switzerland, where he and two accomplices applied for asylum. The Swiss granted the three perpetrators political asylum on the grounds that they had not harmed anyone and their pursuit of 'political freedom' could not have been achieved by other means due to Yugoslavia's closed border regime.[14] While this case prompted Yugoslav officials to liberalize their emigration rules, the Soviet-aligned Eastern Bloc states only tightened their border controls. From the end of the Second World War onward, hijacking as a form of criminal activity was rapidly established as an international crime during which the perpetrator aimed to traverse political spheres and blocs of countries as they sought political asylum

---

[11] Geoffrey Levitt, 'International Counterterrorism Cooperation: The Summit Seven and Air Terrorism', *Vanderbilt Law Review* 20 (1987): 263.

[12] For example, the deliberations over the contents of the convention are made actorless in M. Cherif Bassiouni and Edward Martin Wise, *Aut Dedere Aut Judicare: The Duty to Extradite or Prosecute in International Law* (Leiden: Martinus Nijhoff, 1995), 17. The Soviet Union is treated as an impediment to anti-terrorism law until the late 1980s in Ben Saul, *Defining Terrorism in International Law* (Oxford: Oxford University Press, 2006); Non-Western states are present, but inactive in Bernhard Blumenau and Johannes-Alexander Müller, 'International Organisations and Terrorism. Multilateral Antiterrorism Efforts, 1960–1990', *Terrorism and Political Violence* 35, no. 2 (2021): 1–19.

[13] This mythmaking can be traced to a blog post from the Romanian Securitate defector Ion Mihai Pacepa, who first recalled a conversation with KGB General Aleksandr Sakharovsky who said, 'Airplane hijacking is my own invention', more than three decades after this allegedly took place. 'Russian Footprints', *National Review* (24 August 2006). This quote has been repeated credulously in many mainstream sources since, including Nick Lockwood, 'How the Soviet Union Transformed Terrorism', *The Atlantic* (23 December 2011).

[14] Celine Y. November, 'Aircraft Piracy: The Hague Hijacking Convention', *The International Lawyer* 6, no. 3 (1972): 651.

or refuge from the consequences of their crimes. In the postwar period, the hijackings out of the socialist world were initially central to the emerging problem of in-flight criminality. As one exhaustive study on the history of skyjacking found, 'between 1948 and 1958, of the thirty-three attempted or successful hijackings world-wide, twenty-three originated from within the Soviet sphere of influence, and all of these were motivated by an attempt to flee the Iron Curtain'.[15] The vast majority of these flights were on small planes and many were conducted by military personnel in military aircraft as opposed to large civilian airliners as in the case of the Yugoslavians. The Cuban Revolution only increased the centrality of crossing ideological boundaries in criminally diverted airplanes: of twenty-one hijackings between 1959 and 1961, thirteen were Cubans fleeing the country to seek asylum in the United States.[16]

When the international community sought to tackle this problem as part of the first postwar air law conference on crime in Tokyo in 1963, state socialist Eastern European states played a crucial role in the decolonization of international air law and set the stage for later developments in terms of opening up conventions to universal membership, not just members of the United Nations (UN). In 1944, the Chicago Convention on International Civil Aviation created the International Civil Aviation Organization (ICAO) as a special organization of the UN, but it did not anticipate the problem of in-flight criminal activity.[17] As civil aviation proliferated in the late 1950s, the ICAO's legal committee decided that an international treaty was needed to deal with a variety of jurisdictional and definitional problems associated with crime in the skies. Furthermore, 'the object of the convention would be the recognition, by international agreement, of the competence of States to establish jurisdiction of their courts under national laws', in cases of crimes committed on board airplanes which were often located at high altitude over areas with no territorial sovereignty.[18] In 1959, the ICAO legal committee adopted the Draft Convention on Offences and Other Acts Occurring on Board Aircraft in Munich, and in 1963 an international conference was held in Tokyo so that more than the select members on the committee could debate its contents.[19]

Neither the USSR nor the rest of the Eastern Bloc had signed the Chicago Convention or joined the ICAO. The USSR sent a delegation to the Chicago conference in 1944, but it was actually turned back en route—on orders from Moscow—when they reached the city of Winnipeg in Canada with the explanation that they could not abide the attendance of 'countries that have conducted a pro-Fascist

[15] Yannick Veilleux-Lepage, *How Terror Evolves: The Emergence and Spread of Terrorist Techniques* (Lanham, MD: Rowman & Littlefield, 2020), 64.
[16] Veilleux-Lepage, *How Terror Evolves*, 65.
[17] The Convention on International Civil Aviation.
[18] The Sub-Committee on the Legal Status of the Aircraft 1956. Cited in ICAO, Doc 8565-LC/152-2 International Conference on Air Law, Tokyo, August–September 1963, vol. II (hereafter ICAO Tokyo II), 30.
[19] History of drafting, in ICAO Tokyo II, 23–27.

policy hostile to the Soviet Union', including Switzerland, Portugal, and Spain.[20] In the early postwar years, the Soviets viewed even the minimal obligations set out by the Chicago Convention regarding access to airspace as an intolerable violation of their state sovereignty; in keeping with the USSR's boycott of any international organization that seemed political rather than purely technical, it chose not to sign or join the ICAO until 1970.[21] Of the socialist Eastern European states, only Poland and Czechoslovakia signed the Chicago Convention in the immediate postwar period (in 1945 and 1947 respectively), Yugoslavia delayed until 1954 and the rest until 1965. Seven European socialist delegations came to the Tokyo conference in 1963 as members of the UN: the USSR, the Byelorussian Soviet Socialist Republic, the Ukrainian Soviet Socialist Republic, the Polish People's Republic, the Hungarian People's Republic, and the Romanian People's Republic, as well as non-aligned Yugoslavia.[22]

The Eastern Bloc came with a series of proposals which met with mixed results. In their opening statements, both the Soviet and the Polish delegates spoke in favour of a limited treaty on 'minimal international standards' that only include offences endangering the safety of the flight itself, rather than all forms of criminal activity that one could partake in while on an airplane, to increase the potential for the widest possible acceptability to all states.[23] The UK delegation agreed that they should avoid drafting a general code relating to prosecution of criminal offences committed in the air.[24] The Soviet delegation also found general support for their demand that the treaty explicitly recognize both state-owned and private civil aviation so that they and other countries with nationalized airlines would not be excluded. This was framed as a necessary act for 'peaceful co-existence' so that the Convention could be 'adhered to by all countries, both socialistic and capitalistic which had State property and those which permitted private property'.[25] Several African delegations and even the United States accepted this corrective, since state airways were never meant to be excluded, only state aircraft such as those used by the military or police.[26]

---

[20] David MacKenzie, *ICAO: A History of the International Civil Aviation Organization* (Toronto: University of Toronto Press, 2010), 25. US and British delegates speculated that either the Soviets did not want to get involved in an impending dispute between the two anglophone powers or they simply did not think they were in a position to play a decisive role, so chose to not play any part at all.

[21] Christopher Osakwe, *The Participation of the Soviet Union in Universal International Organizations: A Political and Legal Analysis of Soviet Strategies and Aspirations Inside ILO, UNESCO and WHO* (Leiden: A. W. Sijthoff, 1972), 41.

[22] The Byelorussian Soviet Socialist Republic and the Ukrainian Soviet Socialist Republic were members of the United Nations separate from that of the USSR although they were part of the Soviet Union so they were afforded the right to send their own delegations.

[23] ICAO, Doc 8565-LC/152-1 International Conference on Air Law, Tokyo, August–September 1963, Volume II (hereafter ICAO Tokyo I), 12, 16. Polish Delegation, ICAO Tokyo I, 19.

[24] ICAO Tokyo I, 23.

[25] Ibid., 62.

[26] Ibid., 64.

Yet when the Soviets put forward an amendment to make the convention open to all states, they met with stiff resistance. As drafted, the agreement was only open to be signed according to the so-called 'Vienna formula', which held that only members of the UN or its specialized agencies could be signatories to UN treaties.[27] The Eastern Bloc states protested that this excluded of the People's Republic of China (PRC), in favour of the Republic of China (Taiwan) which continued to hold the UN seat for the nation of China, and the German Democratic Republic (GDR). Neither German state was a member of the UN until 1973, but West Germany was able to attend the conference and could sign the eventual convention as it was already a member of UN special organizations such as the World Health Organization in contrast to its diplomatically isolated socialist counterpart. While Mali—ruled by African socialist Modibo Keïta— initially spoke out in support of the Eastern Bloc proposal, Venezuela, West Germany, and the United States openly opposed it. When it came to a vote, the Soviet proposal lost twenty-two to seven—while the votes of individual states were not recorded, the yes votes equalled the Eastern Bloc plus one (likely Mali or Yugoslavia).[28]

Although the countries of the Global South had little interest in pushing for universal eligibility to help unrecognized socialist states gain access to international negotiations, they were able to collaborate with the Eastern Bloc towards decolonializing air law. Article F of the draft agreement allowed all states to agree to the Convention on behalf of any dependent territories or territories whose foreign policy they controlled. The delegation from the Republic of Congo called for it to be deleted on the grounds that this was effectively a 'colonial clause' and an implicit legitimization of ongoing Portuguese colonialism.[29] The colonial clause had been used in earlier international conventions to create a dual system of law that gave imperial states the ability to sign treaties while stipulating that those treaties did not apply in colonial territories—most infamously in the 1926 Convention to Suppress the Slave Trade and Slavery.[30] The Soviets and their allies had already successfully removed the colonial clause from the Convention for the Suppression of the Traffic in Persons and the Exploitation of the Prostitution of Others in 1949 (see Sonja Dolinsek and Philippa Hetherington, Chapter 9 in this volume). In Tokyo, the Soviets backed the Congolese, citing the 1960 'historic resolution on the rights of oppressed and colonial peoples to obtain their independence' and the precedent of the General Assembly voting to strip the colonial clause from the 1961 draft of the Convention on Marriage.[31] The Soviets had earlier proposed the

---

[27] It was only later that the term 'Vienna formula' was given to this set of criteria based on the Vienna Convention on the Law of Treaties (1969), but it is used here as a shorthand for the sake of clarity.
[28] ICAO Tokyo I, 355.
[29] Ibid., 357.
[30] This usage in 1926 was in turn based on the Constitution of the International Labor Organization. Kevin Grant, 'The League of Nations, the International Labour Organization, and Slavery in Africa', in *Oxford Research Encyclopaedia of African History*.
[31] The full name was the Draft Convention and Draft Recommendation on Consent to Marriage, Minimum Age of Marriage and Registration of Marriages. ICAO Tokyo I, 357.

deletion of an identical Article F at the more sparsely attended deliberations over the Guadalajara Convention on cargo flights in 1961.[32] At that time, the Soviet Bloc was supported only by India and the United Arab Republic (the short-lived union between Egypt and Syria), and with so few recently decolonized Afro-Asian states in attendance, the socialist amendment was overwhelmingly rejected by a vote of seventeen to eight.[33]

In Tokyo, several Western states defended Article F on the grounds that it was a technical legal tool that would extend the reach of the treaty and not a traditional colonial clause to limit applicability in colonial territories. The Dutch delegation sought to assure the others that its dependent territories were in no way colonies and the Australians cited the example of the remote and barely populated Cocos Islands in the Indian Ocean, an external territory, which was home to an important airstrip.[34] Several states with extensive colonial and external territories including Portugal, France, and the United States all supported the inclusion of Article F as a technical matter of law, not politics.[35] The United Kingdom, still a major colonial power, argued that Article F was identical to one included in the Guadalajara Convention—so precedent was on their side. Conversely, Nigeria, Ceylon (Sri Lanka), Mali, Liberia, Ivory Coast, Guatemala, Indonesia, India, and Panama all spoke out against it. The delegation from Upper Volta (Burkina Faso) said that while they were barely willing to tolerate the participation of Portugal at the conference (due to its fascist politics and unapologetic imperialism), a colonial clause was too much to stomach. European socialist states also spoke out against the inclusion of Article F, with the Poles arguing that it sanctioned the colonial system and the Yugoslavians declaring solidarity with the Congolese.[36] Only two years after negotiations in Guadalajara had upheld an identical clause, the situation was very different in Tokyo, as decolonization had rapidly shifted the centre of power away from the West towards the Afro-Asian states. When Mali called for a roll call vote, the Congolese proposal to delete Article F was passed twenty-six to nineteen with two abstentions. Without the votes of the seven Eastern European socialist states, the result would have been a tie.[37]

The debates about hijacking as a specific crime proved far less contentious and the socialist states barely spoke on the subject. Most hijackings from the socialist world were of small military aircraft rather than civilian airliners, so the Tokyo Convention did not address the type of airplane diversion that affected the Eastern

---

[32] The conference led to the creation of the Guadalajara Convention, Supplementary to The Warsaw Convention, for the Unification of Certain Rules Relating to International Carriage by Air Performed by a Person Other than the Contracting Carrier (1961). It made no mention of hijacking or crime.
[33] ICAO, Doc 8301-LC/149-1 International Conference on Private Air Law, Guadalajara, August–September 1961, 231.
[34] ICAO Tokyo I, 359.
[35] Ibid., 358.
[36] Ibid., 361–62.
[37] Ibid., 361.

Bloc. The discussion centred mostly on the exact terminology around the use of force in seizing an airplane. The conference ultimately agreed to a set of general rules on hijacking acceptable to all: the signatories were obligated to assist in restoring control of a hijacked plane as soon as possible, to allow passengers to continue their journey in a timely manner and to return stolen airplanes and cargo to their rightful owners. As for the hijackers themselves, all states were obliged to allow airplane commanders to disembark anyone who had endangered a flight, to conduct preliminary inquiries in cases of hijacking, and to report this information to the country of registration of the affected airplane. The agreement allowed states to take suspected hijackers into custody when they landed in their country but made no obligations as to what should happen next. The convention provided room for states to continue to grant asylum on political grounds and did not compel prosecution or extradition.[38]

Despite the influence they had over the negotiations, Eastern European socialist states did not bother to actually sign or ratify the final document. Preventing illicit emigration was of high priority across the Eastern Bloc— the Berlin Wall had been constructed by East Germany just two years earlier to forestall such movement— but the hijacking of civilian airliners was not yet a serious problem in Eastern Europe. Cuba did not participate in the conference for reasons that remain unclear. As such, civilian airline hijacking was considered primarily a crime of the capitalist world that did not warrant a commitment to further international legal obligations.[39] After using the conference as an opportunity to strike a blow against colonialism in international law, socialist Eastern European states saw little to gain in acceding to the resulting Convention.

Hijacking Goes Global

The 1968 hijacking of the El Al Flight 426 by the People's Front for the Liberation of Palestine (PFLP) revolutionized the problem of hijacking in both politics and law. The Marxist–Leninist faction of the Palestinian Liberation Organization (PLO) diverted the Israeli flight from Rome to Lod Airport near Tel Aviv to land in Algeria, at the time a self-described radical socialist state.[40] This was the first hijacking to

---

[38] Allan I. Mendelsohn, 'In-Flight Crime: The International and Domestic Picture under the Tokyo Convention', *Virginia Law Review* 53, no. 3 (1967): 509–63.

[39] This paralleled the Eastern Bloc's approach to prostitution and drugs, which were also instrumentalized towards anticolonial political aims but also dismissed as a pathologies of capitalist society. See Sonja Dolinsek and Philippa Hetherington, Chapter 9 in this volume and Ned Richardson-Little, 'The Drug War in a Land Without Drugs: East Germany and the Socialist Embrace of International Narcotics Law', *Journal of the History of International Law* 21, no. 2 (2019): 270–98.

[40] Dan Porat, 'The Hijacking of El Al Flight 426: The Advent of Air Terrorism', *Journal of Contemporary History* 57, no. 4 (2022). On Algeria and socialism in the 1960s, see Jeffrey James Byrne, 'Our Own Special Brand of Socialism: Algeria and the Contest of Modernities in the 1960s', *Diplomatic History* 33, no. 3 (2009): 427–47.

use passengers as hostages for political ends. By the late 1960s, hijacking transformed from an occasional problem to a veritable epidemic. At first the majority of hijackings were of American flights diverted primarily to Cuba. Hijackers ranging from Black political revolutionaries to petty criminals saw the communist island as a safe haven where they could avoid prosecution and persecution by American authorities. But this wave of hijackings in the West moved beyond the US–Cuba axis in 1968 with a series of hijackings by Palestinian militants starting with El Al Flight 426. This wave expanded to include the Eastern Bloc in 1970 when the Soviet Union was faced with the problem of those seeking to emigrate turning to the hijacking of large civilian airliners, rather than the earlier incidents of defectors seizing small military aircraft.

The hijackings of American planes to Cuba and Algeria and out of the Soviet Union generated international conflicts that demonstrated the problem of finding cross-bloc legal remedies and prompted the international community to seek a multilateral solution. All three trends—hijackings to Cuba, by Palestinian militants and by Soviet emigrationists—hit upon the same issues of what to do with the hijacked planes and passengers, how to deal with perpetrators, and how to handle the question of extradition. While Cuban authorities accommodated the arrival of hijacked planes, the hijackers were seen as unstable—and possibly as spies—and most were sent to workhouses or imprisoned. Although African American radicals had assumed that Cuba would be a reliable safe haven, it became clear that few if any hijackers would be welcomed on the island nation. Eldridge Cleaver of the Marxist–Leninist Black Panther Party came to see Cuba as a prison: a 'sort of a San Quentin with palm trees, an Alcatraz with sugar cane'.[41] As the United States sought negotiations with Cuba to create a bilateral treaty on hijacking to ensure punishment for perpetrators and the return of vehicles and passengers, National Security Adviser Henry Kissinger warned President Richard Nixon that the United States had already rebuffed a similar proposal from Che Guevara earlier that decade. It was the United States that had been delinquent in refusing to prosecute Cuban hijackers and return planes hijacked by Cubans fleeing to the United States. In a memo, Kissinger observed that 'Cuba has now become one the best-behaved of the hijacking states, since it immediately allows the planes and passengers to return and often jails the hijackers.'[42]

By contrast, in the case of the PFLP hijacking of El Al Flight 426, the Algerian government assisted the hijackers and held the Israeli passengers as hostages for the duration of negotiations.[43] Although the Cuban ambassador had advised the

---

[41] Sean L. Malloy, *Out of Oakland: Black Panther Party Internationalism during the Cold War* (Ithaca: Cornell University Press, 2017), 142.
[42] Quoted in Teishan A. Latner, 'Take Me to Havana! Airline Hijacking, U.S.-Cuba Relations, and Political Protest in Late Sixties' America', *Diplomatic History* 39, no. 1 (2015): 39. American legal literature in this era erased the period of hijackings from Cuba to the United States and portrayed the wave in the other direction as entirely novel. See e.g. November, 'Aircraft Piracy'.
[43] Porat, 'The Hijacking of El Al Flight 426', 2.

Algerians to quickly return the plane and its passengers, they refused to do so prompting an international backlash, primarily in the West but also from African states such as Ghana, which denounced it as an act of piracy. When negotiations over the release of the Israeli passengers brokered by Italy appeared to break down, the International Federation of Air Line Pilots' Associations (IFALPA) called on its global membership to boycott Algeria on the grounds that it was violating the Tokyo Convention (which had not actually come into effect due to lack of signatories, and which Algeria had not signed). When French pilots signed onto the boycott threatening to cut off Algeria from the world, as Air France operated most flights to and from the country, Arab states threatened a counter-boycott of flights to Europe. Shortly before the boycott could take effect, the Algerian government came up with a solution to release the remaining hostages and the plane.[44] While forced to concede, Algeria replaced Cuba as the hope for African American radicals, who now began to congregate in Algiers where the Black Panther Party provided a refuge for hijackers from the United States.[45] Although the crisis in Algeria had been resolved, in that same year, Leila Khaled and Salim Issawi of the PFLP seized flight TWA 840 and diverted it to Damascus, Syria, where they detonated the nose of the plane, killing four passengers and injuring several others. In 1970, the PFLP simultaneously hijacked four planes, landing three at a remote airstrip in Dawson's Field in Jordan, where they were emptied of passengers and then blown up with images of the destruction broadcast around the world.[46] Airliner hijackings had become a global spectacle as the technologies of the developed world, both aircraft and television, were now being used against it.[47] While air power had earlier been a key factor in the spread of imperialism in the Middle East, it was now being hijacked by anticolonial militants.[48]

As hijacking had become a weapon of choice for Marxist–Leninist revolutionaries, the Soviet Union and its Eastern European allies were faced with those who wanted to seize airplanes to exit the Eastern Bloc. In 1969, two East Germans had hijacked an LOT Polish Airlines flight from Warsaw to Brussels when it made at stopover at East Berlin's Schönefeld Airport. By landing in West Berlin, they hoped to claim asylum due to the policy of treating all East Germans as automatic West German citizens; they had, however, arrived at Tegel Airport in the French sector of occupation and were thus referred to a French military court and imprisoned

---

[44] Ibid., 11.
[45] Malloy, *Out of Oakland*, 198.
[46] The Dawson's Field incident prompted the Jordanian crackdown on Palestinian militants that became known as Black September.
[47] On hijacking as a media spectacle, see Annette Vowinckel, *Flugzeugentführungen: Eine Kulturgeschichte* (Göttingen: Wallstein Verlag, 2012), 59–82.
[48] Priya Satia, 'The Defense of Inhumanity: Air Control and the British Idea of Arabia', *American Historical Review* 111, no. 1 (2006): 16–51.

for two years.[49] That same year, another LOT Polish Airlines flight was diverted to Vienna, Austria by two Poles who were tried and convicted by an Austrian court. The following year, a group of nine Czechs on a plane bound for Prague diverted it to land in Nuremberg where a West German court sentenced the ringleader to more than two years in prison.[50] In June 1970, sixteen people, mostly Soviet Jews, were arrested in Leningrad for planning to hijack a plane to emigrate to Israel. Later that same year, Aeroflot Flight 244 from Batumi in Georgia to the Russian city of Krasnodar was hijacked by an armed Lithuanian father and son, Pranas and Algirdas Brazinskas. When the crew tried to stop them by making a rapid descent, the hijackers began to fire their pistols, killing a nineteen-year-old flight attendant, Nadezhda Kurchenko, and wounding the captain and another member of the cabin crew. The plane was diverted to Turkey where the Soviets unsuccessfully demanded their extradition to the USSR. A Turkish court found that the Brazinskases had a legitimate political claim to emigration as the Soviet annexation of Lithuania remained disputed and an appeals court affirmed the political character of the crime, allowing both men to go free. Although their bid for asylum in the United States was rejected, the two hijackers eventually made it there via Italy, Venezuela, and Canada, crossing the border illicitly to the United States where the Lithuanian diaspora welcomed them as heroes. With extradition to the USSR deemed too politically problematic, they were allowed to stay, which was also protested by Soviet officials, who again unsuccessfully demanded their return to face trial for murder and hijacking.[51]

In response to this rash of international hijackings, ICAO aimed to revise the Tokyo Convention to make the earlier agreement more punitive and act as a deterrent. At a conference held in The Hague in December 1970, a wide range of possible legal solutions were proposed. UN Secretary General U Thant suggested that since hijacking was a crime of a 'totally different category', which targeted an international service affecting so many different nations, it required an international tribunal to go beyond the limitations of national courts.[52] While Thant's proposal found support among some legal academics (one of whom suggested that hijackers could be detained in West Berlin's Spandau Prison, now that all the Nazi war criminals convicted at the Nuremberg Trials had been released), the idea that a non-political tribunal could be entrusted with prosecuting such crimes was endorsed only by the IFALPA and Belgium.[53] At The Hague conference, debate

[49] Hans von Mangoldt, 'Das Urteil des Tribunal du Gouvernement Militaire Français de Berlin zur Entführung einer polnischen Verkehrsmaschine nach Berlin', *Zeitschrift für ausländisches öffentliches Recht und Völkerrecht* (1970): 528–41.
[50] For details of the LOT and Czech hijackings, see Jacob Sundberg, 'The Case for an International Criminal Court', *Journal of Air Law and Commerce* 37, no. 2 (1971): 218.
[51] Erik R. Scott, 'The Hijacking of Aeroflot Flight 244: States and Statelessness in the Late Cold War', *Past & Present* 243, no. 1 (2019): 213–45.
[52] November, 'Aircraft Piracy', 654–55.
[53] Spandau Prison was at that time still home to one Nazi war criminal, former Deputy Führer Rudolf Hess, who remained there until his death in 1987 due to the Soviet refusal to allow his release. See

hinged primarily on the questions of obligations of states to prosecute or extradite perpetrators and the limits of political discretion for states in dealing with such cases. The question of asylum in particular led to cracks along a North–South axis among socialist states, while the Eastern Bloc and the West found new common ground due to their shared problem of domestic airliner hijackings.

The socialist states of Eastern Europe and the Global South were initially able to work together on the question of making the treaty universally accessible, against the Western states which demanded it remain open according to the Vienna formula. The Hague conference began, as had Tokyo, with protests from the socialist states over the participation of the Republic of China (Taiwan) rather than the PRC and the continued exclusion of East Germany. The Romanian delegation also called for the inclusion of both the Provisional Government of South Vietnam and the Cambodian government of Prince Norodom Sihanouk, in exile in Beijing after a coup earlier that year.[54] By contrast, the Federal Republic of Germany was particularly adamant that the Convention follow the Vienna formula to ensure the ongoing exclusion of East Germany. The combined weight of the Eastern Bloc with the delegations from the Global South, however, made the treaty open to all states. Western states emphasized that their signatures on this treaty in no way represented a recognition of any socialist state with which they did not already have diplomatic ties but which had also signed the agreement.[55]

The designation of hijacking as a grave crime was uncontroversial among the delegations, but divisions emerged over what was to be done about it. The United States and the Soviet Union agreed that the priority was to create an international convention that would demand punishment for hijackers—not just permit their prosecution as in the Tokyo Convention—without regard to their politics. Many African and Asian countries were equally concerned about the problem of hijacking—for example, Ethiopia spoke out against it as a threat to its economic future given the importance of air transportation for its connections to the wider world. The most hardline rhetoric at the conference came from Israel, which declared that hijackers had to be targeted 'in much the same spirit of international concern in which piracy at sea had once been eliminated', and Thailand, which

---

Chester Leo Smith, 'The Probable Necessity of an International Prison in Solving Aircraft Hijacking', *The International Lawyer* 269, no. 5 (1971). See also Sundberg, 'The Case for an International Criminal Court'. The IFALPA brought up the proposal in Montréal in 1971, citing the precedent of the Conventions on the Creation of an International Criminal Court and on the Prevention and Punishment of Terrorism, both from 1937, and neither ever brought into force with sufficient signatures. ICAO, Doc 9081-LC/170-1 International Conference on Air Law, Montréal, September 1971, 16. Belgian advocacy for the plan came later at the Rome conference. See ICAO, Doc 9225-LC/178 International Conference on Air Law, Rome, August–September 1973 (hereafter ICAO Rome), 44. Neither the proposal by the IFALPA nor Belgium elicited a response from any other delegates.

[54] ICAO, Doc 8979-LC/165-1 International Conference on Air Law, The Hague, December 1970, vol. I (hereafter ICAO The Hague), 8.
[55] Ibid., 200–01.

argued that 'hijackers should be regarded as enemies of humankind'.[56] Although the use of the 'pirate analogy' had become commonplace in the postwar era as a shorthand for international law that could apply to *hostis humani generis* (enemies of all mankind)—as Cicero had once denounced the maritime pirates of the Mediterranean in Ancient Rome—it ironically failed to gain widespread purchase in the codification of modern day 'aerial piracy'.[57]

Although the United States sought mandatory prosecution in the country where hijackers were arrested, the Soviets aimed for mandatory extradition to the country where the planes were registered.[58] For the Eastern Bloc states this was the only means to assure that hijackers would face justice and could not be granted leniency on political grounds in a foreign country. The Soviets explicitly courted and found support from the observers of the International Air Transport Association (IATA) and the IFALPA, who sought maximalist measures against hijackers—but they had no vote.[59] IATA did have LOT Polish Airlines and ČSA Czechoslovak State Airlines as founding members, but the vast majority of member airlines were based in the West. Most Western states rejected mandatory extradition since it could mean sending perpetrators back to countries where they may face execution—not just in Eastern European but also in the United States, though this was not said explicitly at the conference. The proposal was also rejected by the leading socialist African states including Senegal, Tanzania, and the People's Republic of Congo.[60] Mandatory extradition not only posed a threat to African agreements on refugees but the inclusion of South Africa as a signatory to the convention would create a binding extradition treaty to that country.[61] Although liberation fighters were not explicitly mentioned, the threat of being forced to extradite hijackers to the apartheid state was clearly a concern. Tanzania in particular closely allied itself to the PRC in its push for the recognition of national liberation movements under international humanitarian law, so it is highly probable this was a strong if unstated

---

[56] Ibid., 18–19.

[57] On the invocation of pirates as universally despised figures subject to self-evident universal jurisdiction as a trope of postwar legal scholarship, see Eugene Kontorovich, 'The Piracy Analogy: Modern Universal Jurisdiction's Hollow Foundation', *Harvard International Law Journal* 45, no. 1 (2004): 183–237. Although a convenient analogy denoting universal scorn, the evolution of actual piracy law was similar marked by the historical problem of states seeking exceptions for privateering that benefitted their state interests. See Michael Kempe, '"Even in the Remotest Corners of the World": Globalized Piracy and International Law, 1500–1900', *Journal of Global History* 5, no. 3 (2010): 353–72. Michael J. Kelly, 'The Pre-History of Piracy as a Crime & Its Definitional Odyssey', *Case Western Reserve Journal of International Law* 46, no. 25 (2013), 25-42.

[58] Scott claims that both the United States and the Soviet Union did not seek mandatory extradition as 'neither of the superpowers wanted to cede control over people who entered their respective spheres of influence', but when it came to international negotiations, the Soviets were willing to return Westerners if it meant the return of its own people: Scott, *Defectors*, 203.

[59] ICAO The Hague, 127.

[60] Ibid., 104.

[61] Ibid., Uganda comment, 129.

motivation.[62] In the end, the socialist proposal for mandatory extradition failed forty-seven to ten with eight abstentions.

In contrast, East and West found a point of common concern on the question of asylum, as both sought to explicitly forbid excusing hijacking on political grounds, even though in practice the United States had often provided refuge to hijackers from Cuba.[63] Much of this debate centred on Article 7 concerning jurisdiction for the prosecution of hijacking. The United States asked for 'an unequivocal statement that hijacking was not considered to be a political offence and should be treated as any other grave, common and criminal offence'.[64] The Soviets took a similar line stating that 'hijacking should be considered an offence in itself and no account should be taken of any political motives behind it'.[65] Other Eastern Bloc delegations rejected any possibility of mitigation on political grounds. The Polish delegate argued that 'anyone engaged in truly political activities would hardly commit the crime of hijacking, thereby gravely endangering the lives of innocent people'.[66] By definition, the act of hijacking invalidated the political cause of the hijackers.

Although Yugoslavia had legalized emigration, the socialist, but non-aligned, state still followed the same line as Moscow. Nationalist movements, particularly Croatian separatists, sought to use hijacking and attacks on airplanes as a weapon against the central government of Josip Broz Tito in Belgrade. This included the famous case of JAT Flight 367 that was bombed in mid-air killing everyone on board except for cabin crew member Vesna Vulović, who miraculously survived the fall from over 10,000 metres. As a result, Yugoslavia took a hardline position on extradition with no possibility of asylum.[67] At private talks during a state visit by US President Richard Nixon, Tito denounced hijackings as 'criminal acts jeopardizing the lives of innocent people'. He reported that a recent incident where Algerian hijackers had landed their plane in Dubrovnik was going to be met with local prosecution before the perpetrators were deported to Algeria to face further charges. The Yugoslavian Secretary of State for Foreign Affairs Mirko Tepavac told his American counterpart that he had already informed his Palestinian contacts that 'terrorist and hijacking escapades were damaging their cause before world

---

[62] Georges Abi-Saab, 'The Third World Intellectual in Praxis: Confrontation, Participation, or Operation behind Enemy Lines?', *Third World Quarterly* 37, no. 11 (2016): 1957–71,
[63] Western support for freedom of movement from their own states and for 'escapees' fleeing the Eastern Bloc was never as concrete in practice as it was in Cold War propaganda. See Susan L. Carruthers, 'Between Camps: Eastern Bloc "Escapees" and Cold War Borderlands', *American Quarterly* 57, no. 3 (2005): 911–42; Sebastian Gehrig, 'The Difficulty of Leaving: Freedom of Movement and the National Security State in Cold War West Germany', *Journal of Modern European History* 21, no. 1 (2023): 133–52
[64] ICAO The Hague, 10.
[65] Ibid., 12.
[66] Ibid., 126.
[67] On the Yugoslav position against political discretion, see ibid., 136. On Croatian terrorism, see Mate Nikola Tokić, *Croatian Radical Separatism and Diaspora Terrorism During the Cold War* (West Lafayette: Purdue University Press, 2020).

public opinion'.[68] The imperative to stop hijacking was placed ahead of the needs of ideological allies like the PFLP or national liberation movements in the colonized world.

The US–Soviet proposals for Article 7 met with resistance from across the Global South, including those in the socialist camp, who agreed that hijacking was a severe problem but were unwilling to sacrifice the right to claim political asylum to combat it. Most states in the Global South saw the issue as less urgent than those in the West, and while emigration was also a concern for many developing countries, it was an issue of brain drain rather than individual cases of plane hijackings.[69] At the UN General Assembly in 1970, the pugilistic Saudi representative Jamil Baroody defended Palestinian hijackers stating: 'the British hijacked colonies and nobody says anything. [...] Although planes have been hijacked to Cuba time and again, it was only when the Palestinian people hijack planes that you went to the Sixth Committee with certain draft resolutions on hijacking'.[70] While no states were willing to explicitly defend hijacking as a tactic at The Hague conference, certain African delegations did defend the idea that motivations could legitimize a case of airplane diversion into a political crime that would be exempt from mandatory prosecution or extradition. The representative from Tanzania, led at the time by African socialist Julius Nyerere, argued that the treaty should be written 'so that States should have the possibility of granting asylum in cases of political hijackings'.[71] This discretionary power would be rooted in the need to recognize state sovereignty as the basis for the international order. The delegate from Chile—under the democratic socialist government of Salvador Allende—argued for a change in language of the text so that Article 7 referred to the 'decision whether to prosecute' rather than assuming prosecution was mandatory. Although backed by Tanzania, this was fiercely opposed by the United Kingdom, the Soviet Union, and Romania. In a vote, the Chilean amendment was defeated twenty-two to forty-one.[72]

Although the Soviet Union and its allies were normally staunch defenders of state sovereignty at such conferences, in this instance they made the case that their proposals represented an appropriate and voluntary restriction on state power.

---

[68] Foreign Relations of the United States, 1969–1976, vol. XXIX, Eastern Europe; Eastern Mediterranean, 1969–1972, Document 221, Memorandum of Conversation. National Archives, RG 59, Yugoslav Desk Files: Lot 79 D 230, POL 7 Nixon Visit, 550, On the precarious position of Yugoslavia between cooperation with the United States and solidarity with liberation movements, see Milorad Lazic, *Unmaking Détente: Yugoslavia, the United States, and the Global Cold War, 1968–1980* (Lanham, MD: Rowman & Littlefield, 2022).

[69] Sara Dehm, 'Contesting the Right to Leave in International Law: The Berlin Wall, the Third World Brain Drain and the Politics of Emigration in the 1960s', in *International Law and the Cold War*, edited by Matthew Craven, Sundhya Pahuja, and Gerry Simpson (Cambridge: Cambridge University Press, 2019), 159–88.

[70] UN General Assembly, 25th Session, 1915th Plenary Meeting, (30 November 1970), 7.

[71] ICAO The Hague, 104.

[72] Ibid., 180–81.

As the Hungarian delegate said, 'the principle of national sovereignty raised by many delegations did not mean that countries could not agree to deal jointly with universal problems. Rather than a loss of sovereignty, adoption of that proposal would mean the assumption of certain rights stemming from national sovereignty'.[73] Other socialist states rejected the idea that fighting hijacking required giving up any aspect of national sovereignty. Cuba did not attend The Hague conference, and generally rejected multilateral solutions to hijacking, but a representative did speak at a special session of ICAO in 1970.[74] In his speech, Major Claudio Rey Marin defended Cuba's 'sovereign prerogative' to provide asylum to hijackers who were 'politically persecuted [and] had no choice but to resort to such an extreme remedy'.[75] Placing the island in the camp of the Global South defending the importance of political discretion with regards to political criminals, Marin cited the right to asylum in the Universal Declaration of Human Rights. At The Hague, the Marxist–Leninist People's Republic of Congo, African socialist Tanzania, and the nominally socialist dictatorship of Milton Obote in Uganda all prioritized state sovereignty and African solidarity over the Soviet proposals.

While the United States and the Soviets aimed to include the phrase 'irrespective of its motivation' to the section on the obligation to prosecute or extradite, they were countered by the Kenyan delegation who suggested instead 'without exception whatsoever', as this terminology was already present in a relevant UN resolution.[76] The Kenyan proposal ultimately gained general acceptance from all sides, and the result was a compromise where all cases had to be referred to for extradition or local prosecution—the legal principle of *aut dedere aut judicare*. Nevertheless, national courts could ultimately still decide not to press charges, or to find other means to exonerate hijackers if they chose to do so.[77] Although functionally close to declaring hijacking to be a crime prosecutable through universal jurisdiction, the term is not mentioned, and some courts have classified the terms of The Hague Convention as a form of 'obligatory territorial jurisdiction', as the Convention creates a 'treaty-based broad extraterritorial jurisdiction' where the hijacked plane lands.[78] The Convention thus created a model for subsequent Cold

---

[73] Ibid., 129.
[74] Cuba was the only country to vote against a 1969 UN Resolution calling on all member states to take action to ensure hijackers could be legally punished. Haro F. van Panhuys, 'Aircraft Hijacking and International Law', *Columbia Journal of Transnational Law* 9 (1970): 1.
[75] Latner, 'Take Me to Havana!', 27. See text of Marin's speech at the XVII Special Assembly of ICAO, Montréal, Canada, June 1970 in Cuba Ministerio de Relaciones Exteriores, *Hijacking of Aircraft: A Boomerang Hurled at Cuba by the Imperialist Government of the United States of America* (Havana: Cuban Ministry of Foreign Relations, 1970).
[76] ICAO The Hague, 177. See Resolution 2264 (XXV) of the UN General Assembly.
[77] R. H. Mankiewicz, 'The 1970 Hague Convention', *Journal of Air Law and Commerce*, 37: 2 (1971), 204–05.
[78] Mitsue Inazumi, *Universal Jurisdiction in Modern International Law: Expansion of National Jurisdiction for Prosecuting Serious Crimes Under International Law* (Antwerp: Intersentia, 2005), 70, fn 69.

War era agreements including the Protection of Diplomats Convention (1973), the Hostage Convention (1979), the Torture Convention (1984), and the Mercenaries Convention (1989).[79]

The superpowers were in close alignment in promoting the final document as an effective tool against hijacking. The American delegation praised the convention as an 'important international reaction to lawless acts which, regardless of motivation, must be subject to punishment'.[80] This sentiment was echoed by the Soviet delegation, which spoke of the expectations from people around the world who hoped 'that the Conference would work out an international instrument which would put an end to such criminal acts, regardless of the pretence and the motive thereof, and would establish severe punishment of the offenders and their accomplices and would define conditions for their extradition'.[81] While there was near universal agreement, Algeria and Tanzania rejected the convention as an impingement on their right to grant asylum to political hijackers.[82] The Algerian delegation abstained in the final vote as it 'could not support an inclusion of a reference to motives for the act in the Convention', because this question should be left to individual governments.[83] As with the earlier Tanzanian objections, the Algerian dissent in favour of greater political latitude for states in dealing with hijackers signalled the growing split between the Eastern Bloc, which sought punishment without exception, and those states—primarily African socialist—which saw this as a threat to freedom fighters and radical militant movements.

Although the Eastern Bloc had failed to sign the Tokyo Convention, the concerns over airliner hijackings in the USSR led, within a year of The Hague conference, to full ratifications being deposited by the Soviet Union, Bulgaria, Hungary, and Mongolia.[84] While only Vienna formula countries had been invited to take part in the talks, The Hague Convention was made open to all signatories and was ratified by East Germany in 1971—two years before it joined the UN. The North–South split between the Eastern Bloc and African socialist states over the problem of extradition and asylum continued at a 1971 follow-up conference held in Montréal. This conferecne aimed to supplement The Hague Convention to deal with attacks on airplanes and acts of violence committed on board a plane that could endanger its safety.[85] Once again, the Soviets and their allies pushed

---

[79] Bassiouni and Wise, *Aut Dedere Aut Judicare*, 17. Formally, the Convention on the Prevention and Punishment of Crimes Against Internationally Protected Persons, Including Diplomatic Agents; International Convention against the Taking of Hostages; Convention Against Torture and Other Cruel, Inhuman or Degrading Treatment or Punishment; International Convention against the Recruitment, Use, Financing and Training of Mercenaries.
[80] ICAO The Hague, 204.
[81] Ibid., 198–99.
[82] Ibid., 182.
[83] Ibid., 200.
[84] Horlick, 'The Public and Private International Response to Aircraft Hijacking', 176.
[85] In 1970, the Action Organization for the Liberation of Palestine and the Popular Democratic Front for the Liberation of Palestine attacked an El Al bus at Munich airport, killing one passenger and injuring eleven.

for mandatory extradition, but this had no support in the West outside of IATA and the IFALPA, and it was uniformly rejected by the delegations from the Global South. The People's Republic of Congo in particular spoke out against the proposal on the grounds that it would upset the delicate balance agreed to at The Hague.[86] The conference successfully led to a minor convention that expanded the scope of the acts and perpetrators The Hague Convention could apply to, but there was no progress on the issues of prosecution, asylum, and extradition. Although universal membership and the absence of a colonial clause had now become standard for such agreements, the productive collaboration between the Eastern Bloc and the Global South was effectively at an end.

Failure in Rome and the Turn to Terrorism

In 1972, five members of the Black Liberation Army took over Delta Air Lines Flight 841 from Detroit to Miami; after collecting a million-dollar ransom, they flew to Algeria. Fearing further boycott threats and tiring of the Black radicals who were living in exile in the country, the Algerian government returned the plane, its passengers, and the ransom money to the United States but allowed the hijackers to flee to France (four of five were caught a few years later but not extradited as French courts believed Black radicals would not receive a fair trial in the United States and face possible execution).[87] That same year, the PFLP expanded its campaign against air travel through an attack on Israel's Lod Airport by a team of Japanese Red Army members, killing twenty-six and injuring eighty. On 19 June 1972, the IFALPA held a near global strike day as pilots protested inaction on the problem of hijackings.[88] In the USSR in 1973, there were three failed hijackings, one of which was stopped by an armed police response personally led by the minister for civil aviation—a fact loudly broadcast to the international media to demonstrate the seriousness of the Soviet response.[89]

Although once isolated as a problem of crime against civil aviation, hijacking had now been integrated into the emerging international legal disputes over the definition of terrorism. Following the Munich massacre of Israeli athletes by Palestinian

---

[86] ICAO, Doc 9081-LC/170-1 International Conference on Air Law, Montréal, September 1971, 62. It is probable that the People's Republic of the Congo's position on hijacking led the Black Panther Party to request that its international section be able to set up a base there in 1971. They received no response from the government in Brazzaville. Malloy, *Out of Oakland*, 192.

[87] Fearing that further cooperation with hijackers could endanger a pending natural gas deal, the Algerian government refused the request of the Black Panthers to keep the ransom to fund their activities. The conflict over the hijacking led to the breakdown of relations between Algeria and the Party. Malloy, *Out of Oakland*, 203–7.

[88] Alona E. Evans, 'Aircraft Hijacking: What Is To Be Done?', *American Journal of International Law* 66, no. 5 (1972): 819.

[89] 'Soviet Air Ministers Personally Oversees Foiling of Hijacking', *The New York Times* (6 November 1973), 74.

militants in 1972, Western efforts to make terrorism into a generally condemned crime were met with demands from the Third World to recognize the existence of 'state terrorism', and the need to distinguish criminality from legally recognized acts of violence by national liberation movements.[90] The relationship of the Eastern Bloc to terrorism was complex: while offering material support to militant organizations such as the PFLP and others, the Soviets called on them to refrain from international terrorism, cutting off funding at one point in the late 1970s to try to force the issue.[91] Terrorist attacks were seen through the lens of anticolonialism but also viewed by many Eastern European socialist officials as a distasteful tool of far-left Maoist extremists and far-right reactionaries, both of which threatened progressive socialist forces in the West.[92] As one Bulgarian official declared to an Eastern Bloc meeting on tackling international terrorism in 1979, 'terrorism is alien to the essence of the theory of scientific communism and the practice of socialist society itself'.[93] Just as the Eastern European states had successfully lobbied for national liberation movements to be given international protection under international humanitarian law according to the 1977 Geneva Convention Protocols, they now lobbied for similar exemptions in international negotiations over criminalizing specific forms of terrorism, including the International Convention against the Taking of Hostages (1979).[94] But hijacking remained outside of this umbrella of protection, and the Eastern Bloc continued to treat it as a form of intolerable piracy, not a possibly justifiable form of revolutionary violence. Unlike the other legal categories of terrorism such as hostage-taking or attacks on diplomats which took place in an individual location, hijacking for political purposes was inseparable from the use of hijacking for migration.

Negotiations at the UN over terrorism resulted in major clashes between East and West, but behind the scenes, the legal and bureaucratic tools for anti-hijacking cooperation proliferated as part of the relaxation of Cold War tensions during

---

[90] Kendall W. Stiles, 'The Power of Procedure and the Procedures of the Powerful: Anti-Terror Law in the United Nations', *Journal of Peace Research* 43, no. 1 (2006): 40. Bernhard Blumenau, 'The Other Battleground of the Cold War: The UN and the Struggle against International Terrorism in the 1970s', *Journal of Cold War Studies* 16, no. 1 (2014): 61–84. Negotiations over a terrorism convention in the interwar period had also been plagued by the problem of the right of states to offer asylum in cases of 'political crimes'. Ben Saul, 'The Legal Response of the League of Nations to Terrorism', *Journal of International Criminal Justice* 4, no. 1 (2006): 78–102.

[91] Adrian Hänni, 'State Support for Terrorist Actors in the Cold War—Myths and Reality (Part 1)', in *Terrorism in the Cold War: State Support in Eastern Europe and the Soviet Sphere of Influence*, edited by Adrian Hänni, Thomas Riegler, and Przemyslaw Gasztold (London: Bloomsbury Academic, 2022), 6–7.

[92] See Soviet academic studies denouncing terrorism such as I. Blitschenko and N. Zhdanov, 'Terrorism: An International Crime', *International Association of Democratic Lawyers—Review of Contemporary Law*, Issue 2, 1978, 9–13 and I. Karpetz, 'On International Terrorism', *International Association of Democratic Lawyers—Review of Contemporary Law* 2 (1981), 47–52.

[93] Deputy Minister Lieutenant General G. Sopov, Ágnes in Hankiss (ed.), *Terrorists in Budapest: The Communist State Security Services and Europe* (Budapest: Hamvas Institute, 2011), 24.

[94] Giovanni Mantilla, 'The Protagonism of the USSR and Socialist States in the Revision of International Humanitarian Law', *Journal of the History of International Law* 21, no. 2 (2019): 181–211.

Détente. This latest wave of airplane seizures led to a series of cross-bloc bilateral agreements on hijacking. Already in 1970, Bulgaria and Italy entered into talks to discuss a possible collaboration on the problem of 'acts of air piracy', after several minor incidents between the two nations.[95] In 1973, the United States and Cuba came to a formal agreement on the extradition of hijackers, bringing an end to Havana as the primary destination for stolen American airplanes.[96] That same year, the Soviet Union signed agreements with Turkey and Afghanistan; and the following year, one with Finland.[97]

Seeking to strengthen the enforcement regime of The Hague and Montréal Conventions, ICAO held another conference in Rome in 1973, which was the first to fail to produce a new convention.[98] Cooperation between the Soviets and the United States fell apart as the Americans sought to create a system to punish states, including non-signatories, for non-compliance through blockades on civilian air traffic. While the Soviets and their allies still pushed for a mandatory extradition regime, they opposed any system of coerced compliance for states that were not signatories on the grounds that this was a violation of sovereignty norms established by the UN Charter and would set a dangerous precedent for all other fields of law. The French and the British representatives agreed with the Soviets that the American proposal was a threat to usurp their powers as permanent members of the UN Security Council.[99]

As the United States found itself isolated, the North–South split in the socialist world also became more pronounced. The rhetoric of Eastern Bloc states had only increased in vitriol since the previous conferences. The Czechoslovakian delegate referred to their collective work as the 'war against air pirates', while the Polish delegation denounced the Israeli seizure of a Lebanese aircraft as state terrorism.[100] The Hungarian delegate said that he was convinced that 'compulsory extradition represents the best deterrent and most effective solution' and compared the problem of hijacking to maritime piracy, which was defeated by ensuring that 'the pirates enjoyed no rights of asylum in any country and all States imposed the severest penalties on them without regard to their nationality.'[101] Soviet initiatives

---

[95] Jordan Baev, 'Bulgarian State Security and International Terrorism', in *Terrorism in the Cold War: State Support in Eastern Europe and the Soviet Sphere of Influence*, edited by Adrian Hänni, Thomas Riegler, and Przemyslaw Gasztold (London: Bloomsbury, 2022), 144. Bulgarian officials also worked with Turkey during repeated hijacking landings by the Marxist liberation group Dev Cenc, who mistakenly hoped that fellow socialists would provide them refuge.

[96] The Cuba–United States Memorandum of Understanding on Hijacking of Aircraft and Vessels and Other Offenses. Latner, 'Take Me to Havana!' 40.

[97] Abraham Abramovsky, 'Multilateral Conventions for the Suppression of Unlawful Seizure and Interference with Aircraft Part III: The Legality and Political Feasibility of a Multilateral Air Security Enforcement Convention', *Columbia Journal of Transnational Law* 14, no. 3 (1975): 463

[98] After years of fighting to enable the GDR to attend ICAO conferences, the country was able to take part right when aviation law became deadlocked.

[99] McWhinney, *Aerial Piracy and International Law*, 52.

[100] ICAO Rome, 37, 50.

[101] Ibid., 57–58.

were better received by some in the West, but even then, support was qualified and limited. The Belgian delegation said that they were open to an amendment making political motivations inadmissible, but only in extreme cases.[102] The West German government, however, rejected the possibility of mandatory extradition as the right of asylum was in its constitution, the Basic Law.[103] The strongest support for the Eastern Bloc proposals came from IATA, a non-voting observer.[104]

By contrast, African socialists emphasized the need to tackle the root causes of terrorism and the importance of defending national liberation movements.[105] The delegation from Senegal, under the African socialist government of Léopold Senghor, emphasized his state's support for liberation movements and 'the national sovereignty of States, that inalienable and sacred right which is universally recognized'.[106] Socialist-leaning Burundi also mentioned its recognition of 'the just struggle of the liberation movements, which are in a position of legitimate defence'.[107] The delegate of the Marxist–Leninist People's Republic of Congo challenged the need for an additional convention on hijacking and also rebuked the conference for its hubris. He compared the delegates to a doctor who was treating an illness it did not understand and denounced 'state terrorism at present encouraged and practised in the world', referencing the Israeli seizure of Lebanese aircraft and the US bombing campaign in Vietnam.[108] The Congolese had essentially adopted the position of Jamil Baroody, exonerating individual airline hijackers by contrasting their actions with those of Western and imperial powers using aviation as a tool of war against colonial peoples.

The arguments of the Congolese found widespread approval among Global South states with a variety of ideological outlooks. The delegate from Kenya, at the time ruled by the pro-capitalist government of Jomo Kenyatta echoed these sentiments, albeit with less invective. Previously, many African states had viewed hijacking as a threat to civil aviation and in turn their own prospects for economic development, but now air law appeared as a backdoor means of criminalizing national liberation movements as terrorists.[109] The Algerian delegation demanded that the conference confront the root causes of terrorism and criticized the Montréal negotiations as a 'dialogue between the deaf'.[110] Non-socialist Upper Volta openly rejected Soviet plans for mandatory extradition as a threat to 'African liberation movements, which Upper Volta recognizes and actively supports'.[111]

---

[102] Ibid., 44.
[103] Ibid., 53.
[104] Ibid., 133.
[105] See statements from the Republic of Congo, Burundi, and Kenya at the ICAO legal committee meetings prior to the Rome Conference in Abraham Abramovsky, 'Multilateral Conventions for the Suppression of Unlawful Seizure and Interference with Aircraft Part III', 462–63
[106] ICAO Rome, 41.
[107] Ibid., 64.
[108] Ibid., 40.
[109] Ibid., 48–49.
[110] Ibid., 76.
[111] Ibid., 69.

The Pakistani delegation described hijacking as 'wrong and inadmissible' but 'nothing is more reprehensible than any attempt to use hijacking as an excuse for inflicting arbitrary and punitive measures on weaker countries'.[112] The Afro-Asian states were backed by a joint declaration of twelve Latin American delegations that they would not do anything to endanger the right to asylum 'to which their countries attached a great deal of importance'.[113] The instrumentalization of hijacking by states in the Global North was now viewed as a greater threat than hijacking itself for states in the Global South seeking to defend their sovereignty.

With Afro-Asian states pushing for more attention to the root causes of terror, Latin American states demanding the right to asylum, everyone outside the Eastern Bloc rejecting mandatory extradition, and many Western countries expressing scepticism that US plans were legal, the Rome conference was deadlocked. In a last minute plea from the Soviet representative that the 'people of the world [are] expecting positive results', they were rebuked by the People's Republic of the Congo that 'this evil was not to be eradicated by a proliferation of documents, a flood of amendments to certain conventions'.[114] When Poland tried to pass an amendment to lower the votes needed for a final agreement from two-thirds to half, they were rebuked by Tanzania. With no agreement possible, the conference ended in failure. The passage of Resolution 3103 by the UN General Assembly later that year, entitled 'Basic Principles of the Legal Status of Combatants Struggling Against Colonial and Alien Domination and Racist Regimes', moved to recognize national liberation movements as recognized fighters under international humanitarian law, paving the way towards enshrining this principle in law in the Geneva Convention Additional Protocols of 1977.[115] The problem of hijacking could no longer be isolated from the laws concerning national liberation and terrorism.

Despite the collapse of multilateral negotiations, there continued to be some efforts to realize East–West cooperation on hijackings. When West German counterterrorism police retook Lufthansa Flight 181 from a PFLP commando seeking the release of German Red Army Faction prisoners in a raid at the Mogadishu, Somalia, airport in 1977, this was supported by Eastern Bloc states. Soviet media denounced the hijacking as a 'provocative act of isolated elements of the anarchist-leftist band' (but also used it as an opportunity to criticize the United States for providing a home to the Lithuanian hijackers of Aeroflot Flight 244).[116] Polish news coverage of the event expressed sympathy for the West Germans in facing the problem of hijacking and admiration for the effectiveness of the counter-terrorism raid that

---

[112] Ibid., 60.
[113] Ibid., Colombia on behalf of Latin American states, 318.
[114] Ibid., 301
[115] Jochen von Bernstorff, 'The Battle for the Recognition of Wars of National Liberation', in *The Battle for International Law: South-North Perspectives on the Decolonization Era*, edited by Jochen von Bernstorff and Philipp Dann (Oxford: Oxford University Press, 2019), 52–70.
[116] Soviet press coverage summary from NARA Central Foreign Policy Files, Electronic Telegrams, 1977, D770392-0097.

ended the standoff in Mogadishu.[117] That year, the Soviets repeatedly pressed the United States and West Germany to sign bilateral agreements for the mutual return of escapees and defectors who committed acts of hijacking, but without success.[118]

Hijackings were on the decline from a highpoint in 1970, when there had been nearly a hundred incidents worldwide. However, when Ugandan dictator Idi Amin allowed an Air France flight hijacked by the PFLP and the far-left German group Revolutionary Cells to land in his country (leading to an Israeli special forces raid to rescue the hostages at Entebbe Airport), Western states became increasingly concerned that hijacked flights would be welcomed in friendly African and Middle Eastern states. At a Group of Seven (G7) Summit in 1978 in the West German capital of Bonn, the participants issued a declaration that each would conduct a flight boycott against any country that failed to prosecute or extradite hijackers, or failed to returned seized airplanes.[119] Such tactics had successfully pressured Algeria to shift its policies earlier in the decade and while the United States had not been able to enshrine this strategy in a multilateral agreement at the Rome conference, it could be undertaken voluntarily by the major Western states. This was enough to bring the United Kingdom and France on board (even though they had objected to this plan in multilateral negotiations), but no other states aside from the G7 signed on.[120] Ultimately, the Bonn Declaration was only put into effect twice: once against Afghanistan for harbouring Pakistani communist hijackers and then later as a threat against South Africa for refusing to prosecute mercenaries who had attempted a coup against a socialist government in the Seychelles.

From the late 1970s to the end of the Cold War, there was no more political will for further international law regarding hijacking. Although Eastern Bloc demands for the extradition of escapees were never met, Western states consistently prosecuted hijackers even if they were fleeing communism. The lenient treatment of East German hijackers Detlev Tiede and Ingrid Ruske who diverted a LOT Polish Airlines flight to Tempelhof Airport in West Berlin in 1978 (as mentioned in the introduction of this chapter) was the exception, not the rule. Even after the 1981 declaration of martial law in Poland, Western states continued to prosecute hijackers fleeing Poland and refused claims of asylum.[121] Terrorism related to aircraft

---

[117] Jakub Szumski, 'Międzynarodowy terroryzm w polskiej literaturze i prasie lat siedemdziesiątych XX wieku (wybrane przykłady)' *Polska 1944/45–1989: Studia i Materiały XIV/2016* (Warsaw: Institute of History of the Polish Academy of Sciences, 2016), 174–75.

[118] Blumenau, 'The Other Battleground of the Cold War', 70.

[119] James J. Busuttil, 'The Bonn Declaration on International Terrorism: A Non-Binding International Agreement on Aircraft Hijacking', *International and Comparative Law Quarterly* 31, no. 3 (1982): 474–87.

[120] See Bernhard Blumenau, 'The Group of 7 and International Terrorism: The Snowball Effect That Never Materialized', *Journal of Contemporary History* 51, no. 2 (2016): 316–34; Geoffrey Levitt, 'International Counterterrorism Cooperation: The Summit Seven and Air Terrorism', *Vanderbilt Law Review* 20, no. 2 (1987), 259-287.

[121] Jin-Tai Choi and Robert B. Munson, *Aviation Terrorism: Historical Survey, Perspectives and Responses* (Berlin: Springer, 1993), 104.

moved away from hostage-taking towards mass killing—as with the bombing of Air India Flight 182 in 1985 by Sikh militants over the Atlantic Ocean, the Lockerbie bombing of 1988, and the destruction of Avianca Flight 103 by the Medellin Cartel in 1989. After the attacks of 11 September 2001, the actual act of hijacking itself was less important than the use of the hijacked planes as weapons. As a result, ICAO set out to update the international hijacking conventions. In 2010, The Hague and Montréal Conventions were updated with the Beijing Convention, which now covered the transport of weapons of mass destruction by airplane and the use of airplanes as weapons. Although the PRC had been excluded from the Tokyo, The Hague, and Montréal conferences, its capital city was now home to the conference that brought air law into the twenty-first century.

Conclusion

The split on the importance of suppressing migration versus protecting national liberation movements meant that there was no consistent global socialist perspective on the problem of hijacking. The problem of illicit emigration (or in the case of Yugoslavia, separatist nationalism) was deemed enough of a threat to Eastern European socialist states that the defence of national sovereignty against overarching Western legal ambitions took a back seat to the punishment of hijackers and the goal of mandatory extradition. The international legal agreements on hijacking that made prosecution or extradition mandatory were made possible by the brief window of time where Western and Eastern Bloc concerns over migration came into alignment, but before states in the Global South had fully mobilized to defend national liberation movements in connection to hijacking.

Although the Eastern Bloc was instrumental in eliminating the colonial clause and allowing for universal membership in the treaties, the agreement between East and West on the intolerability of hijacking regardless of political motive helped to cement the crime as universal enough that even non-signatories to the air law conventions such as Algeria found themselves under tremendous pressure to conform to this new international norm. But the Soviets could not realize their maximalist agenda: hijackers were not widely accepted as self-evident enemies of humankind and not subject to mandatory extradition. The political initiatives of the Eastern Bloc were ultimately undermined by its fixation on illicit emigration, which put it into direct conflict with Western states for whom mandatory extradition was politically untenable and with African socialist states, which prioritized the support of national liberation movements. Most importantly, it led Eastern European states to abandon the spheres of international law where it found the greatest success in the collaboration with the Global South as a whole, namely anticolonialism and the defence of state sovereignty.

Acknowledgements

This research was supported by the Romanian National Authority for Scientific Research and Innovation, CNCS-UEFISCDI, project number PN-III-P4-ID-PCE-2020-1337. Thanks to Elise Schmidt for research assistance and to my colleagues in Department V at the ZZF for feedback on an earlier draft of this chapter.

12
Socialisms and International Law: Epilogue

Paul Betts

For decades socialist law and justice were routinely dismissed as being nothing but an ideological fig leaf obscuring brute communist power and were typically met in the West with dark rounds of laughter and forgetting. Karl Marx's idea that law was fundamentally class warfare by other means confirmed to many observers that even socialist legal theorists and lawyers did not take socialist law—whether international or domestic—all that seriously. Law, by contrast, was lionized as autonomous and disinterested under liberal regimes, whose conception of a distant relationship between law and politics (as well as state and citizen) was identified as one of the fundamental features distinguishing West from East, especially during the Cold War. That Eastern European states devoted such intense energy to dismantling their old Soviet-style legal systems after the fall of state socialism as the unwanted inheritance from Moscow further fuelled post-Cold War antipathy towards communist era law as a contradiction in terms unworthy of serious study.

Such a polemic view has changed dramatically in recent years, as historians and legal scholars have reconsidered the legacy of socialist law from fresh perspectives, with surprising results. This pioneering volume revisits the synergies between international law and socialism, and it reveals how socialist legal experts advanced profound critiques of the development of international legal norms, practices, and laws governing interstate conduct. The Soviet contribution to the Nuremberg Trials and the 1949 Geneva Conventions are two well-known examples from the early post-1945 period, but Soviet engagement with international law started a generation before, as several authors in this volume point out.[1] There were many other innovations that originated in various settings and contexts, and not just from the Soviet Union. International law and norm-making also linked socialist countries across the Second and Third Worlds and helped to forge political, normative, and moral partnerships with the developing world in the era of decolonization and 'alternative globalization'.[2]

---

[1] Francine Hirsch, *The Soviets at Nuremberg: A New History of the International Military Tribunal after World War II* (Oxford: Oxford University Press, 2020); Scott Newton, *Law and the Making of the Soviet World. The Red Demiurge* (London: Routledge, 2015).

[2] James Mark, Artemy M. Kalinovsky, and Steffi Marung (eds.), *Alternative Globalizations: Eastern Europe and the Postcolonial World* (Bloomington, IN: University of Indiana Press, 2020).

Michelle Penn reminds us of international socialism's changing attitudes towards international law long before Nuremberg. Much early Soviet legal theory wrestled with the issue of universalism, as leading legal theorists (Evgeny Pashukanis, Yevgeny Korovin, and Andrey Vyshinsky) grappled with the problem of whether Soviet law was, in essence, separate or universal. Initially they argued (as did Carl Schmitt from the other side of the political spectrum) that there was no such thing as one-size-fits-all international law and therefore rejected any family resemblance with the universalizing thrust of bourgeois law, usually in the name of national sovereignty. With time this changed, however, after which national self-determination was embraced as a go-to political concept to challenge Western imperial dominion and solicit support among those who suffered under the yoke of Western empires. With it the Soviet Union and its allies positioned themselves as the guardians of a limited and largely non-interventionist understanding of international law. Sebastian Gehrig develops this theme by showing how socialist internationalism not only took aim at the very foundations of liberal order but also sought to use law to consolidate the broader socialist project. Socialist law was based on linking domestic and international justice as an extension of state-driven political transformation. For this reason, Korovin (and even Pashukanis to a certain extent) rejected the idea that international law would wither away after the victorious socialist revolution, and endorsed a strategic use of international law within a 'socialist world system'. After the death of Stalin in 1953, Soviet and East German legal scholars, including Grigory Tunkin and Peter Alfons Steiniger, embraced a universal system of international law in the mid-1960s, yet one inflected with socialist meaning, such as the principle of peaceful coexistence. Law was thus identified not as a separatist socialist alternative but rather as a means to secure the socialist world's integration into the international system.

Sonja Dolinsek and Philippa Hetherington address the growth of international socialist law, but do so from a different angle. They explore how socialist governments in the 1940s proclaimed that commercial sex did not exist under socialism and were enthusiastic participants in the drafting of a new UN 1949 Convention for the Suppression of the Traffic in Persons and the Exploitation of the Prostitution of Others. Their contribution tracks state socialist involvement in the global moral reform drive behind the 1949 Convention. There were always socialist differences of emphasis, most famously with the Soviet call for the eradication of the draft Convention's 'colonial clause' that enabled imperial states to withdraw from international instruments on behalf of 'non-self-governing territories' if they so desired. Gender too was identified as an arena of rights and justice in which the East nominally outpaced the West in terms of issues of legal equality and anti-discrimination.[3]

---

[3] Celia Donert, 'From Communist Internationalism to Human Rights: Gender, Violence, and International Law in the Women's International Democratic Federation Mission to North Korea, 1951', *Contemporary European History* 25, no. 2 (2016): 313–33; Kristen Ghodsee, *Second World,*

This was an issue that linked the legal cultures of Eastern European socialist states (as evidenced the presence of equal gender rights in all Eastern European constitutions), but unlike race it was less a point of convergence with socialist regimes in the Global South. Gender equality was very low down on the rights agenda for these new Asian and African countries, and the chequered response to calls for gender equality underscored the limitations of cooperative rights work between Eastern Europe and the developing world in the early postwar period.

That said, this was a strange form of socialist international law. As Bradley Simpson writes, at least for much of the twentieth century it was built on the defence of the nation-state, not international socialism. As early as 1903, Lenin argued that the territorial nation-state was the true foundation of the international order, insomuch as 'self-determination of the nations' signalled 'political self-determination and state independence, and the formation of a national state', as Simpson discusses. Nevertheless, socialist self-determination was used as a justification for the annexation of the Baltic states and military occupation of Eastern Europe and Central Asia, as evidenced by the Soviet invasions of Hungary (1956), Prague (1968), and Afghanistan (1979). Such actions were legitimized by the controversial principle that the USSR and constitutive republics had already exercised their right to self-determination by choosing to federate with the Soviet Union. By the late 1960s, the newly minted Brezhnev Doctrine held that the older Soviet principle of peaceful coexistence had been replaced by a coercive idea of 'socialist internationalism', in which socialist states had the duty to assist other socialist states to preserve their independence and sovereignty. Imperial threats overrode the principle of state sovereignty, as the Monroe Doctrine was extended across the globe. This Brezhnev Era defence of socialist federalism served as the late Soviet vernacular of international law until Gorbachev's assumption of power. The consequence was that the tension between empire and self-determination—which characterized liberal internationalism since the end of the Great War and spurred ideas of Soviet exceptionalism—was effectively reproduced in the socialist world over the course of the last century and beyond.

In this respect, the volume makes key contributions to three areas. First, it is clear that the socialist world did not speak with one voice. At first this may seem obvious enough, but the volume's attention to the plurality of perspectives underlines the great variety of socialist legal culture. By 1949, Moscow's monopoly on international communism had been broken by Belgrade and Beijing, which found expression in international socialist law. In the 1950s and beyond, numerous socialist countries—including those in Eastern Europe—worked to combine Soviet internationalism and national legal culture, as noted in Jakub Szumski's discussion of how Poland's Poznań School rehabilitated interwar Polish legal traditions to blend

Second Sex: Socialist Women's Activism and Global Solidarity during the Cold War (Durham, NC: Duke University Press, 2019).

national and international justice with a distinctly Polish accent. In other contexts, international law was a source of more open antagonism between socialist countries such as the Soviet Union, China, and Yugoslavia, especially in the domains of trade, sovereignty, and borders disputes.[4] This meant that international law was not just an object of dispute between East and West but also between East and East. It was in the 1960s when the People's Republic of China (PRC) rejected the Soviet line and began to forge its own path in international socialist justice. This gave rise to a broader international geography of international socialist law, one in which the Poznań School suggested a kind of socialist multilateralism in legal affairs. Just as there were national roads to socialism, there were national roads to socialist international law.

The same went for the development of Chinese international law and norm-making, as noted in Ryan Martínez Mitchell's contribution. The old idea that China's path to superpower status was understood as international communism with Chinese characters was common to all of the communist regimes over the decades.[5] Cold War socialist internationalism featured a wide spectrum of forms and laws ranging from the Soviet Union to China, and even within Eastern Europe. The contributors show how Eastern European countries carved out surprising autonomy in legal matters, as long as it did not cross swords with overarching Soviet ideas about the relationship between socialism and law, power and authority. In the early twenty-first century Chinese attitudes towards international law reflected a nominally Marxist–Leninist superpower's quest to reconcile anticolonial legacies, geopolitical interests, and liberal ideas of global governance. In areas ranging from dispute resolution to the laws of war, trade, and the sea, Beijing's path towards institutionalized multilateralism has reconfigured its traditional agenda of anticolonialism and preserving state autonomy. It has built on China's increasing commitment to international law since the early twentieth century through the Korean War (1950–53), Bandung (1955), and the joining of the World Trade Organization (2001), often borrowing Western models of globalization to shore up national authority and statist sovereignty.

But this is not to say that socialist international law remained static. It underwent tremendous change from the 1930s through the 1980s, generally in response to seismic international events, such as the Second World War, the expansion and fracturing of the communist world, decolonization and the changing geopolitical fortunes of the socialist superpowers. The meaning of socialist international law changed dramatically from the universalism of the 1948 Universal Declaration of Human Rights (UDHR) to the Brezhnev Doctrine after the Soviet invasion of

---

[4] Arno Trültzsch, *Sozialismus und Blockfreiheit: Der Beitrag Jugoslawiens zum Völkerrecht 1948–1980/91* (Göttingen: Wallstein, 2021).

[5] Jennifer Altehenger, *Legal Lessons: Popularising Laws in the People's Republic of China 1949–1989* (Cambridge, MA: Harvard University Asia Center, 2018).

Prague in 1968. It was partly liberalized with the 1975 Helsinki Accords, but, as Ned Richardson-Little argues in his contribution, it hardened again in the 1970s and 1980s around the thorny issue of illegal border-crossing, in particular in connection with hijacking, emigration, and extradition, which in effect undermined Eastern Europe's good relations with its socialist partners in the Global South. These developments drove home the extent to which international law and norm-making were movable feasts and changed directions according to the shifting geopolitical interests of the socialist powers at the time. In this sense, socialist international law was no different from other forms of international law, insomuch as they were both indelibly recast by shifting political imperatives.

This diversity of forms reflected one of the underlying tensions of socialist international law at the time, namely the issue of universalism. As noted by several contributors, communist legal authorities long suspected that such universalism was a bourgeois political tool to advance the liberal West's geopolitical class-based interests. John Stuart Mill's dismissal of human rights as 'nonsense on stilts' was part of a broader late nineteenth-century anti-liberal antipathy towards woolly internationalism, one that ran from Marx to the Austro–Marxists of the 1920s. That said, the socialist world increasingly championed universalism when it served its interests, especially if it helped to build bridges to the developing world, particularly around the rallying causes of peace and anticolonialism. Anti-imperial communist internationalism first took wing in reaction to Fascist Italy's military conquest of Abyssinia in the 1930s and Hitler's assault on Eastern Europe, then in support of national liberation struggles in Africa and Asia in the 1950s and 1960s. Soviet involvement in the drafting of the UDHR in 1948 was a milestone in the socialist enlistment of universalism for the sake of anti-Western emancipation, and was extended in the UN International Covenant on Civil and Political Rights of 1966.[6]

Once decolonization had been achieved, the banner cause of socialist international law to build links between communist Eastern Europe and the Global South shifted from anti-imperialism to race and anti-apartheid. As Raluca Grosescu explains, socialist activists had worked to bundle together racial discrimination, self-determination, and anti-imperialism since the 1930s, but in the late 1960s and 1970s they directed increasing attention towards the criminalization of apartheid, culminating with the 1973 UN Convention on the Suppression and Punishment of the Crime of Apartheid. This campaign was jointly spearheaded by UN representatives from Eastern Europe and Africa, supported by the leftist-oriented International Association of Democratic Lawyers. A variety of new East–South coalitions sprung up around the international fight for racial justice,

---

[6] Jennifer Amos, 'Embracing and Contesting: The Soviet Union and the Universal Declaration of Human Rights, 1948–1958', in *Human Rights in the Twentieth Century*, edited by Stefan-Ludwig Hoffmann (Cambridge: Cambridge University Press, 2011): 147–65; Alexander Dallin, *The Soviet Union at the United Nations* (London: Methuen, 1962); Chris Osakwe, *The Participation of the Soviet Union in Universal International Organizations* (Leiden: AW Sijthoff, 1972).

not least because the celebrated 1955 Bandung Conference in Indonesia, in which twenty-nine African and Asian states gathered to discuss colonialism, did not address apartheid. Calling attention to racial injustice became a way for socialist activists to use anti-discriminatory international law to shame the West and to deflect scrutiny away from draconian practices at home among many of these authoritarian socialist regimes.[7]

Another salient theme of this volume is the significance of international organizations in brokering the norm-making of socialist internationalism. For decades, international organizations—ranging from the UN to Amnesty International—have been treated as the loose change of the post-1945 international order, with varying degrees of authority and influence depending on the leadership and moral cause du jour. The UN, for example, certainly played a central role in the Congo Crisis, Biafra War, and first Iraq War, but it did comparatively little in Afghanistan, Poland, or the break-up of Yugoslavia. Recently, scholars have persuasively argued that international organizations were not just by-products of the international settlements after both world wars but in time became especially vital in a world of Cold War bipolarity, to the extent that they served as unique bridges of communication, networking, and norm-making at the international level.[8] This could be seen in the UN General Assemblies, which provided the socialist and developing world with an unprecedented platform to have their voices heard and to form coalitions of moral politics with like-minded allies against the West.

The socialist world's efforts to position itself as the defender of international law and norm-making was particularly successful around the issue of peace. This was certainly the case with Soviet participation in the drafting of the Geneva Conventions in 1949, in which Soviet lawyers pushed successfully for a broader definition of crimes against peace.[9] Such politicking took on concrete form in the USSR's campaign against atomic warfare and weapons of mass destruction, issues that were of pivotal importance to the developing world and helped consolidate support for socialist critiques of Western war-making and arms build-up. Socialist conceptions of peace also pivoted on non-intervention and the inviolability of the territorial nation-state. Peace politics in the socialist world—especially in Eastern Europe—was not restricted to foreign policy, however, but assumed domestic expression in the constitutions and educational policies of people's republics across the region.

Socialist ideas of international peace were not confined to the technology of war or domestic education. In her contribution, Nelly Bekus recalls how one of the

---

[7] Sebastian Gehrig, Paul Betts, James Mark, Kim Christiaens, and Idesbald Goddeeris, 'The Eastern Bloc, Human Rights, and the Global Fight against Apartheid', *East Central Europe* 46, no. 2–3 (2019): 290–317.

[8] Sandrine Kott, *Gouverner le monde: Une autre histoire de la guerre froide* (Paris: Seuil, 2021).

[9] Boyd van Dijk, *Preparing for War: The Making of the Geneva Conventions* (Oxford: Oxford University Press, 2022).

distinctive domains of socialist peace politics was cultural protection and heritage management. The departure point was to preserve and protect the cultural patrimony of Eastern Europe that was all but destroyed by Nazi military expansion and occupation, especially in the capitals of Eastern Europe. Socialist representatives at UNESCO (established in 1946) were decisive in rebuilding badly damaged cultural artefacts in those cities, and elsewhere across the world. As such socialist countries not only promoted themselves as the guardians of tradition they did so in the belief that conserving the past was a step towards international peace, based on the recognition, respect, and equality of all cultures in the face of what was called 'cultural genocide' at the time. Their preservation campaign led to the enshrinement of the 1954 Hague Convention to safeguard cultural property during war. The cultural convention became a pendant to the Geneva Conventions passed five years before, and socialist countries were at the forefront of getting these conventions on the books. The initiative represented another form of socialist universalism at the time and spurred the desire to codify international conventions to oversee international activity, in this case the management of damaged cultural pasts.

Less well known is that the Cold War development of socialist international law was inseparable from the growth of what was called 'socialist legality' across the socialist world in the 1960s, most noticeably in the Soviet Union, Eastern Europe, Yugoslavia, and China. The impetus was Khrushchev's effort to put Soviet everyday life on a more consistent legal footing, in stark contrast to Stalin's legacy of terrorism and arbitrary rule. Whilst similar pleas were mooted in the 1950s, most famously by Hungary's reformist leader, Imre Nagy, they grew and spread in the 1960s as a visible yardstick of de-Stalinization. The 1960s was the Golden Age of socialist domestic courts, laws, and regulations designed to rationalize the development of a more stable and law-abiding socialist society. Domestically, international law found expression as social justice, as socialist countries sought to make good on their hallmark values—egalitarianism, equality before the law, and even human rights.[10] So advanced was this model that it eventually became the target of criticism by socialist citizens—the Prague Spring of 1968 was largely an effort to restore 'socialism with a human face' so as to counter the heavy bureaucratization of everyday life, as well as the widening gap between the government and the governed. There were always tensions in its application, as justice—and law—remained heavily party-centric until the very end, and closely associated with the regimes' social engineering project. This was a far cry from Stalin's law

---

[10] Sebastian Gehrig, *Legal Entanglements: Law, Rights and the Battle for Legitimacy in Divided Germany* (New York: Berghahn, 2021); Robert Brier, *Poland's Solidarity Movement and the Global Politics of Human Rights* (Cambridge: Cambridge University Press, 2021); Ned Richardson-Little, *The Human Rights Dictatorship: Socialism, Global Solidarity and Revolution in East Germany* (Cambridge: Cambridge University Press, 2020); Dina Moyal, 'Did Law Matter? Law, State and Individual in the USSR, 1953–1982', PhD dissertation, Stanford University (2010).

and justice from the 1930s, and a model that continued to evolve under 'real existing socialism' from the 1960s through the 1980s.

Striking too is that socialism flagged its domestic welfare state provisioning as a feature of its progressive modernity and campaigned for international conventions of health and hygiene as new global norms. As Bogdan Iacob writes, European socialist health professionals worked with their counterparts in various international organizations, such as the World Health Organization and UNICEF, to develop basic standards of healthcare in the Global South as human rights, combining anticolonialism and anti-racism. In their work, hunger was blamed on colonial rule, as public health was identified as an international measure of good governance. These claims may not have added up to enforceable laws but they—like the preservation conventions—were significant in advancing international awareness and improvement, and they became one of the most prized aspects of the practicalities of international socialism during the Cold War.

At the moment, it is timely to revisit the social aspects of international socialist law, not least because so much of it has disappeared. It evolved as a set of norms and conventions that accompanied ideologies of peace, welfare, and anti-imperialism; and for much of the Cold War it offered a serious alternative to Western law, development, and international relations. And in a moment when liberalism and liberal law find themselves endlessly in crisis,[11] in which the 1990s sense of liberal universalism has lost its lustre internationally in a new era of expanding international wars, the once powerful socialist legacy may be a distant past but aspects of its heritage offer some relevance for a possible future, ranging from peace to universal healthcare.

---

[11] Ivan Krastev and Stephen Holmes, *The Light that Failed: A Reckoning* (London: Penguin, 2020).

Index

For the benefit of digital users, indexed terms that span two pages (e.g., 52–53) may, on occasion, appear on only one of those pages.

Abdel Nasser, Gamal 31, 146, 207–8
Afghanistan
  and health 151–52
  and hijacking 254
  and international organizations 262
  Soviet invasion of 42, 54–55, 62, 66–67
  US invasion of 130–31
African Regional Committee (WHO) 144–45, 154
African socialism 1, 12–13, 31–32, 50, 205–12, 223, 237, 244–49, 252, 255
African Union *see* Organisation of African Unity
aggression, crime of
  and banditry 80, 87
  and China 130–31
  and cultural destruction 80, 170
  and health 143
  and the Korean War 86, 87–88, 121–22
  and mistreatment of POWs 80
  and national liberation movements 89–90
  and the Non-Aligned Movement 83–84
  and propaganda 70, 72, 73–74, 87
  and socialist definition of 72–73
  and socialist international law 38–39, 69–90
  and Trainin 23–24, 69–90
air law 231–55 *see also* Beijing Convention; Bonn Declaration; Chicago Convention; Montreal Convention; The Hague Convention; Tokyo Convention
Algeria 13, 27, 224–25, 226–27, 239–42, 245–46, 248–50, 252–53, 254, 255
Allende, Salvador 4–5, 246
Alma-Ata Declaration (1978) 137, 159–60
Amin, Hafizullah 66
Amin, Idi 222, 254
Angola 58, 219, 222, 223, 225–26
anticolonialism
  and apartheid 207–8
  and China 32–33, 124
  and cultural genocide 173–74
  and cultural heritage 165, 177–78
  and health 138, 140–45, 147, 148–49, 152–56
  and hijacking 239–49, 254–55
  and the IADL 224–27

  and international law 7–8, 27, 31–32, 59
  and Resolution 1514 55–56
  and self-determination 46–68
antifascism 22–23, 146, 165
antisemitism 26, 84–85, 98–99, 105–6, 169, 170–71, 209
apartheid *see also* UN Apartheid Convention; individual countries
  and air law 244–45
  and crime of genocide 87–88
  and health 154–56, 161
  and international law 205–29
  and Rome Statute (ICC) 228
Argentina *see* Latin America
asylum law 231, 232–33, 234–35, 238–39, 241–43, 245–49, 251–55
Atlantic Charter (1941) 50–52
Australia
  and apartheid 210–11, 215, 216–18, 222–23, 238
  and culture 166–67, 176, 181, 182
  and health 150
  and prostitution 187–88
Austria 26–27, 97–98, 171, 216, 222–23, 241–42
  see also Habsburg Empire
Austro-Marxism 261
Awami League (Bangladesh) 60–61
Azmi Bey, Mahmud 149

Baltic states
  and emigration 241–42
  and independence movements 48–49, 57, 65–66, 67–68
  occupation of 23, 50–52, 54–55, 79
Bandung Conference (1955) 33, 55, 122–23
Bangladesh (East Pakistan) 60–61
Baroody, Jamil 53, 54–55, 246, 252
Bebel, August 193–95
Bedjaoui, Mohamed 27
Beijing Convention (2010) 254–55
Belarus 168–69, 179–81
Belgium (Belgian Empire) 34, 152–53, 168, 178–79, 225–26, 242–43
Benin 154, 221

Bentoumi, Amar 226–27
Bermann, Gregorio 142
Biafra (Nigeria) 59–60, 262
Bokhari, Ahmed Shah 200–1
Bolshevik Revolution (1917) *see* Russian Revolution
Bonn Declaration (1978) 254
Borisov, Aleksandr 193–95, 198–99
Bose, Vivian 226
Brazil *see* Latin America
Brazinskas, Pranas & Algirdas 241–42, 253–54
Brezhnev Doctrine
  and Afghanistan 66–67
  and China 126
  and Prague Spring 37–38, 39, 63–65
  and socialist internationalism 259
British Empire 13, 27, 144, 152–53, 199–201, 238 *see also* United Kingdom
Buhler, Josef 170–71
Bulgaria
  and apartheid 221
  and cultural heritage 164
  and health 144, 156–57, 158–59
  and hijacking 248–51
  and legal education 30–31, 111–12
  and narcotics 8
  and terrorism 249–50
Burkina Faso (Upper Volta) 238, 252–53
Burma 122–23, 201
Burundi 252
Butler, William E. 39–41

Cambodia 75–76, 243
Cambournac, Francisco 144–45
Cameroon 215, 221
Canada 142, 145–46, 154–55, 176, 180–81, 241–42
Canary Islands 223–24
Čančik, Joseph 140–41
Candau, Marcolino Gomes 148
Casanueva, Diaz 151–52
Cassin, René 146–47
Catholicism 97–99, 100–1, 112–13
Central Treaty Organization (CENTO) 88–89
Čepelka, Čestmír 110–11
Chagos Islands 134
  Charta 77 (Czechoslovakia) 160
Charvin, Robert 226–27
Chechnya 45
Chen Tiqiang 121
Chiang Kai-shek 117–18, 120
Chicago Convention on International Civil Aviation (1944) 235–36
Chile *see* Latin America

China
  and 1989 36
  and air law 237
  and Biafra 60
  and cultural genocide 173, 174
  and the Cultural Revolution 36, 124, 125–26
  and de-Stalinization 125
  and health 142, 150
  and hijacking 254–55
  and India 122–24
  and international law 2, 4, 12–13, 32–34, 115–35, 260
  and legal education 36, 117, 120
  and legal formalism 130–34
  and legal innovation 129, 131, 135
  and multilateralism 130–31, 254–55, 260
  and national liberation movements 33–34, 126–27
  and North Korea 121–22, 260
  and Palestine 134–35
  and peaceful coexistence 122–23
  and Prague Spring 126
  and self-determination 60, 120, 134–35
  and the UN Security Council 118–19, 126, 129, 132
Chinese Society of International Law 11
Chisholm, Brock 142, 148, 149–50
Cleaver, Eldridge 240
climate change 130, 131, 133–34, 135
Cocos Islands 238
colonial clause *see also* individual countries, individual treaties
  and apartheid 208
  and culture 164–65, 177–79
  and health 147
  and hijacking 234–39, 248–49, 255
  and international law 7
  and narcotics 198–99
  and prostitution 186–87, 197–204, 258–59
  and Trainin 76–77
colonialism *see* imperialism
Congo (Zaire) 8, 31, 34, 59–60, 216, 262
Congo, People's Republic (Brazzaville) 13, 15, 237–38, 244–45, 246–47, 248–49, 252–53
Convention to Suppress the Slave Trade and Slavery (1926) 237–38
Corley-Smith, Gerard 199–200
Council for Mutual Economic Assistance (COMECON) 28–29, 95–96
Croatia 245–46
Cuba *see also* Latin America
  and cultural heritage 182
  and health 152–53, 156–57

and hijacking 234–35, 239–41, 245, 246–47, 250–51
and the invasion of Afghanistan 66–67
and missile crisis 34, 37–38
and national liberation movements 58
and Ogaden War 61
cultural heritage *see also* genocide, crime of
and Cold War divide 178–82, 183–84
and crime of aggression 80
and France 180–81
and internationalism 163–65
and Jewish victimhood 170–71, 173, 177–78, 183
Czechoslovakia
and air law 235–36, 251–52
and antisemitism 26
and apartheid 214, 221
and cultural genocide 173, 174
and cultural heritage 166–72, 176–84
and dissidents 160
and Germanization 166, 168, 172
and health 140–41, 147, 156–57, 158–59, 160
and hijacking 241–42, 244–45
and legal education 110–11
and Prague Spring 12–13, 37–38, 39, 62, 63–65
and prostitution 186, 191–95, 201
and racism 154–55
and self-determination 62–63
and the UNWCC 78–79

Darul Islam (Indonesia) 59
David, Vladislav 110–11
Deng Xiaoping 35–36, 128
Denmark *see* Scandinavian states
diplomats, protection of 247–48, 249–50
discrimination *see* racism
disease
epidemic 140, 143–44, 152, 155
and human rights 137, 144–45
social conditions of 139–41, 142–43, 147–48, 150–52, 156–58
venereal 190–91, 193–95, 197
dissident movement, Eastern Europe
and Baltic states 57
and health 160
and post-1989 100–1
and self-determination 64–65, 67–68
Draper, Gerald 222–23
Du Bois, W.E.B. 87–88, 173–74
Dubček, Alexander 63–64
Dutch Empire 59, 238 *see also* Netherlands

East Germany *see* German Democratic Republic
Ečer, Bohuslav 78–79, 167

Ecuador *see* Latin America
Egypt *see also* United Arab Republic
and apartheid 216, 217–18, 225–26
and the colonial clause 201
and crime of aggression 83–84
and cultural genocide 174
and decolonialisation 27, 31, 207–8
and health 139, 144–45, 149, 150–51, 154
and prostitution 203
and right of return 217–18
and self-determination 55
Ehrlich, Ludwik 30–31
Ehrlich, Stanisław 107
Eritrea 12–13, 61
Estonia *see* Baltic states
Ethiopia 12–13, 61, 71–72, 174, 210–11, 243–44
Eurocentrism 1–15, 111, 112–13, 115, 163, 206–7, 211, 213, 215, 216–17
Evang, Karl 142, 148, 155–56
extradition
and air law 232–33, 240, 241–42, 244–45, 246–49, 250–55, 260–61
and Nazi criminals 171
and the Soviet Union 197–98
and White Russians 74–75

Ferguson, Clarence Clyde 216–17, 219–20
Finland *see* Scandinavian states
Fischer, Ludwig 170–71
Ford, James W. 50
France (French Empire) *see also* Algeria
and anticolonialism 27, 144, 152–53, 157–58, 210–11, 226–27
and apartheid 214, 216–17, 225–26
and the colonial clause 25–26, 178–79, 180–81, 186–87, 199–200, 201–2
and crime of aggression 72–74
and cultural destruction 168
and cultural genocide 173–74
and health 144, 150, 156–57
and hijacking 238, 254
and prostitution 187–88, 196
and self-determination 54–55
and statutory limitations 212–13
Frank, Hans 169–70, 171–72
Friendly Relations Declaration (1970) 7–8, 56–57, 58–59, 65–66, 113

Gabon 153
Gadkowski, Tadeusz 100–1
Ganji, Manouchehr 159
Garvey, Marcus 49–50
gender 258–59

Geneva Conventions (1949)
  Additional Protocols (1977) 89, 126–27, 128, 132, 205–7, 221–24, 228–29, 253
  and cultural heritage 182
  and the Korean War 121–22
  and the Soviet Union 257, 262
genocide, crime of *see also* UN Genocide Convention
  and apartheid 87–88
  and crimes against peace 70–71
  and culture 172–76
  and Jim Crow race laws 87–88
German Democratic Republic
  and air law 237, 243, 248–49
  and apartheid 221
  and emigration from 239, 241–42
  and health 158–59
  and international law 12, 28, 113–14
  and legal education 13–14, 107–10
  and legal theory 93–94
  and self-determination 53, 62–63, 68, 242–43
  and the Socialist Declaration of Human Rights 68
  and war crimes trials 26
German Empire 118, 146
Germany, Federal Republic of
  and air law 231, 237, 243
  and apartheid 216–17
  and extradition 251–52
  and hijacking 241–42
  and the IADL 226–27
  and international law 12
  and the Red Army Faction 253–54
  and the Revolutionary Cells 254
  and self-determination 53
  and statutory limitations 212–13
Germany, Nazi
  and crimes against peace 70, 71–72
  and cultural destruction 164–65, 168, 170, 171, 172, 180–81, 262–63
  and Germanization 166, 168, 172
  and the Nuremberg Trials 26, 77–82
  and occupation 13–14, 164–65, 166–72
  and the Soviet Union 23
Ghana 31, 55, 152–53, 207–8, 219, 240–41
Glaser, Edwin 111
Goering, Hermann 169–70
Gorbachev, Mikhail 42, 259
Graefrath, Bernhard 109–10
Greiser, Artur 170–71
Guadalajara Convention on Cargo Flights (1961) 237–38
Guevara, Che 240
Guinea 12–13, 31, 207–8, 215, 216, 221

Haas, Ernst B. 28–29
Habsburg Empire 48–49, 62–63, 111–12
  see also Austria
Hager, Kurt 68
The Hague Hijacking Convention (1970) 242–49
Haiti 217
Haldane Society of Socialist Lawyers (United Kingdom) 226–27
Harvey, Richard 226–27
Haywood, Harry 50
Hazard, John 17, 20, 23, 41
health *see also* disease; medicine; public health; welfare state; individual countries
  and comparisons to Nazism 143, 154–55
  as a human right 14, 137–62
  and international law 13
Helsinki Accords 41, 65–66, 67–68, 260–61
Ho Chi Minh 75–76
Hobza, Antonín 110–11
Höjer, Axel 149–50
Holocaust 82–83, 170–71, 173, 177–78
hostage-taking, crime of 231, 232–33, 239–41, 247–48, 249–50, 254–55
Houdek, Vladimir 193–95
crimes against humanity
  and apartheid 209, 212–29
  and banditry 80
  and crime of aggression 86
  and crimes against civilians 81
  and crimes against peace 70–71
  and the Nuremberg Trials 77–82
human rights *see* health; International Year for Human Rights; self-determination; Socialist Declaration of Human Rights; socialist law; UN Human Rights Covenants; Universal Declaration of Human Rights
Humphrey, John 145–46
Hungarian Revolution (1956) 30, 62, 63, 111–12, 113
Hungarian-Polish Convention (1948) 28–29
Hungary
  and apartheid 221
  and cultural heritage 164, 180–81
  and health 141–42, 156–57, 158–59
  and hijacking 246–47, 248–49, 251–52
  and legal education 111–12
Hyde, Henry van Zile 149–50

immigration law 191, 231–32 *see also* asylum law
imperialism *see also* colonial clause
  and capitalism 87–89, 186
  and China 117–19
  and comparisons to Nazi Germany 177–78

INDEX   269

and crime of aggression 83–84
and epidemics 143–44
and health 140–41, 144–46
and hijacking 240–41, 255
and international law 19–20, 21–22, 25–26
and multi-ethnic states 62–63
and non-intervention 111
and prisoners of war 223–24
and self-determination 46–52
and the Soviet Union 23
impunity 181, 215
India
  and air law 237–38
  and Bangladesh 60–61
  and China 122–23
  and health 141–43, 144–47, 148–50
  and independence 75–76
  and the Non-Aligned Movement 33
  and peaceful coexistence 122–23
Indigenous activism *see also* minorities, rights of
  and cultural genocide 176
Indonesia 59
International Air Transport Association (IATA) 244–45, 248–49, 251–52
International Association of Democratic Lawyers (IADL)
  and apartheid 14, 205–6, 224–28
  and health 146–47
  and socialist international law 11
  and the Soviet Union 224–25
International Civil Aviation Organization (ICAO) 235–55
International Commission of Jurists (CIJ) 224–27
International Court of Justice (ICJ)
  and anticolonialism 210–11
  and China 119, 128, 131, 134
  and Poland 98–99
  and prostitution 197–98
  and *South-West Africa* case 210
  and sovereignty 220
  and the Soviet Union 29
International Covenant on Civil and Political Rights *see* UN Human Rights Covenants
International Covenant on Economic, Social & Cultural Rights *see* UN Human Rights Covenants
International Criminal Court (ICC)
  and apartheid 228
  and China 129–30, 131, 132, 135
  and crime of aggression 89–90
International Criminal Tribunal for Rwanda (ICTR) 128–29

International Criminal Tribunals for Yugoslavia (ICTY) 128–29
International Federation of Air Lines Pilots' Associations (IFALPA) 240–41, 242–43, 244–45, 248–49
International Labour Organization 150–51
international law *see also* aggression, crime of; extradition; genocide; hostage-taking, crime of; humanity, crimes against; looting; peace, crimes against; propaganda, crime of; terrorism; trafficking; universal jurisdiction; war crimes
  and bourgeois law 20–22, 258
  and China 32–34, 35–36, 115–35, 254–55
  and Christianity 112–13
  and cultural heritage 163–84
  and customary law 69, 76–77, 110–11, 213–14
  and decolonization 38, 134, 138, 197, 257
  and the Eastern Bloc 53, 62–63, 91–114, 163–72, 176–84
  and economic relations 30, 55, 59, 65–66, 68, 123, 205, 216–21, 226–27
  and enforcement mechanisms 9–10, 129, 186–87, 251
  and environmental law 133–34
  and extraterritoriality 118, 228–29, 247–48
  and fragmentation 10–15, 91–114, 134
  and global socialism 6–8
  and health 137–62
  and hijacking 231–55
  and imperialism 19–20, 40–41, 116
  and legal universalism 10–15, 33–34, 110–11, 113–14, 177–82
  and the nation-state 38–39
  and national pluralism 10–15, 91–114
  as propaganda 22–23
  and prostitution 185–204
  and the Soviet Union 17–43, 69–90
  and structural adjustment 160–61
International Military Tribunal (IMT) *see* Nuremberg Trials
International Military Tribunal (IMT) for the Far East *see* Tokyo War Crimes Trials
international police cooperation 191–92, 193–96, 197–98
International Tribunal on the Law of the Sea (ITLOS) 133–34
International Year for Human Rights (1968) 156, 158–59
internationalism
  anti-racist 212
  cultural 163–64
  health 152
  liberal 211–12, 258, 259

internationalism, socialist
   and apartheid 205, 208
   and international organizations 262
   and Korovin 28–29
   and the liberal order 258
   and national liberation 33, 261
   and national particularism 91–114, 260
   and non-intervention 9–10
   and peaceful coexistence 63
   and prostitution 185–204
   and self-determination 64–65, 66–67, 68
   and Tunkin 37–38, 39, 40–41
Iran 8, 55, 83–84, 159, 177–78, 180–81
Iraq 130–31, 151–53, 180–81, 201, 221, 262
Ireland 180–81, 182, 223–24
Israel
   and crime of apartheid 217–18, 226–27, 228
   and crimes against humanity 213
   and Eastern Bloc Jews 84, 105–6, 241–42
   and emigration to 241–42
   and hijacking 239–42, 243–44, 249, 254
   and military necessity 181, 182
   and nuclear weapons 180–81
   and terrorism 249–50, 251–52
Issawi, Salim 240–41
Italy 250–51, 261

Jablensky, Assen 157
Jackson, Robert 77–78
James, C.L.R. 50
Japan 117, 249
Jessup, Philip 94, 210–12
Jodl, Alfred 169–70
Jordan 240–41

Kacic, Ivo 234–35
Kacprzak, Marcin 140–41
Kader, Asmal 226–27
Katanga (Congo) 59–60
Katz-Suchy, Juliusz 102–3, 105–6
Kaur, Rajkumari Amrit 143
Kazakhstan 159
Keïta, Modibo 237
Keitel, Wilhelm 169–70
Kellogg-Briand Pact (1928) 71–73
Kelly, Walter 50
Kelsen, Hans 121–22
Kemenov, Vladimir Semyonovich 177–78, 179
Kenya 213–14, 219, 247–48, 252–53
Kenyatta, Jomo 252–53
Khaled, Leila 240–41
Khrushchev, Nikita 35, 55, 59–60, 62, 63–64
Kissinger, Henry 240

Klafkowski, Alfons 91, 99–101, 104, 105–6, 112–13
Klenner, Hermann 109–10
Kollontai, Aleksandra 193–95
Korean War 34, 121–23, 166
Korea, Democratic People's Republic of (North) 25–26, 228
Korea, Republic of (South) 25–26
Koretsky, Vladimir 210–11
Korovin, Yevgeny (Evgeny) 20–22, 27, 28–29, 30, 36–37, 48–49, 108–9, 258
Kosovo 130–31
Kozhevnikov, Fyodor 24–25, 29
Krylov, S.B. 24–25
Kurchenko, Nadezhda 241–42

Latin America *see also* Cuba
   and anti-racism 153–54
   and apartheid 155–56, 215, 216, 218, 221
   and cultural genocide 173, 174
   and health 14, 139, 140–44, 145–46, 148, 149–52, 154–55, 157–58, 162
   and hijacking 246, 252–53
   and impunity 228–29
   and military necessity 182
   and *Nicaragua v USA* 128
   and the NIEO 4–5
   and the Non-Aligned Movement 125
   and propaganda 73–74
   and socialist law 15
   and the welfare state 13, 137–38
Latvia *see* Baltic states
Lauterpacht, Hersch 73, 94
Lazareanu, Alexandru 179–80, 181
League against Imperialism 46, 49–50
League of Nations *see also* UN Trust Territories
   and aggression 23–24
   and mandates 49–50, 210, 211
   and prostitution 187–88, 191–92
   and socialist international law 71–72
League of Nations Health Organization (LNHO) 140–42
Lebanon 150, 173
legal education *see* individual countries
legal expertise
   and African lawyers 225–27
   and apartheid 224–27
   and China 33–34, 119, 120, 124, 126, 128–29
   and health 145–46
   and the Eastern Bloc 39, 98–101, 107–13
   and legal innovation 39–40, 102, 131
   and the Soviet Union 29, 42–43
legal formalism
   and China 129–34
   and the Soviet Union 93–94

legal universalism
  and cultural heritage 176–82
  and the liberal tradition 18, 211–12
  and Polish international law 94–95, 112–13
  and socialist law 258, 262–63
  and Soviet international law 19–20, 21, 24–25, 36–39, 41
Lemkin, Raphael 82–83, 170, 172, 174, 176, 183
Lenin, Vladimir 45–47
Li Haopei 128–29
liberalism, Western
  and China 116, 120
  and the CIJ 224–27
  in crisis 264
  and internationalism 211–12
  and the law 1–6, 18, 94–95
Liberia 210–11
Libya 132, 180–81, 221
Lin Biao 125–26
Lipson, Leon 34–35
Lithuania *see* Baltic states
Litvinov, Maxim 72–73
Liu Daqun 128–29
Liu Shaoqi 32–34
looting, crime of 166–67, 168, 169–70, 171–72
Lopez-Rey, Manuel 190–91
Lorentz, Stanislaw 179–80, 181
Lumumba, Patrice 31
Lutorowich, Pavel 179–80
Luxemburg, Rosa 45–47

Ma Xinmin 133–34
MacDermot, Niall 226
Mali 237, 238
Mao Zedong 35, 120, 121, 128, 160
Marinescu, Voinea 155
maritime law 133–34 *see also* Philippines; piracy; UN Convention on the Law of the Sea (UNCLOS)
Marxism-Leninism
  and Africa 15, 207–12
  and fascism 71, 72
  and law 11–12, 18–22, 69, 92, 93–94, 101–9, 113–14, 257
  and prostitution 193–95
  and revisionism 125–26
  and socialist internationalism 205
  and the Stalin Constitution 17–18
  and terrorism 240–42
Mazzini, Giuseppe 46–47
medicine *see also* health
  preventative 139–41, 143–44, 149, 151–52, 155, 156–58, 160, 161–62

  social 11–12, 137–38, 140–43, 144, 148, 150, 159, 161
  socialized 141–42, 264
mercenaries 247–48, 254
Mexico 137–38, 143–44, 152–53
military necessity clause 6–7, 164–65, 176–77, 181–84
minorities, rights of 9, 57–59, 62–63, 164–65, 166–67, 173–76, 209, 215
Mitrany, David 28–29
Molotov-Ribbentrop Pact (1939) 23, 50–51, 79
Mongolia 156–57, 221–22, 248–49
Montreal Convention for the Suppression of Unlawful Acts against Civil Aviation (1971) 248–49, 251, 252–53, 254–55
Morozov, Platon 149
Mozambique 15, 58–59, 219, 223
Muszkat (Mushkat), Marian (Marion) 102–3, 104–6

Nagy, Imre 63
Namibia 58–59, 207–8, 210–11, 222, 225–26
narcotics 8, 198–99, 201–2
national liberation movements
  and African socialism 207–8, 253
  and air law 244–45
  and crime of aggression 83–84, 89–90, 126–27
  and cultural heritage 182
  and health 152
  and hijacking 13, 232–33, 239–55
  as international conflicts 221–24
  and prostitution 197–202
  and self-determination 51–52, 57–59, 126–27
  and terrorism 57–58, 75–76
Nehru, Jawaharlal 33, 122–23
Netherlands 152–53, 168, 173–74, 180–82, 210–11, 216 *see also* Dutch Empire
Neto, Agostinho 225–26
Neumann, Franz 17–18
New International Economic Order (NIEO) 4–5, 7–8, 27, 31–32
New Zealand 176
Ni Zhengyu 128
Nicaragua *see* Latin America
Nigeria 31–32, 35, 59–60, 216, 219, 238
Nixon, Richard 240, 243–46
Nkrumah, Kwame 31, 152–53, 207–8, 218
Non-Aligned Movement
  and apartheid 206–7
  and crime of aggression 83–84
  and health 147, 148
  and international law 2–5
  origins of 26–27
  and self-determination 55–57, 66–67

non-intervention 5, 7-8, 9-10, 30, 33, 60-61, 65-66, 111, 122-23, 125, 232, 258, 262
North-Atlantic Treaty Organization (NATO) 87-89, 132-33
Norway *see* Scandinavian states
nuclear weapons 85-86, 164-65, 176-77, 179-81, 184, 224-25, 262
Nujoma, Sam 225-26
Nuremberg Trials
  and anticolonialism 173-74, 216-17
  and crimes against humanity 212-13, 214-15
  and cultural heritage 164-65, 166-71
  and international law 77-83
  and Poland 102-3
  and socialist law 2-4, 17-18, 21, 24-25, 69-71
  and the Soviet Union 257
Nyerere, Julius 12-13, 207-8, 213, 218, 222, 246

Obote, Milton 246-47
October Revolution *see* Russian Revolution
Oeser, Edith 109-10
Ogaden 12-13, 61
Ojukwu, Chukwuemeka Odumegwu 60
Organisation of African Unity 31-32, 59-60, 67-68, 221-22
Organization for Security and Cooperation in Europe (OSCE) 65-66
Ottoman Empire *see also* Turkey 48-49
Outrata, Vladimír 110-11

Pakistan
  and China 123
  and the colonial clause 198-99
  and cultural genocide 174
  and health 142-43, 150
  and hijacking 252-53, 254
  and prostitution 193-95, 200-1
Pal, Radhabinod 83-84
Palestine
  and apartheid 215, 217-18, 223-24, 228
  and crimes against humanity 213
  and hijacking 232-34, 239-41, 245-46, 253
  and national liberation 58-59
  and self-determination 134-35
  and terrorism 249-50
Pan-Asian Conference on Rural Hygiene (1937) 141-42
Paniushkin, Aleksandr 195-96
Paris Agreement 130, 133-34
Parisot, Jacques 144
Parran, Thomas 142
Parsons, Anthony 216-17

Pashukanis, Evgeny 17, 21-23, 69
Pazhwak, Abdul Rahman 54-55
peace, crimes against 23-24, 69-90
peaceful coexistence
  and the Bandung Conference 33, 122-23
  and international law 42, 56-57, 236, 258
  and socialist internationalism 63-64
  and the Soviet Union 34-35, 37-39, 56-57, 62, 63, 108-9
Pella, Vespasian 73, 75
Philippines 78-79, 133-34, 151-52, 181, 216
Pierson-Mathy, Paulette 225-27
piracy 233-34, 243-44, 249-52
Poeggel, Walter 109-10
Poland *see also* Poznań School of Law; University of Warsaw
  and air law 235-36, 253
  and colonialism 211
  and cultural genocide 173, 174
  and cultural heritage 166-72, 176-84
  and health 140-41, 150-51
  and hijacking 245
  invasion of 23
  and Katyn Forest Massacre 80
  and legal education 98-101, 102-3, 104, 107-9, 112-13, 211
  and prostitution 201
  and socialist law 91-114
  and Stalinization 105-6
  and Supreme National Tribunal (SNT) 170-72
political prisoners 224-26, 227-28, 253-54
Portugal (Portuguese Empire)
  and apartheid 207-8, 213-14, 215, 219, 220-22, 224-26
  and the colonial clause 237-38
  and health 144-45, 152-53, 154
  and national liberation movements 58-59
Poznań School of Law 13-14, 91-114, 211, 259-60
prisoners of war 80, 121-22, 223-24
propaganda, crime of 6-7, 70, 72, 73-74, 82, 87, 209, 216, 218
prostitution
  and abolition 13, 192-95
  and criminalization 190, 191-93, 195-96, 203
  and international law 185-204
  and pimping 189, 190, 191-92, 195-96, 198-99
public health 156-61, 264
Putin, Vladimir 45

Qatar 221
Quenum, Alfred Comlan 154

racism *see also* antisemitism; UN Convention on
    the Elimination of Racism
  and African students 153–54
  and apartheid 206–7, 209, 223
  and capitalism 87–88
  and cultural genocide 174
  and cultural heritage 165, 177–78
  in Eastern Europe 153–54
  and health 138–40, 152–56, 157
  and self-determination 50
Rajchman, Ludwig 140–41
Reagan, Ronald 42
Responsibility to Protect (R2P) 132
Rhodesia (Zimbabwe) 58–59, 213–14, 222, 223
right of return 217–18
right to development 130–31
Roma community 9, 209
Romania
  and apartheid 220, 225–26
  and crime of aggression 73
  and cultural heritage 164, 176–78, 179–81
  and health 151–52, 155–56
  and hijacking 235–36, 243, 246
  and legal education 30–31, 111
  and legal expertise 111
  and sovereignty 12
  and the WHO 160–61
Romashkin, Pyotr 70–71, 83–90
Roosevelt, Eleanor 145–47, 150
Rosenberg, Alfred 169–70
Ruske, Ingrid 231, 254–55
Russia *see* Soviet Union
Russian Empire 48–49, 187–88
Russian Revolution (1917) 17, 48, 85–86, 107

Salmon, Jean 225–26
Sand, René 142
Saudi Arabia 54–55, 150–51, 246
    see also Baroody, Jamil
Scandinavian states
  and apartheid 213–14, 220–21, 222–23
  and cultural destruction 168
  and health 139–40, 141–42, 149–50, 155–56
  and hijacking 250–51
  and self-determination 48–49
Schmitt, Carl 258
Schönefeld Airport (East Berlin) 241–42
Schweisfurth, Theodor 93–94
Schwelb, Egon 167
secession movements *see* national liberation
    movements; self-determination
Sékou Touré, Ahmed 12–13, 31, 207–8, 216
self-defence 45, 75–76, 89, 128
self-determination *see also* individual countries
  and anti-trafficking 197–98
  and apartheid 207–12
  and China 60, 117, 120, 134–35
  and crime of aggression 89–90
  and health 138–39, 140–44, 145–56, 161
  and human rights 24–25, 32
  and the IADL 225–26
  and international relations 31
  and Tito 62–63
  and Palestine 58, 134–35
  and socialist law 30, 45–68, 75–76, 259
  and sovereignty 116, 135
Senegal 153, 252
Senghor, Leopold 252
sex, commercial *see* prostitution
Seychelles 254
Shawcross, Hartley 201–2
Sheen, Martin 231–32
show trials 26, 69, 79
Shurshalov, Vladimir 63
Sihanouk, Norodom 243
Sino-Soviet Friendship Treaty (1950) 28–29, 121
Sino-Soviet Split 33–34, 35, 125–26
Skubiszewski, Krzysztof 100–1, 104, 112–13
Slovenia 62–63
Šnejdárek, Antonín 62
social welfare 143–44, 186, 190–91
socialism, scientific 29, 249–50
Socialist Declaration of Human Rights 42, 68
socialist law *see also* internationalism, socialist;
    legal universalism
  and anticolonialism 146, 257, 261–62
  and apartheid 207–12
  and bourgeois law 19–21, 23, 40, 41, 108–9, 261
  and China 115–16
  after the Cold War 257
  and crime of aggression 72–73
  and crime of conspiracy 78–79
  and crime of genocide 82–83
  and crimes against peace 72, 82–83, 86–90
  and cultural heritage 165–66, 175–81, 183–84, 262–63
  and the Eastern Bloc 28, 30–31, 42, 91–114
  and enforcement mechanisms 9–10, 129, 138–39
  and global engagements 1–6, 21–22, 23
  and health 137–62, 264
  and hijacking 232–34
  and human rights 38, 137–62
  and international relations 28–29, 39–40
  and its contradictions 8–11, 62–68
  and the Korean War 87–88

socialist law (*cont.*)
  and legal education 21–22, 29, 30–31
  and legal innovation 4–8, 41, 70–71, 131
  and national pluralism 39, 91–114, 259–60
  as a new type 18, 27, 32
  and the Nuremberg Trials 77–82, 166–72
  and peace 262–63
  and peaceful coexistence 33, 40–41, 56–57
  and prostitution 185–204
  and self-determination 30, 40–41, 62–68, 75–76, 259
  and show trials 26, 69, 79
  and the Socialist Declaration of Human Rights 42
  and sovereignty 40–41, 135
  and terrorism 249–50
  as a tool for governance 18
  as a tool of revolution 17–18, 69
  and trade 30, 125, 259–60
socialist legality 18–19, 207, 263–64
Somalia 12–13, 61, 221, 253–54
songbun (North Korea) 228
South Africa 50, 57, 58–59, 87–88, 154–56, 205–29, 244–45, 254
South Molucca, Republic of 59
Southeast Asia Treaty Organization (SEATO) 88–89, 123
sovereignty
  and African Americans 50
  and the Brezhnev Doctrine 12–13, 37–38, 63–65, 259
  and China 117–20, 130–35
  and culture 165–66
  and decolonization 30–31, 83–84
  and the Eastern Bloc 12, 19–20, 98–99
  and economic independence 55, 59, 65–66, 68, 123
  and enforcement mechanisms 9, 130
  and hijacking 232–34, 246–47
  and international law 35, 40–41, 76–77
  and the invasion of Afghanistan 42
  and Palestine 134–35
  and Prague Spring 37–38
  and self-determination 116
Soviet Union *see also* asylum law; Baltic states, and occupation; peaceful coexistence
  and air law 235–39, 244–49, 251
  and apartheid 205–6, 208, 214, 221–22
  and cultural heritage 178–84
  and emigration 240, 255
  and ethnic minorities 175–76
  and extradition 252–53
  and hijacking 246, 248–49
  and the IADL 224–27

  and imperialism 116, 152, 209
  and legal formalism 93–94
  and neo-colonialism 31, 54–55, 63–65, 75–76, 154–55
  and the Nuremberg Trials 77–82, 257
  and prostitution 185–204
  and purges 22–24, 73–74, 193–95
  and Resolution 1514 55–56
  and self-determination 24–25, 55–57, 59–61, 63–68
Spain 223–24, 235–36
Spandau Prison (Berlin) 242–43
Sri Lanka (Ceylon) 144–45, 238
Stalin *see also* Soviet Union, purges
  and Stalinization 22, 45–46, 48–49, 193–95
  death 55, 84–85
  and de-Stalinization 11, 36–37, 263–64
Stalin Constitution (1936) 17, 22–23
Štampar, Andrija 140–42, 148, 156–57
statutory limitations 6–7, 14, 87, 205, 212–15, 227–28
Steiniger, Peter Alfons 258
Stern, Herbert Jay 231–32
Stuby, Gerhard 226–27
Sun Yat-sen 117–18
Sweden *see* Scandinavian states
Switzerland 180–81, 234–36
Syria 174, 180–81, 201–2, 221, 240–41
  see also United Arab Republic
Szeming Sze 142

Taiwan 120–21, 126, 237
Tanzania
  and apartheid 207–8, 213–15, 219, 221–23
  and national liberation movements 13, 244–45, 246–47, 248, 253
  and self-determination 12–13
Taylor, Telford 166–67, 170
Tegel Airport (West Berlin) 241–42
Tempelhof Airport (West Berlin) 231, 254–55
Tepavac, Mirko 245–46
terrorism
  and crime of aggression 72, 74–75
  and global war on 131
  and hijacking 8, 231–34, 239–55
  and self-defence 75–76
  and self-determination 57–59
Thailand 149–50, 243–44
Third World
  Approaches to International Law (TWAIL) 42–43, 89
  and international law 1–6, 12–15
  and Prague Spring 64–65, 126

Third Worldism
  and China 35, 121–25
  and the Soviet Union 38
Tibet 122–23
Tiede, Detlev 231, 254–55
Tito, Josip B. 26–27, 32–33, 62–63, 245–46
Togba, J.N. 144–45
Tokyo Convention on Offences Committed on Board Aircraft (1963) 166–67, 235–41, 242–44, 248–49, 254–55
Tokyo War Crimes Trials 2–4, 78–79, 119, 128, 166–67, 173–74
torture 161–62, 226, 248
trafficking, crime of 187–91 *see also* prostitution
Trainin, Aron N. 23–25, 29, 69–90, 167–69
Treaty of Versailles 48, 98, 117–18, 120, 211
Tricontinental Conference (1966) 35, 125
Tunkin, Grigory (Grigorij) 29, 34–35, 36–41, 48–49, 64–65, 108–9, 258
Turkey 72–73, 181, 182, 241–42, 250–51
  see also Ottoman Empire

U Thant 242–43
Uganda 221–22, 223, 246–47, 254
Ukraine
  and apartheid 221–22
  and banditry 80
  and China 132–33
  and the colonial clause 199–200
  and culture 168–69, 180–81
  and health 147, 150
  and hijacking 235–36
  and prostitution 199–202
  and self-determination 45
UN Apartheid Convention (1973) 7–8, 35, 205–7, 216–21
UN Charter (1945)
  and apartheid 210–11
  and China 9–10, 118–21, 128, 132
  and non-self-governing territories 197–98
  and self-determination 46, 51–53, 208
  and sovereignty 251
UN Convention on the Elimination of Racism (1965) 209, 216–17, 218
UN Convention on the Law of the Sea (UNCLOS) 5, 127, 128, 129, 133–34
UN Convention on the Non-Applicability of Statutory Limitations (1968) 87, 205–7, 212–15, 222–23, 228–29
UN Economic and Social Council (ECOSOC) 57–58, 185–90, 198–99, 201
UN Genocide Convention (1948)
  and apartheid 213, 216, 217
  and Aron Trainin 82–86

  and China 119, 132–33
  and the colonial clause 198–99, 201–2
  and cultural genocide 6–7, 164–65, 170, 172–75, 183–84
  and the Soviet Union 70–71
UN Hague Convention for the Protection of Cultural Property (1954) 164–65, 176–82
UN Human Rights Covenants (1966)
  and the colonial clause 201–2
  and health 137–39, 146–47, 148–49, 150–53, 155, 156–59, 161–62
  and self-determination 32, 46, 68
  and universalism 261
UN International Law Commission 29–30, 36–37, 82–83, 89–90, 119
UN Resolution 1514 55–56
UN Trafficking Convention (1949) 185–204, 208, 237–38
UN Trust Territories 7, 51–52, 54–55, 140, 142, 144–46, 150–51, 178, 197–200
  see also colonial clause
UN War Crimes Commission (UNWCC) 166–68, 171, 183
Union of Soviet Socialist Republics
  see Soviet Union
United Arab Republic 152–53, 214, 237–38
United Kingdom *see also* British Empire
  and air law 236, 246, 251, 254
  and anticolonialism 210–11
  and apartheid 215, 216–17, 219–21, 222–24, 226–27
  and atomic weapons 180–81
  and Biafra 60
  and China 118
  and the colonial clause 198–201, 238
  and extradition 171
  and health 144, 145–47, 150, 152–53, 156–58
  and the IRA 223–24
  and legal expertise 226–27
  and military necessity 181
  and prostitution 171, 187–88, 195–96
  and racism 209
  and self-determination 55–57
United Nations *see also* UN Charter; UN Conventions
  Security Council 35, 89–90, 110–19, 132, 251
  Social Defense section 188–91, 193–95
  and Western dominance 24–25
United States of America *see also* Korean War
  and African American radicals 173–74, 239–41, 249
  and air law 243–45, 251, 254
  and apartheid 213–17, 220–21
  and the CIJ 224–25

United States of America (*cont.*)
  and the colonial clause 178–79, 201–2, 238
  and the Communist Party (CPUSA) 50
  and Cuba 234–35, 240–41, 250–51
  and cultural destruction 171, 184
  and cultural genocide 172–76
  and genocide 87–88
  and health as a right 137–38, 141–42, 145–46, 147, 158
  and hijacking 231–34, 236–37, 239–40, 244–49
  and Indigenous rights 176
  and legal education 211–12
  and military imperialism 87–89
  and the New Deal 137–38, 141–42
  and *Nicaragua v USA* 128
  and the Nuremberg Trials 78
  and prostitution 195–96, 201
  and racism 87–88, 209
  and SEATO 123
  and segregation 207
  and self-determination 46, 52–53, 54–55, 57
  and Taiwan 120
  and the WHO 147–48, 150, 152–53, 156
Universal Declaration of Human Rights (UDHR)
  and the colonial clause 201–2
  creation of 24–25
  and cultural genocide 174–76
  and health 137–62
  and hijacking 246–47
  and self-determination 52–53
  and universalism 260–61
universal jurisdiction 9, 205, 216–21, 227–29, 247–48
University of Warsaw 102–3
Uruguay 139, 143–44, 149–50

Venediktov, Dmitry 158
Venezuela 154–55, 172, 173, 174, 237
Vienna Convention on the Laws of Treaties (1969) 34–35, 237, 243, 248–49
Vietnam 15, 75–76, 125–27, 221–22, 243, 252
Vinogradov, Nikolai 143–44
Vulović, Vesna 245–46
Vyshinsky, Andrei 17, 22–24, 29, 36–37, 69, 79, 103–4

Wang Tieya 128–29
war crimes *see also* aggression, crime of; Nuremberg Trials; Tokyo War Crimes Trials
  and apartheid 221–24
  and banditry 80
  and cultural destruction 168–70
  and Nazi Germany 70–71, 78–79
  and socialist law 6–7, 85–86
  and statutory limitations 6–7, 14, 87, 205, 212–15, 227–28
wars of national liberation *see* national liberation movements
Warsaw Pact 28–29, 68, 95–96, 125
weapons of mass destruction *see* nuclear weapons
welfare state 13, 142–44, 146–47, 149–51, 156–57, 159, 186, 190–91, 264 *see also* social welfare
West Germany *see* Germany, Federal Republic of
white slavery *see* prostitution
Wiewióra, Bolesław 104
Wilson, Woodrow 45–46, 48
Winiarski, Bohdan 13–14, 98–104, 210–12
World Bank 160–61
World Health Assembly (WHA) 140, 142–44, 151–53, 154–58, 159–61
World Health Organization (WHO) 137–62
World Trade Organization (WTO) 130, 260

Xue Hanqin 131

Yugoslavia
  and air law 235–36, 238
  and apartheid 221–22, 225–26
  and asylum 234–35, 255
  and cultural genocide 174, 175–76
  and cultural heritage 175–76, 178, 180–81
  and health 146, 147, 148–52
  and hijacking 245–46
  and international organizations 147, 262
  and narcotics 8
  and national liberation 75–76
  and peaceful coexistence 56–57
  and racism 153–54
  and self-determination 62–63
  and socialist legality 4–5, 263–64
  and Soviet imperialism 26–27, 32–34, 83–84, 259–60

Zetkin, Clara 193–95
Zhou Enlai 122–23, 125–26
zhuquan 117–19, 120–21, 122, 132–34, 135
Zimbabwe *see* Rhodesia
Zonov, Vasilii 195–96